MORE TRADITIONAL BALLADS
OF VIRGINIA

MORE TRADITIONAL BALLADS
OF VIRGINIA

Collected with the Cooperation of Members of
The Virginia Folklore Society

Edited by
ARTHUR KYLE DAVIS, JR.
Professor of English Literature, University of Virginia

With the Editorial Assistance of
MATTHEW JOSEPH BRUCCOLI
GEORGE WALTON WILLIAMS
PAUL CLAYTON WORTHINGTON

Chapel Hill
THE UNIVERSITY OF NORTH CAROLINA PRESS

To the Memory of

C. ALPHONSO SMITH
MARTHA M. DAVIS
JULIET FAUNTLEROY
ALFREDA M. PEEL
JOHN STONE

TABLE OF CONTENTS

	PAGE
Introduction	ix
Acknowledgments	xxv

BALLADS

1. Riddles Wisely Expounded (Child, No. 1)	3
2. The Elfin Knight (Child, No. 2)	8
3. The Fause Knight upon the Road (Child, No. 3)	14
4. Lady Isabel and the Elf-Knight (Child, No. 4)	16
5. Earl Brand (Child, No. 7)	26
6. The Twa Sisters (Child, No. 10)	35
7. Lord Randal (Child, No. 12)	51
8. Edward (Child, No. 13)	61
9. Babylon (Child, No. 14)	68
10. Sir Lionel (Child, No. 18)	72
11. King Orfeo (Child, No. 19)	79
12. The Cruel Mother (Child, No. 20)	81
13. The Three Ravens (Child, No. 26)	84
14. The Whummil Bore (Child, No. 27)	89
15. The Twa Brothers (Child, No. 49)	92
16. Young Beichan (Child, No. 53)	102
17. Young Hunting (Child, No. 68)	111
18. Lord Thomas and Fair Annet (Child, No. 73)	123
19. Fair Margaret and Sweet William (Child, No. 74)	138
20. Lord Lovel (Child, No. 75)	146

PAGE

21. Sweet William's Ghost (Child, No. 77)   152

22. The Unquiet Grave (Child, No. 78)   157

23. The Wife of Usher's Well (Child, No. 79)   161

24. Little Musgrave and Lady Barnard (Child, No. 81)   170

25. Bonny Barbara Allan (Child, No. 84)   182

26. Lady Alice (Child, No. 85)   199

27. Jellon Grame (Child, No. 90)   207

28. Lamkin (Child, No. 93)   214

29. The Maid Freed from the Gallows (Child, No. 95)   221

30. Sir Hugh, or The Jew's Daughter (Child, No. 155)   229

31. The Hunting of the Cheviot (Child, No. 162)   239

32. Mary Hamilton (Child, No. 173)   245

33. The Gypsy Laddie (Child, No. 200)   253

34. Geordie (Child, No. 209)   262

35. Bonnie James Campbell (Child, No. 210)   267

36. James Harris (The Dæmon Lover) (Child, No. 243)   270

37. Henry Martyn (Child, No. 250)   290

38. Our Goodman (Child, No. 274)   300

39. The Wife Wrapt in Wether's Skin (Child, No. 277)   305

40. The Farmer's Curst Wife (Child, No. 278)   316

41. The Jolly Beggar (Child, No. 279)   328

42. The Gaberlunyie-Man, or The Gaberlunzie-Man
(Child, No. 279A)   333

43. The Sweet Trinity (The Golden Vanity) (Child, No. 286)   339

44. The Mermaid (Child, No. 289)   344

45. John of Hazelgreen (Child, No. 293)   350

46. Trooper and Maid (Child, No. 299)   356

Bibliography   361

Index of Titles and First Lines   367

INTRODUCTION

I. Prospectus

It is the purpose of this book to present, with appropriate editorial attention, an adequate selection of the older traditional ballads ("Child" ballads), texts and tunes, assembled at the University of Virginia, with the cooperation of members of the Virginia Folklore Society, since the publication of *Traditional Ballads of Virginia* in 1929. These ballads were listed and described in the first major section (Section I) of *Folk-Songs of Virginia: A Descriptive Index and Classification,* published in 1949, but no texts or tunes were there printed. These two earlier books, especially the former, are, of course, important background references for the present volume. This volume is, however, fully independent and self-sustaining, though its headnotes often look backward to establish a continuity with its predecessors under the same editorship.

Other types of ballads and songs in the Virginia collection remain to be published. It is arguable that the Child ballads, sometimes known as "the aristocrats of the folk-song field," are as interesting and valuable as any portion of the Virginia collection. Whether or not this is so, they are certainly the proper starting point for publication from a very large and miscellaneous collection from American sources. There is no intent here, except as a matter of convenience and of established editorial practice, to draw any hard-and-fast distinction between the Child ballads and other types of ballads and folk-songs. The Child collection is itself an extremely varied one, and its canon is by no means definitive. The reasons for the *de facto* acceptance of the Child canon in editorial practice are fully stated in the introductions to the two volumes cited above, and have recently been convincingly and authoritatively restated by Bertrand H. Bronson in his Introduction to Volume I of *The Traditional Tunes of the Child Ballads* (p. xviii).

Apart from the question of the significance or acceptability of the Child canon, the importance of the present work would seem to consist in its abundance of fresh material recently collected from traditional sources, largely by the most modern methods (aluminum discs, tape recordings, etc.). Upon three principal grounds the value of the book may be said to rest: the number of rare or unusual ballads, some of them virtually or actually new in recent traditional forms either in Virginia or in America, or in Britain and America; the number of significant new versions or variants, many of them with hitherto unrecorded tunes, added to the previous account; the number of excellent tunes and the scrupulous care of the musical transcriptions, with all significant variants, made from phonographic or tape recordings by experts in folk music and scientifically verifiable by comparison with these records. In addition, each of the forty-six ballads and its accompanying tunes is prefaced by an essay relating the texts and tunes to the total known tradition of the ballad and containing material of interest to the amateur and general reader as well as to the specialist.

II. Historical

It seems hardly necessary to repeat here what has been said at some length in the introductions to the two previous books cited above and dealing with ballads and folk-songs collected in Virginia. A brief retrospect is, however, in order.

The beginnings of this book hark back almost to the turn of the century, to the time when, following the publication of Francis James Child's five-volume edition of *The English and Scottish Popular Ballads,* other American scholars and collectors became aware of the presence in oral American tradition of many of the old story-songs of European origin widely known and sung in many parts of America. In Virginia the movement to collect these old songs directly from the lips of the singers, and thus to preserve them accurately from tradition, owed most to C. Alphonso Smith, who was Edgar Allan Poe Professor of English in the University of Virginia from 1909 to 1917. On his own initiative, Professor Smith founded the Virginia Folklore Society in Richmond on April 17, 1913, and gave to it until shortly before his death in 1924 a leadership and a magnetism that assured the fulfillment of its purposes.

The zealous members and workers of the Society were drawn chiefly from the school and college teachers of the state. Both the organization meeting and the annual meetings of the Society were held for some years in connection with the annual meetings of the Virginia Education Association, in Richmond. The Society set as its first objective—the objective in which Professor Smith was chiefly interested—the collection and preservation of the older

English and Scottish popular or folk ballads ("Child" ballads) surviving in oral tradition in Virginia. Despite the interruption of World War I, especially after America's entry into it in 1917, the campaign proceeded with great vigor and effectiveness under Professor Smith's enthusiastic direction for just over ten years, until his failing health and the wealth of the Society's ballad collection pointed to the need for another archivist and editor to undertake the publication of the material in book form. The editor of the present volume was fortunate enough to be chosen to take up that task.

In 1929 the Harvard University Press published a large octavo volume of 634 pages with the title *Traditional Ballads of Virginia* In it were printed some 440 versions or variants (out of 650 items then available) of 51 Child ballads, with 148 tunes. Its elaborate Introduction canvassed a number of preliminary matters, such as the definition of the ballad, the now somewhat out-dated controversy about ballad origins, and the history of the ballad in America; explained the content and editorial procedure of the volume; and presented a detailed history of the ballad movement in Virginia up to that time, with extensive quotations from the letters and recorded experiences of collectors. This Introduction and the volume as a whole constitute perhaps, despite the lapse of thirty-one years, the best and fullest introduction to the present volume. Obviously, *Traditional Ballads of Virginia* is of basic importance to *More Traditional Ballads of Virginia*. Unhappily, the earlier volume is now out of print, but is available in many libraries.

Other types of ballads and folk-songs remained to be collected. In 1929 and the years following, the present editor revived the relatively inactive Virginia Folklore Society and initiated a new drive for all types of traditional songs and for the miscellaneous folklore of the state. With the help of several grants from the University of Virginia's Research Committee and a larger grant from the American Council of Learned Societies, he personally toured the more promising ballad sections of the state and, often with the assistance of local collectors who were or had been members of the Virginia Folklore Society, made phonographic recordings of genuine folk singing.

Although the primary purpose of the new campaign was to extend the Virginia collection to include other varieties of folk-song than the already copiously collected Child ballads, the collector-editor was careful also to receive and to record wherever they presented themselves versions or variants of Child ballads, whether new or old to the Virginia collection. With the number and quality of the new ballads, new versions, and new tunes of the Child canon, many or most of them on verifiable phonographic records, it soon became apparent that the continuation or extension of the earlier phase of collecting was almost if not quite as important as the shift of emphasis to hitherto uncollected types of songs. The by-product began to assume an importance comparable to that of the product directly aimed at.

By the time that the war clouds of World War II were gathering, the Virginia collection had grown to some 3200 versions or variants of almost a thousand folk-songs of all sorts, including Child ballads, with many notations of tunes and some 325 phonographic records from which both texts and tunes could be accurately transcribed. Of these, the more recent quest had added to the Child-ballad materials published or described in *Traditional Ballads of Virginia* some 248 versions or variants of forty-six Child ballads, at least ten (with perhaps a trace of an eleventh) of them newly discovered in Virginia tradition, and with 111 tunes, most of them phonographically recorded.

The problem of publishing any considerable portion of this mass of material was deferred by the coming of World War II, and actual publication was deferred even longer by the postwar backlog of books to be printed. In place of *in extenso* publication of whole or part, it was decided to issue first a full descriptive census or check-list of the entire collection. *Folk-Songs of Virginia: A Descriptive Index and Classification* (Duke University Press, 1949) is a 450-page book listing, describing, and classifying each of the almost 3200 items of the collection. A sixty-four page Introduction sketches the history of the collection and explains and discusses critically the very elaborate system of classification applied to the material. There are eighteen major categories and numerous subdivisions.

The material there listed and described runs the gamut of folk-song types: old English and Scottish ballad survivals; later broadside and other narrative songs; more lyrical songs; humorous ballads; comic or nonsense songs; songs of married and single life; nursery and children's songs; play-party songs; dance songs, banjo and fiddle tunes; sea songs; American historical songs; crime songs; ballads and songs of the West; railroad songs; White religious songs; Negro songs; fragments; and some more literary ballads, doubtful and miscellaneous songs. There is obviously some overlapping between certain but not all of the categories, and there are difficulties of classification and sub-classification. It will be noted that the Child ballads constitute the first of the eighteen major categories. It is from this first group only that the material of the present book is drawn.

A powerful impetus toward the preparation of this book was given during the University of Virginia session of 1955-56, when the editor offered an advanced graduate course in "Ballad, Folksong, Folklore." There were in the class three very alert and interested students, each of whom had some ability in music as well as in literary scholarship. After a semester devoted to a study of the Child ballads and the scholarly problems of oral tradition, each student was given an assignment of actually editing and preparing for publication a single ballad and its variants, textual and musical. The process began, quite properly, with the more recently collected Child ballads of the Virginia archives. The class responded with enthusiasm, and soon there was formulated (even at the expense of the detailed study of certain later American types of folksong) a sort of class project to edit and prepare for eventual publication all of the Child ballads of more recent collection. As an encouragement, the editor-professor agreed to put the names of all three students upon the title page as collaborators or assistants under his general editorship. Under this arrangement good progress was made and a manuscript assembled, to be worked over, added to, and revised by the editor from that time to this (1960).

Seventeen perhaps lesser sections of the Virginia collection of folk-songs remain to be published. But the appearance of this first major section of Child ballads is the necessary first step. Whatever other contribution it may make, the present volume, added to the previously published *Traditional Ballads of Virginia,* at least shows the extraordinary richness of one American state or ballad locality in these rare traditional ballads, many of which are no longer current in the countries of their origin. In these old story-songs, the voices of our "contemporary ancestors" speak, or rather sing, to us movingly in an idiom and often with a beauty scarcely to be equaled by other popular artists of today.

III. Editorial Procedure

Inclusions and Exclusions

Since a ballad is not a single text or tune but embraces a number of extant texts and tunes, ideally no available specimen should go unrecognized. But time and printer's ink being in short or expensive supply, it is necessary to curtail such full representation. It has been deemed unnecessary to print here texts or tunes which merely repeat, with a minimum of variation, those previously published, especially those previously published in *Traditional Ballads of Virginia*. Similarly, items which are subject to any kind of question have either been excluded or the reader put on his guard with respect to them. On these and like grounds, a total of one hundred of the available newly collected texts have been excluded, bringing the total of inclusions to 148.

The tunes, however, long comparatively neglected and now available on verifiable records and in authoritative transcriptions, seemed to deserve fuller recognition. Of the 111 tunes available, only ten have been discarded, leaving a total of 101. A high priority has thus been given to texts with tunes, and more particularly to versions, texts and tunes, taken down from phonographic recording. No highly distinctive text without tune has been discarded, but in general the tuneless texts have had to prove their worth. Naturally, no really rare ballad has been sacrificed, even though it is imperfect textually and without tune, and one or two mere "traces" or fragments have been reluctantly admitted for lack of anything better. It is regrettable that some of the rarest of the ballads here included are without tunes, though they are known to have been sung. Yet it is pleasing to note that the balance of texts and tunes is closer here than in most collections, with the exception of collections primarily musical, like those of Sharp-Karpeles and Bronson. The ratio here is 148 texts to 101 tunes.

It should perhaps be made clear that no manuscript collection has been tapped for this book other than that brought together at the University of Virginia under the direction of the present editor. If any of several other known collections from Virginia sources had been added to the present collection, the totals for Virginia would have been considerably swelled.

Headnotes, Footnotes, Texts

No effort has been made to standardize the headnotes. There is, of course, a certain similarity of content, but each ballad seemed to call for its own approach and treatment. Sometimes the procedure is from the present material backward, but more often it is the reverse, from the Child background as a foundation, forward through more recent British and American versions to the previous Virginia texts or tunes, then on to the fresh items now presented. Usually, but not always, the story of the ballad is either summarized or hinted at, in the interest of the reader who is less of a specialist and as a quick means of focusing the attention of the specialist on the ballad at hand.

Some effort is made, but seldom by any approximation to a complete bibliography which would engulf the headnote, to indicate the comparative popularity, dissemination, or rarity of the ballad in British and American tradition. Fuller bibliographical helps are available in many places: in Margaret Dean-Smith's *Guide;* in Gavin Greig and Alexander Keith's *Last Leaves;* in Tristram P. Coffin's *The British Traditional Ballad in North America;* and the like. With Child's help, the dissemination of the European analogues of the ballad is often suggested. With the help of Wimberly and others, any interesting superstitions or folklore survivals are pointed out.

Explanation is frequently given for the particular inclusions and exclusions and for any ordering or grouping of those included. A brief summary of certain interesting points found in excluded items is added when it seems called for. The selected material is generally classified in accordance with Coffin's Story Types A, B, C, etc.

An eleventh-hour task of some importance has been the effort to take into account the just published first volume (three volumes presumably to follow) of Bertrand H. Bronson's major study of the tunes, *The Traditional Tunes of the Child Ballads,* dated 1959. Since his first volume includes only Child ballads 1 to 53, only those headnotes which fall between these numbers have profited by communion with him. Bronson's statistics of tunes (plus texts) are indicated. His classification of the tunes into certain groups in accordance with their melodic patterns has been briefly explained, with a minimum of technical musical language. Next, his actual classification of the tunes published in *Traditional Ballads of Virginia* has been reported, and any specific comments of his on the Virginia tunes have been quoted or paraphrased. Finally, so far as his system of classification seemed clearly applicable, it has been applied to the new tunes of this volume. But no effort has been made to force all the present tunes into his groupings. Where classification is uncertain, or where elaborate explanation or qualification would have been necessary, silence has been observed and the tune or tunes left unclassified. This is not a reflection upon Bronson's categories. It represents rather a recognition of the often extreme delicacy of judgment involved and an unwillingness to run the risk of misrepresenting Bronson's intent or of making him speak more positively than he would wish to. The same caution might be voiced as to the necessarily abbreviated and less technical explanations of his groupings, which are here suggested rather than fully delineated. It is hoped and believed that, with these qualifications, the relevant material from Bronson has been accurately and adequately presented. It is a matter of regret that his later volumes are not now available.

Wherever the study of a particular ballad has brought to light special problems or controversial points, these have been commented upon and an effort made to resolve them. See, for instance, the detailed examination of the relationship of "Sir Andrew Barton" (Child, No. 167) to "Henry Martyn" (Child, No. 250) in the headnote to the latter ballad, with the conclusion (contrary to Barry and others) that the two ballads, though related, are distinct and that recent traditional copies all belong to "Henry Martyn" and not to "Sir Andrew Barton." See also the long headnote to "Mary Hamilton" (Child, No. 173), where the effort is made to adjudicate between the claims of a Scottish or a Russian origin for the ballad. Many general problems of balladry are dealt with when relevant: for instance, the relationship of traditional specimens to broadsides; the question of what degree of difference distinguishes a separate ballad from a somewhat distant version of the same ballad; the ballad's use of history; the problem of ribaldry in ballads; and the like.

With these and other such matters to be canvassed, it is not surprising that many of the headnotes that follow are considerably longer than their predecessors have customarily been. Varying as they do in content, in procedure, and in length, each constitutes a prefatory essay relating the texts and tunes to the total known tradition of the ballad and pointing up any matters of especial interest.

The individual headnotes to particular versions or variants present the essential information about the particular text or tune: its local title, name and address of collector or contributor, name and address of singer, the Virginia county in which the song was sung, the date of collection or receipt, the person by whom the tune (if any) was noted or transcribed, and any interesting or significant facts of provenience. If the source of the item is a phonographic recording, the type of the record and the name of the recorder are also given. Attention is directed to matters of particular interest in either text or tune, with any comments available from either collector or musical transcriber. Occasionally material thought worthy of inclusion in the general headnote will be repeated in the more specific context of the individual headnote.

With so much opportunity for editorial comment in general and particular headnotes, footnotes have been reduced to a minimum. They are occasionally useful, however, in making specific textual comments, in supplying variant readings, in explaining doubtful or omitted words or phrases, in pointing out irregularities, in offering comparisons with other texts, and the like.

Occasionally there will be noted a slight discrepancy between the text of the stanza interwoven with the music and the text of the same stanza as given with the full text apart from the music. The discrepancy arises chiefly from the fact that the musical transcriber has heard the words differently from the textual transcriber. Where one or the other was obviously in error, the two have been brought into conformity, but in a few cases, rather than make an arbitrary decision, the two readings have been allowed to stand as self-declared variants. The remaining differences are slight, and both readings are phonetically possible.

It need hardly be said that few or no editorial liberties have been taken with either verbal or musical texts, and that where any appreciable liberty is taken with the texts, notice is given. The editor has felt free to correct spelling (except where a misspelling seemed to represent the singer's pronunciation), to alter punctuation, to supply capitalization and quotation marks, to change line divisions or stanza divisions where change is obviously called for— anything, in fact, which does not endanger the text as an accurate record of the original performance or rendition. One obvious error of musical notation has been corrected. But editorial prerogative has been exercised with caution and with explanatory notice. After all, we are in the post-Child era of scientific folklore, not in the less responsible era of Bishop Percy, Sir Walter Scott, and other expert but too liberal emenders. Without undue subservience to manuscript detail, but also without undue editorial tampering, the effort has been to present the song as it was actually sung, so far as can be determined. This hardly needs saying by a responsible editor of today.

IV. The Tunes: Their Sources and Treatment

The music has already been touched upon in the historical section of this Introduction and in the section dealing with general editorial procedure. It will also be dealt with in connection with certain acknowledgments, to follow. But its particular problems and their solution must be indicated here in more technical detail.

Although a score or more of competent musicians have contributed to the music of this book, the musicians chiefly responsible are three, all knowing in the specific ways of folk music: George W. Williams, one of the three student collaborators, now of the English faculty at Duke University; Winston Wilkinson, concert violinist and sometime Fellow in Folk Music in the University of Virginia; and Ernest C. Mead, Jr., scholarly Chairman of the Music Department of the University of Virginia and with a special interest in folk music. The specific notations of each, as of the other musical contributors, are indicated in the headnotes to individual versions or variants. To Mr. Mead fell the task of reviewing and checking the entire body of tunes and of making recommendations, which have in the main been followed. No effort has been made to standardize the musical transcriptions from different sources.

The tunes fall into four major groups: (1) tunes taken down by Winston Wilkinson or John Powell from live performance; (2) tunes transcribed by Winston Wilkinson from phonographic recordings; (3) tunes transcribed by George Williams or Ernest Mead, or both, from tape recordings of phonograph records; and (4) tunes taken down by various other collectors from live performance.

The tunes of group (1) are given without change. Those of group (2) also are practically unchanged, since the Wilkinson transcriptions are models of accuracy and musical insight. Those of group (4) occasionally needed editorial revision. A few have been excluded as untrustworthy; a few have been retained with a hint of suspicion; the rest are presented with some confidence. The difficulty here is, of course, the impossibility of verification. A few noteworthy and unexceptionable tunes still survive in group (4).

The largest and most representative group is group (3), all tunes of which received particular attention from Ernest Mead. It seems wise, with the help of Mr. Mead and for the most part in his words, to indicate his procedure in some detail. The same general procedure, with perhaps minor modifications, would seem to apply to the Wilkinson notations from records, and therefore to the bulk of the music in the volume.

According to Mr. Mead, his purpose was to represent in notational symbols as approximately as possible the pitch shape and rhythmic shape of the melodies as he heard them from the tape recordings.

Except in the case of tunes that are quite simple and that remain consistent throughout the stanzas, he transcribed all the stanzas and compared them to arrive at what might be considered the essential skeleton of the melody. If, after this, the first stanza seemed on the whole characteristic, that stanza was selected for printing, followed by significant variants that occurred in the remaining stanzas. In some tunes the first stanza was either unreliable or not representative, in which case another stanza was chosen for publication. Occasionally there was a wide divergence between the melodies of different stanzas, in which case the melodies of several representative stanzas are given.

Undoubtedly, one of the most striking aspects of many of these tunes is their subtle, organic rhythmic complexity. All rhythmic values of the transcriptions have been checked many times, and when a rhythmic value was definitely measurable it was so transcribed, even though the resulting time signature might seem exotic. Most probably some readers will desire, and are at liberty, to simplify the metrical scansion by considering certain values as "pauses." The purpose of the barring has been to indicate, first, an interpretation of the upbeat and downbeat qualities of the tune and, second, the component parts of the rhythmic movement. Admittedly, the barring is in several instances conjectural, and in the case of Mr. Russell's "Geordie," which defies scansion unless forced into a straightjacket, no time signature has been given and the bar lines are offered only as a suggestion. The metronome marks are, of course, only approximate.

In the first transcription of a tune, the absolute pitch heard by the transcriber was noted. In the final copy, however, the tune has in many cases been pitched where it would lie conveniently on the staff and not obstruct the lay reader with too many accidentals. The justification for this is as follows: first, in the oral tradition a singer does not hesitate to pitch a tune where it is convenient for him to sing it; second, in the course of several stanzas a singer will vary the pitch location; and third, in the recording process that lay between the actual performance and what the transcriber heard, the pitch location had very probably changed.

In the original process of notation, each tune in groups (1), (2), and (3) was classified with respect to its scale, modal characteristics, tonal center, and other strong scale degrees. However, in the final copy—and hence in this book—no modal classifications are indicated, since to give them would necessitate a lengthy exposition on the complicated matter of the modal classification of traditional music, a discussion which would far exceed the purpose and the physical limits of this Introduction. Another reason for abstention has been the expected publication of Bronson's book on the Child tunes.

In the key signature of a tune, only those accidentals that actually occur in the melody have been given. For pentatonic or hexatonic tunes, the reader may, if he wishes, supply his own modal classification and consequently add whatever is necessary to the key signature—though the editor understands that this is something of a controversial point among musicologists.

The style of certain singers involves various types of ornamentation. Although these ornaments seldom have any rhythmic weight, they constitute an essential part of the beauty of the melodic style. Frequently their pitch is too uncertain, their rhythm too subtle, to be caught in notation. Whenever possible these ornaments are represented by grace notes, their position on the page indicating their temporal relation with the melodic line.

Several of the singers represented in this collection have very individual and idiomatic styles. There is no way of representing on paper many of the characteristic and intrinsically beautiful features of these styles, such as the subtle rhythmic nuances, the slight pitch inflections, the peculiar nasal disguise of one singer's voice, the impersonal objectivity of another singer, or the lyric charm of another. In these cases the transcription is hardly more than a melodic skeleton. It is consoling, however, that the recordings in the archives will preserve these inimitable styles for future generations.

Finally, at the request of the editor, Mr. Mead, who has studied these tunes more carefully than anyone else and who is most competent to evaluate them, has written a brief statement about their quality, with a few specific examples:

This collection of ballad tunes from Virginia includes some of the finest traditional melodies found in the British and American oral tradition, melodies that exhibit a wealth of rhythmic vitality and expressive melodic line. The tunes present a great variety of modal designs and reflect the striking idomatic styles of different singers.

There is the vigorous, direct rhythmic style of Mrs. Whitehead's "Love Henry" and, in contrast, the subtle, organic rhythmic flow of Mr. Russell's "Geordie" that almost defies scansion. Between these extremes one finds the completely natural alternation of metrical groupings in Miss Bowman's "Lord Bacon" and the complex rhythmic style of Victoria Morris' "The Turkish Lady."

Hardly less exciting is the variety of melodic lines: the simple melodic arch of Mrs. Keeton's "Two Brothers," the wide pitch range and interesting structure of Mr. Keesee's "Cruel Mother," and the intensely expressive line of Mrs. Hicks's "Two Brothers." Particularly arresting are the varying stanzas of Mrs. Starke's "The Jewses' Daughter" which, taken as a whole, constitute in effect a set of melodic variations. The tunes present also a variety of modes, ranging from the more commonplace pentatonic patterns to Mrs. Victoria Morris's rich Dorian tune, "The Seven Sleepers," or Miss Purcell's fine Mixolydian tunes, "Sir Hugh" and "The Two Sisters."

Represented in this collection are singers with individual and fascinating styles, styles that can be only faintly suggested in writing. No system of notation can adequately catch the subtle charm of Horton Barker's lyric style with its decorative line and syncopation, or the epic quality of Victoria Morris' severe yet intense and figured style, or the freedom and objective simplicity of Mr. Russell's singing.

In every respect this collection of melodies will be a source of musical enjoyment as well as a valuable contribution to the printed repertory of traditional music.

This considered and documented judgment corroborates the opinion of Cecil Sharp expressed in a letter to C. Alphonso Smith and quoted in the Introduction to *Traditional Ballads of Virginia* (p. 43), as follows: "I have found the tunes in Virginia extraordinarily beautiful; I think of greater musical value than those that I have taken down elsewhere in America."

There can be little doubt that the tunes themselves and the trustworthiness of their presentation constitute a major feature of this volume.

V. A Note on Fundamentals

It is late in the day and late in this Introduction to undertake a discussion of the nature of ballads and folk-songs. In general, folk-song is the broader term and may be applied to all types of traditional songs—that is to say, to all songs passed on by word of mouth from person to person or from generation to generation and undergoing in the course of this passage some variation or change that tends to give them certain distinctive characteristics. The ballad is the more narrative, impersonal or objective type of folk-song, and since the folk is fond of narrative and of the impersonal way of telling a story, the ballad acounts for a considerable portion of the folk-song field. The less narrative, more emotional or personal type of folk-song is often referred to, confusingly enough, as folk-song in a narrower and more lyrical sense, in contradistinction to the more narrative and impersonal ballad. The broadside or stall ballad is a bit of narrative verse, often of known authorship and intended to be sold, printed on a broadside or broadsheet. It has no necessary connection with the more traditional specimens, but it is possible that a traditional piece might be so printed and preserved or that a broadside creation might subsequently attain a traditional life of its own. There is also the so-called literary ballad or ballad imitation, such as "The Rime of the Ancient Mariner" or "La Belle Dame sans Merci," in which the conscious literary artist utilizes the ballad form or technique for his own poetic purposes—a type to be sharply distinguished from the genuine traditional or folk ballad. The ballads of this volume are folk-songs in the broader sense only, and ballads in the more traditional sense.

Informative discussions of the general problems of balladry will be found in the introductions to most ballad collections, including the two previously published Virginia volumes. George Lyman Kittredge's introduction to the one-volume *English and Scottish Popular Ballads* retains its flavor and much but not all of its authority. For a fuller and more recent scholarly presentation, Gordon Hall Gerould's *The Ballad of Tradition* is the best book. Somewhat more popular, but also dependable, is *The Ballad Tree* of Evelyn Kendrick Wells. Brief but reliable information is supplied by the introductions to two recent popular collections: MacEdward Leach's *The Ballad Book* and Albert B. Friedman's *The Viking Book of Ballads*. Other volumes cited in the bibliography would also be useful. The editor surrenders with regret the privilege of discussing here the background of ballads. But in the pages to follow he will have his say on many important ballad matters.

VI. Ballad Roster

One final word. Since both *Traditional Ballads of Virginia* and *Folk-Songs of Virginia* are out of print, it should be pointed out that for the full roster of Child ballads in the University of Virginia collection the following sixteen titles represented in the earlier volumes but not represented here should be added: "The Cherry-Tree Carol" (Child, No. 54), "Dives and Lazarus" (Child, No. 56), "Fair Annie" (Child, No. 62), "Lady Maisry" (Child, No. 65), "The Lass of Roch Royal" (Child, No. 76), "The Bailiff's Daughter of Islington" (Child, No. 105), "Johnie Cock" (Child, No. 114), "Robin Hood's Death" (Child, No. 120), "Robin Hood and the Tanner" (Child, No. 126), "Robin Hood Rescuing Will Stutly" (Child, No. 141), "The Death of Queen Jane" (Child,

No. 170), "Bessy Bell and Mary Gray" (Child, No. 201), "The Heir of Linne" (Child, No. 267), "The Suffolk Miracle" (Child, No. 272), "Get Up and Bar the Door" (Child, No. 275), and "The Brown Girl" (Child, No. 295).

Similarly, the eleven new ballads represented here but not in *Traditional Ballads of Virginia* are the following: "The Elfin Knight" (Child, No. 2), "Babylon" (Child, No. 14), "King Orfeo" (Child, No. 19), "The Whummil Bore" (Child, No. 27), "Sweet William's Ghost" (Child, No. 77), "The Unquiet Grave" (Child, No. 78), "Jellon Grame" (Child, No. 90), "Bonnie James Campbell" (Child, No. 210), "Henry Martyn" (Child, No. 250), "The Jolly Beggar" (Child, No. 279), and "The Gaberlunyie-Man, or The Gaberlunzie-Man" (Child, No. 279A).

These twenty-seven rarer ballads, added to the thirty-five titles common to the earlier and later volumes, bring the total of Child ballads for the Virginia collection to sixty-two.

University of Virginia   ARTHUR KYLE DAVIS, JR.
Charlottesville, Virginia.

ACKNOWLEDGMENTS

Since this book is in part a memorial of a very pleasant class-room association, my first acknowledgment is to the three younger men whose contribution is indicated on the title page and throughout the book. Not the least of their contributions was the laborious but indispensable and exacting one of accurately transcribing from records or manuscripts both texts and tunes of the songs. Messrs. Bruccoli and Worthington worked mainly on the texts, and Mr. Williams, the best equipped musician of the four of us, on the tunes not previously transcribed. Nor did their services end with transcription, as has been indicated already in the Introduction. However, the final product of this work and the final responsibility belong to the editor alone.

Next, I am deeply indebted to the several gifted musicians and musicologists whose contributions, visible and acknowledged in detail on almost every page, have enabled this volume to claim some genuine musical distinction. Two musicians, in addition to Mr. Williams cited above, deserve especial thanks. One is Winston Wilkinson, because of his scrupulous transcriptions from records made during the 1930's, and also for his painstaking revision of the Purcell family tunes. Without that revision from Miss Purcell's singing it is doubtful that these valuable tunes could have been used. The appearance of these Wilkinson notations, following the publication by Bronson of many of his manuscript tunes in the University of Virginia Library (an enterprise in which the present editor was glad to have a part), will confirm Winston Wilkinson's reputation as a master in the field of folk music. I am grateful for the opportunity to present a considerable number of his immaculate notations.

Next, and with a special warmth of gratitude, I cite the really crucial contribution of my colleague and friend, Ernest C. Mead, Jr., Chairman of the Music Department in the University of Virginia and deeply versed in the idioms of folk music. Not only has he himself transcribed many of the tunes, with microscopic attention to all variants, but the entire musical content of the volume has been reviewed by him, with recommendations and comments and with occasional revisions from the records. In the Introduction and in the headnotes (general and particular) I am privileged to include some of his comments. He has given confidence in the music of the book and added distinction to it.

Mrs. Whitwell W. Coxe, of Roanoke, and Mrs. Paul Cheatham, of Lynchburg, have kindly lent their musical talents to help those great collectors, Miss Alfreda Peel and Miss Juliet Fauntleroy, respectively, to retrieve a number of the tunes of their localities.

Fred F. Knobloch, formerly of Crozet and now of Fincastle, deserves a special citation not only for his dedicated work as a collector, but also for his friendly cooperation on several fruitful recording trips. Also deserving of special mention here are E. J. Sutherland, of Clintwood; Mrs. Annabel Morris Buchanan, of Richmond; Miss Margaret Purcell, of Greenwood; and the late R. E. Lee Smith, of Palmyra, without whose notable contribution this book would lack some of its rarer ballads.

To my unfailing benefactor, the University of Virginia Research Committee, I am indebted for much encouragement and for several grants-in-aid.

To the Old Dominion Foundation, and to the special University of Virginia committee allocating its funds, I owe major thanks for their confidence in the form of a very substantial publication subsidy.

I wish also to acknowledge my indebtedness to the Ford Foundation for a grant under its program for assisting American university presses in the publication of works in the humanities and the social sciences.

Though the debt has been previously acknowledged, I am still grateful to the American Council of Learned Societies for its sponsorship of the field trips during which the records represented here (and others) were made.

To the Harvard University Press thanks are due for permission to cite or to quote from *Traditional Ballads of Virginia* as much as might be expected in a follow-up volume entitled *More Traditional Ballads of Virginia*.

Similarly, the Duke University Press has granted permission to cite or to quote from *Folk-Songs of Virginia: A Descriptive Index and Classification*.

The Princeton University Press and Bertrand H. Bronson have generously allowed citations and quotations from Volume I (alas, the only volume published as we go to press!) of Bronson's *The Traditional Tunes of the Child Ballads*.

To the Alderman Library of the University of Virginia, and especially Francis L. Berkeley, Jr., Curator, and his staff, of the Manuscript Division, I am beholden for photographic help and for permission to use certain unpublished manuscripts.

Again I have been able to avail myself of the expert typing ability of Miss Nella V. Dickinson, of Charlottesville.

It is a privilege to use as jacket illustration an appropriate and decorative woodcut by my talented colleague and friend, Charles Smith, Chairman of the University of Virginia's McIntire Department of Art.

And finally, I speak a word of appreciation and gratitude to all those—collectors, singers, musicians, transcribers—whose names appear in the headnotes to follow. Especially would I pay tribute to the distinguished "Old Guard" of Virginia balladry, to whom this book, like its predecessors, has owed so much, and to whose memory this book is appropriately, almost inevitably, dedicated.

A. K. D., Jr.

MORE TRADITIONAL BALLADS
OF VIRGINIA

RIDDLES WISELY EXPOUNDED
(Child, No. 1)

Since the publication of *TBVa* in 1929, only two new stanzas and one phonographic recording of this rare ballad have been added to the Virginia collection.

AA is essentially the same text and tune published in *TBVa*, except that a new first stanza from the same singer has been added, and the stanza is important since it makes explicit the character of the Devil in the text of the song and not merely in the title and (by implication only) in the (former) first and last stanzas (possibly also in the next-to-last stanza). The version now clearly conforms to Coffin's Story Type A, with the inquisitor now unmistakably the Devil and no mere cavalier come a-courting. The new stanza is obviously influenced by or imported (with appropriate variations) from such ballads as "Sir Lionel" or "Old Bangum" (Child, No. 18) or the (non-Child) "Frog Went A-Courting" song. Such is the way of oral tradition!

Miss Peel's phonographic recording, BB, offers still another and a quite different first stanza, in which the Devil has become a knight, whether actually or merely as a disguise is not quite clear. At any rate, it is possible up to the last stanza to understand the ballad as a courting type of riddle song, like most of the versions of "The Elfin Knight" (Child, No. 2) and indeed like many of the Child versions of this ballad. But the last stanza's, "Oh, you are God's, you're not my own," seems to reestablish the identity of the Devil. In any case, BB, with its differing first stanza, is closer to Coffin's Story Type C, except that there is only one girl, the weaver's bonny, not three pretty maids in search of a man, with the youngest, who knows the answers, triumphant.

The source of Miss Peel's first stanza is not clear. It is obviously not from Mrs. Rill Martin, from whom the rest of her text, with minor variations, seems to come. It is unlike any other opening stanza of the ballad known to the editor, though one might find a slight resemblance to Child C 1. (Cf. also Bronson I, 8, Appendix.) If the new stanza leaves the character of the Knight (the Devil?) in doubt, it certainly sets the stage effectively for the riddles and answers to follow. It is of interest, though of no traditional importance, that a neighbor of Miss Peel and an admirer of her ballad work, S. H. McVitty, of Salem, commissioned a handsomely decorated broadside panel of Miss Peel's version of this ballad, including the present first stanza. A photostatic copy of this broadside is in the Virginia collection.

Miss Peel has herself told the exciting story of her original finding of AA, minus its present first stanza—the first discovery in America of this ballad which is still extremely rare both in British and in American tradition. See *TBVa,* pp. 46-47, and Coffin, pp. 29-30.

The relationship of the Virginia text(s) to the several Child versions is complex and is discussed in some detail in the *TBVa* headnote (p. 59) and in Coffin (pp. 29-30). There is no very close relationship to any particular Child text. In number and in subject matter of questions, the resemblance is to Child C, but in the alternation of questions and answers in pairs, the resemblance is to Child B, not to C, where the whole series of questions is followed by the whole series of answers. The antecedent action about the three sisters, found in Child A, B, and C, but by no means essential to the ballad, is lacking in Virginia.

Bronson (I, 3-8) prints a total of six tunes (and texts), plus a seventh somewhat anomalous version as an appendix. His four variants of Group A are all British (English), the earliest and apparently ancestral musical record coming from Restoration broadsides and first printed in full by D'Urfey in *Wit and Mirth; or, Pills to Purge Melancholy,* 1719-20, IV, 129-32. The two members of Bronson's Group B are both from Virginia, the first being AA below, minus its first stanza, from *TBVa.* The second Virginia variant, from a record made by the Lomaxes in 1941, is sung by Mrs. Texas Gladden, a neighbor and friend of Miss Peel, the collector of AA and the singer of the BB record. According to Miss Peel, Mrs. Gladden, a gifted singer, learned the song from her, Miss Peel, as seems corroborated by the texts and tunes, despite some interesting variations. The present editor, who recorded Mrs. Gladden's songs during the 1930's, did not find this ballad in her repertory at that time. It is clearly a variant of AA and BB below, and stems directly from them.

Bronson's headnote, having commented upon the British tunes from D'Urfey's to Gilbert's, adds this comment upon AA, below: "It would be very difficult to make out a connection between the

Virginia tune and the foregoing airs.   Up to this point, however, the melodic tradition for this ballad, so far as the scanty record reveals it, has been remarkably single-tracked for the span of time which it covers.   If the tune was dropped overboard when the ballad came west, we might reasonably surmise that the ballad was transported on paper, rather than in the head, for the Bell Robertsons who remember only the words are black swans in balladry.   It is possible, however, that the Davis tune represents an unrecorded, but genuine, tradition, for which the refrain may provide a clue. The connection of the ballad-text and refrain is not at all clear. The new air is of stuff familiar in the Appalachians, and perhaps the song was inundated by a more vigorous melodic tradition, such as that of 'Barbara Allan' (Child, No. 84) or 'Geordie' (Child, No. 209), both of which often begin similarly and have the characteristic feminine upward swing at the middle of the final cadence.   Such a case is doubtless of frequent occurrence, and probably one of the chief ways in which ballads acquire a new melodic direction.   Nowhere today is the present ballad known to be strongly rooted." It is a privilege to be able to record these very reasonable speculations about the present tune.   AA quite definitely falls into Bronson's Group B.

The two final stanzas of the ballad may reflect the old folklore idea that naming the Devil frightens him away.   See Wimberly, p. 87.

AA

"The Devil and the Nine Questions" or "The Devil's Nine Questions." Collected by Miss Alfreda M. Peel, of Salem, Va. Sung by Mrs. Rill Martin, of Mechanicsburg, Va. Bland County (formerly of Giles County). The original text and tune collected September 11, 1922, the additional stanza October 22, 1933. Tune noted by Miss Evelyn Rex. Cf. *TBVa*, pp. 59-60, 549.

The dev-il went a-court-ing and   he did ride, Sing nine-ty-nine and nine-ty,

A sword and pis-tol   by his side, And you're the weav-er's   bon - ny.

  1   The Devil went a-courting and he did ride,
      Sing ninety-nine and ninety,
    A sword and a pistol by his side,
      And you're the weaver's bonny.

2 "If you don't answer me questions nine,
      Sing ninety-nine and ninety,
   I'll take you off to hell alive,
      And you are the weaver's bonny.[1]

3 "What is whiter than milk?[2]
      Sing ninety-nine and ninety;
   What is softer than silk?[2]
      Say you're the weaver's bonny."

4 "Snow is whiter than milk,
      Sing ninety-nine and ninety;
   Down is softer than silk,
      And I'm the weaver's bonny."

5 "What is louder than a horn?
      Sing ninety-nine and ninety;
   What is sharper than a thorn?
      Sing I am the weaver's bonny."

6 "Thunder's louder than a horn,
      Sing ninety-nine and ninety;
   Death is sharper than a thorn,
      Sing I'm the weaver's bonny."

7 "What is higher than a tree?
      Sing ninety-nine and ninety;
   What is deeper than the sea?
      Sing I'm the weaver's bonny."

8 "Heaven's higher than a tree,
      Sing ninety-nine and ninety;
   And hell is deeper than the sea,
      Sing I am the weaver's bonny."

9 "What is innocenter than a lamb,
      Sing ninety-nine and ninety;
   What is worse than woman kind?
      Say I'm the weaver's bonny."

10 "A babe is innocenter than a lamb,
      Sing ninety-nine and ninety;
   The[3] Devil's worse than woman kind,
      Sing I'm the weaver's bonny."

11 "You have answered me questions nine,
      Sing ninety-nine and ninety,

Oh, you are God's, you're not my own,
And you're the weaver's bonny."

1. Variant line: "An-a you the weaver's bonny."
2. Miss Peel in BB sings "the milk" and "the silk."
3. A misreading of Miss Peel's original manuscript is here corrected from "She" to "The." Incidentally, a certain popular singer of ballads has perpetuated the error on a commercial record, thus revealing the source of his text (also tune)! The editor regrets the necessity of parting with the picturesque and distinctive variant.

BB

"The Devil and the Nine Questions." Phonograph record (aluminum) made by A. K. Davis, Jr. Sung by Miss Alfreda M. Peel, of Salem, Va. Roanoke County. August 9, 1932. Text transcribed by P. C. Worthington. The rest of the ballad, and the tune, are almost (but not quite) identical with Mrs. Rill Martin's version, AA. Hence they are not reproduced here. See headnote.

1   There was a knight came riding by,
        Sing ninety-nine and ninety,
     And there he spied a weaver's lass,
        And she the weaver's bonny.

THE ELFIN KNIGHT
(CHILD, No. 2)

This ballad has been widely collected in Britain and America. Coffin states that it is "the best remembered of the Child riddle songs both in America and Europe." It is not surprising, then, that version J of Child is an American text, and that Child cites two more American texts from *JAFL*, VII, in his Volume V. All of these are of Massachusetts origin.

After a discussion of the clever woman in European and Oriental song and tale, Child says of his versions: "The first three or four stanzas of A-E form the beginning of 'Lady Isabel and the Elf-Knight,' and are especially appropriate to that ballad, but not to this. The last two stanzas of A, B, make no kind of sense here, and these at least, probably the opening verses as well, must belong to some other and lost ballad. An elf setting tasks, or even giving riddles, is unknown, I believe, in Northern tradition, and in no form of this story, except the English, is a preternatural personage of any kind the hero. Still it is better to urge nothing more than that the elf is an intruder in this particular ballad, for riddle-craft is practised by a variety of preternatural beings. . . ."

The story in Child A and B is as follows: An elf knight sits on a hill and blows his horn. A maiden wishes that it and he might be hers. He appears to her, but tells her that she is too young to marry. She replies that a sister younger than she was married yesterday. He then tells her that if she would be married with him, she must do him a "courtesie." He gives her the task of making a shirt but imposes numerous restrictions. She in turn tells him that she has an acre of land and he must plant and harvest it but also with difficult restrictions; then she will give him his shirt. In the last two stanzas which Child speaks of above, the elf knight tells her that he has a wife and children, and she tells him that she will keep her maidenhead. C and D tell a similar story without the two concluding stanzas. (In D she is actually the younger sister.) E follows this type but is fragmentary. The elfin knight has become an "auld auld man" and she must answer or go with him; the old man is clearly the Devil, and the situation is reminiscent of "Riddles Wisely Expounded." F, G, and H have a pair of mortal lovers presenting tasks to one another; only the love story remains. J has a woman presenting tasks involving land for a man, but none are given her in return. K and L have lost sight of the story completely: in these versions the speaker has inherited land and tells of cultivating it. There is no shirt motif, and no indication of a love story. Besides these texts, there are others added by Child in Additions and Corrections to Volumes I, II, IV, and V. Volume I gives M, a text of the F, G, H, type, and two more of this type are found in Volume II. Volume IV has an interesting text in which the dead lover returns and would have taken his lover "away with the dead" had she not been able to answer him. "The dead lover represents the auld man in I," states Child. Four more texts and variations are given in Volume V.

Coffin notes that "in this country, the elf, an interloper in Britain, has been universally rationalized to a mortal lover. Frequently, nothing remains but the riddle, sometimes even the love affair being absent." This seems to be the case also with texts recently collected from oral tradition in Britain. The ballad in its modified form has been found in Ireland, Aberdeenshire, Northumberland, Yorkshire, Wilkshire, Sussex, and Somerset, and in this country from Maine to Florida, Texas to California. With its wide popularity, it is curious that the ballad has not been more often found in Virginia. No texts of this ballad appear in *TBVa*. At present, three versions from three singers have been recovered. All are fragmentary, but all preserve to some extent the love element of the tasks. The refrain lines indicate the usual deviations from such lines as "Parsley, sage, rosemary and thyme" of Child G. Wimberly suggests: "The plant refrain in *The Elfin Knight* (2G) is a very probable survival of an incantation used against the demon-suitor. . . ." See Wimberly, pp. 345-62, for a general discussion of name magic, verbal charms, and herbal magic.

The meager records of this ballad in Virginia—no record in *TBVa* and only the three incomplete texts here without tunes—are all the more remarkable in view of the twenty texts printed by Child and the no less than fifty-five tunes (and texts) printed by Bronson (I, 9-33).

Bronson divides his musical records into three main groups: Group A, with six variants surviving from Scotland, New England, and Texas; Group B, the sturdiest branch, with forty representatives, all having the "True Lover of Mine" refrain; and Group C, with only five variants, wholly English and with the "Acre of Land" and "Ivy" refrain. Since Bronson's classifications are based primarily on musical considerations, it is impossible to relate the three tuneless fragments here to his groups. On the basis of the refrains, however, they would seem to lie closest to his large middle group, B. But what Bronson says of his third group, C, is certainly true of all three of the fragments given here: "So far as concerns the words," he says, "this group has pretty completely descended to the nursery: the riddles have lost their dramatic function, and the story is a straight-forward recounting of impossibles, with no challenging from opponents. Here there is little to bolster a theory of evolution from simple to complex." Only CC has the lady reply to the gentleman with a series of tasks equally impossible.

The three fragments given below are at least proof that the ballad, apparently more vigorous elsewhere in Britain and in America, especially in New England, is by no means extinct in Virginia.

AA

No local title. Collected by Miss Alfreda M. Peel, of Salem, Va. Sung by Minter Grubb, of Back Creek, Va. Roanoke County. Miss Peel collected this ballad first in 1932, when she sent in six stanzas of two lines, each without chorus. On July 8, 1935, she sent a text as she had re-collected it from Mr. Grubb. This text contained only four stanzas (all of which were included in the six sent earlier), but after each was an indication of a two-line chorus. Since the later text is better metrically, it is accepted as the basic text here. Stanzas 3 and 4, which were not sent with the later text, are supplied from the earlier one. The chorus is supplied throughout as indicated in the later manuscript. When there is any variation in wording between the earlier and later texts, the whole line as it was sent earlier is given in a footnote.

  1 "Go buy to me an acre of land
     Between salt water and sea sand.
        Let every rose grow merry in time,
        And you shall be a true lover of mine.

  2 "Go plow it all up with one cow's horn,[1]
     Plant it all down with one peck of corn.[2]
        Let every rose grow merry in time,
        And you shall be a true lover of mine.

  3 "Go cut it down with a goose quill,
     Go stack it up in an egg shell.
        Let every rose grow merry in time,
        And you shall be a true lover of mine."

4   "Many a question you have asked me,
       And many I'll ask of thee.
          Let every rose grow merry in time,
          And you shall be a true lover of mine.

5   "Go buy to me a cambric shirt,
       Go stitch it all 'round without needle or work.[3]
          Let every rose grow merry in time,
          And you shall be a true lover of mine.

6   "Go wash it out in yonder well
       Where water never run nor rain never fell.[4]
          Let every rose grow merry in time,
          And you shall be a true lover of mine."

1. "Go plow it with a cow horn."
2. "Go plant it down with one peck of corn."
3. "Go stitch it around without needle or work."
4. "Where rains nor waters never fell."

BB

No local title. Collected by Miss Alfreda M. Peel, of Salem, Va. Sung by Mrs. William Horton, of Roanoke, Va. Roanoke County. Miss Peel sent in two texts of this ballad taken from Mrs. Horton's singing. With the second text which was sent March 31, 1931, Miss Peel wrote: "I think this ballad has been sent in by me from the same source years ago. But the old lady's sister came with her, and there may be changes, as she helped her sing it." Miss Peel's comment is indeed an understatement. The two versions are quite different, and their fragmentary, irregular quality makes it extremely difficult to establish an authoritative single text. The earlier version, though more fragmentary, is more regular. It has therefore been thought best to give her earlier version in full. The editor offers a reconstruction based upon the earlier text with its refrain, and utilizing all the lines in both versions. "Saving" in the refrain line of this ballad probably is a variation of the herb "savoury" mentioned in herbal refrains.

Earlier Version

1   "Tell her to sew it up with a white thorn,
          Saving a rose that grows merry in time,
       And not let the needle touch the shirt,
          Thus she shall be a true lover of me.

2   " . . . .
       . . . .
       Nor let a drop of water fall on,
          Then she shall be a true lover of mine.

3   "Tell her to sew it up with a goose quill,
          Saving a rose that grows merry in time,

. . . .
Then she shall be a true lover of mine."

Later Version

1 There was an old woman lived over the sea
    Refrain: Saver a rose that grows merry in time,
        And you shall be a true lover of mine.

2 "Tell her to buy a yard of white cloth,
    Saver a rose, *etc.*
Tell her to sew it with a white thorn,
And not let the needle touch the shirt,
    Then she shall be a true lover of mine.

3 "Tell her to buy a half acre of land
    That lieth low by the salt sea sand,
Tell her to plow it with a goose quill,
Tell her to get a grain of corn,
    And thrash it out with a goose quill."

Reconstruction

1 There was an old woman lived over the sea,
    Saving a rose that grows merry in time,
"Tell her to buy a yard of white cloth,
    Then she shall be a true lover of mine.

2 "Tell her to sew it up with a white thorn,[1]
    Saving a rose that grows merry in time,
And not let the needle touch the shirt,
    Then she shall be a true lover of mine.

3 "Tell her to buy a half acre of land,
    Saving a rose that grows merry in time,
That lieth low by the salt sea sand,
    Then she shall be a true lover of mine.

4 "Tell her to plow it with a goose quill,
    Saving a rose that grows merry in time,
And thrash it out with a goose quill,
    Then she shall be a true lover of mine.

5 "Tell her to get a grain of corn,
    Saving a rose that grows merry in time,
Nor let a drop of water fall on,
    Then she shall be a true lover of mine."

1. Cf. "Tell her to sew it up with a goose quill" of the earlier version.

CC

"The Cambric Shirt." Collected by Miss Corita Sloane, of Merryfield, Va. Learned from an old Negro woman in Fairfax County. Fairfax County. January 10, 1915. The manuscript presents the ballad divided into two stanzas of seven lines each, and although several possibilities of more usual division are apparent, it has been thought best to retain this unusual but consistent manuscript presentation.

1 "Carry a lady a letter from me
   And tell her to make a fine cambric shirt
   With nary a stitch in nor nary a stitch out,
   Wash it in yonder well where never a drop of rain fell,
   Iron it all over with a cold flint stone
   And put a gloss on it for me to be married in,
   And I'll be a true lover of hers."

2 "Now carry that gent a letter from me
   And tell him to buy me an acre of ground
   'Twixt the salt sea and the shore side,
   Plow it all over with an old cow's horn,
   Plant it all over with one grain of corn,
   And raise a barrel of corn for me,
   And he can be a true lover of mine."

3

THE FAUSE KNIGHT UPON THE ROAD
(CHILD, No. 3)

Child prints only three versions of "this singular ballad," one
a briefer fragment than the text below : it contains only one question
and answer. The basic theme of the ballad is that the Fause
Knight or Devil may carry the child off if he can nonplus him. The
child is consistently successful in outwitting the Fause Knight, and
in some American texts finally throws his questioner into a well.
It has not been widely found in the United States, and many of the
better texts emanate from Virginia. A fuller version with distinctive tune was published in *TBVa,* and the text here given of two
statements and responses is the only one subsequently discovered
in Virginia. The present text does not duplicate that in *TBVa.*
It may be compared with the two concluding stanzas of Child A :

'I wiss ye were in yon sie :'
'And a gude bottom under me.'

'And the bottom for to break :'
'And ye to be drowned.'

All three of Child's texts are Scottish. Two of them come from
Motherwell's *Minstrelsy,* the third, with tune, from an aunt of the in-
defatigable Mr. Macmath. Margaret Dean-Smith reports no version from more recent British Isles tradition. From North America, texts or tunes or both have been reported from Nova Scotia,
Maine, Vermont, Virginia, Missouri, Indiana, Tennessee, and
North Carolina.

Bronson (I, 34-38) has found a total of ten tunes. He remarks that the song is "rooted in Scottish tradition. . . . The tunes
that are recorded all seem to have the same ancestry, yet they have
developed into surprisingly diversified variants." Of the *TBVa*
text and tune he notes : "The copies from Virginia and Indiana,
respectively, seem fairly close to each other, and show vaguer likeness to the rest of the family, rather more distinctly to North Carolina than to the others. Neither record, however, inspires much
confidence in its accuracy. The Indiana variant is at best a sadly

worn-down affair." No other tune or full text have more recently been recovered from Virginia.

AA

"The Boy and the Devil." Collected by Miss Alfreda M. Peel, of Salem, Va. Sung by Mrs. Ninninger, of Roanoke, Va. Roanoke County. November 6, 1941. "Am trying to get rest of song," writes Miss Peel on the manuscript, but no addition seems to have been forthcoming.

> Devil: "I wish you out in yonder sea."
> Boy: "With a good boat under me."
>
> Devil: "And the bottom would drop out."
> Boy: "And you were in and I were out."

4

LADY ISABEL AND THE ELF-KNIGHT
(Child, No. 4)

Child observed that "of all ballads this has perhaps obtained the widest circulation" over all of Europe. It has similarly in the present century been found in oral tradition in many shires of England, in Australia, Newfoundland, Nova Scotia, New Brunswick, and spread generally through the eastern half of the United States. This international popularity is reflected in the twenty-eight earlier Virginia texts, of which nineteen, plus seven tunes, were printed in *TBVa,* and in the twelve new items described in *FSVa,* of which only three are here presented, two of them with recorded tunes.

The new texts add little to the body of information already presented. The common confusion of the names of the heroine and her bird will be found again, as will the rarer confusion of parent and parrot (*TBVa,* D). Version AA, however, retains the proper name "Collin" as found in Child D and H. The name occurs infrequently in America, where it is also represented by the form "colleen." Also preserved in AA is the initial "following" stanza (as in *TBVa,* A, B, C, D, E). This stanza may be a survival of a demonic enchantment formula (Child D) or of an aspect of courtship or seduction (Child C). If the former is correct, the stanza exhibits the only trace in the ballad of the supernatural character of the would-be murderer. The legendary and fantastic bird, blessed with the gifts of reason and conversation, has dwindled to a mere talking parrot—an obvious rationalization of the primitive belief in the "bird-soul." See Wimberly, pp. 44 ff.

The newer Virginia texts still seem to correspond more closely to the Child series C-G (and Sargent and Kittredge H) than to A and B. They represent Coffin's Story Type A. The narrative is developed in three scenes or stages, separated by the two journeys forth and back: the seduction or elopement, the waterside scene ending in the drowning of the man, the girl's return home and the dialogue with the parrot. In spite of resemblances, the three texts printed here are quite distinct variants: notice, for instance, the complete difference in the three first stanzas, which begin, respectively, as follows:

He followed me up and he followed me down   [AA]
"Go bring me a portion of your father's gold   [BB]
There was a man out in the land   [CC]

Other differences of diction, stanzaic structure, dialect, and tunes
will be noted.   All three end, however, with the parrot's "cover-
up" remark about the cats.

The excluded items add little beyond verbal variants, though
the singer of one variant reports that once, when he was a boy (in
Southampton County?), he attended an evening wedding and that
after the ceremony and during the wedding supper the groom sang
this long "ballet-song" to the bride.   A not too appropriate selection for the occasion, one would think.

Bronson (I, 39-100) has amassed no fewer than 141 tunes
(with texts) for this widely disseminated ballad, though all musical
records of it are subsequent to the first quarter of the nineteenth
century.   He divides the tunes into two large classes, ninety-seven
in Group A and forty-four in Group B.   Of the seven Virginia
tunes printed in *TBVa,* four are classified in Group A, which contains both British and American variants, and three in Group B,
which includes the more distinctive American melodic tradition of
the ballad, "not shared by England, but probably imported from
Scotland."   Of the two new recorded tunes from Virginia, AA
especially seems to add something of value to the musical tradition
of the ballad.   Both AA and BB clearly belong to Bronson's Group
B, although AA lacks the characteristic first cadential pause on the
fourth degree of the scale.

AA

"Salt Water Sea."   Phonograph record (aluminum) made by A. K.
Davis, Jr.   Sung by Mrs. Martha Elizabeth Gibson, of Crozet, Va.   Albe-
marle County.   April 13, 1933.   Text transcribed by P. C. Worthington.
Tune noted by E. C. Mead.   Text independently collected by Fred F.
Knobloch.   May 1, 1931.

The variation between the manuscript and the recording is frequent but
on the whole not significant.   In the composite text here printed, the wording of the record and the order of stanzas of the manuscript have been
followed.   Variants are footnoted.

Apparently the angle of narration shifts from the first person in stanza
1 to the third person in stanza 3, back to the first person in stanza 8, and
to the third person again in stanza 12—a type of shift not uncommon in
ballads, especially those sung by older singers, as here.   Stanzas 1 and 8
seem to be examples of "an impersonal kind of I" mentioned by MacEdward
Leach (p. 8), and scarcely to be distinguished from the third person.

These two stanzas obviously differ from the quoted speeches of the ballad, and they are therefore left unquoted.

As usual with Mrs. Gibson's difficult but impressive performance, there are problems of stanzaic division and structure, enunciation, dialect. There is still some confusion of speakers in stanza 14 in spite of the change in the girl's name from Polly to Miss Collin. The second stanza has been selected for notation as most typical. "A beautiful tune and impressive rhythm" (E. C. Mead).

1   He followed me up and he followed me down,
      And he followed me onto the room;
    I neither had the heart to speak unto him,
      Nor the tongue for to tell him my name.

2   "Away, away to yonders field,
      There stands twenty-two or three,
    And pick out two of the best work horses,
      And come and go along with me, with me,
      And come and go along with me,

I will take you to some forent town[1]
  And married we will be, will be,
  And married we will be."

3 They rode, they rode that live long night,
  Till they came to the salt water sea;
And when they came to that salt water sea,
  All the chickens were crowing for day, for day,[2]
  All the chickens were crowing for day.

[4 "Get you down, get you down, my Miss Collin,
  Get you down I earnest pray,
For here I have drownded six king's daughters,
  And you are the seventh for to be."

5 "Is this the promise you made me?
  You promised to carry me
To some forent land
  And married we will be."][3]

6 "Pull off, pull off that gay, gay clothing
  And hang on there willow tree,
For they air too nice and they air too fine
  For to rot in the salt water sea, sea,
  For to rot in the salt water sea.
[For here I have drowned the six king's daughters
  And you are the seventh for to be, for to be,
  And you are the seventh for to be."][4]

7 "Oh, turn your back all around and about,
  Oh, turn your back on me,
For that is a sin and an open shame
  That a naked woman you should see, you should see,
  All naked woman you should see."

8 So he turned his back all around and about,[5]
  And he turned his back on me,
I picked him up in my arms so strong,
  And I lied him into the sea, sea,
  I lied him into the sea.

9 "Lie thar, lie there, you false-hearted villyun,
  Lie thar in the place of me,
For here you have drownded six king's daughters,
  And you are the seventh for to be, for to be,
  And you are the seventh for to be."

10 "Some help, some help, my Miss Collin,
  Some help I earnest pray,

> For every promise I made you
> I'll double it into three, lady,
> I'll double it into three."[6]

11 "Lie thar, lie thar, you false-hearted villyun,[7]
> Lie thar in the place of me,
> For thar you have drownded six king daughters,
> And you are the seventh for to be, for to be,
> And you are the seventh for to be."[8]

12 She jump-ed on her bonny, bonny brown,
> And she led her die-apple gray,
> And when she came to her father's hall,
> All the chickens were crowing for day, for day,
> All the chickens were crowing for day.

13 "Oh, where have you been, my Miss Collin,
> Made you stir so soon ['fore day?"
> "Hush, oh hush, my pretty parrot,
> And tell no tales on me,
> And your cage shall be made of beautiful gold
> And hung on the willow tree."][9]

14 "Oh, where have you been, my Miss Collin,
> Made you stir so soon 'fore day?"
> "Oh, the cat she came to my cage window,
> And swore[10] she would worry[11] me;
> I call-ed out my Miss Collin
> For to drive the cats away."

1. MS. has "land."
2. MS. has "Three hours before it was day."
3. Stanzas 4 and 5 omitted on recording, but apparently sung by **Mrs. Gibson** on other occasions.
4. MS. omits bracketed section.
5. MS. has "He turned hisself all around and about."
6. MS. has for this stanza:
> "Some help, some help, my Miss Collin,
> Some help I earnest pray,
> If I ever live to get out o' here,
> O married we will be."

7. MS. has "wretch."
8. MS. adds here a second "Some help" stanza, following the second "Lie there" stanza:
> "Some help, some help, my Miss Collin,
> Some earnest help I pray,
> For every promise I made you,
> I'll double it into three."

9. Bracketed section omitted on recording.
10. Possibly "said" or "sore"; MS. has "So she would worry me."
11. For a comparable use of this verb, cf. Child C and also Child, No. 62, A, stanzas 23-24.

BB

"Miss Mary's Parrot." Phonograph record (aluminum) made by A. K. Davis, Jr. Sung by Mrs. Kit Williamson, of Yellow Branch, Va. Campbell County. August 4, 1932. Text transcribed by P. C. Worthington. Tune noted by Winston Wilkinson.

This text is actually a later variant of *TBVa* H collected from Mrs. Williamson (then Mrs. Sprouse). The recorded text has disclosed a refrain. The tune is very similar to that given for version D (*TBVa*, p. 550), but it is even closer to the Sharp and Karpeles series A, B, D, and G (I, 5-12). It is here transcribed from the record, with variants, and can be verified.

1   "Go bring me a portion of your father's gold,
      And some of your mother's fee,
   And bring me your father's choice horse,
      That stands on sixty-three, my love,
      That stands on sixty-three."

2   She brought him a portion of her father's gold,
      And some of her mother's fee,
   She brought him her father's choice horse,
      That stands on sixty-three, my love,
      That stands on sixty-three.

3   So he mounted upon the milk-white steed,
    She on her i-ron gray,
And they arrived at the salt sea side,
    At the length of a long summer's day, my love,
    At the length of a long summer's day.

4   "I would like you down, Miss Mary, dear,"
    Was the words he said to me,
"I've drownded six of the king's daughters here,
    And the seventh one you shall be, my love,
    And the seventh one you shall be.

5   "Take off your robe of silk, Miss Mary,
    It's pinned with a golden pin,
It cost your father too much money,
    For to drownd your body in, my love,
    For to drownd your body in."

6   "So it's turn your back to the broad sea side,
    Your face to the leaves on the trees,"
She picked him up in her lily-white arms,
    And plunged him in the deep sea, my love,
    And plunged him in the deep sea.

7   "Hand down your hand to me, Miss Mary,
    Hand down it bitterly,
That promise I made to you last night,
    I'll double it over," says he, "My love,
    I'll double it over," says he.

8   "Is this what you promised me, my love?
    Is this what you promised me?
You promised to carry me to Old Scotland,
    And thar you'd marry me, my love,
    And thar you'd marry me."

9   "Now lie there, you false-hearted wretch,
    Lie there in the place of me,
'Twas never intended for no such a villian,
    To drownd such a lady as me, my love,
    To drownd such a lady as me.

10   "You know the promise you made me,
    On yonders greenwood side,
You promised that you'd marry me,
    And make me a truthful bride, true love,
    And make me a truthful bride."

11 "If ever I made such a promise as that,
        It's more'n I intend to do,
    I never promised man such a thing as that,
        As easy found out as you, my love,
        As easy found out as you."

12 So she mounted upon that milk-white steed,
        And led the i-ron gray,
    And she arrived at her father's gate,
        One hour before it was day, my love,
        One hour before it was day.[1]

13 Out stepped Miss Mary's pretty little parrot,
        In his cage of ivory,
    "What makes you ride so soon, Miss Mary?
        What makes you ride 'fore day, my love?
        What makes you ride 'fore day?"

14 "Oh hush your mouth you pretty little parrot,
        Tell no tales on me,
    I'll make you a cage of the purest gold,
        And doors of ivory, my love,
        And doors of ivory."

15 Out stepped Miss Mary's wretched old father,
        Come walking out o' his room,
    "What's the matter with you, my pretty little parrot,
        What makes you talk so soon, my love?
        What makes you talk so soon?"

16 "Those cats they are now at my window,
        Wishing to weary[2] me,
    And I have called on Miss Mary,
        For to drive those cats away, my love,
        For to drive those cats away."

1. On the recording the singer intrudes this stanza after stanza 8 and then
repeats it here.
2. Cf. "worry" of AA 14.

CC

"A Man in the Land" or "The Dapple Gray." Collected by Miss Juliet
Fauntleroy, of Altavista, Va. Sung by Miss Caroline Reid, of Altavista,
Va., who learned it from Mrs. Leftwich in Bedford County. Campbell
County. October, 1921.

This version follows *TBVa* F but adds the concluding stanzas describing
the return home and the conversation with the parrot.

The curious participial construction of stanzas 12 and 14 recalls Child
E, and the nonsense line at 7c may reflect phonetically the word "ruffian"
as found in the same version.

1   There was a man out in the land
     Who courted the maiden fair,
     And promised to take her out to the North land
     And there their marriage should be.

2   Says, "Get some of your father's gold
     And some of your mother's feed,
     And two the best horses that stands in the stall,
     That stands by forty and three."

3   She got some of her father's gold
     And some of her mother's feed,
     And two the best horses that stood in the stall,
     That stood by forty and three.

4   She mounted all on her milky white horse
     And led her dapple gray,
     And rode till she came to the great salt sea,
     Three hours before it was day.

5   "Dismount, dismount your milky white horse,
     Deliver them unto me,
     For six pretty maidens I drownded here,
     And the seventh one you shall be.

6   "Take off, take off your silky white clothes
     And deliver them unto me,
     For they are too great, too grand, too rich,
     To rock in this great salt sea."

7   "If I must take off my silky white clothes,
     Please turn your back on me,
     For I think it not fit, for as often as you,
     An undressed lady to see."

8   He turned his back all unto her,
     And she wept bitterly.
     She grabbed him around his waist so small
     And tumbled him into the sea.

9   He waved, oh, high, and he waved, oh, low,
     And waved till he came to her side.
     "Take hold my hand, my pretty Polly,
     And you shall be my bride."

10   "Lie there, lie there, you horrid old wretch,
     Lie there, lie there," said she,
     "For six pretty maidens you drownded in there,
     And the seventh one drownded you."

11   She mounted all on her milky white horse
          And led her dapple gray
      And rode till she came to her father's house
          One hour before it was day.

12   A parrot being up in his cage so high
          And unto her did say,
      "What is the matter, my pretty Polly,
          You tarry so long before day?"

13   "Hold your tongue, hold your tongue, my pretty parrot,
          Don't tell no tales on me.
      Your cage shall be lined with glittering gold
          And the doors with ivory."

14   The father being up at his window so high
          And unto her did say,
      "What is the matter, my pretty parrot,
          You tarry so long before day?"

15   "There's matter enough," the parrot replies,
          "There's matter enough," said she.
      "Two cats have been up in my cage so high,
          And I'm afraid they will catch me."

5

EARL BRAND

(CHILD, No. 7)

Like the Virginia versions already published, these additional texts seem to follow Child B, Sir Walter Scott's version of "The Douglas Tragedy." Again like their predecessors, they also lack the last three stanzas, the "rose-and-briar" ending. All Virginia versions have clung tenaciously to the detail of the lady holding the horse while the knight kills her family; this with other characteristics unites the ballad to a vast European tradition, extending over most of the continent. No variant here or in *TBVa* has the rare interlaced refrain of Child A or of Bronson's Group A.

The AA and BB versions listed below both derive from Albemarle County. They bear marked resemblances to *TBVa* A from Greene County. As the two counties are contiguous, it may well be that the three texts constitute variants of the same version. Both in tunes and in language, however, AA and BB differ considerably. They follow the Coffin Story Type A or B, as they include the death of Lord William's (Lord Thomas's) mother. The second stanza of CC is a contamination from "Lord Thomas and Fair Annet" (Child, No. 73). The matter-of-fact accounting of the mortality rate at the conclusion of the ballad is common in Virginia though seldom more prosaically stated than here. The last line of BB and of *TBVa* A seem to be phonetically similar.

E. C. Mead writes enthusiastically about several of the tunes to this ballad. AA he describes as "certainly one of the outstanding tunes in the collection," and urges that all variants be printed. Every text here printed has its tune, at least three of the four excellent tunes from phonographic recordings.

That this ballad has long been popular in Scotland is clear enough from the sources of Child's texts—Scott, Motherwell (three), Kinloch, Cambell, and Edinburgh, with only two English versions. Gavin Greig has shown that it still persists in Scottish tradition. See *Folk-Song of the North East*, I, 64, and *Last Leaves of Traditional Ballads and Ballad Airs*, pp. 5-7. It is also among the *Bothy Songs* collected by Ord. In contrast, there is no twentieth-century record of the song in English tradition in Margaret

Dean-Smith's *Guide* or in the *Journal of the English Folk Dance and Song Society*. Child surveys an impressive list of Continental affiliations of this ballad in many languages.

In Virginia the ballad is reasonably rare. *TBVa* printed four variants, of five available, and two tunes. Of five items (not counting two overlapping ones) more recently collected and listed in *FSVa,* four are here presented, all of them with tunes. The one omitted item contributed by R. E. Lee Smith and Thomas P. Smith, though long resident in Virginia, comes ultimately from North Carolina and is printed in Brown, II, 29-30. It is also a good full text available in the Virginia collection.

Bronson (I, 106-27) finds "a marked formal cleavage" in the musical tradition of "this impressive ballad." He divides his forty tunes into six groups of one, two, fourteen, seven, three, and thirteen members, respectively. His fourth group of seven variants consists of texts and tunes collected in Virginia by either Sharp and Karpeles, Winston Wilkinson, or the present editor. "Group D," he says, "is a comparatively small gathering of Virginia variants with mid-cadence consistently on the flat seventh. All are authentic Dorian tunes. The group as a whole begins to display marks of the omnipresent 'Gypsy Laddie' scheme, which appears much more clearly in the next group." *TBVa* B he classifies in this Group D, while *TBVa* D appears in his final "aberrant" Group F. Of the four new tunes here given, he would certainly find both AA and BB highly distinctive specimens in any grouping. Incidentally, DD below is a later recording and transcription from the same singer as *TBVa* D (Bronson's Group F, No. 40), interestingly varied and now verifiable. Of the tunes below, AA belongs in Bronson's Group D, of which it is a fine example; CC shows a similarity to Bronson's Group A, 1a; and DD falls clearly into Bronson's Group F.

AA

"The Seven Sleepers." Phonograph record (aluminum) made by A. K. Davis, Jr. Sung by Mrs. Victoria Morris, of Mt. Fair, Va. Albemarle County. November 21, 1932. Text transcribed by P. C. Worthington. Tune noted by Winston Wilkinson.

"A rich Dorian tune," writes E. C. Mead, "in every respect one of the most beautiful tunes in the tradition," and he goes on to specify its distinctions as "fascinating rhythmic irregularities, expressive line, movement largely diatonic, figured melodic style." The editor can vouch, less technically, for the moving quality of the performance.

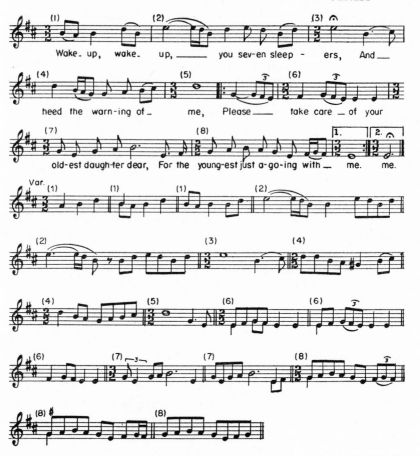

1   "Wake up, wake up, you seven sleepers,
      And heed the warning of me,
    Please[1] take care of your oldest daughter dear,
      For the youngest[2] just a-going with me."

2   He mounted up on a milk-white steed,
      Herself upon the dapple gray,
    He drew his buckle down by his side,
      And away went a-singing away.

3   "Wake up, wake up, my seven sons bold,
      And put on your armor so bright,
    I'll never have it said that a daughter of mine
      Shall stay with a lord all night."

4   He rode, he rode, he better, better rode,
      Along with his lady so dear,
    Until she saw her seven brothers bold,
      And her father a-walking so near,
    Until she saw her seven brothers bold,
      And her father a-walking so near.

5   "Get you down, get you down, Lady Margret," he said,
      "And hold my steed for a while,
    Until I fight your seven brothers bold,
      And your father a-walking so near."

6   She held, she held, a better, better hold,
      And she never shedded a tear,
    Until she saw her seven brothers fall,
      And her father she loved so dear,
    Until she saw her seven brothers fall,
      And her father she loved so dear.

7   He mounted up on the milk-white steed,
      And herself upon the dapple gray,
    He drew his buckle down by his side
      And away went a-bleeding away.

8   He rode, he rode, a better, better rode,
      Along with his lady so dear,
    Until he came to his own mother's stile,
      Where he did love so dear.

9   "O Mother, Mother, go make my bed,
      And make it soft and wide,
    And lay my lady down by my side
      That I may rest for a while."

10 Lord William he died about midnight,
      Lady Margret before it was day,
    And the old woman died for the loss of her son,
      So there was eleven lives lost.

1. Possibly "To."
2. Possibly "youngest's."

BB

"The Seventh Brother." Phonograph record (aluminum) made by A. K.
Davis, Jr. Sung by Mrs. Martha Elizabeth Gibson, of Crozet, Va. Albemarle County. April 13, 1933. Text transcribed by P. C. Worthington. Tune noted by E. C. Mead. Text independently collected by Fred
F. Knobloch. May 1, 1931. Significant variants footnoted. "A beautiful
tune, fluid rhythm," remarks Mead. A few of Mrs. Gibson's dialectical
peculiarities are phonetically suggested in the text.

1 "Get you up, get you up, you seventh sleeper,
   And do take warning of me,
   Oh, do take keer of your oldest daughter dear,
   For the youngest going on with me."

2 He mounted her up on his bonny, bonny brown,
   Himself on the die-apple gray.
   He grewed his buckles down by his side,
   And away he went whistling away.[1]

3 "Get you up, get you up, my seven sleepers,[2]
   And get in your arms so bright,

For it never shall be said that a daughter of mine
    Should lie with a lord all night.

4 He rode, he rode, that live-long day[3]
    Along with his lady so dear,
  Until she saw her seventh brother bold
    And her father was walking so near.

5 "Get you down, get you down,[4] Lady Margaret," he cried,
    "And hold my horse for a while,
  Until I can fight your seventh brother bold
    And your father is walking so nigh."

6 She helt, she helt, she better, better helt,
    She never shedded one tear,[5]
  Ontill she saw her seventh brother fall,
    And her father she loved so dear.

7 "Do you choose for to go, Lady Margaret," he said,
    "Do you choose for to go or stay?"
  "I'll go, I'll go, Lord Thomas," she cried,
    "For you've left me without any guide."

8 He mounted her up on the bonny, bonny brown,
    Himself on the die-apple gray,
  He grewed his buckles down by his side,
    And away he went bleeding away.

9 He rode till he came to his mother's stile
    Three hours 'fore hit was day.[6]
  "Get you down, get you down, Lady Margaret," he cried,
    "So that we can rest for a while.

10 "It's mother, mother, make my bed,
    And fix that smooth and wide
  And lie my lady down by my side,
    While we can rest for a while."

11 Lady Margaret she died about midnight,
    Lord Thomas 'fore it was day,[7]
  And the old woman died for the lost of a son,
    And there was several lives lost.

1. MS. has "And he went singing away."
2. MS. has "sons bold."
3. MS. has "night."
4. MS. has "Get you down" once only.
5. MS. has "And never shed a tear."

6. MS. has:

> He rode, he rode, the live-long night,
> Till he came to his mother's stile.

7. MS. has:

> Lord Thomas he died about midnight,
> Lady Margaret before it was day.

CC

"Seven Horsemen." Collected by Miss Alfreda M. Peel. Sung by W. H. Thomas, of Salem, Va. Roanoke County. September 16, 1940. Tune noted by Miss Lee Robertson Peters. The tune seems less interesting than the other three, but worth recording.

It was ear-ly in the month of May When the mead-ows they lie green,

He hung his bu-gle a-round his neck And so went rid-ing a-way.

1 It was early in the month of May,
 When the meadows they lie green,
He hung his bugle around his neck
 And so went riding away.

2 He rode till he came to Fair Ellender's hall,
 He blared both loud and shrill;
"Asleep or awake, fair Ellender," he cried,
 "Arise and let me in."

3 He mounted her on his milk-white steed,
 Himself the iron gray,
He hung his bugle around his neck
 And so went riding away.

4 He had not rode far from town,
 When he turned himself all round,
And who should he spy but seven horsemen
 Come tripping over the ground.

5 "Let yourself down, fair Ellender," he cried,
 "And take my steed in hand,
Till I go back to yonder spring
 And fight the seven horsemen."

6 She stood till she saw her seven brothers fall,
 Her father she could not revere,
"So hold your hands, sweet William," she cried,
 "Your licks are most severe."

7 She drew a white handkerchief from her side
   To wipe poor William's wound,
   And the blood came twinkling from his side
   As red as any wine.

8 He mounted her on his milk-white steed,
   Himself the iron gray,
   He hung his bugle around his neck
   And so went riding away.

9 He rode till he came to his mother's hall
   And blared both loud and shrill;
   "Asleep or awake, dear mother," he cried,
   "Arise and let me in.

10 "Listen, dear sister, come bind up my head,
   You'll never bind it again."
   Sweet William he died from the wounds he received
   In fighting those seven horsemen.

DD

"The Seven Brothers" or "Lord William." Phonograph record (aluminum) made by A. K. Davis, Jr. Sung by Mrs. J. B. Crawford, of Altavista, Va. Campbell County. August 4, 1932. Text transcribed by P. C. Worthington. Tune noted by Winston Wilkinson. "Good tune" (E. C. Mead). A comparison of the 1915 text and tune from the same source with the 1932 recording will reveal what has happened to the ballad during the seventeen-year interval. The new and more elaborate notation is now verifiable. Cf. *TBVa*, pp. 552 and 90-91.

1 Lord William he rose about four o'clock,
   And kissed his mother goodbye.

He drew his sword and pistol down by his side,
And he went singing away.

2 He mounted her upon a milk-white steed,
And him upon a iron gray,
He drew his sword and pistol down by his side,
And they went a-riding away.

3 He rode, he rode, he better had a-rode,
Along with his lady so gay,
Until he met her seven brothers bold,
And her father she loved so dear.

4 "Get you down, get you down, Lady Margret," says he,
"And hold my horse for a while;
That I may fight your seven brothers bold,
And you father she loves, loves so dear."

5 She held, she held, she better had a-held,
And she never shedded a tear,
Until she saw her seven brothers fall,
And the father she loved so dear.

6 "Hold your hand, hold your hand, Lord William," says she,
"Hold your hand, hold your hand, for a while,
For you have slain my seven brothers bold,
And the father I loved so dear."

7 "You can choose, you can choose, Lady Margret," says he,
"You can choose to go or to stay."
"Oh yes, Lord William, you know I will go,
For you've left me without my kind."

8 He mounted her upon the milk-white steed,
And him upon a iron gray,
He drew his sword and pistol down by his side,
And they went a-riding away.

9 He rode, he rode, he better had a-rode,
Along with his lady so gay,
For when he reached his own mother's house,
It was just four hours 'fore the day.

10 "O Mother, Mother, go make my bed,
Go make it soft and wide,
That I may lay down for to rest a while,
With a new bride by my side."

11 Lord William died before four o'clock,
Lady Margret died 'fore day,
The old lady died for the loss of her son,
And there was eleven lives lost.

6

THE TWA SISTERS
(CHILD, No. 10)

One of the few old ballads that Child found to be still extant in oral tradition, "The Twa Sisters" is rich in American texts. Coffin, moreover, accredits it with "more American story variations than any other ballad."

The narratives of the English and Scottish versions fall into two broad categories on the basis of the action after the older sister, motivated by jealousy, pushes the younger into the sea: one in which the body of the drowned girl is brought ashore by a miller, and some part of it is made into a musical instrument which reveals the murder; and the other in which the girl is rescued by a miller who robs her, then pushes her in again, and is subsequently hanged for the deed. In general, the American texts preserve the second form and omit the musical instrument material, which is preserved in only one exceptional Virginia version, AA. This version resembles Child B in its narrative detail, but has the "bow down, true to my love" refrain of Child R, S, U, Y, Z. The wicked sister, previously unnamed in Virginia, is here named Elinder (compare with Ellen of Child B), and this may possibly be a variant introduced from "Lord Thomas and Fair Annet." AA is truly a collector's item, as a glance at Coffin's survey will show.

As evidenced by narrative detail and refrain, the Virginia versions of "The Twa Sisters" normally belong with Child, R, S, U, Y, Z, in which the villainous miller is executed for murdering the girl (although the method of discovery is not revealed)—a form of the ballad which Child considered "entirely wanting in ancient authority." FF, a fragment with a "Hey ho, my honey O" refrain, belongs with Child G and J. Most of the Virginia texts belong to Coffin's Story Type A, except that AA and possibly FF represent story types not recognized by him.

There is a tendency in both the British and American versions for this ballad to become abbreviated by the loss of narrative material subsequent to the lines in which the older sister pushes the younger into the sea, or the lines in which the miller pushes her in again. The closing of the ballad on these scenes introduces a comic effect which is heightened when the tune is not sung in a completely traditional manner. JJ verges dangerously close to burlesque, and for this reason has been relegated to last place among the newly collected material.

The many variants of the "true to my love" refrain lend a moving and simple lyrical quality much more appropriate to the traditional nature of the ballad. The refrains have received considerable scholarly attention: see Barry, *BFSSNE,* III, 11; Mellinger, *JAFL,* XLV, 2; and for a discussion of the use of the refrain in dance games, see Botkin, *The American Play Party Song,* pp. 59 ff.

Following the extremely rare text AA, without tune, this ballad offers a number of beautiful tunes, most of them meticulously transcribed with all significant variants, from phonographic recordings. See the headnotes to individual versions or variants to follow. There are also interesting textual variations.

Since Child printed a larger number of versions of this ballad (twenty-seven) than of any other ballad except one ("Mary Hamilton," No. 173), since this ballad has more American story variants than any other ballad, and especially since eight of the ten texts given here have distinctive tunes and the two without tunes (AA and II) are significant variants, it has seemed impossible to exclude any of the ten. *TBVa* printed ten of a dozen available texts, plus six tunes. The ten given here represent fully the subsequent Virginia collection.

The ballad survives vigorously in recent English and Scottish tradition, especially Scottish, and has Continental affiliates in many languages. See Dean-Smith, Greig-Keith, Child.

Bronson (I, 143-84) prints a total of 97 musical versions or variants (plus texts), divided into four major groups: Group A, with twenty-two variants, contains most of the older or Scottish records, with the "Binnorie" refrain; Group B, by far the largest group of fifty variants subdivided into six parts, includes a few English and the greater portion of recent American variants, which generally keep the elaborate and repetitious "Bow down" refrains; Group C, of only three variants, is entirely Scottish and has the "Edinburgh, Edinburgh" refrain; Group D, with a sparse seven variants from Scotland, Ireland, and the United States, has the swan-refrain; and Group E contains a total of nine "anomalies." Here, as always with Bronson, the basic principle of classification is musical and rather too complicated and technical for satisfactory

summary. All six of the Virginia tunes of *TBVa* he classifies under
one or another subdivision of Group B. Under the rarer Group
D he lists the text of *TBVa* K, which here reappears, with its tune
now supplied, as FF below, a rarity of Scottish extraction. Of the
seven tunes below, six (BB, CC, DD, EE, GG, and JJ) belong to
one or another subdivision of Bronson's Group B; the seventh, FF,
falls into Bronson's Group D.

AA

"The Fair Sisters." Contributed by R. E. Lee Smith, of Palmyra, Va.
Sung by his brother, Thomas P. Smith, of Palmyra, and himself. They
learned it from the singing of their father, Bennet Smith, who "learned
it over seventy years ago from Cox Ladier." Fluvanna County. February,
1914.

The refrain lines are repeated because they show some variation from
stanza to stanza.

1   There was a king lived in the west,
     Bow down, bow down,
   There was a king lived in the west,
     Bow down once to me,
   There was a king lived in the west,
   He had two daughters of the best.
     I will be true to my love,
     And my love will be true to me.

2   A brave knight courted the eldest one,
     Bow down, bow down,
  [A brave knight courted the eldest one,
     Bow down once to me,][1]
   The knight courted the eldest one,
   But he dearly loved the youngest one.
     I will be true to my love,
     And my love will be true to me.

3   He gave the youngest a fine gold ring,
     Bow down, bow down,
   He gave the youngest a fine gold ring,
     Bow once to me,
   He gave the youngest a fine gold ring,
   And to the eldest he gave not a thing.
     I will be true to my love,
     And my love will be true to me.

4   He gave the youngest a silken dress,
     Bow down, bow down,
   He gave the youngest a silken dress,
     Bow once to me,

[He gave the youngest a silken dress,]²
The eldest got mad at that.
    I will be true to my love,
    And my love will be true to me.

5 One day as they walked by the riverside,
    Bow down, bow down,
   One day as they walked by the riverside,
    Bow once more to me,
   One day as they walked by the riverside,
   [The eldest she pushed the youngest in.
    I will be true to my love,
    And my love will be true to me.]³

6 The eldest she pushed the youngest in,
    Bow down, bow down,
   The eldest she pushed the youngest in,
    Bow once to me,
   The eldest she pushed the youngest in,
   The youngest said it was a sin.
    I will be true to my love,
    And my love will be true to me.

7 She swam till she came to the miller's pond,
    Bow down, bow down,
   She swam till she came to the miller's pond,
    Bow once to me,
   She swam till she came to the miller's pond,
   And there she swam all round and round.
    I will be true to my love,
    And my love will be true to me.

8 Out came the miller's son,
    Bow down, bow down,
   Out came the miller's son,
    Bow once to me,
   Out came the miller's son,
   And saw the fair maid swimmin' in.
    I will be true to my love,
    And my love will be true to me.

9 "O father, father, draw your dam,"
    Bow down, bow down,
   "Oh father, father, draw your dam,"
    Bow once to me,

"Oh father, father, draw your dam,
There's either a merimaid or a swan."
 I will be true to my love,
 And my love will be true to me.

10 The miller quickly drawed the dam,
  Bow down, bow down,
The miller quickly drawed the dam,
  Bow once to me,
The miller quickly drawed the dam,
And there he found a dead maid within.
 I will be true to my love,
 And my love will be true to me.

11 And by there came a harper fine,
  Bow down, bow down,
And by there came a harper fine,
  Bow once to me,
And by there came a harper fine,
That harper to this king to dine.
 I will be true to my love,
 And my love will be true to me.

12 He took three locks off her yellow hair,
  Bow down, bow down,
He took three locks off her yellow hair,
  Bow once to me,
He took three locks off her yellow hair,
And with them strung his harp so fair.
 I will be true to my love,
 And my love will be true to me.

13 The first tune he plays and sings,
  Bow down, bow down,
The first tune he plays and sings,
  Bow once more to me,
The first tune he plays and sings,
"Alas, farewell, my father the king."
 I will be true to my love,
 And my love will be true to me.

14 The next in that he played soon,
  Bow down, bow down,
The next in that he played soon,
  Bow once more to me,

The next in that he played soon,
"Alas, farewell to my mother the queen."
I will be true to my love,
And my love will be true to me.

15   The last tune that he played them,
Bow down, bow down,
The last tune he played them,
Bow once to me,
The last tune that he played them,
Was, "Woe to my sister, fair Elinder."
I will be true to my love,
And my love will be true to me.

1., 2., 3. These lines are lacking in the MS. and have been supplied by the editor.

BB

"The Two Sisters." Phonograph record (aluminum) made by A. K. Davis, Jr. Sung by Mrs. Kit Williamson, of Yellow Branch, Va. Campbell County. August 4, 1932. Text transcribed by P. C. Worthington. Tune noted by Winston Wilkinson. "Beautiful tune" (E. C. Mead).

Independently collected by Miss Juliet Fauntleroy, of Altavista, Va. Sung by Mrs. Williamson. March 15, 1934. Tune noted by Mrs. Paul Cheatham, of Lynchurg, Va. Two stanzas.

Though Mrs. Cheatham's notation is corroborative, only the Wilkinson transcription from the record is presented here. Mrs. Williamson's beautiful voice and fine folk style, with strict timing, make her presentation of this excellent tune a most appealing performance. The musical variants are worth noting (in both senses!). Mrs. Williamson here (and elsewhere) makes effective use of a subtle variety of ornamentation known as a "glottal catch" or sometimes a slur to a falsetto note above—an embellishment which not even Mr. Wilkinson's careful notation has been able to reproduce.

In subsequent stanzas and repetitions of lines there are minor variations such as the addition or omission of an "O," the change of an "and" to an "oh" or a "so," etc., but these minor variations hardly justify the printing of the repetitions in full. The singer, of course, gives full value to these repetitions.

That 'll be true, true, true to my love— to you.

1 There was an old man in our town,
   Bow down,
   There was an old man in our town,
   And there it's been to me,
   There was an old man in our town,
   And he had daughters one, two, three.
       That'll be true, true, true to my love, to you.

2 There was a young man went courting there,
   And he took choice of the youngest fair.

3 "Sister, O sister, let's we walk out,
   And view them brooks[1] on the water's bay."

4 As they was walking down the water's bay,
   The eldest pushed the youngest in.

5 "Sister, O sister, just loan me your hand,
   And you may have my house and land.

6 "Sister, O sister, just loan me your glove,
   And you shall have my own true love."

7 "I'll neither loan you my hand nor my glove,
   But I will marry your own true love."

8 So down she sank and away she swam,
   She swum into a miller's mill dam.[2]

9 "Miller, O miller, yon swims a swan,
   There comes a maiden on."[3]

10 The miller he got his fishing hook,
   And fish-ed the maiden from the brook.

1. "Brooks" is indistinct and might be "ducks."
2. The last words of this line are indistinct; they might be "miller's mill dam" or "miller's dam."
3. This line is uncertain.

CC

"The Old Woman by the Seashore." Phonograph record (aluminum) made by A. K. Davis, Jr. Sung by Horton Barker, of near Chilhowie, Va. Washington County. August 15, 1932. Text transcribed by P. C. Worthington. Tune noted by Winston Wilkinson.

The tune (pentatonic), with its wealth of variation, is an excellent example of "Horton Barker's lyric style with its decorative line and syncopation" (E. C. Mead). Although it is perhaps true that no system of notation can adequately catch the subtle charm of this kind of singing, Winston Wilkinson's scrupulous notation comes very close to doing so. The importance of printing all the musical variants is here clearly apparent. Mr. Barker's melodious tenor voice effectively supports the spell of his singing style.

1 There was an old woman lived on the seashore,
  Bowing to me,
There was an old woman lived on the seashore,
Her number of daughters, one, two, three, four,
  And I'll be true to my love,
  If my love will be true to me.

2 There was a young man came there to see them,
And the oldest one got struck on him.

3 He bought the youngest a beaver hat,
And the oldest one got mad at that.

4 "O sister, O sister, let's walk the seashore,
And see the ships as they sail o'er."

5 While these two sisters were walking the shore,
The oldest pushed the youngest o'er.[1]

6 "O sister, O sister, please lend me your hand,"
  Bowing to me,
"Sister, O sister, lend me your hand,
And you may have Willie and all of his land,"
  And I'll be true to my love,
  If my love will be true to me.

7 "Oh no, I'll never lend you my hand,
But I'll have Willie and all of his land."

8 The miller he got his fishing hook,
And fished the maiden out of the brook.

9 "O miller, O miller, here's five gold rings,
To push the maiden in again."

10 The miller received those five gold rings,
And pushed the maiden in again.

11 The miller was hung at his own mill gate
For drowning little Sister Kate.

1. Mr. Barker, in this particular rendition of the song, sang this stanza after the seventh stanza. This was obviously a confusion due to phonographic recording, and the stanza is here placed in its proper position.

DD

"There Was an Old Woman." Phonograph record (fiber base) made by
Fred F. Knobloch, of Crozet, Va. Sung by Mrs. Edna Ethel McAlexander,
of Meadows of Dan, Va. Patrick County. April 1, 1948. Text transcribed
by M. J. Bruccoli. Tune noted by G. W. Williams. "Hexatonic, with
cadential raised 7th" (Mead).

1   There was an old woman who lived on the sea,
      Bow down,
    There was an old woman who lived on the sea,
      Bows they bend to me,
    There was an old woman who lived on the sea,
    Daughters she had one, two, three.
      I'll be true to my love,
      My love be true to me.

2   There was a young sailor to see them came,
    Just for his love, the youngest one.

3   He gave to her a beaver hat,
    The oldest she thought hard of that.

4   He gave to her a ring of gold,
    Which made the oldest fret and scold.

5   "Sister, sister, come down to the shore,
    And watch the waves go rolling o'er."

6   As they were walking near briney rim,[1]
    The oldest pushed the youngest in.

7 "Sister, sister, give me your hand,
   And I will give you my house and land."

8 "I'll give you neither hand nor glove,
   All I want's your own true love."

1. These last three words are indistinct.

EE

"The Twa Sisters." Collected by Miss Martha M. Davis, of Harrisonburg, Va. Rockingham County. 1931. Tune noted by Miss Eunice L. Kettering, of Harrisonburg State Teachers College. Miss Davis writes, "The words and air of this fragment of 'The Twa Sisters' were picked up by us in Harrisonburg, Va., many years ago when we were children." Mead finds the notation "in some respects suspicious," but since it is all we have it is retained with this warning.

1 There was an old woman in the North Countree,
      Bow down, bow down.
   There was an old woman in the North Countree,
      The bow was bent to me.
   There was an old woman in the North Countree,
      And she had daughters one, two, three.
   Lover be true, lover be true, I will be true to thee.

2 There came a young man went courting there,
   And he did choose the youngest fair.

3 He bought for her a beaver hat,
   The oldest thought quite hard of that.

4 "O sister, O sister, let's we walk out,
   To see the ships go sailing about."

5 So 'way they walked by the seaside,

. . . .

6 The oldest pushed the youngest in,
   And said to her, "Now, sink or swim."

FF

"The Twa Sisters." Collected by Miss Martha M. Davis, of Harrisonburg, Va., as sung by her grandmother. Rockingham County. 1931. Tune noted by Miss Eunice L. Kettering, of Harrisonburg State Teachers College.

"My grandmother sang this ballad in broad Scotch," writes Miss Davis, "but this is all we can recover." Except for the Scotticism *sae* in line four, only the tune is new, as the text, contributed by Miss Davis in 1914, appeared in *TBVa* as version K (p. 104). Here are put together for the first time text and tune of this highly distinctive Scottish version, which seems worth preserving even though its notation cannot now be verified. Miss Kettering, who noted the tune, was a college teacher of music. Cf. Bronson, I, 180.

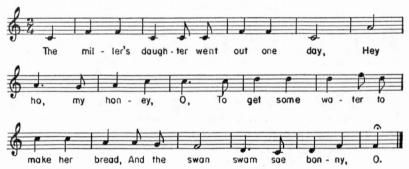

1 The miller's daughter went out one day,
   Hey ho, my honey, O,
   To get some water to make her bread,
   And the swan swam sae bonny, O.

   .   .   .   .

2 The miller went and stopped his dam,
   Hey ho, my honey, O,
   And placed the king's daughter on dry land,
   And the swan swam sae bonny, O.

GG

No local title. Collected by Miss Margaret Purcell, of Greenwood, Va. Sung by her grandmother, Elizabeth Ashton Garrett Purcell (Mrs. S. H.

Purcell), of Greenwood, Va., in the early nineties. **Albemarle County.**
May, 1934. Tune noted by Winston Wilkinson. "A fine Mixolydian tune
. . . . Occasional and cadential Major 7th" (Mead).

1   "O sister, O sister, give me your hand,"
     Bow down, bow down,
     "O sister, O sister, give me your hand,"
     And bow down to me,[1]
     "O sister, O sister, give me your hand,
     And I will give you my house and land."
     I'll be true, true to my love,
     And my love be true to me.

   1. Variant line (see music, above): "And bough, bend to me."

HH

"The Twa Sisters." Collected by Miss Martha M. Davis, of Harrisonburg, Va. Sung by Mrs. Sarah Finchum, "a mountain woman," of Elkton,
Va. Rockingham County. November, 1913.

1   There was an old woman lived on a seashore,
     Bow down, bow down,
     There was an old woman lived on a seashore,
     Of daughters she had two or more,
     And I'll be true to my love,
     If my love will be true to me.

2   There was a young man went to see them,
     And he fell[1] in love with the youngest one.

3   He bought the youngest a beaver hat,
     And the oldest one thought much of that.

4   As they were walking on the seaside,
    The oldest pushed the youngest one in.

5   "Oh, sister, oh, sister, give me your hand,
    And you can have my house and land."

6   "I'll neither give you my hand nor glove,
    You shall not have my own true love."

7   Oh, down she sank and away she swam,
    She swam right into the miller's mill dam.

8   The miller he ran with his grab hook,
    And pulled the fair maiden out of the brook.

9   "Oh, miller, oh, miller, I have gold stamps,
    That's brought me safe unto the banks."

10 The miller pulled off her golden stamps,
    And pushed her into the dam again.

11 The miller was hung on his mill gate,
    For drowning of poor sister Kate.

1. Miss Davis's typescript has "feel," evidently an error.

II

"The Wed Lady."   Collected by Miss Juliet Fauntleroy, of Altavista, Va.
Sung by Mrs. Maggie Sandidge, of Leesville, Va., who learned it from
her mother, Mrs. Zach Ogden, of Amherst County.   Campbell County.
April 27, 1934.

Note the comic last stanza, which does not properly belong to this ballad
—except by the folk singer's basic freedom of appropriation and expropria-
tion.   But note that this particular sequestration is not unique in this version.
See the version that follows, JJ, where the comic character of the ballad
is intensified.

1   There was a wed lady lived on the seashore,
        I will send to thee,
    There was a wed lady lived on the seashore,
    She had daughters three or four.
        I'll be true to my love,
        My love will be true to me.

2   The youngest one she had a beau,
    The oldest one and she had none.

3   "Oh sister, dear sister, let's walk the seashore,
    And watch the proud waves roll o'er and o'er."

4   So they took hand in hand and walked the sea brim,
    The oldest shoved the youngest in.

5   "Oh sister, dear sister, give me your hand,
    And you may have my house and land."

6   "I'll neither give you my hand nor my glove,
    For all I want is your old true love."

7   She waved her hand and she swum away,
    She swum on down to the miller's bay.

8   The miller cast in his iron hook,
    And safely drew her to the brook.

9   He taken from her a golden chain,
    And then he shoved her back again.

10 The miller was hung on the old gate post,
    For drowndin' of my sister Luce.

11 If you want any more song sung, you must sing it yourself,
    For the fife and the fiddle both lie on the shelf.

JJ

"Bow Ye Down." Phonograph record (aluminum) made by A. K. Davis, Jr. Sung by Mrs. Orpha Pedneau, of Radford, Va. Montgomery County. August 15, 1932. Text transcribed by P. C. Worthington. Tune noted by G. W. Williams and E. C. Mead.

Independently collected by Miss Alfreda M. Peel, of Salem, Va. Sung by Mrs. Pedneau. February 11, 1932. The text and rendition verge on comedy throughout and topple into it at the end. The last stanza is a commonplace importation from other and generally more comic songs. This interesting version has come a long way from the ancient tragedy of "Binnorie, O Binnorie."

true to my love, And my love will be true to me. ___

Var. (1) (2)

(3) (4)

1 There was a man lived in the West,
       Come bow you down, come bow you down,
   There was a man lived in the West,
       Come bow you down to me,
   There was a man lived in the West,
   He had two daughters he loved the best,
       And I'll be true, true to my love,
       And my love will be true to me.

2 The squire he courted the oldest one,
   But still he loved the youngest one.

3 He bought the oldest a gay gold ring,
   And the youngest one didn't get anything.

4 He bought the youngest a velvet hat,
   And the oldest one got mad at that.[1]

5 They all went down to the riverside,
   And there they all sat down and cried.

6 The oldest pushed the youngest in,
   And round and round they did swim.[2]

7 Now I lay my book on the shelf,
   If you want any more you can sing it yourself.

1. Miss Peel's MS. has:
             He bought the oldest a velvet hat,
             And the youngest one got mad at that.
2. The MS. has "And round and round she did swim."

LORD RANDAL
(CHILD, No. 12)

Despite the great popularity of this ballad in America, the basic story of the sweetheart's murderous treachery, revealed through a question-and-answer sequence between a mother and her dying son, has remained surprisingly uncorrupted. Except for AA, the newly collected Virginia texts follow Child B in omitting information about the death of Randal's dogs, and all follow either Child A or B in the use of the gallows or hell-fire motif.

The concluding stanza of AA giving the detail of the punishment of the faithless sweetheart represents a story variant different from any classified by Coffin. Although of interest to the collector, this information seems rather superfluous, since "Lord Randal" ends far more dramatically on the bleak note of the betrayed lover's curse. Other texts given here follow Coffin's Story Type A, with many verbal variants.

Child prints twenty-five versions of the ballad, and points out its Continental relations. Gerould (pp. 17-20) remarks that the ballad has been found "as far east as Czecho-Slovakia and Hungary, as far north as Scotland and Sweden, and as far south as Calabria." He shows the close parallel between an Italian version recently collected near Pisa and traced back to a broadside printed in Verona in 1629, and an eighteenth-century Scottish version.

TBVa prints fourteen texts out of sixteen available, with four tunes. More recent collecting in Virginia has produced six additional items, including four tunes (one lost). All six versions, with three tunes, are presented here.

Bronson (I, 191-225) has found and prints 103 tunes (with texts), and divides them into three major groups, commenting that "most of the divisions suggesting themselves within the larger body of tunes are subdivisions rather than actual cleavages." Group A, with 81 variants, represents the main melodic tradition of the ballad, which Bronson subdivides into four varieties, plus an appendix of anomalies, the oldest copy coming from Robert Burns in Ayrshire before 1792. Group B, with 16 variants divided into two almost equal parts, is the "Henry" group, mainly English, but with representatives from the west of Scotland and America. Group C, the "Croodin' Doo" version, with six variants, has two varieties, one Scottish and Aeolian, the other English. All four Virginia tunes from *TBVa* are classified under one or another subdivision of Bronson's major Group A. Of the tunes below, FF belongs to Bronson's Group Ac.

AA

"Lord Randall." Contributed by R. E. Lee Smith, of Palmyra, Va. Sung by his brother, Thomas P. Smith, of Palmyra, and himself. They learned it from the recitation of Mrs. Polly J. Rayfield, of Zionville, N. C. "She heard it sung now over sixty years ago by her mother, Mrs. Chaney Smith." Fluvanna County. January 11, 1915.

1 "Oh, where have you been, Lord Randall, my son,
And where have you been, my handsome young man?"
"I have been in Silverwood;
Mother, make my bed soon,
For I am tired with hunting
And want to lay down."

2 "And who did you meet there, Lord Randall, my son,
And who met you there, my handsome young man?"
"I met my true love, Mother;
Make my bed soon,
For I am tired of hunting
And want to lay down."

3 "And what did she give you, Lord Randall, my son,
And what did she give you, my handsome young man?"
"Fried fish, Mother;
Make my bed soon,
For I am tired of hunting
And want to lay down."

4 "And what did you do with your game, Lord Randall,
my son,
And what got your game, my handsome young man?"
"My hounds and hawks, Mother;
Make my bed soon,
For I am tired of hunting
And want to lay down."

5 "And what became of them, Lord Randall, my son,
And what became of them, my handsome young man?"
"They died, Mother;
Make my bed soon,
For I am tired of hunting
And want to lay down."

6 "Oh, I fear you are poisoned, Lord Randall, my son,
   I fear you are poisoned, my handsome young man."
      "O, yes, I am poisoned, Mother dear;
      Make my bed soon,
      For I am sick in the heart
      And want to lay down."

7 "What are ye going to leave to your mother, Lord Randall,
            my son,
   What are you going to leave to your mother, my handsome
            young man?"
      "Four and twenty milk cows;
      Please make my bed soon,
      For I am sick at heart
      And want to lay down."

8 "What will you leave to your sister, Lord Randall, my son,
   What will you leave to your sister, my handsome young
            man?"
      "My silver and gold, O Mother;
      Make my bed soon,
      For I am sick at heart
      And about to fall down."

9 "What will you leave to your brother, Lord Randall, my
            son,
   What will you leave to your brother, my handsome young
            man?"
      "My houses and my lands, O Mother;
      Please make my bed soon,
      For I am sick at the heart
      And want to lay down."

10 "What do you leave to your true love, Lord Randall, my
            son,
   "What do you leave to your true love, my handsome
            young man?"
      "I leave her hell and fire;
      O Mother, make my bed soon,
      For I am sick at the heart
      And want to lay down."

11 Lord Randall was buried in a church yard close by.
   His wicked love was hanged to a gallows so high.

BB

"Where Have You Been?" Collected by Miss Margaret Purcell, of Greenwood, Va. Sung by her mother, Elizabeth Ashton Garret Purcell (Mrs.

S. H. Purcell), of Greenwood, Va., in the early nineties. Albemarle County. May, 1934. Tune noted by Winston Wilkinson. Mead comments: "Beautiful tune: combination of leaps and diatonic movement."

This is substantially the same text as *TBVa* E, collected by Miss Evelyn Purcell, Miss Margaret Purcell's sister, in 1913. The earlier text, however, was without music, and the order of stanzas 4 and 5 was there reversed. See *TBVa*, pp. 110-11.

1   "Where have you been[1] to, my dear son?
       Where have you been to, my dear son?"
       "Courting, Mother, courting, Mother; make my bed smooth,
       For I'm sick at my heart and fain would lie down."

2   "What did you have for your supper, my son?
       What did you have for your supper, my son?"
       "Eel's broth, Mother, eel's broth, Mother; make my bed
            smooth,
       For I'm sick at my heart and fain would lie down."

3   "What sort of eel's broth was it, my son?
       What sort of eel's broth was it, my son?"
       "Black back, Mother, speckled breast, Mother; make my bed
            smooth,
       For I'm sick at my heart and fain would lie down."

4   "What will you leave to your mother, my son?
       What will you leave to your mother, my son?"
       "Carriage and horses, Mother; make my bed smooth,
       For I'm sick at my heart and fain would lie down."

5 "What will you leave to your father, my son?
   What will you leave to your father, my son?"
   "House and plantation, Mother; make my bed smooth,
   For I'm sick at my heart and fain would lie down."

6 "What will you leave to your sister, my son?
   What will you leave to your sister, my son?"
   "Hook, crook, and a bag net, Mother; make my bed smooth,
   For I'm sick at my heart and fain would lie down."

7 "What will you leave to your brother, my son?
   What will you leave to your brother, my son?"
   "Horse, saddle, and bridle, Mother; make my bed smooth,
   For I'm sick at my heart and fain would lie down."

8 "What will you leave to your sweetheart, my son?
   What will you leave to your sweetheart, my son?"
   "Brimstone and fire for to burn her heart brown
   For she was the cause of my lying down."

1. Earlier text reads "ban."

CC

"Johnny Randolph, My Son." Collected by Miss Martha M. Davis, of
Harrisonburg, Va. Sung by Edgar Steele. Rockingham County. 1931.
Tune noted by Miss Eunice L. Kettering, of Harrisonburg State Teachers
College.

The full text of this fragment is to be found as *TBVa* H (p. 113); the
tune subsequently contributed is here printed for the first time. Mead
finds the tune interesting, but in some respects suspicious. It is retained
with this warning.

The *TBVa* headnote points out the possibility of a ballad "tribute" to a
distinguished Virginian, John Randolph of Roanoke, himself an early collector of old ballads. In view of ballad ways, this possibility is not to be
taken too seriously. But Cf. *TBVa*, p. 23.

1   "What did you have for your supper,
     Johnny Randolph, my son?"
     "Eels fried in butter, Mother,
     Make my bed soon,
     I've a pain in my heart,
     And I want to lie down."

DD

"Johnny Randal." Collected by Weston O. McDaniel, of Fairview, Va.
Sung by Mrs. Murvil Dick, of Frederick County, Va. Frederick County.
March 14, 1933. A tune was sent with this version, but the editor cannot
locate it. Variations in the text justify its inclusion, without the tune.

1   "Where was you last night [nigh-height],
     Johnny Randal, my son?
     Where was you last night,
     My dear little one?"

2   "I was a-courtin' my sweetheart,
     Mother, make my bed soon,
     I have a pain in my heart [har-art],
     I want to lie down."

3   "What had you for supper,
     Johnny Randal, my son?
     What had you for supper,
     My dear little one?"

4   "Fresh eels fried in butter,
     Mother, make my bed soon,
     I have a pain in my heart
     I want to lie down."

5   "Do you think you are dyin',
     Johnny Randal, my son?
     Do you think you are dyin',
     My dear little one?"

6   "Yes, I think I am dyin',
     Mother, make my bed soon,
     I have a pain in my heart,
     I want to lie down."

7   "What do you will to your father,
     Johnny Randal, my son?
     What do you will to your father,
     My dear little one?"

8   "My farm and utensils,
     Mother, make my bed soon,

I have a pain in my heart,
 I want to lie down."

9 "What do you will to your sister,
 Johnny Randal, my son?
What do you will to your sister,
 My dear little one?"

10 "My bed and bed clothin',
 Mother, make my bed soon,
I have a pain in my heart,
 I want to lie down."

11 "What do you will to your brother,
 Johnny Randal, my son?
What do you will to your brother,
 My dear little one?"

12 "My horse and my saddle,
 Mother, make my bed soon,
I have a pain in my heart,
 I want to lie down."

13 "What do you will to your sweetheart,
 Johnny Randal, my son?
What do you will to your sweetheart,
 My dear little one?"

14 "Hell fire[r] and brimstone
 That will scorch her light brow,
For she's the cause of this pain [pay-ain],
 I want to lie down."

EE

"Jeems Randal." Collected by E. J. Sutherland, of Clintwood, Va. Contributed by Miss Ada Rose, of Clinchco, Va., who learned it from Mrs. Betty Sexton, her great-grandmother. Dickenson County. March 12, 1932. Interesting text variants.

1 "What did you have for your breakfast,
 Jeems Randal, my son?
What did you eat for your breakfast,
 My sweet and fair one?"
"Fried eel and fresh butter,
 Mother, fix my bed soon,
I am sick at my heart,
 And it faints or lie down."

2 "What did you eat for your dinner,
　　Jeems Randal, my son?
What did you eat for your dinner,
　　My sweet and fair one?"
"Sweet milk and roast venison,
　　Mother, fix my bed soon,
I am sick at my heart,
　　And it faints or lie down."

3 "What did you eat for your supper,
　　Jeems Randal, my son?
What did you eat for your supper,
　　My sweet and fair one?"
"Baked ham and fried onions,
　　Mother, fix my bed soon,
I am sick at my heart,
　　And it faints or lie down."

4 "What do you will to your mother,
　　Jeems Randal, my son?
What do you will to your mother,
　　My sweet and fair one?"
"The house and the garden,
　　Mother, fix my bed soon,
I am sick at my heart,
　　And it faints or lie down."

5 "What do you will to your sister,
　　Jeems Randal, my son?
What do you will to your sister,
　　My sweet and fair one?"
"My trunk and my money,
　　Mother, fix my bed soon,
I am sick at my heart,
　　And it faints or lie down."

6 "What do you will to your brother,
　　Jeems Randal, my son?
What do you will to your brother,
　　My sweet and fair one?"
"My rope and my saddle,
　　Mother, fix my bed soon,
I am sick at my heart,
　　And it faints or lie down."

7   "What do you will to your father,
Jeems Randal, my son?
What do you will to your father,
My sweet and fair one?"
"The me-ans to bury me,
Mother, fix my bed soon,
I am sick at my heart,
And it faints or lie down."

8   "What do you will to your sweetheart,
Jeems Randal, my son?
What do you will to your sweetheart,
My sweet and fair one?"
"The rope and the gallows,
Mother, fix my bed soon,
I am sick at my heart,
And it faints or lie down."

FF

"John Willow, My Son." Phonograph record (aluminum) made by A. K. Davis, Jr. Sung by Mrs. J B. Crawford, of Altavista, Va. Campbell County. August 4, 1932. Text transcribed by P. C. Worthington. Tune noted by Winston Wilkinson.

This version is the same as *TBVa* A, with the exception that a stanza relating the death of the dogs has been dropped. The tune, here faithfully transcribed from phonographic singing, may be compared to the earlier notation from the same singer in *TBVa*, p. 556.

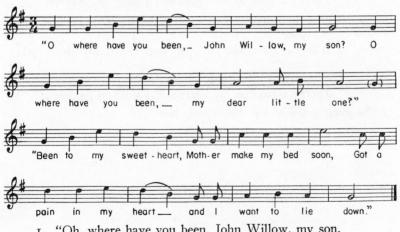

1   "Oh, where have you been, John Willow, my son,
Oh, where have you been, my dear little one?"
"Been to my sweetheart's, Mother make my bed soon,
There's a pain on my heart and I want to lie down."

2 "What'd you have for your supper, John Willow, my son,
       What'd you have for your supper, my dear little one?"
   "Eels fried in batter, Mother make my bed soon,
       There's a pain on my heart and I want to lie down."

3 "What'd you do with your leavings, John Willow, my son,
       What'd you do with your leavings, my dear little one?"
   "Gave them to my dogs, Mother make my bed soon,
       There's a pain on my heart and I want to lie down."

4 "I believe you are poisoned, John Willow, my son,
       I believe you are poisoned, my dear little one,"
   "Yes, Mother, I'm poisoned, Mother make my bed soon,
       There's a pain on my heart and I want to lie down."

5 "What do you will to your father, John Willow, my son,
       What do you will to your father, my dear little one?"
   "My house and my land, Mother make my bed soon,
       There's a pain on my heart and I want to lie down."

6 "What do you will to your mother, John Willow, my son,
       "What do you will to your mother, my dear little one?"
   "Wish a home in heaven, Mother make my bed soon,
       There's a rill[1] in my heart and I want to lie down."

7 "What do you will to your sister, John Willow, my son,
       What do you will to your sister, my dear little one?"
   "My horse and my saddle, Mother make my bed soon,
       There's a pain on my heart and I want to lie down."

8 "What do you will to your sweetheart, John Willow, my
       son,
       What do you will to your sweetheart, my dear little
       one?"
   "Hell fire and brimstone, Mother make my bed soon,
       There's a pain on my heart and I want to lie down."

1. The singer seems to say "rill" clearly here.

EDWARD
(Child, No. 13)

Despite the remarkable dramatic power of this ballad in which a mother pries from her son a confession that he has murdered his father or brother, relatively few texts have been found in Britain and America. The versions in *TBVa* and the present versions, with one exception, follow Child A in presenting the crime as fratricide rather than patricide; in BB Edward appears to have murdered his sweetheart.

It is likely that AA is the first uncorrupted American text to follow Child A and B in implicating the mother. Previously, only a garbled text from Vermont (*Vt. Hist. Society, Proceedings,* N. S., VII, 1939, 102), which was a combination of "The Twa Brothers" and "Edward," involved the mother in the crime. AA, however, is a fine text which is remarkably close to the language and detail of Child A—particularly in the concluding "fire of coals" speech. In spite of the possible ambiguity of this speech, it seems clear that the son would gladly see his mother burn in hell for her complicity. The title "Percy" and the address to "Son Percy, Son Percy" seem to be unique in this version.

BB is a fragmentary but distinctive text with a tune verifiable from the record. The text of CC from the same source appeared as *TBVa* B, but the tune is new and of interest.

Child prints only two versions of this ballad, from Motherwell and Percy, respectively, plus an 1829 manuscript fragment of Alexander Laing. Continental counterparts seem to be limited to Northern Europe—Sweden, Denmark, Finland, Norway. These versions, plus the English, Scottish, and American, have been carefully studied by Professor Archer Taylor in *Edward and Sven i Rosengaard* (University of Chicago Press, 1931).

No record of this ballad in recent British tradition appears either in Margaret Dean-Smith's *Guide* or in Greig and Keith's *Last Leaves*. American texts and tunes are fairly well known (Sharp-Karpeles print ten), but Coffin has shown the ballad to be less common than most in American tradition, and less varied in story types. *TBVa* printed only five out of an available six texts, with two tunes. *FSVa* lists only three items, with two tunes, all of which are presented here.

The poetic and dramatic excellence of this ballad has led some scholars and critics to question whether it may not be rather the product of conscious art than of folk tradition (see Bertrand H. Bronson, *SFQ, IV* [1940], 1-13 and 159-61, and Arthur K. Moore, *Comparative Literature,* X [Winter, 1958], 16). The appearance of so many and varied American texts and tunes from authentic oral tradition—including the three that follow—should go far toward a solution of the problem, even without the authority of Child. But the voice of Child is also clear: " 'Edward' is not only unimpeachable, but has ever been regarded as one of the noblest and most sterling specimens of the popular ballad." Perhaps it is only Percy's version, with its antique spelling and dramatic climax, that is subject to some question.

Bronson (I, 237-47) prints a limited twenty-four tunes (with texts) of this ballad first given to the world by Percy. Mother-well fails to give a promised tune, so that "all the tunes that have been found for this ballad, save one or two, come from the Appalachians, and all have been recovered only in the present century." No recent Scottish version has been found, and only very recently a copy from Hampshire in England. Bronson distinguishes three groups: Group A, with six members, composed of Appalachian variants and their derivatives; Group B, with thirteen items, composed of variants with tunes (three) traditionally associated with other ballads ("Gypsy Laddie" or "Lady Isabel," "Boyne Water," or "The House Carpenter"); and a somewhat arbitrary Group C, of five variants, developing from "The House Carpenter" and with other connections. Of the two tunes of *TBVa,* C is classified in Group B, D in Group C.

AA

"Percy." Collected by R. E. Lee Smith, of Palmyra, Va. Sung by his brother, Thomas P. Smith, of Palmyra, Va., and himself. They learned it January 22, 1916, from the singing of "M. A. Yarber, of Mast, N. C., who had heard it sang now of sixty-five years by his father." Fluvanna County. Smith adds, "One person, Mrs. P. J. Roper [?], said it was called 'Edward.' "

> 1   "What blood is that on your coat lap,
>   My son Percy, my son Percy?
> What blood is that on your coat lap,
>   And the truth please tell to me."

2 "It is the blood of my great falcon,
   Mother Lady, Mother Lady,
   It is the blood of my great falcon,
   And the truth I have told ye."

3 "Falcon's blood was never that red,
   Son Percy, son Percy,
   Falcon blood was never that red,
   And the truth to me."

4 "It is the blood of my greyhound,
   Mother Lady, Mother Lady,
   It is the blood of my greyhound,
   As he would not hunt for me."

5 "Dog's blood was never that red,
   Son Percy, son Percy,
   Dog's blood was never that red,
   And the truth tell to me."

6 "It is the blood of my brother John,
   Mother Lady, Mother Lady,
   It is the blood of my brother John,
   And the truth I have told ye."

7 "What plea have you to give,
   Son Percy, son Percy?"
   "It began by cutting an elm tree,
   That tree I did not want cut."

8 "What death do you wish to die,
   Son Percy, son Percy?
   What death do you wish to die,
   And the truth tell to me."

9 "I would like to sink in the sea,
   Mother Lady, Mother Lady,
   I will set my foot in a bottomless ship
   And you will see any more of me."

10 "What will you leave your poor wife,
   Son Percy, son Percy?"
   "Grief and trouble all her life,
   And she I will never see again."

11 "What will you leave to your old son,
   Son Percy, son Percy?"
   "I will leave him the world to wander up and down,
   And he will never get more from me."

12 "What will you leave to your mother dear,
    Son Percy, son Percy?"
"A fire of coals to burn her hearty cheer,
    And she will never get more from me."

BB

"Edward." Phonograph record (aluminum) made by A. K. Davis, Jr. Sung
by Mrs. S. A. Bishop, of Marion, Va. Smyth County. August 16, 1932.
Text transcribed by P. C. Worthington. Tune noted by G. W. Williams
and E. C. Mead.

1   "How come this blood on your shirt sleeve,
        My son, pray tell on to me?"
    "It is the blood of the little gray mare
        That plowed those fields for me,
        That plowed those fields for me."

2   "It's too red a blood for the little gray mare,
        Plowed those fields for me."
    "It is the blood of the little dear girl
        That walked and talked with me,
        That walked and talked with me."

3   "What you gonna do when your father comes home,
        My son, pray tell on to me?"

"I'll set my foot on the yonders ship,[1]
And I'll sail across the sea,
I'll sail across the sea."

4   "When you coming back, my son, to me,[2]
My son, pray tell on to me?"
"When the moon and the sun goes down upon the green,[3]
And nobody else but me,
And nobody else but me."[4]

1. "Yonders" is uncertain.
2. These last four words are uncertain.
3. Singer starts "When the sun . . .," hesitates, and continues "moon and the sun."
4. Last lines unclear.

CC

"What's on Your Sword?"   Collected by Miss Margaret Purcell, of Greenwood, Va.   Sung by her mother, Elizabeth Ashton Garrett Purcell (Mrs. S. H. Purcell), of Greenwood, Va., in the early nineties.   Albemarle County.   May, 1934.   Tune noted by Winston Wilkinson.
This text is very close to TBVa B (pp. 121-23), collected by Miss Evelyn Purcell, the sister of Miss Margaret Purcell, in 1913.   The previously collected text was, however, without tune.   The order of stanzas 4, 5, 6 is reversed in the TBVa text, and there are minor verbal changes.

1   "What is that on the end of your sword
My dear son, tell to me,
What is that on the end of your sword,
My dear son, tell to me?"
" 'Tis the very blood of an English crane
My father sent to me,
'Tis the very blood of an English crane
My father sent to me."

2   "Crane's blood is not so red,
        My dear son, tell to me,
    Crane's blood is not so red,
        My dear son, tell to me."
    " 'Tis the very blood of my dear little brother,
        And I wish it had never been,
    'Tis the very blood of my dear little brother,
        And I wish it had never been."

3   "What will your father say to you,
        My dear son, tell to me,
    What will your father say to you,
        My dear son, tell to me?"
    "I will put my foot in the bottom of the boat,
        And sail away to sea,
    I will put my foot in the bottom of the boat,
        And sail away to sea."

4   "What will you do with your pretty little girl,
        My dear son, tell to me,
    What will you do with your pretty little girl,
        My dear son, tell to me?"
    "I will leave her with her grandmother
        To make her think of me,
    I will leave her with her grandmother
        To make her think of me."

5   "What will you do with your dear little boy,
        My dear son, tell to me,
    What will you do with your dear little boy,
        My dear son, tell to me?"
    "I will leave him with his grandfather
        To make him think of me.
    I will leave him with his grandfather
        To make him think of me."

6   "What will you do with your sweet little wife,
        My dear son, tell to me,
    What will you do with your sweet little wife,
        My dear son, tell to me?"
    "She shall put her foot in the bottom of the boat,
        And sail away with me,
    She shall put her foot in the bottom of the boat,
        And sail away with me."

7 "When do you expect to return again,
　　My dear son, tell to me,
When do you expect to return again,
　　My dear son, tell to me?"
"When the sun and the moon set on yonder hill,
　　And that will never be,
When the sun and the moon set on yonder hill,
　　And that will never be."

9

BABYLON; or, THE BONNIE BANKS O FORDIE
(CHILD, No. 14)

Child prints six texts of this ballad which tell substantially the following story: Three maidens go out together or singly to a wood, when up starts a robber or banished man. One by one he turns them around and makes them stand, demanding that they wed him or die by his wee penknife. The first and second refuse, and die. The third warns him of her brother who is in the wood, and who will avenge them. He realizes that he is the brother, and now aware of having killed his two sisters, he commits suicide. Sometimes there are three brothers, and their occupations are given. In Child E, the third sister is saved by a *deus ex machina* brother, John. Child F has two brothers, among other changes, but is closely related to Child A. Child apparently considered this ballad, by structure, to be one of the older ballads. It preserves such interesting folklore as the idea of a tabooed sacred wood or grove; here the maidens summon an outlaw by picking flowers, leaves, etc. (see Wimberly, pp. 314-20).

The ballad has not been widely collected in tradition. Greig-Keith publish a two-stanza fragment, and Barry reports that there is an excellent text with tune in the *Miscellanea of the Rymour Club*. These seem to be the only British survivals. In North America, versions of this ballad have been printed from Newfoundland (Greenleaf and Mansfield; Karpeles; Fowke), Maine (Barry —a one stanza fragment), Vermont (Flanders: *Ballads Migrant in New England*), New York (*BFSSNE,* No. 7), Tennessee (*TFSB,* VIII), and North Carolina (Brown). In the only texts which name the robber, he is called Baby Lon in the North Carolina and Tennessee versions, Robey in the New York version, and Little Lon in the present Virginia version. In addition to preserving a name for the robber, these are the only four texts which preserve the talisman of pulling the flowers. The robber is named in only two Child versions. In Child F he is either John or James; in Child A he is Baby Lon. It is curious that Child should combine the two names into one, Babylon, in his title, when the only time this name appears in a text (Child A, 15) it is given as two

words.   He evidently follows the title as given in Motherwell's
Minstrelsy and risks confusion with the ancient city.

The Virginia version of this ballad was contributed October
20, 1932, by R. E. Lee Smith, then of Bumpass, Va., as he and
his brother Thomas P. Smith collected it from Moses A. Yarber, of
Mast, N. C., February 11, 1914.   Mr. Smith writes on the manuscript:

Mr. Yarber heard this song sung over 45 years before by his father
John Yarber.   Bennett Smith, my father, recalled hearing part of this
song over 40 years before the above date 1914, and he said the last
verse: "And that was (wur) the last of Baby Lon," instead of Little
Lon, but I thought it was best to use it as Mr. Yarber sang it, as he
knowed more of the song than my father.

The Virginia text follows Child A closely, with some abridgement.
It preserves much of the best of Child's version, such as "to bear
the fair rose company," while adding a vigor and color from its
American oral tradition.   The "rank robber" of Child has become
a "bloody robber" with a "keen sharp knife" instead of a "wee
penknife."   Child's "banisht man" is replaced by a "mean looking
man," and in the sixteenth stanza "he fell to the ground dead" has
an immediacy which we do not find in Child, whose villain "twyned
himsel o his ain sweet life."   The final stanza, with its retrospect
and termination of the story, seems to be in the tradition of this
ballad.   The local title "Three Sisters" is also unique for this
ballad, though it is a very natural extraction from the first line of
this and other versions.

Bronson (I, 248-52) can muster only eight tunes (with texts)
of this rare ballad, six in Group A and two "by courtesy" in a
separate Group B.   No version appeared in *TBVa*.   The present
text, even without a tune, is a great rarity.

AA

"Three Sisters."   Collected by R. E. Lee Smith, of Palmyra, Va.   Sung
by his brother, Thomas P. Smith, of Palmyra, Va., and himself.   Fluvanna
County.   October 20, 1932.   They learned the ballad from Moses A. Yarber,
of Mast, N. C., on February 11, 1914.   The state of the manuscript leaves
much to be desired, but there is clear indication that the stanzaic division
Mr. Smith favored was a two-line stanza as given below.   The only other
text of North Carolina origin (Brown Collection, pp. 44-45) also is made
up of two-line stanzas and has no refrain.   There is no indication of a refrain in the Virginia text, but the manuscript leaves the possibility that the
second line of stanza one, and the second line of stanza two, might have
been interpolated as refrain lines throughout, though this seems unlikely.

In the absence of music, the two-line stanzaic rendering of the ballad and the present stanzaic division seem to have best manuscript authority, even if they lack absolute finality. The possibility of certain refrain lines remains: "They was handsome to behold" is a not impossible parallel to Child A's "Eh vow bonnie," and "On ye banks of ye river Mordie" is even closer to Child A's "On the bonnie banks o Fordie," and is echoed with a somewhat refrain-like effect in the final line, "The robber of river Mordie." But it would be a greater liberty to present these lines as refrain lines than to print the text as it follows, in closer conformity to the (admittedly difficult) manuscript.

1   There was three ladies that lived in a town,
    They was handsome to behold.

2   And one day they went out to pick some flowers
    On ye banks of ye river Mordie.

3   They had picked but a very few flowers,
    When up come a mean looking man.

4   He took the oldest sister by the hand,
    And he turned her around and made her stand.

5   Saying, "Will you be a bloody robber's wife,
    Or will you die by my keen sharp knife?"

6   "I will not be a bloody robber's wife,
    I had ruther die by your keen sharp knife."

7   He killed this lady and laid her down
    For to bear the fair rose company.

8   He took the second sister by the hand,
    And turned her round and made her stand.

9   He said, "Will you be a bloody robber's wife,
    Or will you die by my keen sharp knife?"

10   "I will never be a bloody robber's wife,
    I had ruther die by your keen sharp knife."

11   He killed this lady and laid her down
    For to bear the fair rose company.

12   He took the youngest sister by the hand,
    And turned her round and made her stand.

13   "Will you be a bloody robber's wife,
    Or will you die by my keen sharp knife?"

14   "I will not be a bloody robber's wife.
    I had a brother that lived in the woods.

15   "They called him Little Lon,
    And if he sees you your days will be few."

16　He turned his knife to his heart,
　　And he fell to the ground dead.

17　And that was the last of Little Lon,
　　The robber of river Mordie.

10

SIR LIONEL
(CHILD, No. 18)

In the course of its history, this ballad has run the gamut from "Arthurian romance to semi-burlesqued melodrama in homespun" (*TBVa* headnote, p. 125). The texts that follow reduce the narrative to the single episode of the boar hunt, familiarized even further in BB, CC, and DD as a wild hog hunt. The ballad has become merely a hunting song of a somewhat comic sort or a nursery song used for entertainment, lullaby, or "scare" purposes. A few traces may be found, however, of a chilvalric ancestry known to Child: the knife is still "wooden" (i.e., for use in the woods), the bugle is still in evidence, the vegetation is still oak and ash (Child D), and the hero still receives his "shoes" for his victory (*TBVa* D, F). AA retains the "Temple Hill" found also in *TBVa* B and D; but the trusty knife of the huntsman has succumbed in BB to old age and to rust. The nineteenth-century minstrel stage may in part account for the spread of this song in America.

The nonsense refrains are highly characteristic of this ballad and are no doubt part of its appeal to children. Note, however, the effort of CC and DD (from neighboring counties) to make sense of the last refrain line.

Child prints four more or less full texts and two fragmentary ones, none of them having much in common with the American ones. His texts are all English, except one which is Scottish. A few English texts have been found in recent tradition (see Margaret Dean-Smith) but none in Scotland (see *Last Leaves*). Coffin indicates rather meager gleanings in America. Sharp prints four tunes with very brief texts from the Southern Appalachians. Only one two-stanza text (no tune) appears in the Brown Collection (II, 46). *TBVa* prints seven texts and four tunes. From more recent collection in Virginia, there are six additional items, including four tunes, three of them from records (one not listed in *FSVa*). All four texts with tunes are here presented.

Bronson (I, 265-74) prints seventeen tunes (with texts) and divides them into three groups: Group A, of only two members, one mid-nineteenth-century Scottish and one twentieth-century

American, either retains the more dignified romantic tone of the ballad or the interlaced refrain concerning the hunter; Group B, with only a single specimen from D'Urfey, harks back to the seventeenth-century ballad of "Sir Eglamore" and has a distinctive stanzaic pattern with interlaced refrain lines; and Group C contains fourteen numbers, two British and the rest American, all collected in this century and representing the "Bangum and the Boar" tradition, with stanzaic patterns and elaborate nonsense refrains which suggest either the "Sir Eglamore" pattern or a crossing with "The Frog's Wedding." The four texts with tunes from *TBVa* all fall into Group C.

After a quick survey of older and more recent versions, chiefly with respect to words and stanzaic patterns, Bronson concludes: "Obviously, there has either been a complete break here with older tradition, or the traditional antecedents are not represented in the examples printed by Child." He inclines to the latter alternative, and supports his case by an account of what has happened to the narrative before he proceeds to his musical analysis and classification indicated above.

Of the tunes below, AA, BB, CC, and DD all belong to Bronson's Group C.

AA

"Old Bangem." Contributed by Miss Margaret Purcell, of Greenwood, Va. Sung by her mother, Mrs. S. H. Purcell, of Greenwood, Va. Albemarle County. May, 1934. Tune noted by Winston Wilkinson. A text and tune from the same source were printed in *TBVa*, pp. 127-28, 558-59. A slightly changed text and revised tune, with variants, are here presented.

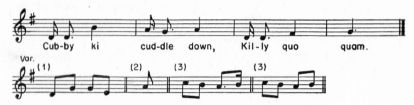

Cub-by ki   cud-dle down,   Kil-ly quo   quam.

1   Old Bangem would a-hunting ride,
      Dillum down dillum,
    Old Bangem would a-hunting ride,
      Dillum down,
    Old Bangem would a-hunting ride,
    Sword and pistol by his side,
      Cubby ki cuddle down,
      Killy quo quam.

2   "There is a wild boar in this wood,
    Will eat your meat and suck your blood."

3   "O how shall I this wild boar see?"
    "Blow a blast and he'll come to thee."

4   Old Bangem blew both loud and shrill,
    The wild boar heard on Temple Hill.

5   The wild boar came with such a rush,
    He tore down hickory, oak and ash.

6   Old Bangem drew his wooden knife,
    He said that he would take his life.

7   "Old Bangem, did you win or lose?"
    He said that he had won the shoes.

BB

"Wild Hog." Phonograph record (aluminum) made by A. K. Davis, Jr.
Sung by Mrs. Martha Elizabeth Gibson, of Crozet, Va. Albemarle County. April 13, 1933. Text transcribed by P. C. Worthington. Tune noted
by E. C. Mead. Mrs. Gibson's stanzaic patterns are somewhat irregular.
Hence Mead has chosen the fourth stanza as most representative of the
tune.

Text independently collected by Fred F. Knobloch. May 1, 1931. Significant variants are footnoted.

Old Lank-tum foll'd him to his den,   Dil-lum down dil-lum,— Old

Lank-tum he fol-low'd him to his den, He found the bones of a thou-sand men

Come to quarl, cud-dle down, kill de qual, quam.

1 There was a wild hog in the woods
    Dillum down dillum,
  He'll eat your meat, he'll drink your blood,
    Come to quarl,[1] cuddle down,
    Kill de qual, quam.

2 Old Lanktum went out on the hill,
    Dillum down dillum,
  He blowed his horn both loud and shrill.
    Come to quarl, cuddle down,
    Kill de qual, quam.

3 That wild hog came in such a dash,
    Dillum down dillum,
  That wild hog came in such a dash,
  He cut his way through oak and ash,
    Come to quarl, cuddle down,
    Kill de qual, quam.

4 Old Lanktum followed him to his den,
    Dillum down dillum,
  Old Lanktum he followed him to his den,
  He found the bones of a thousand men.
    Come to quarl, cuddle down,
    Kill de qual, quam.

5 Old Lanktum drew his rusty[2] knife,
    Dillum down dillum,
  Old Lanktum he drew his rusty knife,
  For to 'prive that wild hog of his life.
    Come to quarl, cuddle down,
    Kill de qual, quam.

1. MS. notes that this is a spelling of "quarrel." Mr. Knobloch's MS. consistently spells this word "quarl" and the word in the line following "qual," but Mrs. Gibson's pronunciations of the the two are hard to distinguish.
2. MS. has "lusty"; cf. "trusty."

CC

"Wild Hog." Phonograph record (fiber base) made by Fred F. Knobloch. Sung by Mrs. Edna Ethel McAlexander, of Meadows of Dan, Va. Patrick County. April 1, 1948. Text transcribed by P. C. Worthington. Tune noted by G. W. Williams and E. C. Mead. Stanza five seems most characteristic musically, hence has been noted as the standard ahead of stanza one.

1   There is a wild hog in the wood,
        Diddle o down, diddle o day,
    There is a wild hog in the wood,
        Diddle o,
    There is a wild hog in the wood,
    He kills their men and drinks his blood,
        Come out Kate, cut him down, kill him if you can.

2   There he comes through yonders marsh,
    He splits his way through oak and ash.

3 Bangum drew his wooden knife,
   To rob that wild hog of his life.

4 They fought four hours of the day,
   At length that wild hog stole away.

5 They followed that wild hog to his den,
   And there they found the bones of a thousand men.

DD

"Wild Hog." Phonograph record (aluminum) made by A. K. Davis, Jr.
Sung by Miss Ruby Bowman, of Laurel Fork, Va. Carroll County. August
11, 1932. Text transcribed by P. C. Worthington. Tune noted by G. W.
Williams. Since there are variations in the repeated lines, the whole text
is given.

1 There's a wild hog in these woods,
       Diddle o down, diddle o day,
   There's a wild hog in these woods,
       Diddle o down today,
   There is a wild hog in these woods
   That kills men and sucks their blood,
   Kill him tell, cut him down, kill him if you can.

2 Do you see him a-comin' through yonders mash,
       Diddle o down, diddle o day,
   See him a-comin' through yonders mash,
       Diddle o down today,

See him a-comin' through yonders mash,
Splittin' his way through oak and ash,
Kill him tell, cut him down, kill him if you can.

3   I fought him with my wooden knife,
       Diddle o down, diddle o day,
   I fought him with my wooden knife,
       Diddle o down today,
   Fought him with my wooden knife,
   Before I'd take that wild hog's life,
   Kill him tell, I cut him down, kill him if I can.

4   I followed that groundhog to yonders bend,
       Diddle o down, diddle o day,
   I followed him to yonders bend,
       Diddle o down today,
   Followed that groundhog to yonders bend,
   And there lay the bones of a thousand men,
   I kill him tell, cut him down, kill him if I can.

11

KING ORFEO
(CHILD, No. 19)

No full text but only a "trace" of this ballad has been found in Virginia. It is true that on November 15, 1934, there was contributed to the Virginia collection an unmistakably old and traditional ballad *entitled* "King Orpheo" or "Orpheo," the first line of which read, "For eight long years I have served the great King Orpheo," and the lady Estelle of which seemed to show some slight phonetic resemblance to the Lady Isabel of Child's "King Orfeo." Hence the discovery of a fragment of Child, No. 19, was announced both in Reed Smith's list, "A Glance at the Ballad and Folksong Field," *SFQ*, I (June, 1937), 7-18, in Branford P. Millar's subsequent list, "The American Ballad List—1952," *SFQ*, XVII (June, 1953), 158-66, and in the intervening (1949) *FSVa* (p. 10). On closer examination, however, in spite of these traces of "King Orfeo," the ballad has turned out to be unmistakably a version not of "King Orfeo" (Child, No. 19) but of "The Whummil Bore" (Child, No. 27). See the headnote and text of the latter ballad in this volume, p. 89.

This whole matter has long since been cleared up in an article by Arthur Kyle Davis, Jr., and Paul Clayton Worthington, "A New Traditional Ballad from Virginia: 'The Whummil Bore' (Child, No. 27)," *SFQ*, XXI (December, 1957), 187-93, where, after correcting the mistaken identification, the Archivist notes: *"Mea culpa,* but in view of the title, the king's name, and other possible traces of the "King Orfeo" ballad, possibly not *mea maxima culpa.* At any rate, the erroneous identification is here corrected." No text, then, but only a trace of "King Orfeo" has been found in Virginia, and it is the only trace of the ballad found in America.

The ballad is almost equally rare in Great Britain. Child prints and apparently knew of only a single version of the song in English or Scottish, itself a fragment obtained some years previously "from the singing of Andrew Coutts, an old man in Unst, Shetland." Only recently has another fragment of the ballad, with tune, turned up from the same locality, collected by Patrick Shuldham-Shaw from John Stickle, of Unst, in April, 1947, and published in the *Journal of the English Folk Dance and Song Society* for 1947, with tune. See *JEFDSS,* V (December, 1947), 77. "Mr. Stickle's ballad is undoubtedly a fragment of Child, No. 19," writes the Librarian of the Society, "which was collected in Unst about 100 years earlier, and was even then imperfectly remembered." We are grateful to the Librarian and the *Journal* of the Society for knowledge of this rarity.

In the circumstances, perhaps the Virginia "trace" is itself a sort of ballad rarity.

The Shuldham-Shaw tune and fragmentary text have not escaped the pantoscopic Bronson (I, 275), who marvels thus: "That a tune should in the midst of the twentieth century be recovered for this whisper from the Middle Ages was as little to be expected as that we should hear 'the horns of Elfland faintly blowing.'" He also reports that the variant has been reprinted, with the Child text, in E. S. Reid Tait's *Shetland Folk Book,* II (1951), 56-57.

12

THE CRUEL MOTHER
(CHILD, No. 20)

Five versions of this ballad with four tunes were printed in
TBVa. Only one new version has been recovered in Virginia since
that time. It most closely resembles *TBVa* B, but its second
stanza is new, and the third stanza of B is omitted. The present
version alternates the refrain lines with the story lines, conforming
in this respect more closely to versions in Child than does B. Its
refrain lines are similar to, though not identical with, those in B,
and both B and AA are distinctive among Virginia texts, AA with
a superb tune taken from the record. Coming from the same neighborhood, they represent the same version.

This text, like all other Virginia texts, is condensed, dealing with
the murdered children's conversation with their mother, and omitting the antecedent action of the babes' birth and their murder. Thus
it is related to Child's versions K, L, M, N, of Vol. I, and the un-
lettered versions, one in Vol. IV, and one in Vol. V. The first
refrain line is not found in any Child version, but the second refrain line appears identically or similarly in E, H, N, of Vol. I, in
N [*sic*] of Vol. II, and in the texts in Vol. IV and Vol. V.

The ballad has been fairly widely collected in the United
States, in versions of varying length and completeness. This condensed Virginia version preserves the essentials of the story and is
especially interesting by reason of its beautiful refrain lines and its
tune, which resembles "Babe of Bethlehem" from *Southern Harmony*. The identical stanzas two and four may represent a confusion on the part of the singer, but they do not detract from the
effectiveness of the words of Mr. Keesee's deliberate and moving
basso singing.

Child prints nineteen versions of the ballad, one of them quaintly (and inappropriately to the Scottish text) called "The Minister's
Daughter of New York," evidently a confusion with old York.
Sharp, Williams and others have found versions in recent English
tradition (see Dean-Smith), and Greig and Keith, quite naturally
since the Child versions are practically all Scottish, find it sur-

viving in Scotland (see *Last Leaves,* pp. 21-23). Among the collectors in America, Sharp-Karpeles print thirteen tunes with texts or partial texts from the Southern Appalachians. There is no version in the Brown Collection, but several versions from North Carolina appear in Cecil Sharp's collections. See Coffin for a fairly extensive, but not too extensive, listing and discussion of American texts.

So condensed is the present text that it may not be clear that the babes are ghosts. The antecedent folklore detail of the mother's binding of the hands and feet of the babes so as to prevent their ghosts from walking, found in several Child texts (C, F, H, I) and in some American texts (see Cox B, p. 30; Sharp-Karpeles A, F, G, Vol. I, 56, 59; etc.), does not appear in the present text or in any other Virginia text. (See Wimberly, pp. 254-55.) The Virginia version is not so detailed about the mother's punishment as some texts, but it does predict hell for her after a normal folklore period of "seven long years on earth."

Bronson (I, 276-96) has brought together a total of fifty-six tunes (with texts), and comments: "For the number of beautiful melodic variations on a basically constant rhythmic pattern, this ballad is exceptional. The binding element of the rhythmical design appears to have been the interlaced refrain at the second and fourth lines." He divides the tunes into five groups, which can only be satisfactorily distinguished by detailed musical technicalities not to be repeated here. But Group A, with twenty-two members, contains some of the oldest copies, as well as recent ones that are Scottish, English, and American; Group B, with eleven variants, contains some good nineteenth- and twentieth-century copies; Group C, with fifteen entries, mostly from America, is predominantly major, but plagal; Group D contains only two related variants in triple time; and Group E, "a group only by courtesy," contains the misfits and leftovers. All four *TBVa* tunes Bronson classifies in his Group C, though he finds one of the four (*TBVa* B) not a strict conformer to the demands of the group.

AA

"The Cruel Mother." Phonograph record (aluminum) made by A. K. Davis, Jr. Sung by Abner Keesee, of Altavista, Va. Campbell County. August 4, 1932. Text transcribed by P. C. Worthington. Tune noted by Winston Wilkinson. "A fine tune, with a wide pitch range and interesting structure" (E. C. Mead).

1 One day I was sitting in my father's hall,
   All day long and I love thee O,
   I saw three babes a-playing their ball,
   Down by the greenwood sidie O.

2 One was dressed in scarlet fine,
   All day long and I love thee O,
   The other two were just like they was born,
   Down by the greenwood sidie O.

3 "O little babes, if you was mine,
   All day long and I love thee O,
   I'd dress you up in scarlet fine,
   Down by the greenwood sidie O."

4 One was dressed in scarlet fine,
   All day long and I love thee O,
   The other two was just like they was born,
   Down by the greenwood sidie O.

5 "O little babes, if you can tell,
   All day long and I love thee O,
   How long on earth am I to dwell,
   Down by the greenwood sidie O?"

6 "Seven long years on earth you'll dwell,
   All day long and I love thee O,
   The balance of your time you will spend it in hell,
   Down by the greenwood sidie O."

13

THE THREE RAVENS
(CHILD, No. 26)

Rather surprisingly, Child prints only a single version of "The Three Ravens" as main entry for the ballad, but he somewhat grudgingly admits another text to the Additions and Corrections in Volume V, 212. He includes in his headnote to the ballad Sir Walter Scott's *Minstrelsy* copy of "The Twa Corbies," which he agrees with Scott in considering rather a counterpart than a traditionary form of "The Three Ravens." He states (V, 212) that traditional copies of the ballad have been far from infrequent, but he apparently finds them too close to the version printed in London in 1611 by Thomas Ravenscroft in his *Melismata, Musical Phantasies, Fitting the Court, Cittie, and Country Humours* (No. 20) and reprinted by Ritson in his *Ancient Songs* of 1790 (p. 155). Child includes a one-stanza variant of his main text from Motherwell's *Minstrelsy* of 1827.

Of recent British collectors (in Britain), only Frank Kidson (*Traditional Tunes*, 1891, and *Folk Songs from the North Countrie*, 1927) seems to have preserved the song, according to Margaret Dean-Smith (p. 111). It is not included in Greig and Keith's *Last Leaves* from Aberdeenshire.

The American texts, with one or two exceptions noted by Coffin, are far removed from the British versions. The change in spirit is symbolized by the change in title to "The Three Crows." The usual American text is certainly less poetical than either the English "The Three Ravens" or the Scottish "The Twa Corbies," though it is closer to the grisliness of the latter than to the tenderness of the former. What was once a human drama, touching or cynical, has become an animal song, comic or gruesome, a nursery song, or "scare" song for children. It is not unlikely that the song has been influenced by the minstrel stage (see Kittredge, *JAFL*, XXXI [1918], 273). But the ballad has by no means lost its appeal for the folk, and continues to be varied and sung.

Seventeen texts (of an available twenty-seven) and four tunes of this ballad—plus two rollicking Civil War parodies—are printed in *TBVa*. Since then, three new texts, two of them with tunes,

have been added to the Virginia collection (one of them unlisted in
FSVa). All three are here presented as interesting brief studies in
minor variation. Only the first, AA, has the "Billy Magee Magaw,"
"Caw, caw, caw" refrain lines. Except for the refrain lines and
their absence in the other two texts, the three obviously belong to
the same version represented by the three Sharp-Karpeles texts
(all three of which, incidentally, come from Virginia—see I, 63-64)
and by most of the texts in *TBVa*. The one Brown Collection text
(II, 46), without tune, is also almost the same. All belong to
Coffin's Story Type A.

The word "bait" in BB 2 comes from the Old Norse and Middle
English word meaning food. Note that the unfamiliar word is
changed to "grub" in AA and to "something to eat" in CC. "Eat,"
incidentally, is pronounced "ate," to rhyme with "mate" and "bait."

Botkin describes the ballad as a play-party game in *American
Play Party Song* (p. 63), and Doerflinger in *Shantymen and Shan-
tyboys* (p. 21) prints a version used as a sea shanty to a "Blow the
Man Down" tune. Only two or three of the American texts—from
Iowa, Pennsylvania, and possibly Maine—retain a trace of the more
elaborate Child version and its primitive superstition concerning
the metamorphosis of the faithful true-love into the fallow doe.
See Coffin, p. 53, and Wimberly, pp. 55-56; also Friedman, p. 23.

Bronson (I, 308-16) prints twenty-one tunes (with texts) and
divides them into seven groups, plus an appendix. Bronson, here
as elsewhere, does not fully explain his groupings, but leaves the
groups to speak for themselves. It would seem, however, that his
Group A, of three members, all British, represents the earlier form
of the ballad: a couplet with first line thrice repeated and interlaced refrain lines; that Group B, of four items, all American, contains later stanzaic and melodic counterparts of the earlier form;
that Group C, with three variants, represents the more cynical
Scottish branch of the ballad; that Groups D, E, and F, of three,
two, and two members, respectively, represent in varying melodic
ways the Scottish tradition in North America; that Group G, a
single American entry, represents a reversion to the older stanzaic
pattern; and that the three occupants of the Appendix are irregular
or questionable in one way or another.

Of the four tunes given in *TBVa*, one (P) is mentioned in
Group D, the other three (I, J, K, the last two almost identical)
compose Group F. Bronson draws attention to the carol or dancing pattern of the better copies of the ballad and their similarity to

the refrain pattern of "The Two Sisters" (Child, No. 10).   Here
—as similarly elsewhere—he properly questions the acceptability,
as tradition related to this ballad, of a Niles text and tune.   Of the
tunes below, AA belongs to Bronson's Group B.

AA

"The Three Crows."   Collected by Miss Margaret Purcell, of Greenwood,
Va.   Sung by her mother, Elizabeth Ashton Garrett Purcell (Mrs. S. H.
Purcell), of Greenwood, Va., in the early nineties.   Albemarle County.
May, 1934.   Tune noted by Winston Wilkinson.

    1   There were three crows sat on a tree,   } *twice*
          O Billy Magee Magaw,
       There were three crows sat on a tree,
       And they were black as crows could be,
       And they all flapped their wings and cried,
          "Caw, caw, caw."

    2   Said one black crow unto his mate,   } *twice*
          O Billy Magee Magaw,
       Said one black crow unto his mate,

"Where shall we get some grub to eat?"
And they all flapped their wings and cried,
    "Caw, caw, caw."

3 "There lies a horse on yonder plain,   } *twice*
     O Billy Magee Magaw,
   There lies a horse on yonder plain,
   And he has just been lately slain."
   And they all flapped their wings and cried,
     "Caw, caw, caw."

4 "We'll perch upon his bare backbone,   } *twice*
     O Billy Magee Magaw,
   We'll perch upon his bare backbone,
   And pick his eyes out one by one."
   And they all flapped their wings and cried,
     "Caw, caw, caw."

BB

"The Three Crows." Phonograph record (aluminum) made by A. K.
Davis, Jr. Sung by Minor Wilson, of Lewisburg, W. Va., and Char-
lottesville, Va. Albemarle County. February, 1932. Text transcribed by
P. C. Worthington. Tune noted by G. W. Williams and E. C. Mead.

There were three crows sat on a tree, And
they were black as black could be. Then one old crow unto his mate: "What shall we have for bait to eat?"

1 There were three crows sat on a tree,
   And they were black as black can be.

2 Said one crow unto his mate,
   "What shall we have for bait to eat?"

3 "I see a horse on yonder plain
   Who looks as though but lately slain.

4 "We'll perch ourselves on his jaw bone
   And pick his eyes out one by one."

CC

"The Three Crows." Collected by Miss Martha M. Davis, of Harrisonburg, Va. Given by Miss Mary Spitzer, a student at State Teachers College, Harrisonburg, Va. Rockingham County. 1931.

1 Three crows they sat upon a tree,
As black as any crows could be.

2 One crow said unto his mate,
"What shall we do for something to eat?"

3 "On the other side of yonders plain
There lies a horse but three days slain.

4 "We'll jump right on to his backbone
And pick his eyes out one by one."

14

THE WHUMMIL BORE
(CHILD, No. 27)

Child prints only one version of this ballad, from Motherwell, and remarks that it "seems not to have been met with, or at least to have been thought worth mention, by anybody but Motherwell." The ballad as Child gives it simply tells how a young man has served the king for seven long years and never glimpsed the king's daughter but once. When he did, it was through a whummil bore or gimlet hole, where he observed her being dressed by her servants. The ballad then describes what he saw. In Volume V, 203, under Fragments, Child gives an interesting fragment sent by Motherwell to Charles Kirkpatrick Sharpe, entitled "King Edelbrode." Child and Motherwell felt that it was related to "The Whummil Bore," and it is interesting that Virginia's version should be titled by a king's name, when the king takes no part in the action of the ballad.

Only one text has been recovered from tradition besides the present Virginia text. That one was published in *JAFL,* XX (1907), by Arthur Beatty, who gave a text as it was collected by Claude H. Eldred from Mrs. McLeod, of Dumfries, Scotland, who was visiting her relatives in Wisconsin. As Barry (who furnishes the most tenuous of traces for this ballad) remarks, it "is a quite dissimilar version" from that of Child. Barry's "trace" is a recognition of the chorus by two different persons (Barry, p. 437).

The present Virginia text is closer to Child than Mrs. McLeod's text, and is the only text which can be said to have been found in American oral tradition. R. E. Lee Smith who contributed the ballad, November 15, 1934, wrote in a letter enclosing the song:

I am sending you a very valuable ballad sing by my grandmother Mrs. Chaney Smith and Mr. M. A. Yarber and old friend. My grandmother heard it sing over 100 years ago by her mother. The song is called Orpheo.

In a letter of November 22, 1934, he refers to "that song called King Orpheo." On the manuscript of the ballad he notes that they sang it in Zionville, North Carolina, in 1912, and that since that time two verses have been lost. It may be presumed that the lost verses would have completed the ballad, possibly indicating what two maidens, then one, were doing. This particular text contains interesting traces of "King Orfeo" (Child, No. 19) in its title, in its first line, and perhaps in the name of the daughter. (See under "King Orfeo," above, p. 79.) How King Orpheo came to be mixed up with a version of "The Whummil Bore" might be a matter of interesting speculation, but hardly in a headnote. Perhaps the simplest and most valid explanation is this: it is a way that ballads have.

This ballad does not seem to have survived in oral tradition in Britain. It is unlisted by Margaret Dean-Smith, and it has not been found by us in any British publications prior to or subsequent to her volume. The Virginia version is the only other version known besides Child's Motherwell text and the McLeod text. Coffin (p. 54) refers only to the McLeod text and to the Barry "traces." The Virginia text seems, therefore, to be the third version discovered anywhere of this rare ballad, and the only text showing any trace of "King Orfeo."

For a more detailed discussion of this text and its problems and relations, see Arthur Kyle Davis, Jr., and Paul Clayton Worthington, "A New Traditional Ballad from Virginia: 'The Whummil Bore' (Child, No. 27)," SFQ, XXI (December, 1957), 187-93.

Even Bronson's assiduity has found (I, 316) only a single tune (with partial text): Motherwell's, not reprinted by Child among his tunes in Vol. V. Bronson first suggests that the ballad "appears to be a further example of pawky fun at the expense of high romance—such another as 'Kempy Kay,' 'The Twa Corbies,' and 'Sir Eglamore,' " then expresses his suspicion that it is "a by-blow of a serious romantic ballad; and the evidence of the tune would suggest 'Hind Horn' (17)."

Even in the absence of a tune, the Virginia text from tradition is an almost supreme rarity, as has been intimated above.

AA

"King Orpheo." Contributed by R. E. Lee Smith, of Palmyra and Bumpass, Va. Sung by his brother, Thomas P. Smith, of Palmyra, Va., and himself. Learned from his grandmother, Mrs. Chaney Smith, and M. A. Yarber, of Zionville, N. C., in 1912. Fluvanna County, Va. November 15, 1934.

1   For eight long years I have served the great King Orpheo,
     La fol da lil lilum,
     O fa da la lil lilio.

2   And I have seen his daughter Estelle only once.
     La fol da lil lilum,
     O fa da la lil lilio.

3   She was fairer than the sun that shines,
     La fol da lil lilum,
     O fa da la lil lilio.

4   And she wore gold and diamonds rare
     La fol da lil lilum,
     O fa da la lil lilio.

5   From the bottom of her feet to the top of her head.
     La fol da lil lilum,
     O fa da la lil lilio.

6   I saw her through the key hole of the door.
     La fol da lil lilum,
     O fa da la lil lilio.

7   Five was combing her hear [sic] golden hair,
     La fol da lil lilum,
     O fa da la lil lilio.

8   And four was buckling on her shoes,
     La fol da lil lilum,
     O fa da la lil lilio.

9   And three was putting on her clothes.
     La fol da lil lilum,
     O fa da la lil lilio.

15

THE TWA BROTHERS
(CHILD, No. 49)

Child prints ten versions of this ballad, one of the few known to him in an American version. It does not seem to persist in present-day tradition in either England or Scotland; at least it does not appear in either Margaret Dean-Smith's *Survey* or Gavin Greig's *Last Leaves*. Bronson (I, 384) confirms this observation. The ballad has often been collected in the United States, and eleven texts (all available) with six tunes were published in *TBVa*. The story changes little. Two brothers wrestle while coming home from school, and one is mortally wounded by the other's knife as a result of accident or jealousy, as in Child texts. Most Virginia texts indicate purposeful murder and are related to Child B; even when the wounding is accidental, the texts are verbally closer to Child B than to Child A.

Five versions have been collected since the publication of *TBVa*, one of them, EE, a later phonograph recording of version G in *TBVa*, there given without its tune. Of these five versions, only AA and DD retain the supernatural calling of the murdered brother from his grave by his sweetheart. In DD the idea is badly garbled, but the version is unusual in the names given the participants. The sweetheart is Fair Ellen, and the murderer Lord Thomas, seemingly taken over from "Lord Thomas and Fair Annet," while the murdered brother is named Ben. In AA the blow is apparently struck from passion. In BB the murder weapon is a tomahawk, and the weapon is apparently used merely because the brother will not "play ball/Nor roll the marble stone." The bow and arrow which the dying youth wishes buried with him, coupled with the toma-hawk, suggest Indian lore, but actually the bow and arrow request is English and is found in Child B, leaving only the tomahawk as an American addition. In DD and EE the killing is intentional, but no clear motive is indicated. CC is the only version in which the wound seems to be accidental, but even here the dying brother seems to hint at jealousy as the motive by asking his brother to tell his sweetheart "it's for her sake I'm gone."

Interesting folklore beliefs are preserved in the ending of AA and perhaps DD: Young Susie's supernatural power to charm birds and fishes and Young Johnny out of his grave, and the notion that the kissing of the dead is fatal. (See Wimberly, pp. 282-83.) In other texts (BB, CC) the ending is religious. EE is incomplete.

This ballad presents some of the finest tunes of the collection, with a tune for every text, all except one tune minutely transcribed from phonograph records, and the one exception taken down from live performance by no less a hand than that of John Powell.

Bronson (I, 384-402) prints forty tunes (with texts), plus a single variant as Appendix, and divides the forty into five groups, divided quite strictly according to the middle cadence. All forty-one variants are from American sources. Group A, of eight members, has a middle cadence on the tonic; Group B, with twelve variants, has a middle cadence on the supertonic; Group C, of ten entries, has a middle cadence on the dominant; Group D, seven members, has a middle cadence on the octave above; Group E, with three variants, contains anomalous cases; the single Appendix version is a too literary combination of "The Two Brothers" and "Edward" and is "disturbingly independent," both melodically and textually.

Of the six tunes from *TBVa,* Bronson classifies E in Group A, H in Group B, A and I in Group C, and D and F in Group D: a very representative distribution, minus anomalies and questionable items. This Virginia record seems to corroborate Bronson's remark that "No marked regional distinctions are discernible" in his groupings. Of the tunes below, AA falls into Bronson's Group C, EE into his Group A.

AA

"The Two Brothers." Phonograph record (aluminum) made by A. K. Davis, Jr. Sung by Mrs. Orilla Keeton, of Mt. Fair, Va. Albemarle County. March, 1933. Text transcribed by P. C. Worthington. Tune noted by Winston Wilkinson. This version is extremely close to *TBVa* A, but there are a certain number of variations. The similarity is possibly explained by the fact that the two singers were neighbors in Albemarle County. Mrs. Keeton is one of the older Albemarle County singers, many of whose songs were taken down by Cecil Sharp and Maud Karpeles in 1916. They seem to have missed her version of this ballad. E. C. Mead cites approvingly "the simple melodic arch" of this tune.

There were two broth - ers in one school. One

eve - ning com - ing home _____ The _ old - est said to the young - est one: "Let's have _ a wres - tle and fall." _____

1 There were two brothers in one school.
    One evening coming home
    The oldest said to the youngest one,
    "Let's have a wrestle and fall."

2 The oldest threw the youngest one,
    He threw him to the ground,
    And out of his pocket he drew a penknife
    And gave him a deadly wound.

3 "Pull off, pull off, your woolen shirt,
    And tear it from gore to gore,
    And wrap it around your bleeding wound,
    Then you will bleed no more."

4 So he pulled off his woolen shirt,
    And tore it from gore to gore,
    An-a wrapped it around his bleeding wound,
    Till he did bleed no more.

5 "Pick me all up upon your back,
    And carry me to yonders churchyard,
    And dig my grave both wide and deep,
    And gently lay me down."

6 "What must I tell your loving father,
    When he calls for his son John?"
    "Tell him I'm in some lonely green wood,
    Teaching young hounds to run."

7 "What must I tell your loving mother,
    When she calls for her son John?"
    "Tell her I'm in some graded school,
    Say, 'A good scholar never returns.' "

8 "What must I tell your loving Sue,
      When she calls for her dear John?"
   "Tell her I'm in my lowly grave,
      My books to carry back home."

9 When-a this young Susy heard of this,
      She took the horn and blew,
   She charmed the birds all from the nest
      And the fishes out of the sea.

10 She charmed young Johnny from his grave,
      Said, "Susy, what do you want?"
   "One sweet kiss from your sweet lips
      Is all my heart does crave."

11 "Go home, go home, my loving Susy,
      And weep no more for me,
   For one sweet kiss from my sweet lips
      Will solve your day short on."

BB

"Jessel Town." Phonograph record (aluminum) made by A. K. Davis, Jr. Sung by Mrs. Texas Gladden, of near Roanoke, Va. Roanoke County. August 7, 1932. Text transcribed by P. C. Worthington. Tune noted by Winston Wilkinson. Text independently collected by Miss Alfreda M. Peel, of Salem, Va. May 27, 1917. The independently collected text varies only slightly from the words of the record. In Miss Peel's text, stanzas six and seven, below, are transposed, and stanza nine does not appear. After stanza seven, below, Miss Peel's text has a stanza of incremental repetition:

> He picked him up on his back
>   And carried him to Jessel town,
> And dug a hole and laid him in
>   That he might sleep so sound.

Miss Peel uses a different local title: "Brother's Murder." Though the town has very little to do with the ballad (even less without the above stanza), Mrs. Gladden's title is definitely "Jessel Town," which no available atlas locates.

The tune is a delightful one, especially when rendered in strict time by Mrs. Gladden's strong and melodious voice, which at last hearing showed no signs even of middle-age.

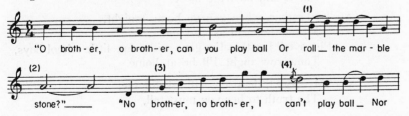

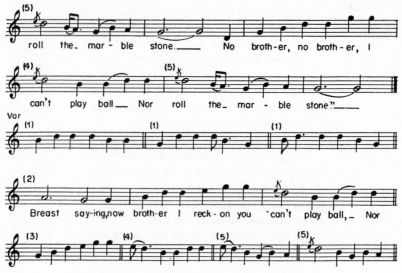

roll   the_ mar - ble stone._____   No   broth-er, no broth-er, I
can't   play ball__   Nor   roll   the_ mar - ble   stone."_____

Var

Breast   say-ing, now broth-er I   reck-on you   'can't play ball,_   Nor

1   "O brother, O brother, can you play ball
        Or roll the marble stone?"
    "No brother, no brother, I can't play ball
        Nor roll the marble stone.
    No brother, no brother, I can't play ball
        Nor roll the marble stone."

2   He took his tomahawk from him
        And hacked him across the breast,
    Saying, "Now brother, I reckon you can't play ball
        Nor roll the marble stone."

3   "Oh, take my hunting shirt from me
        And tear it from gore to gore
    And wrap it around my bleeding breast,
        That it might bleed no more."

4   He took his hunting shirt from him
        And tore it from gore to gore
    And wrapped it around his bleeding breast,
        But it still bled the more.

5   "O brother, when you go home tonight,
        My mother will ask for me,
    Please tell her that I'm gone with some little school boys,
        Tomorrow night I'll be at home.

6   "My dear little sister will ask for me,
        The truth to her you must tell,

Please tell her that I'm dead and in grave laid
    And buried at Jessel town.

7 "O take me up all on your back
    And carry me to Jessel town,
And dig a hole and lay me in,
    That I might sleep so sound.

8 "O lay my Bible under my head,
    My tomahawk at my feet,
My bow and arrow across my breast,
    That I might sleep so sweet."

9 He laid his Bible under his head,
    His tomahawk at his feet,
His bow and arrow across his breast,
    That he might sleep so sweet.

CC

"Two Little Brothers from School One Day." Phonograph record (aluminum) made by A. K. Davis, Jr. Sung by S. F. Russell, of Marion, Va. Smyth County. August 15, 1932. Text transcribed by P. C. Worthington. Tune noted by E. C. Mead, who describes it as "a fine tune," and urges the importance of all musical variants.

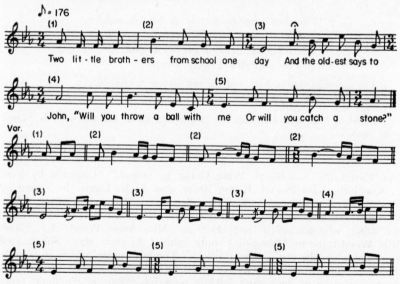

1 Two little brothers from school one day,
    And the oldest says to John,
    "Will you throw a ball with me
        Or will you catch a stone?"

2   "I'll [not][1] throw a ball with you
     Nor neither catch a stone,
   But if you'll go with me to the shady grove[2]
     I'll wrassel you a fall."

3   And when those two little brothers came,[3]
     Johnny wrasseled Willie down,
   In Willie's pocket 'twas a penknife found
     That give Johnny a deadly wound.

4   "O brother, brother, you have wounded me,
     You have wounded me full sore,
   There is a man[4] in this wide world
     Could love my brother any more.

5   "If you meet my mother as you return home,
     And she inquires for her son John,
   Oh, tell her I'm gone to the far-off town,
     You'll bring my new book home.

6   "If you meet my true love as you return home,
     And she inquires for her love John,
   Oh, tell her I'm buried at the old church yard,
     Let her know it's for her sake I'm gone.

7   "Go bury my prayer book by my side,
     My Bible at my feet,
   My little hymn book on my breast,
     The sounder I may sleep."

1. The recording jumps here and the negative is not heard.
2. Could be "cherry big grove."
3. This line is indistinct.
4. Could be "the wretched man" or "the richer man," but the sense is "There
is no man. . . ."

DD

"As Two Little Schoolboys Were Going to School."   Collected by Fred
F. Knobloch, John Powell, Hilton Rufty, and A. K. Davis, Jr.   Sung by
Mrs. Mary E. Hicks, of Charlottesville, Va.   Albemarle County.   May
17, 1931.   Tune noted by John Powell.   Mrs. Hicks learned the ballad from
her father, who learned it from his sister, Miss Annie Wood, in England.
Miss Wood came to Albemarle County "almost 80 years ago.   She was 98
years old when she died" (Mrs. Hicks).   The last stanza, which is scarcely
intelligible and which seems to have little to do with the story, yet suggests
the preservation of interesting folklore material.   "One of the finest tunes
in the collection" (E. C. Mead).   The stanzaic divisions, especially in the
opening stanzas, are a little uncertain.   The words were not fitted to the
tune at the time of collection.   It is clear from Mr. Powell's confident notation that the words fitted the tune at the time.   Perhaps some error was

made in taking down the words or in catching the stanzaic pattern. If so, the last named collector is to blame. (But he did his best!)

1 As two little schoolboys were going to school
      They fell into a play.
   The oldest drew a penknife out of his pocket
      And pierced it into his brother's breast
      Until the blood did flowre.

2 "I am too little, I am too young,
      Oh, brother, let me alone."
   He took his shirt off of his back
      And split it from gore to gore
   And laid it on his bleeding wounds
      As it may bleed no more,
      But it still bled the more.

3 "Oh, brother, when you go home,
      Our father ask after me,
   You may tell him I am to school,
      Gone with my lessons to learn.

4 "Oh, brother, when you go home,
      Our mother ask after me,
   Tell her that I am to London,
      Gone with the boys to play.

5 "Oh, brother, when you go home,
      If Fair Ellen ask after me,
   You may tell her that I am dead and buried
      In the Paul[1] church of the tomb."

6 As Lord Thomas was riding by,
      Was a-riding of an iron grey,
   "Pray tell unto me, Lord Thomas," said she,
      "Where is your brother Ben?"
   "He told me to tell you that he was dead and buried
      In the Paul[1] church of the tombs."

7 "I ain't no living woman,
   I have no nose in my face."
She harped the little fish out of the sea
And swept blood out of stones.

1. "Pall?" is written beneath "Paul" on the MS.

EE

"The Two Brothers." Phonograph record (aluminum) made by A. K. Davis, Jr. Sung by Mrs. Kit Williamson, of Yellow Branch, Va. Campbell County. August 4, 1932. Text transcribed by P. C. Worthington. Tune noted by E. C. Mead. The first stanza with its music was also noted independently by Mrs. Paul Cheatham, of Lynchburg, Va., and the text collected by Miss Juliet Fauntleroy, of Altavista, Va. Campbell County. March 15, 1934. Text and tune given here are taken directly from the record. Mead comments upon the "fine tune and style," and urges—for obvious reasons—that both stanzas of the tune and variants be printed.

An amusing bit of human interest is preserved at the beginning of the record. Mrs. Williamson asks, "Want to turn it?" She starts singing, "Two brothers. . . ," stops and asks, "Is you ready?" and after an audible affirmative reply she begins her song. Such are the charms of untouched field recordings.

1 Two brothers, dear brothers, walked out one day,
     To view the chestnut grove.
   The youngest had a long keen knife,
     And stoved it through the older one's heart.

2 "O brother, dear brother, take off thine shirt,
     And wrap my bleeding wound,
   And bind them up so neat and strong,
     That they won't bleed any more.

3 "O brother, dear brother, go dig my grave,
     Go dig it wide and deep.
   Place my Bible under my head,
     My Testament under my feet,
   My swords and pistols by my side,
     Just like I was[1] sound asleep.

4 "O brother, dear brother, when you go home,
     My mother will ask for me.
   You can tell her I've gone with some little school mates,
     To bear the company home.

5 "O brother, dear brother, when you go home,
     My father will ask for me.
   You can tell him that I'm gone to London town,
     To view the chestnut grove.

6 "O brother, dear brother, when you go home,
     Little Sweetie will ask for me.
   You can tell her that I'm buried in the cold clay ground,
     Whose face she will never more see."

1. Because of the singer's use of the glottal stop, the "was" combines with the "I" and is barely distinguishable.

16

YOUNG BEICHAN
(CHILD, No. 53)

This ballad tells the romantic story of an Englishman released from prison in Turkey by his jailer's daughter, under a pact that neither would marry another for seven long years. At the end of that time she arrives in England in the midst of his wedding feast. Young Beichan sends the bride home (none the worse for him) and takes the Turkish lady for his wife.

Child prints fifteen versions of this very popular ballad, many of them truly traditional forms, some obvious products of the broadside press. The Scottish versions, usually known as "Young Beichan" (or some approximation), are generally more uncorrupted by print that the English versions, usually known as "Lord Bateman" (or some approximation thereto). The ballad survives vigorously both in English and Scottish recent tradition (Margaret Dean-Smith, Gavin Greig). While there are some purely traditional versions, many versions both in England and in Scotland have been influenced by a broadsheet version frequently published in England. Child himself publishes this broadside in his Additions and Corrections (II, 508) and asks that it be substituted for his version L, "The Loving Ballad of Lord Bateman," published in 1839 with illustrations by George Cruikshank. Child evidently thought—and rightly—that the substitute was closer to tradition than the 1839 ballad, but it is evident that he considered both printed ballads to some extent traditional.

Most of the American texts show a close affinity to Child L and its substitute, and may well have been influenced by broadside and songbook publication in America as well as in England. (See Barry, *British Ballads from Maine,* pp. 106-22, and Kittredge, *JAFL,* XXX, 294-97.) Kittredge calls attention to a Massachusetts broadside as a possible influence on some of the American texts and differentiates these from those related to Child L and other Child texts. But the point is that these broadside texts, traditional to an extent at the time of their originial publication (as Child seems to say), have been orally transmitted over a reasonably long period of time without access to print and have taken on a new traditional life.   Examination of the American variants will tend to confirm this.   See Coffin and the texts listed by him, also the present texts and tunes.

TBVa printed nine texts (out of twelve available) of this ballad, with two tunes.   More recent collecting in Virginia has produced only three new items, all three of which are presented here, including two tunes.

The possible connection of this ballad with a familiar legend concerning Gilbert Becket, the father of St. Thomas, has been mentioned by Child and by various collectors and editors (for instance, see *TBVa*, p. 158).   Child concludes: "That our ballad has been *affected* by the legend of Gilbert Becket, is altogether likely .... But the ballad ... is not derived from the legend.   Stories and ballads of the general cast of 'Young Beichan' are extremely frequent."   Continental analogues for this ballad he finds only among Norse, Spanish, and Italian ballads.

As might be expected, the supernatural details of the Billy Blin ("a serviceable household demon") and the miraculous voyage from Turkey to England found in some Scottish versions of the ballad have been dropped from the American texts, including the present Virginia ones.

Bronson (I, 409-65) points out, and by his 112 tunes (with texts) demonstrates, the great popularity of the ballad, a popularity frequently "fortified in its verbal text by the broadside press" but also supported by "a vigorous and consistent musical tradition" which "proves with equal clarity that there has been no interruption in oral tradition."   He continues with a vigorous defence of the service of writing ("song-ballets") and even printing, as well as oral tradition, to the survival of traditional tunes as well as texts. (Cf. Gerould, *The Ballad of Tradition,* pp. 239-45.)

Bronson includes all except one of his 112 tunes in a single very broad Group A, because he feels that "the identity of the tune has persisted with quite remarkable clarity through most of the variants noted."   He does, however, subdivide Group A into three sub-groups according to where the mid-cadences lie.   Group Aa, with fifty-eight members, has the mid-cadence on the fifth; Group Ab, of thirty-six variants, has the mid-cadence on the supertonic; and Group Ac, with seventeen entries, contains seven variants with mid-cadence on the mediant, three on the tonic, five on the octave, and one each on the fourth and sixth.   A single anomalous, perhaps questionable item comprises Group B.

Of the two texts with tunes from *TBVa* (D and I), both are classified in Group Aa, with mid-cadence on the fifth. Of the tunes below, AA, despite some uncertainty, may belong in Bronson's Group Ac, because of the internal cadence on the third; BB clearly falls into Bronson's Group Ab.

AA

"Lord Batesman." Phonograph record (aluminum) made by A. K. Davis, Jr. Sung by Miss Ruby Bowman, of Laurel Fork, Va. Carroll County. August 10, 1932. Text transcribed by P. C. Worthington. Tune noted by E. C. Mead, who points out "the completely natural alternation of metrical groupings" here in contrast to "the complex rhythmic style" of BB, to follow.

1   There was a rich man lived in England,
    And an only son had he,
He never ever could be contented
    Till he must take a voyage on the sea.

2   He sailed to the east, and he sailed to the west,
    He sailed till he come to the Turkish shore,
And there he was taken and put in prison
    Where he could neither see nor hear.

3   That old Turk had an only daughter,
    She was so beautiful and fair,
She stole the keys to her father's prison,
    Saying, "I'll see if Lord Batesman's there.

4 "Now have you land or have you living,
   Have you a castle of high degree;
What would you bestow upon any fair lady,
   Who out of this prison would set you free?"

5 "Yes, I have land and I have living,
   I have a castle of high degree,
All of these I'll bestow upon any fair lady
   Who out of this prison will set me free."

6 She took him to her father's parlor,
   And treated him of her father's wine,
Saying, every health that she drinks unto him,
   "I wish, Lord Batesman, you were mine."

7 "Then seven long years await with patience,
   Seven long years and one day more,
And then if you don't come over to me,
   Some other woman I must adore."

8 Those seven long years were done and over,
   And the eighth was growing nigh,
When she gathered up her rich attire
   And thought she would cross the stormy tide.

9 She sailed till she come to Lord Batesman's castle,
   The ring she made the valley ring,
Saying, "If this is Lord Batesman's castle,
   Surely there's a noble heart within."

10 Then downstairs ran his proud young porter,
   Unlocked and bade the maid come in,
Saying, "Yes, this is Lord Batesman's castle,
   But today he has taken a new bride in."

11 "Go ask him for three crusts of his bread,
   And a bottle of his wine so strong,
And ask him if he does remember
   Who freed him from his dying tomb."

12 Then upstairs ran that proud young porter
   And dropped down at Lord Batesman's knee,
Saying, "At your gate is the prettiest creature
   That ever my two eyes did see."

13 He spread his gold all over the table,
   He cut his loaves in pieces three,
Saying, "I will forfeit my land and labors
   If Susan Pine has crossed the sea."

14   And then up stepped that new bride's father,
         Saying, "Today I rather see'd her died,
     To think that for some other woman
         You would forsake your lawful bride."

15   "It is true, Sir, I married your daughter,
         But she is none the worse of me,
     And Susan came with me on her horse and saddle,
         And pays my way across the stormy sea."

BB

"The Turkish Lady." Phonograph record (aluminum) made by A. K. Davis, Jr. Sung by Mrs. Victoria Morris, of Mt. Fair, Va. Albemarle County. November 21, 1932. Text transcribed by P. C. Worthington. Tune noted by Winston Wilkinson. Mead points out "the complex rhythmic style" of the tune in contrast to "the completely natural alternation of metrical groupings" in AA, preceding. The number of musical variants attests to the rhythmic complexity. The repetitions of the last two lines are irregular, and sometimes slightly varied. A very fine tune, beautifully represented by the intricate notation.

1   I sail-ed east and I sail-ed west,
      I sail-ed over Turkish shore,
    And there was taken and put in prison,
      Where freedom I never expect any more.

2   The jailor had a fairer daughter
      As your two eyes did ever see,
    She stole the keys of her father's treasure,
      And said Lord Batesman she would set free,
    She stole the keys of her father's treasure,
      And she said Lord Batesman she would set free.

3   She went into her father's closet,
      And they was drinkin' of strong wine,
    And every health she drank unto him,
      "I wish, Lord Batesman, he were mine."

4   They went into her father's cellar,
      And there made vows in one, two, three,
    That he were to marry no other lady,
      And she were to marry no other man,
    How he were to marry no other lady,
      And she were to marry no other man.

5   So seven long years been gone on the ocean,
      Oh, seven long years been gone on the sea,
    She pick-did up her golden diamond,
      And said Lord Batesman she would go see,
    She pick-did up her golden diamond,
      And said Lord Batesman she would go see.

6   She rode till she came Lord Batesman's castle,
      So slight-lie she did tap at the ring;

There's some other lady as Lord Batesman's lady
　　To arise and welcome the lady in.

7　"Is this where Lord Batesman lives,
　　Is he at home now or no?"
　"He's sittin' at his supper table,
　　He's just now brought his new bride home."

8　"Tell him to bring me a slice of his bread,
　　And also a glass of wine he'll 'low,
　Tell him to never to forget the lady
　　That freed him from his prison bounds,
　Tell him to never to forget the lady
　　That freed him from his prison bounds."

9　She had one gold ring on her finger,
　　And on the other one, one, two, three,
　The ring[1] of gold around her neck
　　To buy the bride and her company,
　The ring[1] of gold around her neck
　　To buy the bride and her company.

10　"Tell the lord to take your daughter,
　　I'm sure she is none o' the less by me,
　I bid farewell to the land of livin',
　　Since my Susanna has crossed the sea,
　Farewell, farewell, to the land of livin',
　　Since my Susanna has crossed the sea.

1. These words are indistinct.

CC

"Lord Bateman." Collected by Miss Juliet Fauntleroy, of Altavista, Va. Sung by Mrs. Priscilla Hensley, of Meadows of Dan, Va., who learned it from her grandmother, an Englishwoman by birth. Campbell and Patrick Counties. August 13, 1933. The number of verbal variants in this, the fullest of the new texts, seems to justify its retention, even without tune.

1　A rich man who lived in England,
　　He had but one only son;
　He never could be contented
　　Until he taken a voyage on sea.

2　He sailed and he sailed the sea all over
　　Until he came to the Turkish shore,
　And there he was taken and put in prison,
　　Where he could not neither see nor hear.

3　This old Turk had but one daughter,
　　She was beautiful and fair,

She stole the key for her father's prison
And did Lord Bateman go and see.

4 "Have you land or have you living,
     Have you castles of any degree?
   What would you bestow on to any fair lady
     That out of this prison would set you free?"

5 "I have land and I have living,
     I have castles of high degree,
   Which I will bestow to any fair lady
     Which out of this prison will set me free."

6 She put him on horse and saddle,
     Taken him down to the sea shore,
   She paid his way in gold and silver,
     "Lord Bateman, I'll see you no more."

7 "Seven long years I'll wait with pleasure,
     And one day over, and then, oh then,
   If you don't come over,
     Some other fair lady I must adore."

8 Seven long years was past and over,
     The eighth one swiftly rolling on,
   When she gathered up her rich attire
     And thought she'd cross the raging main.

9 She sailed and she sailed the sea all over
     Until she came to Lord Bateman's gate.
   Oh, she knocked so loud she made the valleys ring,
     Then out came a proud young porter.

10 . . . .
     "Who knocked so loud can not come in,
   For I've just come out to tell you
     That today he's his new bride in."

11 "Go ask him for three crumbs of his bread
     And a bottle of his wine so strong,
   Ask him if he does remember
     Who loosed him from his iron bands."

12 Then back went this proud young porter,
     Stooping on his bended knees,
   Says, "At your gate stands the prettiest creature
     That ever my two eyes did see.

13 "She wears a gold ring on every finger,
     On her middle finger three,

The belt she wears around her middle
Would buy your bride and company."

14 He spread the gold all over the table,
Split the leaves in pieces three,
Says, "I forfeit all my land and riches
That Susan Fane has crossed the sea."

15 Then up steps this new bride's father,
"For today I wish you had 'a' died,
Just to think for another woman
That you'd forsake your lawful bride."

16 "It is true I married your daughter,
She's none the worse by me,
She come with me on horse and saddle,
She can go back in coachman free."

17

YOUNG HUNTING
(Child, No. 68)

A young man, back from hunting, is invited by his mistress to come in and spend the night. He declines, explaining that he loves another better than he loves her. As he stoops to give her a farewell kiss, she stabs him mortally. She attempts, sometimes with help, to conceal the body in a well or other water, but her parrot, who will not be cajoled or threatened, presumably reveals her guilt.

Here Child F and most of the American texts end. Child A and other fuller texts go on to tell of the coming of the king's duckers, their finding of the body with the help of the bird, the lady's trial by fire (*judicium ignis*) and burning, while her comparatively innocent bower-woman accomplice escapes unscathed. There are other endings, some of them introduced from other ballads, some of them confused.

Child prints eleven texts of this excellent ballad, most of them of Scottish origin, but, if we may depend upon Margaret Dean-Smith and Gavin Greig's *Last Leaves*, it does not survive in print from recent British sources. It is fairly widely known in America, but chiefly in the South. Sharp-Karpeles (I, 101-14) print fourteen texts and tunes from the Southern Appalachians. *TBVa* presents six of a possible seven texts, with four tunes. More recently the Virginia collection has added nine new items, of which six are here presented, five of them with tunes, the sixth a full and distinctive text. Rather unaccountably, the Brown Collection reports no text from North Carolina.

Like those of *TBVa*, the texts to follow lack the retributive conclusion of the Child collection and terminate before the arrival of the king's duckers. The temptation to confuse this ballad with "Lady Isabel and the Elf Knight" (Child, No. 4)—natural enough, as they share the incidents of a lady drowning her false lover and of the talking bird—has generally been resisted in this series. At least the contamination is not so overt as in *TBVa* E, and the bird stanzas sung here are found also in Child's texts of this ballad. Some contamination from "Sir Hugh" (Child, No. 155) may also be present in the description of the carrying of the corpse to the water.

There are several details of interest here: the moral conclusion of DD is unique in Virginia texts and the retreat to the parlor (BB, FF, and one omitted text) is a curious though not uncommon Americanization. The "other lady" is "in a foreign land" (BB, FF, one other), "in the merry green land" (AA, DD), "in Merry Green Lee" (CC), or (in one omitted text) "in Old Scotland." The victim is "Henry" in all versions except one (see next paragraph). There appears to be some confusion in the purpose of the ring and in the presence of helpers and confidants.

The three omitted texts all come from the same county as FF, Dickenson County, and there is a temptation to print them as showing the extent of variation within a small geographical compass. But FF is the fullest and most distinctive of the four; the other three overlap in large measure with other texts here printed. A few points in the omitted texts may be noted: in one the name of the hero, also the local title, is Scot Eals, and he has a wife "in Old Scotland" (cf. Sharp-Karpeles A, I, 101-2); another, with the more usual title and hero Loving Henry, places the other girl (not wife) "in some Arkansas land" and (like BB and FF) has the kissing and the murder take place "in some parlor room"; in a third, Margaret "leant herself across the fence" (cf. "face" in AA) to do her kissing and stabbing. All three are slightly compressed texts but tell the full story through the dialogue of the girl and the bird, the bird having the last word.

Interesting folk beliefs found in some Child versions have been lost from Virginia and American texts, along with the king's duckers: the belief that the body of a murdered man will emit blood upon being touched or approached by the murderer; the belief that a candle, floated over water, will detect a dead body; belief in justice *via* the ordeal by fire; oaths by corn, grass, or thorn. But the possibility that the talking bird represents a transmigration of the murdered man's soul remains in the texts that follow. See Wimberly, *passim*.

It is with uncommon regret that at this point we must part company with our distinguished companion, fellow-scholar, and friend, Bertrand Harris Bronson, whose great but as yet incomplete work on *The Traditional Tunes of the Child Ballads* (Princeton University Press, 1959) has been drawn upon with such profit in every headnote up to the present one. Unhappily, only the first volume, covering Child ballads 1 to 53, has as yet appeared, and that just before this book's going to press. There is no regret over the eleventh-hour labor involved in these references to him, because they are recognized as a distinct enrichment of this volume. It would have been well, of course, if each of these near-contemporaneous publications could have taken full account of the other. That being impossible, it is consoling that the headnotes up to this point have been able to include all relevant material from his first volume, if not from his subsequent ones. There is also some satisfaction in knowing that sooner or later he will have to take into account the highly relevant new material of this book.

AA

"Love Henry." Phonograph record (aluminum) made by A. K. Davis, Jr. Sung by Mrs. Molly Stinnett Whitehead, of Agricola, Va. Amherst County. August 8, 1935. Text transcribed by M. J. Bruccoli. Tune noted by E. C. Mead.

Mrs. Whitehead is sometimes difficult to understand; this transcription is admittedly uncertain in several places. There is similar uncertainty about the tune; the fourth stanza—perhaps the most typical—has been chosen as the standard for notation. Despite these uncertainties, Mead describes this tune as "one of the finest in the collection," and points to its "vigorous, direct, rhythmic style." Mrs. Whitehead's strong voice, sometimes of nasal quality, with frequent "glottal catches" and slurs, adds to the very genuine "folk" quality of her singing.

1   "Come[1] in, come in, love Henry," said she,
"And spend your night with me,
For I have lodgings of the very best,
And I will comfort thee.
For I have lodgings of the very best,
And I will comfort you."

2   "I won't come in, and I can't call in,
I won't come in," said he,
"For there is a girl in the merry green land
I love far better than thee.
For there is a girl in the merry green land
I love far better than you."

3   She reached across the golden face,[2]
Three kisses she give him sweet,
With the little penknife that she had in her hand
She stuck him to his knee.
With the little penknife that she had in her hand
She stuck him to his knee.

4   "O live, O live, love Henry," said she,
"O live, O if you can,
And all the servants in the Millbor'[3] town
Shall come and wait upon you.
And all the servants in the Millbor'[3]
Shall come and wait upon you."

5   "How can I live? How can I live?
How can I live?" said he,
"And don't you see my only heart blood
Come streaming down by me?
And don't you see my only heart blood
Come streaming down by me?"

6   She taken him by his lily-white hand,
And the knife was in the other,
And into the iron pot of[3] water she threw him
Was both cold and deep.
And into the iron pot of water she threw him
Was both cold and deep.

7   "Lie there, lie there, love Henry," said she,
"Till the flesh drops off your bones,
And the girl that you left in the merry green land
Will think you long coming home.
And the girl that you left in the merry green land
Will think you long coming home.

8 "Call down, call down, little parrot bird,
    And sit-a pon my knee."
    "I won't call down; nor I can't call down;
    I won't call down," said he,
    "For you have killed your love Henry,
    So soon you may kill me.
    For you have killed your love Henry,
    So soon you may kill me."

9 She leaped on her milk-white deed[3]
    And rode off in good speed.
    And every village that she passed through,
    She was taken to be . . .[4]

1. The words "come" and "call" are difficult to distinguish.
2. Perhaps "fence."
3. Unclear.
4. Record ends abruptly. Missing words are probably "some queen."

BB

"Loving Henry." Phonograph record (aluminum) made by A. K. Davis,
Jr. Sung by Wayne Crabtree, of Cleveland, Va. Russell County. August
11, 1932. Text transcribed by P. C. Worthington. Tune noted by G. W.
Williams and E. C. Mead, who says that it is "essentially a pentatonic tune."

1 "Come in, come in, Loving Henry," she said,
    "And stay all night with me.
    Your bed shall be of the finest silk,
    And your pillow gold and silvery."

2 "I can't come in, Little Margaret," he said,
    "Nor stay all night with you.
    For the girl I left in a foreign land
    Will think I've proven untrue."

3 She backed herself in the parlor door
    For to take a kiss or two,
And the knife she held in her right hand,
    She stobbed him through and through.

4 She took him by the curly locks,
    And her sister by the heels.
They drug him down to the river bank,
    And threw him into the deep.

5 "Lie there, lie there, Loving Henry," she said,
    "Till the flesh falls from your bones,
And the girl you left in a foreign land
    Will think you're long coming home.

6 "Fly down, fly down, you pretty little bird,
    And light upon my knee,
For your food shall be of the finest flesh
    And your nest of a golden shield."

7 "I can't fly down, Little Margret," he said,
    "Nor light upon your knee,
You just have murdered your old true love,
    I'm afraid you might kill me."

8 She said to the little girl of the town,
    "You keep this secret true;
And the ring I wear on my right hand
    Shall always belong to you."

CC

"Lady Margaret." Phonograph record (aluminum) made by A. K. Davis, Jr. Sung by Mrs. Orilla Keeton, of Mt. Fair, Va. Albemarle County. March 10, 1933. Text transcribed by M. J. Bruccoli. Tune noted by E. C. Mead, who describes this as "a very beautiful tune with a rhythmic freedom that almost defies scansion. For example: ½ plus ⅝ plus ⅔ or ½ plus ⅘ plus ⅔."

A comparison of the present notation made from the 1933 recording and the notation made by Cecil J. Sharp from life in 1916 and published in *TBVa* will reveal various significant changes which have occurred in Mrs. Keeton's tune in the intervening seventeen years. Similar variants are present in the two texts. (Cf. *TBVa* D, pp. 187-88, 567.) Again, it is possible to check the life of a ballad in the keeping of a given singer over a seventeen-year period. In this case, one can only conclude that the ballad has been preserved with great fidelity.

As La-dy Mar-gret she was go-ing to bed, She heard the sound of a— mu-si - cal—

1   As Lady Margret she was going to bed
      She heard the sound of a musical horn,
    Which made her heart feel glad and sad
      To think that it was her brother, brother John
    Returning from his king,
      But who should it be but her true-love Henery
    Coming in from his wild hunting.

2   "O light, O light, love Henery,
      To stay all night with me,
    And you shall have the cheers of the cheery cold girl,
      The best I can give thee."

3   "I will not light nor I shall not light
      To stay all night with thee,
    For there's a pretty girl in Merry Green Lee
      I love far better than thee."

4   He bended over her soft pillow
      To give her a kiss so sweet,
    But with a penknife in her right hand
      She wounded him down so deep.

5   "Woe be, woe be, Lady Margaret," he cried,
      "Woe be, woe be to thee,
    For don't you see my own heart's blood
      Come twinkling down my knee?"

6   She called unto a maid of hers,
    "Keep a secret, keep a secret on me,
    All of these fine robes on my body
    Shall always be to thee."

7   One taken him by his long yellow hair
    And the other one by his feet,
    And they threw him into the well water
    Which was so cold and deep.

8   "Lie there, lie there, love Henery,
    Till the flesh rots off your bones,
    And that pretty girl in Merry Green Lee
    Thinks long of your coming home."

9   Up spoke, up spoke, a pretty little parrot
    A-sitting on a willow tree,
    "There never was a girl in Merry Green Lee
    He loved so well as thee."

10 "Come down, come down, my pretty little parrot,
    And sit upon my knee,
    And you shall have a cage of a pure, pure gold
    Instead of a willow tree.

11 "If I had my arrow in my hand,
    My bow and tuneful string,
    I'd shoot a dart that would ring your heart,
    So you could no longer sing."

12 "If you had your arrow in your hand,
    Your bow and tuneful string,
    I'd take flight and I'd fly, fly away
    And tune my voice to sing."

DD

"Sir Henry." Phonograph record (aluminum) made by A. K. Davis, Jr. Sung by J. S. Witt, of Salem, Va. Roanoke County. May 31, 1934. Text transcribed by P. C. Worthington. Tune noted by G. W. Williams. Mr. Witt uses the tune also as a basis for a fiddle tune. Cf. *TBVa* B, pp. 184-85, 566.

'Twas late last Fri-day night,— When Mar-gret was go-ing to bed,— She heard the sound of a bu-gle horn, Which

1   'Twas late last Friday night,
     When Margret was going to bed,
  She heard the sound of a bugle horn,
     Which made her heart so glad;
  She heard the sound of a bugle horn,
     Which made her heart so glad.

2   She thought it was Sir Henry
     Returning from his wild hunting,
  With a sword and pistol by his side,
     And a bugle horn 'round his neck.

3   "Get down, get down, Sir Henry,
     And stay all night with me;
  I'll give to you my silver and gold
     To spend at your command."

4   "I won't get down, I won't get down,
     Nor stay all night with thee;
  There is a bonny lass in a merry green land
     That's longing for my return."

5   Bending over his precious breast,
     He gave her kisses three;
  And holding a knife in her right hand
     She pierced him to his heart.

Here two stanzas have been forgotten.

6 Some took him by his feet and hands,
   Some by his long yellow hair,
   And throwed him in the wild waters
   Which run both wide and deep.

7 "Lay there, lay there, Sir Henry,
   Till the flesh rots off your bones,
   And the bonny lass in the merry green land
   Shall long for your return."

8 Then sitting over her head,
   Her parrot sang in a tree,
   "How could you murder your own true love,
   When you then I did see?"

9 "Come down, come down, my pretty parrot,
   And sit in my right hand.
   I'll give to you a cage of gold
   To hang in a willow tree."

10 "I won't come down, I won't come down,
   Nor sit in your right hand;
   For if you would murder your own true love,
   The sooner you'd murder me."

11 "I wish I had my bow to bend,
   My arrow and my string;
   I would pierce you to your heart so deep
   That you would no more sing."

12 "I wish you had your bow to bend,
   Your arrow and your string;
   I would fly from tree to tree,
   You'd always hear me sing."

EE

"Lord Henry." Collected by Miss Alfreda M. Peel, of Salem, Va. Sung
by Mrs. Fanny Grubb, of Back Creek, Va. Roanoke County. September
1933. Tune noted by Mrs. Kathleen Kelly Coxe, of Roanoke, Va.

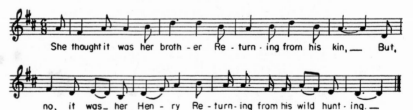

She thought it was her broth - er Re - turn - ing from his kin, ___ But,

no, it was_ her Hen - ry Re - turn - ing from his wild hunt - ing. ___

She thought it was her brother
Returning from his kin,[1]
But, no, it was her Henry
Returning from his wild hunting.

1. King?

FF

"Loving Henry." Collected by E. J. Sutherland, of Clintwood, Va. Given
by Miss Beuna Kiser, of Clinchco, Va., who learned it from her mother,
Mrs. Ida E. Kiser, of Jahile, Va. Dickenson County. March 12, 1932.
This text, somewhat fuller than the recorded versions, is presented both
because of its significant verbal variants and because the distinctive ending
carries through to the death of the girl, Lillie Margaret. It does not
conform to any one of Coffin's seven story types.

1   "Come in, come in, Loving Henry," she said,
        "And stay all night with me.
    Your bed shall be made of finest silk
        And a gold and silver-ee."

2   "No, I can't come in, Lillie [Lady?] Margaret," he said,
        "And stay all night with you,
    For the girl I left in a foreign land
        Will think I am untrue."

3   She seated herself in a parlor neat
        For to take a kiss or two,
    And with the knife she held in her right hand
        She stabbed him through and through.

4   "How long, how long, Lillie Margaret," he said,
        " 'Til you and I must part?
    The purest blood that ever flowed
        Comes flowing from my heart."

5   She called on a girl in this little town
        To keep her secret still,
    "And the ring I place on his right hand
        Shall always belong to him."

6   She took him by his golden locks,
        Her sister at his feet,
    They carried him to the river side
        And threw him in the deep.

7   "Lie there, lie there, Loving Henry," she said,
        " 'Til the meat falls from your bones;
    And the girl you left in a foreign land
        Will think you are long coming home."

8 As Lillie Margaret started on her highway home,
   Some Polly Parrot seemed to say,
"Go home, go home, Lillie Margaret," it said,
   "And stay 'til a sweet summer's day."

9 "Fly down, fly down, Polly Parrot," she said,
   "And rest on my right knee;
I have a cage of the very finest,
   And I'll give it up to thee."

10 "No, I can't fly down, Lillie Margaret," it said,
   "And rest on your right knee;
For you've just killed your own true love,
   And I'm afraid you might kill me."

11 "Have pity on me, Polly Parrot," she said,
   "Don't remind me of my crime,
For the girl he left in a foreign land
   Stole a love that once was mine.

12 "Go make my shroud, dear sister," she said,
   "And bury me by his side;
For here on earth he loved her best,
   And in death I'll be his bride."

13 They found her dead next morning,
   Her face turned up to the sky,
And on her breast a letter pinned,
   Saying, "All dear friends, good-bye."

18

LORD THOMAS AND FAIR ANNET
(CHILD, No. 73)

The *TBVa* headnote points out the kinship between this ballad and the two that immediately follow, "Fair Margaret and Sweet William" and "Lord Lovel," and attempts to distinguish the pure types of the three from the blended texts. All are love tragedies. But in "Lord Thomas" there is a triangle with three violent deaths; in "Fair Margaret" there is a triangle, with two lovers' deaths, neither violent; in "Lord Lovel" the triangle disappears, the lover is not unfaithful, only laggard, returns to find his lady dead of love too long deferred, then himself dies of grief. The "rose-and-brier" ending is often, but not always, attached to all three, more regularly to the two ballads that follow than to this ballad.

The ballad of Lord Thomas plus his variously named sweetheart (generally some form of Eleanor) and her brown-girl rival (sometimes Sally Brown) is one of the more popular ballads still found in tradition in America. Coffin's American bibliography is extensive. *TBVa* printed seventeen texts and omitted seventeen more. *FSVa* lists thirteen items subsequently collected in Virginia, four of them phonographic recordings. Of the thirteen, only six are here presented. Five of the six have tunes.

The new Virginia texts are most closely related to Child D and (with one possible exception to be noted) follow the English rather than the Scottish form of the ballad. All, with variations, follow Coffin's Story Type A, not the extraordinary Type B (if the latter deserves the name of a distinct story type of this ballad).

As usual, it is with a pang that many excellent texts with some distinctive readings have been omitted. One of the discarded texts has this distinctive stanza, somewhat reminiscent of the several Scottish texts in Child:

> The brown girl she come stepping up,
> Her heart was filled with hate.
> "Where did you get your well water
> That washed your skin so white?"

Another has—and the singer insisted upon the readings—"riddler's boat" for "riddle us both," "merriments" for "merry men's," and the following unique last stanza:

> Lord Thomas he commenced cussin' and swearin'
> An' walkin' across the hall.
> Then he cut off the brown girl's head
> And kicked it against the wall.

Another has this variant stanza:

> Lord Thomas called his merry men round,
> He dressed them all in white,
> So that every city he passed through
> They took him to be some knight.

Still another has Lord Thomas reply to Fair Ellen's taunts about the brown girl with, "Throw not your slurs at me, Fair Ellen." And so on. But in the main these discarded versions follow the same story line without too significant variation, except, perhaps, in the eyes of the connoisseur of such variants.

The six texts and five tunes that follow, plus the above notes, will adequately represent the ballad and its variants here.

Child prints nine versions of the ballad and finds room in his Additions and Corrections (III, 509-10) for a variant of his D version "from the singing of a Virginia nurse-maid (helped out by her mother)" communicated by W. H. Babcock to the *Folk-Lore Journal* (VII, 33, 1889). This, like most of the American texts, stems from any one of several seventeenth-century broadside collections (Pepys, Roxburghe, Bagford, and others). Most of the numerous survivals in recent British tradition stem from the same broadside sources. In America, the ballad rivals in popularity "Barbara Allan" and "The House Carpenter." Sharp-Karpeles print an astonishing thirty-one tunes with texts or part-texts (I, 115-31). The Brown Collection prints or comments upon fourteen (II, 69-79), the first from Rockingham County, Virginia. Excellent as the ballad is, it has perhaps less critical and scholarly interest because of its close relationship to broadsides and songbooks (see Barry, p. 134).

AA

"Lord Thomas." Phonograph record (aluminum) made by A. K. Davis, Jr. Sung by Miss Ruby Bowman, of Laurel Fork, Va. Carroll County.

August 10, 1932. Text transcribed by P. C. Worthington. Tune noted by
Winston Wilkinson. As will be seen from the notation, the first stanza is
atypical; the second and succeeding stanzas represent the musical pattern
more closely and repeat the last line, as indicated. There are interesting
verbal variants.

1 Lord Thomas was a brave young man,
       A keeper of bach'lor's hall,
   "Come talk with me, my mother dear,
       Come talk to me of love.

2 "I think I'll quit my rambling round,
       No more I love to roam,
   Shall I marry Fair Ellener now,
       Or bring the brown girl home, home,
       Or bring the brown girl home?"

3 "The brown girl she has house and land,
       Fair Ellener she has none,

My advice to you, my dearest son,
Go bring the brown girl home, home,
Go bring the brown girl home."

4 Fair Ellener dressed herself in white,
Her merry maids in green,
And every station they passed through,
She was taken to be some queen, some queen,
Was taken to be some queen.

5 She rode up to Lord Thomas's hall,
And janged a lovely ring,
No one so ready as Lord Thomas himself,
To open and bid her come in, come in,
To open and bid her come in.

6 He took her by the lily-white hand,
He led her through the hall,
He took her in and set her down,
That she might see them all, them all,
That she might see them all.

7 "Is this your bride, Lord Thomas?" she said,
"I think she's wonderful brown.
You once could have married the fairest-skinned **girl**,
As ever set foot on the ground, the ground,
As ever set foot on the ground."

8 The brown girl had a small penknife,
Its blades were keen and sharp,
She stuck it in Fair Ellender's side,
And it almost reached her heart, her heart,
It almost reached her heart.

9 "Fair Ellen, Fair Ellener," he declared,
"What makes you look so pale?
Your cheeks were once the rosy red,
But all of your color has failed, has failed,
But all of your color has failed."

10 "Lord Thomas, Lord Thomas," she replied,
"O tell me can't you see?
Oh, don't you see my own heart's blood,
Come a-trinkling down so free, so free,
Come a-trinkling down so free?"

11 He took the brown girl by her hand,
He led her from the hall,

And with his sword he cut her throat,
  He flung her head against the wall, the wall,
  Flung her head against the wall.

12 He placed the sword against the wall,
  The point against his breast,
  "Here is the ending of three dear lovers,
  Pray take their souls to rest, to rest,
  Pray take their souls to rest.

13 "Go dig my grave both wide and deep,
  And paint my coffin black,
  Bury Fair Ellender in my arms,
  And the brown girl at my back, my back,
  And the brown girl at my back."

14 They dug his grave both wide and deep,
  And painted his coffin black,
  And buried Fair Ellender in his arms,
  And the brown girl at his back, his back,
  And the brown girl at his back.

BB

"Lord Thomas." Phonograph record (aluminum) made by A. K. Davis, Jr. Sung by Horton Barker, of Chilhowie, Va. Washington County. August 15, 1932. Text transcribed by P. C. Worthington. Tune noted by Winston Wilkinson.

1 "Lord Thomas, Lord Thomas, take my advice,
   Go bring the brown girl home;
For she has land and a house of her own,
   Fair Ellender she has none."

2 He call-ed to his waiting maids,
   By one, by two, by three,
"Go bridle, go saddle, my milky-white speed,
   Fair Ellender I must see."

3 He rode and he rode till he came to her gate,
   So lively he tingled the ring,
And none were so ready as Fair Ellender herself,
   As she rose to let him in.

4 "I've come to ask you to my wedding today."
   "Bad news, Lord Thomas," says she.
"For I your bride I thought I would be.
   Bad news, Lord Thomas," said she.

5 She call-ed to her father and mother
   To make them both as one,
"Shall I go to Lord Thomas's wedding,
   Or tarry at home alone?"

6 She dressed herself so fine in silk,
   Her very maids in green,
And every city that she rode through,
   They took her to be some queen.

7 She rode and she rode till she came to his gate,
   So lively she tingled the ring,
And none were so ready as Lord Thomas himself,
   As he rose to let her in.

8 He took her by the lily-white hand,
   He led her through the hall,
He sat her down at the head of the table,
   Among the quality all.

9 "Lord Thomas," said she, "is this your bride?
   I'm sure she looks very brown.
You might have married as fair a young lady,
   As ever the sun shone on."

10 The brown girl had a penknife in her hand,
   It keen and very sharp,
Betwixt the long ribs and the short,
   She pierced Fair Ellender to the heart.

11 He took the brown girl by the hand,
      He led her through the hall,
    And with a sword he cut her head off,
      And kicked it against the wall.

12 He placed the handle against the ground,
      The point against his breast,
    Saying, "Here's the death of three true lovers,
      God send their souls to rest.

13 "I want my grave dug long and wide,
      And dig it very deep;
    I want Fair Ellender in my arms,
      The brown girl at my feet."

CC

"Lord Thomas." Phonograph record (aluminum) made by A. K. Davis,
Jr. Sung by Mrs. J. F. Hodges, of Roanoke, Va. Roanoke County.
August 8, 1932. Text transcribed by P. C. Worthington. Tune noted by
G. W. Williams and E. C. Mead.

1 He mounted his horse, he rode to fair Ellen,
      He knocked so clear at the ring,
    But who were no ready Fair Ellen herself,
      To rise and let him in.

2 "What's the matter, what's the matter, Lord Thomas?"
        she said,
      "What seems the matter?" said she.
    "I've come to invite you to my wedding,
      Tomorrow it's to be."

3   "Come riddle, come riddle, dear mother," she said,
       "Come riddle us both as one,
    Whether I shall go to Lord Thomas's wedding,
       Or tarry with you at home."

4   "Twelve thousands may be your friends, dear daughter,
       Ten thousand may be your foes,
    I would advise you with my blessing,
       To tarry with me at home."

5   "Twelve thousands may be my friends, dear mother,
       Ten thousand may be my foes,
    But if it is to be my death,
       Lord Thomas's wedding I'll go."

6   She dressed herself in the finest of silk,
       It all trimmed up in green,
    And every town that she passed through,
       She was taken to be the queen.

7   She rode until Lord Thomas's house,
       She knocked so clear at the ring,
    But who were no ready, Lord Thomas himself,
       To rise and let her in.

8   He took her by her lily-white hand,
       As he led her through the hall,
    He take her to the brown girl's chamber
       And placed her above them all.

9   "Is this your bride, Lord Thomas?" she said,
       "I'm sure she's wonderful brown,
    When once you'd of married as fair a young lady
       As ever the sun shone on."

10   The brown girl having a knife in her bosom,
       The point both keen and sharp,
    Between the long ribs and the short,
       She pierced fair Ellender's heart.

11   "What's the matter, what's the matter, Fair Ellen?"
       he said,
       "What makes you look so sad?"
    "Oh, don't you see my own heart's blood,
       Come bleeding out of me?"

12   He took her by the lily-white hand,
       As he led her through the hall,
    He cut the brown girl's head off
       And dashed it against the wall.

13   He placed Fair Ellen by his right side,
       The brown girl at his feet,
     He placed a big Bible right under their head,
       So silently they might sleep.

DD

"The Brown Girl." Collected by Miss Juliet Fauntleroy, of Altavista, Va.
Sung by Mrs. Kit Williamson. First verse and tune collected March 15,
1934, from Mrs. Williamson, then of Yellow Branch, Va.; other stanzas
collected March 20, 1915, from Mrs. Williamson (then Mrs. James Sprouse),
then of Lawyers, Va. Campbell County. Tune noted by Mrs. Paul Cheatham, of Lynchburg, Va. A good full text not included in *TBVa* and now
complete with tune.

1   "Oh Mother, oh Mother, oh Mother," said he,
       "Come and riddle us both as one,
     Whether I must bring fair Ellender home,
       Or bring the brown girl in."

2   "The brown girl has both house and lands,
       Fair Ellender she has none.
     I would advise you as my best son
       To bring the brown girl home."

3   He rode and he rode till he came to the hall,
       He rattled the bell and it rang.
     None was more ready than fair Ellender herself
       To arise and let him in.

4   "What news, what news, Lord Thomas," she cried,
       "What news do you bring to me?"
     "I've come to invite you to my wedding day,
       And is that good news to you?"

5   "Bad news, bad news, Lord Thomas," she cried,
       "Bad news do you bring to me.

I thought that I was to be the bride
And you the bridegroom be.

6 "Oh Mother, oh Mother, come riddle these sports,
Come riddle them all as one,
Whether I shall go to Lord Thomas's wedding
Or tarry at home with you."

7 "Ten thousand of your friends will be there,
Ten thousand of your foes,
Therefore I advise you as my best daughter
To tarry with me at home."

8 She went and dressed herself in white,
Her wait-men all in green,
And every town that she passed through,
She was taken to be a queen.

9 She rode and she rode till she came to the hall,
She rattled the bell and it rang,
None was more ready than Lord Thomas himself
To arise and let her in.

10 He took her by her lily-white hand
And led her across the hall,
And seated her in a bright arm chair
Among the ladies all.

11 "Is that your bride, Lord Thomas?" said she,
"She is most wonderful brown.
You once could have married as fair-skinned a girl
As ever the sun shined on."

12 The brown girl she had a sharp penknife,
It was both keen and sharp;
Right between fair Ellender's ribs and light
She pierced it in her heart.

13 "Fair Ellender, fair Ellender," said he,
"What makes you look so pale?"
"Oh, don't you see my own heart's blood
Run trickling down by me?"

14 Lord Thomas had a sword that hung
In the hall against the wall.
He took it down and cut her head off
And kicked it against the wall.

15 "Mother, oh mother, go dig my grave,
Go dig it both wide and deep,

And bury fair Ellender in my arms
And the brown girl at my feet."

16 He put the sword against the wall,
      The point against his heart,
    Were never three lovers that ever met
      More sooner they did depart.

Alternate Conclusion

Here goes the life of these true loves,
    God take them home to rest.

EE

"Fair Ellen." Phonograph record (aluminum) made by A. K. Davis, Jr.
Sung by Mrs. Sis Sears, of Twelve O'Clock Mountain, Salem, Va. Roanoke
County. August 8, 1932. Text transcribed by M. J. Bruccoli. Tune noted
by G. W. Williams. A comparison of this text and tune transcribed from
the phonograph record of 1932 with the 1915 text and tune from the same
singer printed as *TBVa* D (pp. 198-200, 569) indicates what has happened
to the ballad during the seventeen-year interval. Though the text is somewhat garbled, the tune, with variants, is now verifiable.

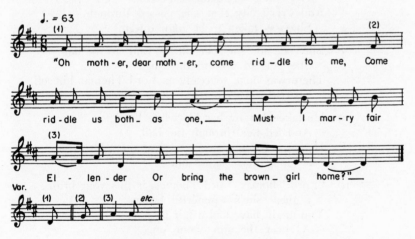

1 "Oh mother, dear mother, come riddle to me,
      Come riddle us both as one,
    Must I marry fair Ellender
      Or bring the brown girl home?"

2 "The brown girl she has house and land,
      Fair Ellen she has none,
    So I'll advise'n my own dear son
      To bring the brown girl home."

3 He rode and he rode till he came to the hall,
 And jangled around the ring,
There was none so ready as fair Ellen herself
 To rise and let him in.

4 "Good news, good news," fair Ellen said she,
 "Good news, good news, you bring to me?"
"I've come to invite you to my wedding,
 And that's sad news to me."

5 . . . .
 . . . .
"I thought I was to be your bride,
 And you the bridegroom to be.

6 . . . .
 . . . .
"I'll venture my life, I'll venture my death,
 At Lord Thomas's wedding I'll be."

7 She dressed up her milk-white steed,
 Her waist was made of green,
And every city that she passed through,
 She was taken to be some queen.

8 She rode and she rode till she came to the hall,
 She jangled around the ring,
There was none so ready as Lord Thomas himself
 To rise and let her in.

9 He taken her by her lily-white hand,
 And led her through the hall,
He set her down at the head of the table,
 A-mong those ladies all.

10 "Lord Thomas, Lord Thomas, is this your bride?
 I guess she's wonderful brown;
You might have had a fair lady
 As ever the sun shone on."

11 The brown girl she had a little penknife,
 Which both keen and sharp,
And thurst it in fair Ellen's breast,
 It entered near her heart.

12 "Oh, what's the matter, my old true love,
 Oh, what's the matter with thee?"
"Oh, don't you see my own heart's blood
 Go tringling down by me?"

13 He taken her by the lily-white hand,
       He led her through the hall,
    He drew a big sword and cut her head off,
       And threw it against the wall.

14 "Oh, mother, dear mother, go dig my grave,
       Go dig it both wide and deep,
    Place fair Ellen in my arms
       And the brown girl at my feet."

15 He put the sword against the wall,
       The point against his breast.
    Oh, here are the death of three true lovers,
       God send them home for rest.

FF

"Lord Thomas." Collected by E. J. Sutherland, of Clintwood, Va. Contributed by Hampton Osborne, of Omaha, Va., who learned it from Misses
Alpha and Lillie Yates, of Omaha. Dickenson County. March 31, 1932.
A full and good text, with some interesting verbal variants. The brown
girl has become Sally Brown.

1 Lord Thomas was a gay young man,
      The lord of many a town;
   He courted a girl called Pretty Fair Ellen,
      And one called Sally Brown.

2 "Come, father, come, mother, I'll ask you both,
      I'll ask you both as one;
   Whether I must marry Pretty Fair Ellen,
      Or bring that Brown girl home?"

3 "The Brown girl has a house and home,
      Fair Ellen she has none.
   But now take warning from a friend,
      And bring that Brown girl home."

4 He rode up to Fair Ellen's gate,
      So loudly toned and called,
   None so ready but Fair Ellen herself
      To rise and ask him in.

5 "Very sad news for you, Fair Ellen,
      And it's very sad news indeed,
   I've come to ask you to my wedding,
      Next Saturday night will be."

6 "Very sad news for me, Lord Thomas,
      It's very sad news indeed;

I was going to be your bride myself,
And you the bride's groom for me.

7 "Come, father, come, mother, I'll ask you both,
I'll ask you both as one;
Whether I can go to Lord Thomas's wedding,
Or tarry with mother at home?"

8 "Many might be there," they say,
"There might be friends and foes;
So now take warning from a friend,
And stay with mother at home."

9 "Many might be there," she said,
"There might be friends and foes;
But I don't care for friends and foes—
To Lord Thomas's wedding I'll go."

10 She dressed herself in scarlet and green,
The fairest colors e'er seen;
And every town that she rode through,
They took her for to be some queen.

11 She rode up to Lord Thomas's gate,
So loudly toned and called;
None was so ready as Lord Thomas himself
To rise and bid her in.

12 He took the Brown girl by the hand,
And led her through the hall,
And sat her on the marble-top table,
Among the ladies all.

13 "Is this your bride?" Fair Ellen said,
"Is this your bride so brown?
You could have married the fairest young girl
That ever rode through this town."

14 "Throw none of your snares at me, Fair Ellen,
Throw none of your snares[1] at me,
For I think more of your little finger
Than the Brown girl's whole body."

15 The Brown girl had a little penknife,
The blade was keen and sharp;
Between the long ribs and the short,
She pierced Fair Ellen's heart.

16 "What makes you look so pale, Fair Ellen?
What makes you look so pale?"

"When I can feel my cold heart's blood,
   Come flowing beside my knees."

17 He took the Brown girl by the hand,
     He led her through the hall;
    And with his knife cut her head clean off,
     And kicked it against the wall.

18 "Papa, Papa, go dig my grave,
     Go dig it long and deep;
    Bury pretty Ellen in my arms,
     And the Brown girl at my feet."

19 He placed the sword against the wall,
     The point against his breast;
    Saying, "Here's the death of three long lovers,
     God send their souls to rest."

1. In other versions from the same section, "slurs," which makes better sense (see headnote).

FAIR MARGARET AND SWEET WILLIAM
(Child, No. 74)

Child printed four versions of this ballad of which one is from Massachusetts (V, 293-94). It is very popular in the United States, but the texts are not very similar to those in Child. It is found in numerous fragmentary forms, but the significant dream sequence is often included. The usual Virginia story has Sweet William arising in the morning and denying any love for Lady Margaret, who later dies or commits suicide upon seeing him ride by with his new bride. In the night Lady Margaret's ghost appears at his bedside, and he confesses that he loves her more than his bride. On the following morning, after portent dreams, usually of swine and blood, he calls upon Lady Margaret and learns of her death. After kissing her he dies of sorrow, and (as elsewhere) sympathetic plants grow from their graves. Child notes that this ballad begins like "Lord Thomas and Fair Annet," that its mid-section is blended with a form of that ballad, and that its catastrophe is repeated in "Lord Lovel."

Fifteen texts (out of twenty-eight available) and eight tunes of this ballad were published in *TBVa*. Since then, seven additional items of the ballad have been collected, of which only three are given here, two of them with tunes. Another item entitled "Lady Margaret" and listed as Item 8 in *FSVa* is a version of "Young Hunting" (Child, No. 68) and is treated in its proper place.

AA, an excellent if less literate full text, has a tune transcribed from live performance by John Powell.

BB, a gapped and compressed text, has a rather more interesting tune taken from the phonograph record.

CC, without tune, is a full and highly distinctive text, with numerous significant variants: stanza 4 hints that Lady Margaret's death is suicide; stanzas 6 and 7 identify the bride as the brown girl, an intrusion from the "Lord Thomas" ballad preceding, a detail unique in Virginia texts and rare in America, though found in Child A and B; stanza 16 is the "funeral feast" stanza rarely found in America (cf. Child A 16); interesting verbal variants abound: "grapevine room," "maiden-maiden all," "snow-white speed," "million alls," etc. Certain stanzas (1, 11, 12) vary from the normal stanzaic pattern, but have been left essentially undoctored, following manuscript.

The excluded texts add little to the story, though each has its characteristic variants: in one the name of Sweet William is changed to William Hall, a corruption from a later well-known British broadside ballad; in another Lady Margaret becomes Liddy Margaret, and the following dialogue takes place between Sweet William and her brother:

> "Good morning, good morning to you,
>   What makes you look so pale and blue?"
> "I'm mourning the loss of my own dear sister
>   Who died for the love of you."

The relationship of the Virginia texts to the Child texts is complex and not very close. See the *TBVa* headnote, and add the information given above. Most of the Virginia texts conform to Coffin's Story Type A, but CC would seem to represent Story Type B.

That the ballad is a rich repository of folklore material is obvious: the ghost, the portent dream, the appearance of blood, swine, and tears in dreams of ill omen, the sympathetic plants of the rose-and-brier ending. See Wimberly, *passim.*

AA

"Sweet William." Collected by Fred F. Knobloch, John Powell, Hilton Rufty, and A. K. Davis, Jr. Sung by Mrs. Martha Elizabeth Gibson, of Crozet, Va. Albemarle County. May 17, 1931. Tune noted by John Powell. The last two lines are repeated except in stanza eighteen. The words were not fitted to the tune at the time of collection, and the editor is unwilling to take any liberty with a John Powell musical transcription from live performance.

(1)

almost

Section *···* is repeated in first stanza

1 Sweet William arose one merry mornin',
   He dressed hisself in blue,
   "Tell on to me of the long, long love
   Betwixt Lady Margaret and you."

2 "I knew nothin' o' Lady Margaret,
   Nor she knew nothin' o' me.
   Befo' de eight o'clock de morrow mornin'
   Lady Margaret my bride shall see."

3 Lady Margaret was standin' at a fine dornin' window,
   Combin' her long yellow hair.
   Who should she spy but sweet William and his bride
   Goin' through the new church yard.

4 Back she tossed her long yellow hair,
   Down she tossed her comb and back she fell
   From her fine dornin' window
   And she never was no mo' seen there.

5 Day bein' gone an' night comin' on,
   And most of them all were asleep,
   Who should he spy but Lady Margaret's ghost
   Standin' at his bed feet.

6 "How do you like your bed," says she,
   "And how do you like your sheet?
   And how do you like your new wedded wife
   Who lies in your arms asleep?"

7 "Very well I like my bride," says he,
   "And better I like my sheet,
   Best of them all that gay lady
   That stands at my bed feet."

8 The night bein' gone an' the day comin' on,
   When the most of them all were awake,
   Sweet William arosed, he was troubled in his mind,
   From the dream that he dreampt last night.

9 "What's that, Sweet William?" they replied,
     "What's that I say unto you?"
   "I dreampt that my room floor was floating in swine
     And my bedside covered with tears."

10 "Bad dream, Sweet William," they replied,
     "Bad dream, I say unto you,
   For some of your nearest 'lations is dead.
     Sweet William, you'd better go and see."

11 He call-ed up his new house maids,
     One and two and three,
   To ask the leave of his new wedded wife
     Of Lady Margaret he could go and see.

12 He rode 'til he came to Lady Margaret's hall,
     He knock-ed so loud at the ring.
   None was so ready as Lady Margaret's brother
     To rise and let him in.

13 "Is Lady Margaret in her kitchen?" says he,
     "Or is she in her hall,
   Or is she in her high chamb-er,
     Amongst those merry maids all?"

14 "Lady Margaret's neither in her kitchen," says he,
     "Nor neither in her hall.
   Lady Margaret's in her coffin made out o' lead,
     And her pale face turned to the wall."

15 "Pull down, pull them fine Hollan' sheets,
     Was made o' the Hollan' so fine,
   Let me git a kiss from her cold, cold lips,
     Where often times has kissed mine."

16 Three times he kissed her lily white breast,
     Four times he kissed her chin,
   Five times he kissed her cold, cold lips,
     Which pleased his heart within.

17 Lady Margaret she died for love,
     Sweet William died for sorrow.
   Sweet William was buried under one willow tree,
     And Lady Margaret under another.

18 From Lady Margaret's grave there sprang a red rose,
     And from Sweet William's a briar.
   O they grew till they came to the church tower
     And they could not grew any higher.
   There they tied in a true lover's knot,
     And there they stayed forever.

BB

"Lady Margret." Phonograph record (aluminum) made by A. K. Davis, Jr. Sung by Mrs. John Webb (née Callie Hogan), of Lynch Station, Va. Campbell County. August 4, 1932. Text transcribed by P. C. Worthington. Tune noted by Winston Wilkinson. Mead comments: "An interesting tune, largely because of the uncertainty of the tonal center." A comparison of this text and tune with those printed in *TBVa* (pp. 237, 537) from the same singer will indicate what has happened to the ballad during the eighteen-year interval.

1   Lady Margret was settin' in her bow'r[1] window,
    Combing out her long yellow hair,
    Who should she spy but Sweet William and his bride
    As they were riding near.

2   Lady Margret fell from her bow'r window,
    Combing out her long yellow hair,
    Who should she spy but Sweet William and his bride
    As they were riding near.

3   "Such a dream, such a dream I dreamed last night,
    Such a dream it may come true,
    I dreamed my bed was full of whitened twine
    And my bride bed was filled with tears."

4   "Hold down, hold down your lily-white cheeks,
    Hold down, hold down so fine,
    Let me get as many kisses from your cold clear lips
    As ever you kissed from mine."

5 Lady Margret died today at twelve o'clock,
  Sweet William died like tomorrow,
  Lady Margret was buried under the tall willow tree,
  Sweet William was buried under another.

1. Pronounced in one syllable like "bow" by the singer.

CC

"Sweet William." Collected by Miss Mettie B. Akers, of Indian Valley,
Va. Sung in her one-room school in 1907. Floyd County. September 19,
1932. For detailed comment upon this text, see the general headnote to this
ballad.

1 Sweet William rose one morning in May.
  He dressed himself in blue.
  His father's reply to him and asked of a long-long-love
  That lies between Lady Margaret and you.

2 "It's I know nothing of Lady Margaret,
  Nor she knows nothing of me,
  But tomorrow by the eight o'clock
  Lady Margaret my bride shall see."

3 Lady Margaret was in her grape-vine room,
  Combing of her yellow hair,
  Who could she see but Sweet William and his bride
  A-walking down the street so fair.

4 She threw aside her wavy combs,
  Folding back her yellow hair.
  She fell out of her grape-vine room,
  No longer could she stay there.

5 The day being spent and the night coming on,
  Although they were asleep,
  Who could he see but Lady's Margaret's ghost,
  Standing over his bed feet.

6 "Sing how do you like your new coverlet,
  It's how do you like your sheet?
  It's how do you like your own brown girl
  Who lies in your arms asleep?"

7 "Very well do I like my new coverlet,
  Very well do I like my sheet,
  But better do I like my own brown girl
  Who lies in my arms asleep."

8 The night being spent and the day coming on,
 Although they were awake
Sweet William called on his maiden-maiden-all,
 If Lady Margaret he might go see.

9 "Such dreams, such dreams as I had last night,
 I fear they will come true,
I dreamed that my vial was filled full of wine
 And my bride's bed a-flowing with blood.

10 "Go saddle up my snow-white speed
 Go saddle him up so fine,

 . . . .
 . . . ."

11 He rode and he rode till he came to Lady Margaret's door,
 He rang the old door bell,
Who was so ready but her own dear brother
 To rise and let him in.

12 "Where is Lady Margaret, oh where is she?
 Is she in her grape-vine room, or is she in her hall?
Or is she in her grave
 Among those million alls?"

13 "She's not in her grape-vine room,
 She's not in her hall,
But she's in her own coffin
 That sits against the wall."

14 "Go fold back those winding sheets,
 Go fold them back so fine,
I want to kiss her cold, pale lips,
 For I'm sure they will never kiss mine."

15 The first he kissed was her red, rosie cheeks,
 The next was her cherry chin,
The next he kissed was her cold pale lips
 That thrilled his heart with pain.

16 "What would you have at Lady Margaret's burial?"
 "Nothing but bread and wine,
And tomorrow by the eight o'clock
 You may have the same at mine."

17 Sweet William was buried in the old church yard,
 Lady Margaret in their choir,
A rose sprang up from Sweet William's breast,
 And from Lady Margaret's a briar.

18   They grew, they grew to the old church top,
      They couldn't grow no higher,
      They both fell down to the cold, clay ground
      With the rose wrapped around the briar.[1]

1. A closely related fragmentary text from the same collector and county, but apparently not from the same singer has "William Hall" for "Sweet William," "Lady Marguerite" for "Lady Margaret," "wavery combs" for "wavy combs," "her own cold coffin" for "her own coffin." It is essentially the same version, but incomplete.

20

LORD LOVEL
(CHILD, No. 75)

The tragic story of this ballad is simple: a young nobleman takes leave of his beloved Lady Nancy Belle and goes off on his travels; after a year and a day he returns and discovers that she has died of grief for his absence, whereupon he kisses her clay-cold lips and dies of sorrow. Child prints ten versions of the ballad. "Lord Lovel" has enjoyed widespread popularity in the United States: there are fifteen versions in *TBVa* (out of thirty-six available). Nearly all the American texts have followed Child H, a London broadside of 1846. "This similarity of texts and the song's popularity," states Coffin (p. 79), "is undoubtedly due to its frequent inclusion in pre-Civil War songbooks and broadsides."

All the Virginia texts are quite close to Child H and preserve the details of the story and the names of the lovers with little variation. This is rather surprising in view of the fact that "Lord Lovel" has frequently blended with "Lord Thomas and Fair Annet" and "Fair Margaret and Sweet William," both of which are also lovers' tragedies often employing the rose-and-brier ending.

"Lord Lovel" has often been parodied, and *TBVa* (pp. 240-41) attributes this in part to the lightness of the tunes to which the ballad has been sung: "They are quite out of harmony with the deep tragedy of the ballad story. To sing the tune is to mitigate the tragedy, perhaps even to run the risk of burlesquing it." Of the many parodies, the most interesting, according to Albert B. Friedman, of Harvard, is "a Southern taunting of Lincoln on his military reverses," which he reproduces from *TBVa* (pp. 258-59) in his recent *Viking Book of Folk Ballads of the English-Speaking World,* pp. 98-99. Barry (pp. 145-47) cites other parodies.

Might a long-time student and lover of these old ballads say that he finds "Lord Lovel" one of the least interesting of the Child ballads, both in text and in tune? Both are fairly standardized (see AA, BB, CC). That London broadside of 1846 (Child H) and other broadsides and songbooks have left too little opportunity for the operations of oral tradition upon this song. It is somewhat consoling that the same standardization of texts and tunes from recent British tradition is noted by Margaret Dean-Smith (p. 85) and by Gavin Greig's *Last Leaves* (pp. 57-58). Yet the ballad continues to be popular with the American folk (see Coffin, pp. 78-79).

AA

"Lord Lovel." Phonograph record (aluminum) made by A. K. Davis, Jr. Sung by Mrs. Margaret Michie Carter, of Charlottesville, Va., and Winston-Salem, N. C. It was taught to her by her grandfather, George Perkins. Albemarle County. 1936. Text transcribed by P. C. Worthington. Tune noted by G. W. Williams and E. C. Mead. Text independently collected by A. L. Hench, of the University of Virginia. Albemarle County. 1930. "An interesting tune and a definite alternation of ⁶⁄₈ and ⁹⁄₈" (E. C. Mead).

1   Lord Lovel he stood at his castle gate,
        A-combing his milk white steed,
    When down came his Lady Nancy Bell,
        A-wishing her lover good speed, good speed,
        A-wishing her lover good speed.

2   "Oh where are you going, Lord Lovel?" she said,
        "Oh where are you going?" said she.
    "I'm going, my lady Nancy Bell,
        Strange countries for to see, see, see,
        Strange countries for to see."

3   "When will you be back, Lord Lovel?" she said,
        "When will you be back?" said she.
    "In a year or two more, or at least three or four,
        I'll return to my lady Nancy, Nancy,
        I'll return to my lady Nancy."

4 He hadn't been gone but a year and a day,
   Strange countries for to see,
When languishing thoughts came into his head,
   Concerning his lady Nancy, Nancy,
   Concerning his lady Nancy.

5 So he rode and he rode on his milk-white steed,
   Till he came to London town,
And there he heard the church bells ring,
   And the people all mourning around, 'round, 'round,
   And the people all mourning around.

6 "Oh what is the matter?" Lord Lovel he said,
   "Oh what is the matter?" said he.
"A beautiful lady, my lord, is dead,
   Some call her the Lady Nancy, Nancy,
   Some call her the Lady Nancy."

7 So he ordered the coffin to be opened wide,
   And the shroud to be turn-ed down,
And there he kissed her clay-cold lips,
   While tears came raining down, down, down,
   While tears came raining down.

8 Lady Nancy she died it might be today,
   Lord Lovel he died tomorrow.
Lady Nancy she died of pure, pure grief,
   Lord Lovel he died of sorrow, sorrow, sorrow,
   Lord Lovel he died of sorrow.

9 Lady Nancy was laid in the nave of the church;
   Lord Lovel was laid in the choir,
And out of her bosom there grew a white rose,
   And out of her lover's a briar, briar, briar,
   And out of her lover's a briar.

10 They grew and they grew till they reached the church top,
   And then they could grow no higher,
And so they entwined in a true lovers' knot,
   For all true lovers to admire, 'mire, 'mire,
   For all true lovers to admire.

BB

"Lord Lovel." Collected by Fred F. Knobloch, of Crozet, Va. Sung by Mrs. Thomas Smith, of Charlottesville, Va., who learned it from her mother, Mrs. Theodore Halleck, of Stroudsburg, Pa. Albemarle County. April 21, 1931. Tune noted by Mr. Knobloch.

Lord Lov - el stood at his cas - tle gate, Comb -ing his milk -white
steed, When a - long came La - dy Nan - cy Belle, Bid - ding her
Much faster to end
lov - er good speed, speed, speed, Bid - ding her lov - er good speed.

1 Lord Lovel stood at his castle gate,
   Combing his milk-white steed,
When along came Lady Nancy Bell,
   Bidding her lover good speed, speed, speed,
   Bidding her lover good speed.

2 "Where are you going, Lord Lovel?" she said,
   "Where are you going?" said she.
"I'm going afar," Lord Lovel replied,
   "Fair countries for to see, see, see,
   Fair countries for to see."

3 "How long will you be gone?" Lady Nancy cried,
   "How long will you be gone?" said she.
"I'm going to be gone a year and a day,
   Fair countries for to see, see, see,
   Fair countries for to see."[1]

4 He hadn't been gone but a year and a day,
   Fair countries for to see,
When languishing thoughts came over him
   Lady Nancy for to see, see, see,
   Lady Nancy for to see.

5 He rode and he rode for a year and a day,
   Till he came to London town,
And there he saw all over the streets
   The people go mourning round and around,
   The people go mourning around.

6 "Is anyone dead?" Lord Lovel said,
   "Is anyone dead?" said he.
"A lady is dead," the people all said,
   "And they call her the Lady Nancee, 'cee, 'cee,
   They call her the Lady Nancee."

7 Lady Nancy died as it were today;
   Lord Lovel he died on the morrow.

Lady Nancy died of a pure broken heart;
Lord Lovel died of sorrow, sorrow, sorrow,
Lord Lovel died of sorrow.

8 They buried Lady Nancy beneath the chancel rail,
And they buried Lord Lovel right by her,
And out of her bosom there grew a red rose,
And out of Lord Lovel's a briar, 'riar, 'riar,
And out of Lord Lovel's a briar.

9 They grew and they grew to church steeple top,
Till they couldn't grow the least bit higher,
And they twined themselves in a true lovers' knot,
For all good folks to admire, 'mire, 'mire,
For all good folks to admire.

1. Mrs. Smith gave the following as a variation of the third stanza:
"How long will you be gone, Lord Lovel?" she said,
"How long will you be gone?" said she.
"A year or two, or three at the most,
And then I'll return to thee, 'ee, 'ee,
And then I'll return to thee."

CC

"Lord Lovell." Collected by Miss Margaret Purcell, of Greenwood, Va.
Sung by her mother, Mrs. Elizabeth Ashton Garrett Purcell (Mrs. S. H.
Purcell), of Greenwood, Va. Albemarle County. May, 1934. Tune noted
by Winston Wilkinson.

1 Lord Lovell he stood at his castle gate,
      A-combing his milk white steed,
   When Lady Nancy Belle came by,
      A-wishing her lover good speed, speed, speed,
      A-wishing her lover good speed.

2 "Oh, where are you going, Lord Lovell?" she said,
      "Oh, where are you going?" said she.
   "I'm going, my dear Lady Nancy Belle,
      Far countries for to see, see, see,
      Far countries for to see."

3 "When will you be back, Lord Lovell?" said she,
      "When will you be back?" said she.
   "In one or two years, or at the most three,
      I'll return to my Lady Nancee, 'cee, 'cee,
      I'll return to my Lady Nancee."

4 He traveled and traveled the whole world around,
      Till he came to London Town,
   And there he met with a funeral,
      And the people all weeping around, 'round, 'round,
      And the people all weeping around.

5 "Who's dead? who's dead?" Lord Lovell he said,
      "Who's dead? who's dead?" said he.
   "Our Lord's only daughter," the people replied,
      "And they called her the Lady Nancee, 'cee, 'cee,
      And they called her the Lady Nancee."

6 Lady Nancy she died as it might be today;
      Lord Lovell as it might be tomorrow.
   Lady Nancy she died of pure, pure grief,
      Lord Lovell he died of sorrow, sorrow, sorrow,
      Lord Lovell he died of sorrow.

7 Lady Nancy was buried in St. Mary's Church;
      Lord Lovell was buried in the choir.
   And out of her bosom there grew a red rose,
      And out of Lord Lovell's a brier, 'rier, 'rier,
      And out of Lord Lovell's a brier.

8 They grew and they grew to the church steeple top,
      And when they could grow no higher,
   They there entwined in a true lovers' knot,
      For all true lovers to admire, 'rire, 'rire,
      For all true lovers to admire.

21

SWEET WILLIAM'S GHOST
(CHILD, No. 77)

This, and the two ballads that follow, are all ghost ballads and the lore of the supernatural is important in them all. As usual in ballads, the ghost is not a wraith or disembodied spirit but simply a person who is dead and who reappears to the living. The living do not usually recognize the ghostly character of the visitant until the ghost declares himself. Wimberly (p. 452) lists the following motives for the walking of ghosts: to admonish the living; to announce the death of the visitant; to carry off the living; to foretell the death of the living; to foretell the punishments in store for the living in the next world, or to punish or reprove the living; to quiet the excessive grief of the living, since the visitant's rest is disturbed thereby; to secure the return of the troth-plight; to succor the children whom a cruel stepmother has mistreated. In some ballads the motives are mixed.

In "Sweet William's Ghost" the primary motive of the dead lover is to ask back his unfulfilled troth-plight, without which he apparently cannot rest quietly in his grave. In "The Unquiet Grave" the primary motive of the revenant is to forbid the living loved one's excessive grief, which disturbs the dead lover's repose. In "The Wife of Usher's Well" the dead children return in answer to the mother's prayers and grief, and in part to warn her against excessive grieving.

When in "Sweet William's Ghost" the lover comes back from the grave to secure the return of his troth, the girl refuses to return it unless he kiss her or wed her, or both. He then informs her that he is no living man. She follows him to the grave and asks if there is any room for her. Usually there is not. In Child A alone does the maiden die. In other texts she is more often curious than compassionate, demanding the answers to such questions about the dead as what becomes of women who die in childbirth; what of unbaptized children, etc. The troth itself is returned in a number of ways: by means of a wand, by striking her lover with a silver key, or by a touch of her hand. A few later versions give a highly allegorical interpretation to the dead man's graveside companions.

"Sweet William's Ghost" is an extremely rare ballad. Though Child prints seven versions, mostly Scottish, the earliest and best (except for the two last stanzas) from Allan Ramsay's *Tea Table Miscellany* of 1740, the ballad does not appear in recent collections from either England or Scotland. Quite recently, however, the ballad has been reported from Northern Ireland. Marie Slocombe in "Some 'English' Ballads and Folk Songs Recorded in Ireland 1952-1954," *JEFDSS*, VII (December, 1955), 239-44, reports that among sixty-five separate songs recorded by the British Broadcasting Corporation in Ireland "there is a high proportion of ballads, including . . . sixteen Child ballads, nearly all represented by at least one very good and complete version." Included in the list that follows is "Sweet William's Ghost." In a continuation of Miss Slocombe's article under the same title in *JEFDSS*, VIII (December, 1956), 16-28, Peter Kennedy and others have more recently published the text of this and other ballads. The interesting version cited there (pp. 16-17) contains seven and a half double stanzas, as sung by Charles O'Boyle, of Belfast, Northern Ireland, on July 7, 1952. The version does not closely resemble any of Child's. At cock-crow Margaret follows her lover to his grave, and when it opens to receive him she strikes her Willy on the breast with her hand, thus returning his faith and troth. In a note on the ballad (*ibid.*, p. 17), A. L. Lloyd remarks upon the rarity of this ballad, cites no other British texts, and remarks that "even Gavin Greig does not seem to have found it."

The ballad has been recently found, but sparingly, both in the United States and in Canada. It does not appear in *TBVa* or in Barry or in Sharp-Karpeles. It is, however, apparently well known in Newfoundland. Both Greenleaf and Mansfield and Miss Karpeles give a text from there. Miss Karpeles writes, "I noted nine variants" (p. 74). She also presents a tune. The earliest text published in the United States appears in *The Green Mountain Songster*, compiled by an old Revolutionary soldier in 1823. The text is printed *literatim* in Flanders' *Vermont Folk-Songs and Ballads* (p. 240) and more recently in Friedman's *The Viking Book of Ballads* (pp. 50-51). It contains an intrusion from "The Maid Freed from the Gallows" (Child, No. 95) and, like the Newfoundland texts, is most closely related to Child C, where several apparitions present at the grave are explained by the ghost. The Brown Collection (II, 92-94) has a fine text resembling Child A, plus a tune (IV, 48). The death of the maiden as in Child A makes this text unique in tradition outside Child. The editors of the Brown Collection are uncertain of the contributor but believe it to be Mrs. Sutton. A comparison of the text with that given in the Maude Minish Manuscripts in the Harvard Library (Miss Minish was later Mrs. Sutton) leaves no doubt that this is the case, though one stanza which the Harvard manuscript contains does not appear in the Brown Collection text. Coffin gives a reference to an article by Josephine McGill in *The North American Review* (CCXXVIII, 222), but this turns out to be a fragmentary quotation used for illustration only and taken from Sir Walter Scott's version of "Clerk Saunders" (Child, No. 69), hence need not be considered here.

The only other known American text is the present Virginia one. It is of five stanzas, two of them imperfect, and is somewhat corrupted. There is no doubt that it is a version of "Sweet William's Ghost," but there are too many intrusions to associate it with confidence with any particular Child version. Stanza one mentions that it was a moonshiny night when "I heard some one at my window sigh." This agrees with all versions of the ballad (except the North Carolina one) in setting the scene at night, and corresponding lines can be found in other versions. Child F has the maiden in a tower "By the lee licht o the moon," and in Child B the ghost appears "With mony a sad sigh and groan," to cite two examples. The second stanza of the Virginia text appears in all versions of this ballad collected, except Child B, F, and G. The third stanza introduces a corruption reminiscent of "Lady Isabel and the Elf Knight," especially in Virginia where the lady in that ballad is often named Polly. More probably, however, it is an interpolation from "The Cruel Ship's Carpenter." In that song the girl is often called Pretty Polly, and the theme of the girl being led to a new-dug grave by her lover, who then kills her, might have resulted in the appearance of this stanza in "Sweet William's Ghost." Ordinarily it is the girl who follows the ghost, not by his request as is indicated here. An exception besides the Virginia text is the Greenleaf and Mansfield text (p. 21), where the ghost takes the girl by the apron strings and says, "Follow, follow me." The fourth stanza of the present version has no parallel in other texts of "Sweet William's Ghost" or in "The Cruel Ship's Carpenter." It is perfectly in keeping with the ballad, however, in having the ghost reach the graveyard and open the gates of the burial ground for his love. The last stanza, unusual in that the ghost wishes to be kissed, when usually in the ballad he discourages the kiss, finds

a parallel of sorts in the Greenleaf and Mansfield text.   Like the
Virginia text, that one lacks any mention of a troth.   Thus the
return seems to be only for a final parting to ensure rest for either
of the lovers.   In Greenleaf and Mansfield the ghost is apparently
concerned for the living sweetheart, for he takes her by the lily-
white hand and presses her to his breast, wishing her rest.   In
the Virginia text, it would seem that this final parting kiss would
ensure rest for the ghost.   It is possible that this stanza has been
taken over from "Fair Margaret and Sweet William," where there
is a similar ghostly appearance, and a later kissing of the corpse.
The stanza is, however, something of a commonplace in ballads
of ghostly apparition and farewell.   The conventional crowing of
the cock as a sign for the dead to return is lacking here.

The rarity of this fragmentary text mitigates its corruption,
though the corruption itself is of some interest.   The even rarer
tune, collected but not located in the Virginia archives, would add
value to a ballad not previously found in Virginia, hence not represented in *TBVa*.

AA

"Sweet Willie's Ghost."   Collected by Miss Alfreda M. Peel, of Salem, Va.
Sung by Mrs. Hattie Dudley, of Franklin, Va.   Nansemond County.   December 17, 1936.   [The tune noted by Mrs. Kathleen Kelly Coxe, of Roanoke, Va., has been lost.]   Miss Peel sent in two texts at the same time,
one a "revised version."   Since the revised version is slightly superior both
metrically and in sense, it is here given, with all the variations indicated in
footnotes.   Where there are deviations, the whole line is given.

1   One night, one night, 'twas a moonshiny night,[1]
      The moon did shine
    And the stars gave light,[2]
      I heard some one at my window sigh.[3]

2   "Is that brother James," said she,
      "Or is it brother John,
    Or is it my sweet true love[4]
      Who has been gone from me so long?"

3   "Oh come, come on now, Pretty Polly,[5]
      And go with me;
    I'll carry you over yonder
      . . . .

4   He opened the gates with his own pale hand
      And let Pretty Polly through
      . . . .
      . . . .

5   He unscrewed the coffin lid
    And threw by the sheet so fine:
    "Come, come Pretty Polly, kiss my clay cold lips
    As you kissed when I left you behind."

1. "One night, one night, was a moon shining bright."
2. Lines two and three of this stanza do not appear in the "unrevised text."
3. "I heard some one at my window sight."
4. "Or is it my own true love."
5. "Oh come on now, Pretty Polly."

22

THE UNQUIET GRAVE
(CHILD, No. 78)

A full discussion of this ballad and a first publication of its
rare Virginia text by the present editor appeared in " 'The Unquiet
Grave': A New-Old Ballad from Virginia," *English Studies in
Honor of James Southall Wilson,* University of Virginia Studies,
IV (Charlottesville, Va., 1951), 99-110.

The ballad seems to be widespread in England, and is known
in Scotland, but is extremely rare in American tradition. Child
prints nine British versions: from Sussex, Suffolk (two), from
Buchan's MSS. (Scotland), 'in Gipsy tents,' from Shropshire, from
Cornwall, from Devonshire, and an additional fragment from
Scotland. More recent English collectors—Cecil Sharp, Lucy E.
Broadwood, A. G. Gilchrist, E. M. Leather, and Alfred Williams,
among others—have added more than a dozen English versions or
variants, many of them with tunes. (See Davis article cited above
for detailed references.) "This ballad, of which I have collected a
large number of variants," says Sharp in *One Hunderd English
Folk Songs* (p. xxvii), "is widely known and sung by English
folksingers." On the other hand, no version of the song appears
in the best known recent collection from Scottish sources, that of
Gavin Greig and Alexander Keith—a fact which points to the
more strongly English character and wider English currency of the
song. Child surveys with his usual impressive scholarship the
counterparts to this ballad in the popular traditions not only of the
Scots but of the Persians, Indians, Celts, Slavs, Greeks, and the
Germanic and Latin races.

Traces of the ballad in North America are few indeed. Greenleaf and Mansfield (pp. 23-24) found it in Newfoundland in 1929
(one full version and a one-stanza fragment, each with a tune);
Niles apparently found it among the Kentucky hill-folk in 1936;
in 1937 Halpert recorded a four-and-a-half-stanza version, plus
tune, in New Jersey; and the Brown Collection of 1952 (II, 94-95)
presents a text, without tune, from North Carolina. The manuscript of the Virginia text states that it was learned by the Smiths in
December, 1912, and was sung by Mrs. Chaney Smith's mother

seventy years before that.   Perhaps the Virginia text may claim some sort of recorded North American priority.

Most versions of the ballad are brief: six or seven stanzas, sometimes less, the longest (Child H) only eleven stanzas.   The fact that several of these stanzas are very nearly repetitions of certain stanzas in "Sweet William's Ghost" (Child, No. 77) and "The Two Brothers" (Child, No. 49) has led Child to a suspicion "that this brief little piece is an aggregation of scraps."   But he puts the suspicion aside, supposing instead that the ballad has survived only in an imperfect form.   "Even such as it is, however," he rightly concludes, "this fragment has a character of its own" (II, 234). He might have spoken even more strongly if he had examined the numerous versions taken down from recent oral tradition, especially in England but also in America.   Cecil Sharp, who knew many more texts and tunes of the ballad, speaks up much more strongly in commendation of it both as folk poetry and as folk music.   See *English Folk Song: Some Conclusions,* pp. 99, 102, and elsewhere.

The ballad is essentially lyrical, but there is a basic story: A lover (man or woman) who has just lost his or her loved one makes a vow of mourning at the loved one's grave for a year and a day.   At the end of that time, the dead lover asks who is weeping at the grave and disturbing his (her) rest.   The living lover then identifies himself (herself) and craves one final kiss of the dead one's lips.   The dead lover refuses, on the ground that the kiss of a dead person will mean death to the living.   The ending is various: a direct end with the dead lover's refusal; a suggestion of the finality of death and the hopelessness of regaining former happiness in the symbol of the beautiful flower now withered; the ghost's more overt forbidding of such excessive mourning; sometimes (and less acceptably), the ghost's suggestion of patience and the consolation of religion.

The Virginia version is most closely related to Child A, but it seems artistically a finer ballad than Child A, because it lacks the pietistic-consolatory and distinctly anticlimactic final stanza of Child A:

> "The stalk is withered dry, my love,
>   So will our hearts decay;
> So make yourself content, my love,
>   Till God calls you away."

In contrast, the Virginia text ends, as one would wish it to, with the moving flower symbolism of the withering of beauty and love in the finality of death. The dead loved one speaks the final words:

> "It is down in yonder fields so green,
>   Love, where we used to walk,
> The beautifulles' flower that ever was seen
>   Is withered now to a stalk."

Otherwise, there is a fairly close correspondency, stanza by stanza, to the first six stanzas of Child A—of course with many verbal variations. The two texts also agree in the important detail of the sex of the dead and living lovers. See the Davis article cited above for fuller detail.

The local Virginia title of "The Broken-Hearted Lover" is quite as appropriate as, if perhaps slightly less poetical than, Child's "The Unquiet Grave" or "The Restless Grave" of the North Carolina text. The Virginia title is, however, one also given to "The Dear Companion" and to other songs of frustrated love. Of the ballad, R. E. Lee Smith writes, "I consider this a good song whether a ballad or not." He is right.

That the ballad is a rich repository of antique folklore or popular beliefs is clear: the talking ghost, the idea that excessive grieving for the dead interferes with their repose, the notion that the breath of a ghost smells strong and that the kiss of a dead person is fatal, the "magic-task" stanzas, the survival of the ancient troth-plight which binds the lovers even after death, and so on. (See Child, Wimberly, Gerould, Davis, and others.) Miss Wells (*The Ballad Tree,* p. 145) even sees a Neoplatonic significance in the kiss of the clay-cold lips, and Miss Harvey (*JEFDSS,* IV, 63-64) asks whether it is permissible to see in the kiss a token of the return of the troth. In contrast to the inanity of many ballad ghosts, Gerould finds in the supernatural visitant of this ballad "exquisite poignancy" (*The Ballad of Tradition,* pp. 63-65). The Virginia text—like other American texts of supernatural ballads—has lost some of these supernatural trappings but preserves the important ones and the essential character of the ballad.

AA

"The Broken-Hearted Lover." Contributed by R. E. Lee Smith, of Palmyra, Va. Sung by his brother, Thomas P. Smith, of Palmyra, Va., and himself. Fluvanna County. December 1912. Learned from the singing of Mrs. Chaney Smith, who heard it sung by her mother seventy years before.

1   "Wind cold today, my love,
    And some wee drops of rain;
I never had but one dear love,
    And in the cruel grave she was lain.

2   "I do is much for my dear love,
    As any young man will say;
I will set and cry on her grave
    For one year and a day."

3   The one year and a day being up,
    The dead began to speak:
"Oh, who's weeping on my grave
    And will not let me sleep?"

4   "It's me, my love, sets on your grave
    And will not let you sleep;
For I crave one kiss from your fair lips
    And that is all I ask."

5   "You crave one kiss from my cold lips,
    But my breath smells earthy strong;
If you have one kiss from my cold lips
    Your days will not be long.

6   "It is down in yonder fields so green,
    Love, where we used to walk;
The beautifulles' flower that ever was seen
    Is withered now to a stalk."

23

THE WIFE OF USHER'S WELL
(CHILD, No. 79)

A mother sends her children away to school. They die before their return home. The mother grieves and prays that they may come back to her. They return at Christmas, of course as ghosts, though the mother seems unaware of this. They refuse to eat or drink. They depart at daybreak, sometimes warning their mother against worldliness and suggesting that her excessive grief for them may disturb their repose.

Child prints only four texts of the ballad, three from Britain and one from America (North Carolina). No additional texts have appeared in English collections since Child's time, according to Miss Dean-Smith, nor have recent texts been found in Scotland or in British America. But the United States is richly supplied with versions or variants, and a great many have been collected, chiefly in the Southern states. For example, Sharp-Karpeles (I, 150-60) present eighteen tunes with texts or partial texts from the Southern Appalachians. The Brown Collection (II, 95-101, and IV, 48-53) reports nine texts, not all of them printed, and seven tunes. *TBVa* prints twelve texts of thirteen available, with two tunes. In contrast, Barry presents no traces from Maine or the Maritime Provinces of Canada. Belden's Missouri collection (pp. 55-57) presents only two texts, and the Ozark collection (I, 122-24) only two texts with tunes. More recent Virginia collecting has produced ten additional items of the ballad, of which only five are here presented, four of them with tunes.

Most, if not all, of the American texts, including the Virginia texts, are more closely related to Child D (V, 294) than to any other Child text, perhaps naturally since Child D comes from North Carolina. Belden (pp. 55-56) has listed the six particulars in which the American texts are to be distinguished from Child A, B, and C. He even suspects some printed source as the explanation of the likeness of the American texts, but he (and others) have been unable to find one. Belden seems to overestimate likeness and to ignore significant variations in the American texts. Perhaps Gerould (p. 177) is on sounder ground when he remarks: "Unquestionably the song has been created anew, as it has been transmitted from singer to singer and has travelled from Scotland to Virginia."

The Virginia texts share with Child C (from Shropshire) as well as with Child D the strongly religious coloring: the presence of the Saviour and the sinfulness of pride, and perhaps the suggestion that the return is made in answer to the mother's prayer. But there are pagan elements also: the belief that spirits return in order to calm the persistent lamentations of the bereaved, the vanishing of the ghosts at cock-crow, and the folk-belief that tears for the dead disturb their rest by wetting their winding-sheet—the note on which all the full texts that follow end.

If Child A from Scott's *Minstrelsy* is the best known and perhaps the most poetic version of the ballad, other versions, including the American, have their poetic claims as well. The essential poetic appeal, shared by all the versions, is the tragic pathos of the mother's failure to understand or unwillingness to believe that her sons are mere ghosts and must depart so soon. It is Child who says (II, 78), "Nothing that we have is more profoundly affecting."

At least three of the four tunes that follow, all three of them transcribed from records, are both musically interesting and fitting musical vehicles for the poetry of the ballad. See the individual headnotes.

AA

"The Three Little Babes." Phonograph record (aluminum) made by A. K. Davis, Jr. Sung by Miss Eunice Yeatts, of Meadows of Dan, Va. Patrick County. August 10, 1932. Text transcribed by P. C. Worthington. Tune noted by E. C. Mead, who comments: "Very beautiful tune: amazing fluid rhythmic irregularities, ⅝, ⅛, ¾. Expressive line; expressive use of the 7th and 3rd degrees as resting points; great variety within pentatonic tonal framework."

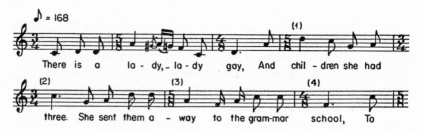

learn __ their_ gram-mer - ey.

1　There is a lady, lady gay,
　　　And children she had three.
　　She sent them away to the grammar school,[1]
　　　To learn their grammercy.

2　They hadn't been gone but a very short while,
　　　Scarcely three weeks to the day,
　　Till death, cold death, came stealing along,
　　　And stole those babes away.

3　"There lives a King in Heaven," she cried,
　　　"A King of a high degree;
　　Oh, send me back my three little babes,
　　　Oh, send them back to me."

4　Christmas time was growing[2] nigh,
　　　The nights being clear and cold,
　　She saw her three little babes come back,
　　　Come back to their mother's home.

5　She set a table of bread and wine,
　　　Just as neat as it could be,
　　"Come eat, come drink, my three little babes,
　　　Come eat and drink with me."

6　"I can't eat your bread," said the oldest one,
　　　"Neither can I drink your wine,
　　For my Saviour dear is standing near,
　　　To him I must resign."

7　She spread them a bed in the back of the room,
　　　And on it a neat white sheet,
　　And over the top spread a golden spread,
　　　That they might better sleep.

8　"Take it off, take it off," cried the oldest one,
　　　"Take it off, take it off," cried one,
　　"What's to become of this wide, wicked world,
　　　Since sin has first begun?"

9 "Cold clay, cold clay, hangs over my head,
   Green grass grows under my feet,
   And every tear that you shed for me,
   Does wet our winding sheet."

1. Possibly "grammercy."
2. Possibly "drawing."

BB

"Three Babes," or "Wife of Usher's Well." Collected by Miss Alfreda M. Peel, of Salem, Va. Contributed by Minter Grubb, of Back Creek, Va. Roanoke County. 1932. Tune noted by Miss Eloise Kelly and Mrs. Kathleen Kelly Coxe, of Marion and Roanoke, Va. Edited by Winston Wilkinson with this cauton: "This looks plausible, but does not ring true."

There was a la - dy, a la - dy _ gay   And chil - dren she had three. She sent them a -way _ to a Nor - thern school   To learn _ their gram-ma - ree.

1 There was a lady, a lady gay,
   And children she had three,
   She sent them away to a northern school
   To learn their grammaree.

2 They had not been gone
   But a very short time,
   Till death, cold death, came hastening along
   And stole her three little babes away.

3 Christmas time was drawing near,
   The nights was cold and clear,
   When her three little babes came hastening in
   Their mother for to cheer.

4 She sot them a table of bread and wine
   As neat as neat could be,
   "Come eat, come eat, my three little babes,
   Come eat and drink with me."

5 "I cannot eat your bread," cried the oldest one,
   "Nor drink your wine,

When my Saviour is standing by
To hear my last resign."

6 She made them a bed in a back wall room,
    And on she spread a sheet,
And over she spread a golden spread,
    That they might better sleep.

7 "Take it off, take it off," cried the oldest one,
    "Take it off, take off," cried they.
"Oh, what is to become of this wide wicked world?
    Oh, what is to become of me?

8 "The cold clay hangs over my head,
    And the green grass at my feet,[1]
And every tear that you shed for me
    Will wet my winding sheet.
And every tear that you shed for me
    Will wet my winding sheet."

1. Text accompanying Mrs. Coxe's notation has this couplet here:
      Cold, cold clay hangs o'er my head,
      Green grass grows round my feet.

CC

"The Three Little Babes." Phonograph record (aluminum) made by A. K. Davis, Jr. Sung by Mrs. W. F. Starke, of Crozet, Va. Albemarle County. November 11, 1932. Text transcribed by P. C. Worthington. Tune noted by E. C. Mead, who comments: "Fascinating rhythm. The melody is different for each stanza, although a melodic skeleton is discernible; 'durchkomponiert.'" Text and tune independently collected by Fred F. Knobloch, of Crozet, Va. May 2, 1931. The stanzaic irregularities apparently reflect the melodic irregularities, or vice versa.

1   There was a lady and a lady gay,
        And children she had three
    But sent them away to the north country
        To learn their grammaree.

2   They had not been gone so very long,
        Perhaps three months and a day,
    When cold death came hastening along
        And stole those babes away.

3   Christmas time was drawing nigh,
        Those three little babes came tripping along,

Down to their mother's home.
"I'll rouse you up," said the eldest one,
"I'll rouse you up, I say,
For the chickens are crowing for day."

4 In the back room she set the table,
On it she put bread and wine,
Saying, "Come eat, come drink, my sweet little babes,
And keep your mother company."

5 But the eldest said, "Put a marble stone at my head,
Put cold clay at my feet,
And the tears my mother will shed for me
Will wet my winding sheet."

DD

"The Three Little Babes." Phonograph record (aluminum) made by A. K. Davis, Jr. Sung by Mrs. Kit Williamson, of Yellow Branch, Va. Campbell County. August 4, 1932. Text transcribed by P. C. Worthington. Tune noted by Winston Wilkinson. First stanza with tune noted by Mrs. Paul Cheatham sent in by Miss Juliet Fauntleroy, of Altavista, Va. March 15, 1934. (Cf. *TBVa*, J, pp. 287, 576.)

1 There was a lady, lady gay,
Who had children,[1] one, two, three,
She sent those babes to the northern country,
To learn the[2] grammaree.

2   They hadn't been there but a month and a day,
        Before swift death came on,
    Before swift death came on,
        And taken those babes away.

3   There is a King that lives in Heaven,
        Where He used to wear a crown,
    "Pray send me back those three little babes,
        Night or in the morning soon.

4   "Come in, come in, my three little babes,
        And eat this bread and wine."
    "O Mother, can I eat your bread,
        Nor can I drink your wine."

1. MS. has "babies."
2. MS. has "their."

EE

"Three Little Babes."   Contributed by R. E. Lee Smith, of Palmyra, Va.
Sung by his brother, Thomas P. Smith, of Palmyra, Va., and himself, and
"many others of Zionville, N. C." Fluvanna County. May 25, 1931.

1   There was a lady of beauty bright,
        And children she had three,
    But she sent them away to the North Countree
        To learn their grammaree.

2   They hadn't been gone so very long,
        Scarce three months and a day,
    When there came a sickness over the land
        And swept them all away.

3   And when she came this to know,
        She wrung her hands full sore,
    Saying, "Alas! alas! what shall I do,
        I shall never see my babes any more.

4   "Isn't there a King in Heaven above
        Who used to wear a crown?
    I pray the Lord will me reward,
        And send my three little babes down."

5   It was a-comin' near Christmas time,
        The nights was long and cold,
    When the three little babes come running down
        To their dear mother's home.

6   She fixed the table for them then
        And covered with cakes and wine,

Saying, "Come and eat, my little babes,
Come eat and drink of mine."

7 "We do not want your cakes, mammie,
We do [not?] want your wine,
For yonder stands our Saviour dear
And with him we will dine."

8 She fixed them in a bed in her best room,
All spread over with clean white sheets,
And over the top a golden one,
That they might soundly sleep.

9 "Take them off, take them off, mammie," the
oldest cried,
"I hear the rooster crow.
Rise up, rise, 'tis coming day
And we must shortly go.

10 "Cold clods lie at our heads, mammie,
Green grass grows at our feet,
And the tears that come down your cheek,
They wet our winding sheets."

24

LITTLE MUSGRAVE AND LADY BARNARD
(Child, No. 81)

"Little Musgrave and Lady Barnard" is one of numerous ballads quoted in old plays of the Elizabethan or seventeenth-century periods. Beaumont and Fletcher's "Knight of the Burning Pestle" (Act V, Scene 3) contains the earliest (about 1611) quotation from this ballad:

> And some they whistled and some they sung,
>> Hey down, down
> And some did loudly say,
> Ever as the lord Barnet's horn blew,
>> Away, Musgrave, away!

Child (II, 243) mentions a number of later seventeenth-century plays in which the ballad is either quoted in part or referred to.

Child prints fifteen versions, some from manuscript, some from broadside or other printed sources. But the ballad does not seem to survive in recent British tradition either in England or in Scotland, according to Miss Dean-Smith's survey or Gavin Greig's *Last Leaves*. In contrast, it is vigorously alive in American tradition, North, South, and Midwest. Sharp-Karpeles (I, 161-82) print seventeen tunes and texts or part texts from the Southern Appalachians. Barry (pp. 150-94) presents nine texts, some with tunes, from Maine. Belden (pp. 59-60) gives three fragments and two tunes from Missouri. The Brown Collection (II, 101-11, and IV, 53-57) gives five texts and seven tunes from North Carolina. *TBVa* (pp. 289-301 and 577) prints six of seven texts then available, plus one tune. Subsequently, five new items of the ballad have been recovered in Virginia. Of these, three texts with two tunes are here included. Miss Beckwith has also found the ballad in Jamaica (see *PMLA,* XXXIX, 455 ff.).

Barry (pp. 150-94) has an elaborate discussion of this ballad, both textually and musically. He is perhaps overbold in presenting a number of interesting conjectures about the ballad as if they were established facts, and he is properly modified or corrected on some points by Helen Pettigrew (*University of West Virginia Studies,*

III [Philological Papers II], 8 ff.).   Barry is perhaps overhasty in dividing American texts into two types, the Lord Banner type and the Lord Arnold (or Daniel) type, with other differentiating details, in asserting that the split antedates the introduction of the ballad into America, in believing that the American texts are nearer to an earlier and better form than that from which the British texts are drawn, and in identifying the King Henry of the ballad too unequivocally with Henry VIII of England.   But one can sympathize with his statement: "The ballad must have been nearly three hundred years in this country, diverging ever farther and farther; but it has never lost its integrity.   We note how well the various American texts are preserved; how well they agree; how spirited they are; how splendidly dramatic, when the folk-singer throws himself into the ballad, and we wonder at the virility of a song which can thus keep itself alive.   Of all the ballad problems that have come to us, that of 'Little Musgrave and Lady Barnard' seems the finest to solve, should it be capable of any solution."   His elaborate grouping of the then (early 1929) known American tunes is ingenious, and we are not inclined to quarrel with his still somewhat speculative conclusion that "the American and British versions of this ballad have come ultimately from a single source, though, if we are to date each by its place in the tradition of the ballad as a whole, the American group, with its fine flavor of unspoiled tradition . . . is not far from a century older than the oldest representative of the British group."   The statement makes very clear the importance of collecting these British ballads in America.   The American "Little Musgrave" is one of the ballads least spoiled by broadside, songster, or print.

The Virginia texts here presented follow in general Coffin's Story Type A, but with varied inclusions and exclusions.

AA, in which the leading characters are little Massey Grove and Lord and Lady Darnell, begins in church on a high holiday, the very first day of the year—a time and place not specified in either BB or CC.   It is a somewhat condensed version, omitting all mention of the warning sent to Lord Darnell and stopping short of the two final killings with their attendant barbarity.   The ending is tragic pathos rather than violence.   Lord Darnell has gone "on top of the king's mountain, Prince Henry for to see."   The tune is a fine one, especially as sung by Miss Bowman.

BB, with Marthyful Globes and Lord and Lady Barney as chief characters, has lost its opening stanzas, but the rest of the story is fully told, with the elaborate exchange between Lord Barney and the little footpage at King Henry's gate, and the full ending in the triple deaths, Lord Barney's barbaric slaying of his unfaithful wife before his own suicide by sword, following his killing of little Marthy in fair fight. There is evidently a euphemism in the line, "This night a bad fellow to be," perhaps representing the singer's effort to clean up what some American folk singers regard as a "dirty" song. (See Randolph, I, 125-26.) Both this text and CC following, but not AA, have the Lord's two swords "cost me deep in purse," a characteristic expression which marks many American texts.

CC, with the main characters identified as Little Mathie Grove and Lord and Lady Daniel, is one of the fullest of American texts, even though it lacks the churchly opening. The messenger to Lord Daniel is not a little footpage, but "one of Lord Daniel's very best friends" and it may or may not be the same friend who "wishing Mathie Grove no harm" blows the warning bugle blast. Rather incongruously, after killing Little Mathie Grove by stroke of sword, Lord Daniel disposes of his wife and himself by pistol shot—obviously a late variant, possibly imported from some later song of the tragic triangle.

An omitted text identifies the principals as Lord and Lady Banner and Little Jack Grover, names which differentiate Barry's Type One of the ballad, as distinguished from his Type Two, to which AA, BB, and CC all belong. But for the names, the text does not seem to differ significantly from the three here printed, a fact which raises some question as to Barry's criteria of classification. The omitted text is fragmentary and without tune.

The excellent text of R. E. Lee Smith and Thomas P. Smith, also contributed to the Virginia collection, has been omitted because it has already been published in the Brown Collection, II, 102-4, with its tune also, IV, 53.

AA

"Little Massey Grove." Phonograph record (aluminum) made by A. K. Davis, Jr. Sung by Miss Ruby Bowman, of Laurel Fork, Va. Carroll County. August 10, 1932. Text transcribed by P. C. Worthington. Tune noted by G. W. Williams and E. C. Mead.

The first one in was a fair la dy, And the next one was a

girl, And the next one was Lord Dar nell's wife, And the fair - est of them all, all, And the fair - est of them all.

1 Now high, now high, now high holiday,
   And the very first day in the year,
The little Massey Grove to the church did go,
   The gospel for to hear, hear,
   The gospel for to hear.

2 The first one in was a fair lady,
   And the next one was a girl,
And the next one was Lord Darnell's wife,
   And the fairest of them all, all,
   And the fairest of them all.

3 Little Massey Grove was a-standing by,
   To him she cast an eye,
Saying, "You must go home with me today,
   All night in my arms to lie, lie,
   All night in my arms to lie."

4 "Oh no, no," said the little Massey Grove,
   "I'm dassn't for my life,
For I can tell by the ring that you wear on your hand,
   That you are Lord Darnell's wife, wife,
   That you are Lord Darnell's wife."

5 "Why should I hold such vows sacred,
   When he's so far away,
He's gone on top of the king's mountain,
   Prince Henry for to see, see,
   Prince Henry for to see."

6 So they went home a-laughin' and a-talkin',
   And when they fell to sleep,
   And when they awoke on the next day's morn,
   Lord Darnell stood at their feet, feet,
   Lord Darnell stood at their feet.

7 Saying, "How do you like my new coverlids,
   Oh, how do you like my sheets,
   And how do you like my fair young wife,
   That lies in your arms and sleeps, sleeps,
   That lies in your arms and sleeps?"

8 "Pretty well do I like your new coverlids,
   Pretty well do I like your sheets,
   Much better do I like your fair young wife,
   Who lies in my arms and sleeps, sleeps,
   Who lies in my arms and sleeps."

9 "Rise up, rise up, little Massey Grove,
   Put on your clothes just as quick as you can,
   Shall never be said in this wide world,
   That I slayed a naked man, man,
   That I slayed a naked man."

10 "Oh no, no," said the little Massey Grove,
   "I'm dassn't for my life,
   For around your waist you have two swords,
   And me not as much as a knife, knife,
   And me not as much as a knife."

11 "If around my waist I have two swords,
   And you not as much as a knife,
   Then you may take the best of them,
   And then I'll take your life, life,
   And then I'll take your life.

12 "And you may strike the first blow,
   Now strike it like a man,
   And I will strike the next blow,
   And I'll kill you if I can, can,
   I'll kill you if I can."

13 The little Massey Grove struck the first blow,
   It wounded deep and sore,
   Lord Darnell struck the next blow,
   Little Massey couldn't fight any more, more,
   Little Massey couldn't fight any more.

14 Then he took his lady by the hand,
   And he set her on his knee,

"Now which one do you love the best,
    Little Massey Grove or me, me,
    Little Massey Grove or me?"

15 "Pretty well do I like your deep blue eyes,
    Pretty well do I like your chin,
  Much better do I love the little Massey Grove,
    Than you and all your kin, kin,
    Than you and all your kin."

BB

"Lord Barney." Collected by Miss Alfreda M. Peel, of Salem, Va. Contributed by Minter Grubb, of Back Creek, Va. Roanoke County. 1932.
Tune noted by Miss Eloise Kelly, of Marion, Va.

Lit-tle foot page was stand-ing by A - hear-ing these words he
said,— "Lord Bar-ney shall hear of this here Be-fore the break of the
day, day, Be-fore the break of the day."

1 Little footpage was standing by,
    A-hearing those words he said,
  "Lord Barney shall hear of this here
    Before the break of day,
    Before the break of day."

2 He run till he came to the bridge broken down,
    He hel' his breath an' he swam,
  He swam till he come to the other side
    And he tied his shoes and he run,
    And he tied his shoes and he run.

3 He run till he come to King Henry's gate,
    He touched the bell an it rung,
  He touched the bell and it rung.

4 "Is any of my castles caught on fire,
    Is any of my castles burnt down?"
  "There's none of your castles caught on fire,
    There's none of your castles burnt down;

Marthyful Globes has gone home with your wife,
This night a bad fellow to be.
This night a bad fellow to be."

5 "If this is the truth you tell unto me,
Which it probably may be,
I have but one daughter in this whole round world
And marry to her you shall be,
And marry to her you shall be.

6 "If this be a lie that you tell unto me,
Which I take it to be,
The very first time that I pass by
I'll hang you high as a tree,
I'll hang you high as a tree."

7 He summoned twenty armed men,
He stood them all in a row,
Never a word was they to say
Until the horn did blow,
Until the horn did blow.

8 "Hark, hark, hark, hark," little Marthy said he,
All so round in fear;
"I think that is Lord Barney's horn
That blows so loud and clear,
That blows so loud and clear."

9 "Lie still, lie still, little Marthy," said she,
"Don't you fear at all.
It's nothing but Lord Barney's horn
A-blowing the sheep to the hall,
A-blowing the sheep to the hall."

10 He turned her over and give her a kiss,
So lovingly they both fell in to sleep,
And the very first thing little Marthy knowed
Lord Barney was at his feet,
Lord Barney was at his feet.

11 "How do you like my fine feather bed,
How do you like my sheet,
How do you like my beautiful bride,
Lies in your arms asleep, asleep,
Lies in your arms asleep?"

12 "I like your fine feather bed very well,
Also your sheet,

Much better do I like your beautiful bride
  Lies in my arms asleep,
  Lies in my arms asleep!"

13 "Rise you up, little Marthy," said he,
    "And put you on some clothes,
  It never shall be said in King Henry's court
    I slain a naked man,
    I slain a naked man.

14 "I have two glitterern swords,
    They cost me deep in the purse,
  You may take the very best one
    And I will take the worst,
    I will take the worst.

15 "You may strike the very first blow,
    And strike it like a man,
  And I will strike the very next one,
    And kill you if I can,
    And kill you if I can."

16 The very first blow little Marthy did make,
    He wounded Lord Barney so,
  So the very first blow Lord Barney did make,
    He killed him dead on the floor,
    He killed him dead on the floor.

17 "Rise up, rise up, my beautiful bride,
    Sit you down on my knee,
  Tell unto me which you like the best
    Little Marthyful Globes or me,
    Little Marthyful Globes or me?"

18 "I like you very well," said she,
    "And all so your kind.
  Much better do I like little Marthyful Globes
    Lies on the floor killed,
    Lies on the floor killed."

19 He took her by the hair of her head,
    And jerked her all over the floor,
  He tore her into ten thousand pieces
    As he did little Marthy before,
    As he did little Marthy before.

20 He put a sword against the wall
    The sharp was against his breast,

Saying, "Fare you well, my merry men all,
I'm going home to rest,
I'm going home to rest."

CC

"Lord Daniel." Collected by E. J. Sutherland, of Clintwood, Va. Contributed by Miss Myrtle Deel, of Clinchco High School, Va., who learned it from Roy Edwards. Dickenson County. May 5, 1932.

1   First came down was dressed in red,
The next came down in green,
The next came down Lord Daniel's wife,
As fine as any queen, queen, queen,
As fine as any queen.

2   She cast her eyes all around and about;
She cast her eyes all through,
She cast her eyes on Little Mathie Grove,
"This night I'll sleep with you, you, you,
This night I'll sleep with you."

3   "How could I dare to sleep with you?
How can I risk my life?
I'll swear by the ring that you wear on your hand
You are Lord Daniel's wife, wife, wife,
You are Lord Daniel's wife."

4   "It makes no difference whose wife I am,
To you nor no other man,
We'll go away and lock ourselves up,
Our hearts be the same as one, one, one,
Our hearts be the same as one."

5   It was one of Lord Daniel's very best friends
Was listening what was done,
He swore Lord Daniel should know this,
Before the rising sun, sun, sun,
Before the rising sun.

6   He had sixteen miles or more to go,
And half of them he run;
He run till he came to the broken down bridge,
He held his breath and swum, swum, swum,
He held his breath and swum.

7   Swum till he came to the grassy side,
He took to his heels and he run,
Till he came to the Keel Gas gate;
He rattled them bells and rung, rung, rung,
Rattled them bells and rung.

8   "What news, what news?" Lord Daniel said,
      "What news have you brought to me?"
    "Little Mathie Grove from fair Scotland
      Is in bed with your lay-dee, -dee, -dee,
      And their hearts the same as one."

9   "If this be a lie you're telling to me,
      Which I do believe it to be,
    A gallows I will build for you,
      And hanged you shall be, be, be,
      And hanged you shall be."

10 "If this be a lie I'm telling to you,
      Which you do believe it to be,
    You need not build a gallows for me,
      Just hang me on a tree, tree, tree,
      Just hang me on a tree."

11 He counted out his very best men,
      It's one, two, by three,
    Saying, "Come along and go with me,
      This happy couple for to see, see, see,
      This happy couple for to see."

12 Was one of Lord Daniel's very best friends
      Was wishing Mathie Grove no harm,
    He blowed Lord Daniel's bugle horn
      To give Mathie Grove a warn, warn, warn,
      To give Mathie Grove a warn.

13 Little Mathie Grove said to this young lady,
      "I must get up and go;
    I hear Lord Daniel coming now,
      I heard his bugle blow, blow, blow,
      I heard his bugle blow."

14 "Lie down, lie down in bed with me,
      And keep my back from the cold,
    For it is my father's shepherd dog
      Driving the sheep to the fold, fold, fold,
      Driving the sheep to the fold."

15 They rolled and tumbled all over the bed,
      Till they both fell asleep;
    And when they woke up next morning,
      Lord Daniel stood at their feet, feet, feet,
      Lord Daniel stood at their feet.

16 "How do you like my curtain fine,
      And how do you like my sheet,
    How do you like my old true love,
      That lies in your arms asleep, sleep, sleep,
      That lies in your arms asleep?"

17 "Very well I like your curtains fine,
      Also do I like your sheets;
    Much better do I like your old true love,
      That lies in my arms asleep, sleep, sleep,
      That lies in my arms asleep."

18 "Rise you up, Little Mathie Grove,
      And put your clothing on,
    It never shall be said that I
      Have slain a naked man, man, man,
      Have slain a naked man."

19 "Oh, how can I dare to fight with you?
      Oh, how can I risk my life?
    You have two swords right by your side,
      And me not as much as a knife, knife, knife,
      And me not as as much as as knife."

20 "I know I have two swords by my side,
      And they cost me deep in purse,
    You may have the very best one,
      And I will take the worst, worst, worst,
      And I will take the worst.

21 "You may strike the very first lick,
      And strike it like a man;
    I will strike the very next lick,
      And kill you if I can, can, can,
      Kill you if I can."

22 Little Mathie Grove struck the very first lick,
      He wounded Lord Daniel sore;
    Lord Daniel struck the very next lick,
      And killed him on the floor, floor, floor,
      Killed him on the floor.

23 He threw his arms around his wife,
      And kisses gave her three,
    "Now tell me which you like the best,
      Little Mathie Grove or me, me, me,
      Little Mathie Grove or me?"

24 "Very well do I like your red rosy cheeks,
    Also do I like your chin,
Much better do I love Little Mathie Grove,
    Than you and all your kin, kin, kin,
    Than you and all your kin."

25 He pulled his pistol out of his pocket;
    It was loaded with powder and lead.
He shot his wife, he shot himself,
    Said, "Here we all three lie dead, dead, dead,
    Here we all three lie dead."

BONNY BARBARA ALLAN
(Child, No. 84)

Samuel Pepys in 1666 and Oliver Goldsmith in 1765 have been so often quoted in appreciation of this ballad that it would be supererogatory to repeat their words here. The earliest known text is Ramsay's of 1740.

Child apparently knew only three versions of "Barbara Allan." This is in marked contrast to its recent English and Scottish currency (Dean-Smith, p. 51 and Greig-Keith, pp. 67-70) and to its extremely widespread currency in America, where it is the most widely known and sung of all the old-world ballads. *TBVa* (pp. 302-45 and 577-81) prints thirty-six of ninety-two available texts, plus twelve tunes, with an elaborate discussion. Sharp-Karpeles (I, 183-95) find room for sixteen tunes and partial texts from the Southern Appalachians. The Brown Collection (II, 111-31, and IV, 57-69) from (mainly) North Carolina prints or lists thirty-one versions, with eighteen tunes. *Ozark Folksongs* (I, 126-39) prints fifteen texts, with six tunes, and Belden (pp. 60-65) lists or presents sixteen texts and four tunes from Missouri. In contrast, Barry (pp. 195-200) presents only four texts and two tunes from Maine. The ballad is obviously much more widely known and sung in the South than in the North. Coffin's bibliography (pp. 87-88) both corroborates this statement and perhaps suggests an explanation in its listing of old Southern song-books (for example, *The Southern Warbler,* Charleston, 1845, and *The Virginia Warbler,* Richmond, 1845).

Since the publication of *TBVa,* twenty-six additional items of "Barbara Allen" have been collected in Virginia. Since the ballad has been so fully represented and discussed in *TBVa* and in other recent American and British publications, it seems reasonable to reduce drastically the number of versions here presented.

Barry comments (p. 196) that " 'Barbara Allan' has proved a hard song to recover in Maine," and goes on to ask the question (p. 200), "Was Barbara Allen a real person? We feel sure of it. No other woman in balladry stands out so 'in the round,' with incident, motive and action all so consistently sequent. If she was not an actual person, then it took genius to invent her." The editors of the Brown Collection report that before Barry's death, he and Mrs. Eckstorm had satisfied themselves that the "Barbara Allen" which Samuel Pepys heard in 1666 from his actress friend Mrs. Knipp "was not a stage song but a libel on Barbara Villiers and her relations with Charles II" (II, 111). But no proof of this has been offered, and it is a dangerous line of commentary.

MacEdward Leach (p. 277) finds a basic weakness in the story in the lack of sufficient motivation for Barbara's action toward the young man. "Can it be," he asks, "that Barbara Allen is a ballad of the type of 'Lord Thomas and Fair Annet,' and that the original story told of Sir John jilting Barbara for another girl, repenting of his action when he was dying, and sending for her?" Such speculation is perhaps legitimate, but folk singers have not been troubled by inadequate motivation, and, especially in America, have found the song most acceptable in any one of its present variations.

Despite a great number of texts and minor variations, the basic narrative framework has remained surprisingly uncorrupted: Barbara Allen is sent for by her lover who is dying of his unrequited passion; she scorns him with the accusation that he has slighted her at a tavern or at a ball, and he dies, whereupon she repents of her cruelty and herself dies or promises soon to die. Barbara's accusation is not always present. Sometimes the lover offers his defense against her accusations. The rose-and-brier ending is often added.

Of the nine story types catalogued by Coffin, the present Virginia texts include three, all of which are represented in *TBVa*: the basic story as outlined above (nine texts); the basic story with the addition of the lover's defense against Barbara's charge that he slighted her (twelve texts); and either of these types with Barbara's claim that her mother is to blame for keeping the lovers apart (one text), the significant stanza of which reads:

> 11 The more she looked the better she loved,
>   Till she fell on the ground a-crying,
>   "Mamma, mamma, you're the one to blame,
>   You wouldn't let me marry him."

The lover's defense, while common in American versions, is absent from the Child texts, which are rather sparse in detail compared to American versions. Commenting on this in his article, "Ballads Surviving in the United States" (*Musical Quarterly*, II,

109-29), C. Alphonso Smith wrote: "The story as story has always seemed to me to be flawed by the silence of Sir John under the accusation brought against him. The reader infers, of course, that Barbara's charge in stanza five [of Child A] is unjust, but, in view of the tragic denouement, artistic balance demands some sort of exculpatory answer from Sir John. It is possible of course that this better constructed version may be as old as any version known to us." Or that it is not.

Although the recent Virginia texts of "Bonny Barbara Allan" present a somewhat overwhelming body of material, some significant points may be singled out. The rose-brier motif appears in twenty of the present texts, but it is absent from all three Child versions. That this commonplace was taken over from "Fair Margaret and Sweet William," another lovers' tragedy, is supported by the fact that in sixteen texts the young man is named Sweet William, Sweet Willie, or William. Three texts include a warning by Barbara to all virgins, exhorting them to avoid her fate, as in *TBVa* M; this detail is lacking in Child. Five preserve the Scarlet Town of Child B; three include the detail of Barbara laughing at the corpse of her lover, as in Child B; and in fourteen Barbara is reproved by the funeral bells, as in Child A and B. Only one displays the shift in person by the narrator, as in *TBVa* D.

Since "Barbara Allen" has been so well represented in *TBVa* and elsewhere, and since the omitted new texts have been surveyed above, only the texts with tunes are here presented—eight in number. With an exception or two the tunes are less interesting than those of many other ballads in this collection.

Since the "Barbara Allen" texts of *TBVa* run from A through JJ, the texts (with tunes) here given are distinguished by an asterisk, thus: AA*—HH*.

It is worth noting that Child finds no Continental analogues to this ballad, which seems purely British, mainly Scottish, and American. Child ignores as not traditional an amplified copy known to Buchan and Motherwell in which the dying lover leaves a number of gifts to Barbara Allen. A recent Scottish version from Aberdeen (Greig, p. 68) repeats in more traditional form this and other details, including requests from various members of Barbara's family that she "take" the dying man. Friedman suggests (p. 88) that "No other text manages the heroine's transition from haughtiness to fatal remorse and repentance so poignantly." There is apparently still a good deal to be learned about Barbara Allen and her ballad, popular as they both are.

AA*

"Barbara Allen." Phonograph record (aluminum) made by A. K. Davis, Jr. Sung by Miss Ruby Bowman, of Laurel Fork, Va. Carroll County. August 10, 1932. Text transcribed by P. C. Worthington. Tunes noted by G. W. Williams and E. C. Mead. Miss Bowman knew three tunes for this ballad; at the collector's request, she sang the first stanza to the first two tunes and then sang the whole ballad to the third tune. The first of the three tunes has most musical interest, mainly because of its varied and flexible rhythm.

man _ I be-lieve you're dy-ing."_ "Oh yes, oh yes, I'm

ve-ry sick, A love.-sick care _ a-dwel-lin, _ No

better, no bet-ter will ev-er I be, If I can't_ get Bar-bra Al - len"

Stanza 5

Stanzas 1, 3, 7, 9: A; stanzas 2, 4, 6, 8, 10, 11: B.

1 All in the merry month of May,
    When the green buds they were swellin',
  Young Jimmy Groves[1] on his death bed lay,
    For the love of Barbra Allen.

2 He sent his servant to a town,
    To the place where she was dwellin',
  "My master's sick and he sends for you,
    If your name be Barbra Allen."

3 Slowly, slowly, she got up,
    And slowly she went to him,
  And all she said when she got there,
    "Young man, I believe you're dying."

4 "Oh yes, oh yes, I'm very sick,
    A lovesick care a-dwellin',
  No better, no better, will ever I be,
    If I can't get Barbra Allen."

5 "Do you remember the other night,
    When we were in the tavern?
  You drank the health to the ladies there,
    But slighted Barbra Allen."

6 He turned his pale face to the wall,
    For death was with him dealin',

"Adieu, adieu, to all o' my friends,
Be kind to Barbra Allen."

7 She had not got one mile from town,
Till she heard his death bell ringing,
"Go bring him here and set him down,
That I might look upon him."

8 The more she looked, the more she grieved,
And she bursted out to crying,
"Just think how easy I could have saved his life,
If only I had been trying.

9 "Mother, mother, make my bed,
Make it both long and narrow.
Young Jimmy died for me today,
I'll die for him tomorrow."

10 Young Jimmy was buried in the old church yard,
And Barbra Allen in the choir,
And out of his grave grew a lily-white rose,
And out of hers a briar.

11 They grew and they grew till they grew so tall,
They could not grow any higher,
Then they both tied in a true love knot,
But the rose grew around the briar.

1. The singer apparently omitted "Groves" in the third repetition of the stanza.
Note other minor variants.

*BB**

"Barbara Allen." Phonograph record (aluminum) made by A. K. Davis,
Jr. Sung by Mrs. W. F. Starke, of Crozet, Va. Albemarle County.
November 11, 1932. Text transcribed by P. C. Worthington. Tune
noted by E. C. Mead.

Text and tune independently collected by Fred F. Knobloch, April 15,
1931.

♩ = 88

'Twas in the mer-ry, mer-ry month of _ May When the green leaf buds were

swel-ling, Young Jim-my Grove on his death-bed lay for the love of Bar-bra

Al - len.

The rhythm of stanzas 9 and 10 is very untrustworthy.

1 'Twas in the merry, merry month of May,
    When the green leaf buds were swelling,
  Young Jimmy Grove on his death bed lay
    For the love of Barbara Allen.

2 He sent his man unto the town
    Where this young maid was dwelling,
  Saying, "Haste unto my master dear,
    If your name be Barbara Allen,"

3 Slowly, slowly she got up,
    Slowly she came nigh him,
  All she said when there she came,
    "Young man, I think you're dying."

4 He turned his face unto the wall,
    His back he turned upon her,
  While all his friends cried out, "Amen,
    Oh cruel Barbara Allen."

5 She had not gone three miles away
    'Fore she heard the death bells nealing.[1]
  Every stroke it seemed to say,
    "Unworthy Barbara Allen."

6 She turned her body round about,
    She spied the corpse a-coming.
  "Lie down, lie down the corpse," she said,
    "And let me look upon him.

7 "Hard-hearted creature him to slight,
    When he loved me so dearly.

I wish that I had been kinder to him
    When he was alive and near me.

8 "Oh mother, mother, make my bed,
    Go make it near and narrow.
My true love has died for me today,
    And I shall die for him tomorrow."

9 So they buried them both in the church graveyard
    Beneath a rosy bower,
Out of his grave there grew a red rose,
    And out of hers a briar.

10 And they grew and they climbed to the church steeple top
    Till they could not grow any higher,
There they twined 'to a true lover's knot
    For all true lovers to admire.

1. MS. has "tolling," but singer apparently combines "pealing" and "knelling"
on the record.

CC

"Barbara Allen." Collected by Miss Juliet Fauntleroy, of Altavista, Va.
Sung by Mrs. Kit Williamson, of Yellow Branch, Va., who learned it from
her mother. Campbell County. August 26, 1933. Tune noted by Mrs.
Paul Cheatham, of Lynchburg, Va.

'Twas in the late sea-son of the year, When
yel-low leaves was fáll-ing, Sweet Wil-liam he ____ was tak-en
sick, ____ For the love of Bar-ba-ra Al-len.

1 'Twas in the late season of the year
    When yellow leaves was fallin',
Sweet William he was taken sick
    For the love of Barbara Allen.

2 He sent a mesenger to the town,
    The town where she was dwellin',
"Rise up, rise up to my master's call,
    If your name be Barbara Allen."

3 Slowly, slowly rose she up,
    And slowly went she to him.

She drew the curtain from his face,
"Young man, I think you're dyin'."

4 "Yes, I'm low, I'm low indeed,
   And death within me dwellin',
No better will I ever be,
   Until I get Barbara Allen."

5 "Yes, you're low, you're low indeed,
   And death within you dwellin',
No better will you ever be
   By getting Barbara Allen."

6 He turned his face unto the wall,
   She turned her back upon him.
"Adieu, adieu to my friends all,
   And adieu to Barbara Allen."

7 "Do you remember in the town,
   The town where you was drinkin',
You treated all the ladies around,
   And slighted Barbara Allen."

8 "Yes, I remember in the town,
   The town where I was drinkin',
I treated all the ladies round,
   And treated Barbara Allen."

9 As she was walkin' down the street,
   She heard a death bell ringin'.
She thought she heard her own heart say,
   "Come back here, Barbara Allen."

10 She looked to east and then to west,
   She spied a corpse a-comin'.
"Lie down, lie down this fair young man,
   And let me gaze upon him."

11 The more she gazed, the more she wept,
   And bursted out a-cryin',
"Take away, take away this fair young man,
   For I think I am a-dyin'.

12 "Oh Mother, Oh Mother, go make my bed,
   Go make it soft and narrow,
Sweet William died for pure, true love,
   And I will die for sorrow.

13 "Oh Father, Oh Father, go dig my grave,
   Go dig it deep and narrow,

Sweet William died for me today,
And I'll die for him tomorrow.

14 "Oh, cursed be my namesay,
   Oh, cursed be my nature,
   For this young man I could have saved
   By using my endeavor."

15 Sweet William was carried to the new church yard,
   And there he was buried,
   And by his side lay his true love,
   By the name of Barbara Allen.

16 Sweet William sprang he up a rose,
   And out of Barb's a brier.
   They linked and grew in a true love's knot,
   For all true loves to admire.

DD*

"Barbry Ellen." Phonograph record (aluminum) made by A. K. Davis, Jr. Sung by Mrs. J. P. McConnell, of State Teachers College, East Radford, Va. Montgomery County. Text transcribed by P. C. Worthington. Tune noted by Winston Wilkinson.

1   'Twas in the merry month of May,
      When the green buds were a-swelling,
    Poor William lay on his death bed,
      For love of Barbry Ellen.
    Poor William lay on his death bed,
      For love of Barbry Ellen.

2   He sent his servants to the town,
      To the place where she was dwelling,
    "My master's sick and he sends for you,
      For you Miss Barbry Ellen."

3   Slowly, slowly she arose,
      Slowly she went unto him,
    And all she said when she got there,
      "Young man, you are a-dying."

4   He turned his face unto the wall,
      For death was in him dwelling,
    "I cannot live to spend a day,
      Without you, Barbry Ellen."

5   "Don't you remember in yonders town,
      When the green buds were a-swelling,
    You drank your health to the ladies around,
      And you slighted Barbry Ellen?"

6   "Yes, I remember in yonders town,
      When the green buds were a-swelling,
    I drank my health to the ladies round,
      And my love to Barbry Ellen."

7   She hadn't gone but a mile from the town.
      When she heard the church bells ringing,
    And as they tolled they seemed to say,
      "Hard-hearted Barbry Ellen."

8   She looked to the east and she looked to the west,
      And she saw some corpse a-coming,
    "Lay down that corpse, that lovely corpse,
      And let me gaze upon him.

9   "O Mother, Mother, make my shroud,
      Go make it long and narrow,
    Sweet William died for me today,
      And I must die tomorrow.

10 "O Father, Father, dig my grave,
      Go dig it deep and narrow,

Sweet William died for me today,
And I must die tomorrow."

11   They buried them down in the old church yard,
The waste was calm and quiet,
And out of his grave there grew a lily-white rose,
And out of hers a brier.

12   They grew and they grew to the church-steeple top,
And there they could grow no higher,
They twisted and they tied till they withered and they died,
With the rose wrapped round the brier.

*EE**

"Barbry Allen." Phonograph record (aluminum) made by A. K. Davis, Jr. Sung by Mrs. Fanny Grubb, of Salem, Va. Roanoke County. May 30, 1934. Text transcribed by M. J. Bruccoli. Tune noted by G. W. Williams and E. C. Mead. This is a very poor rendition, and the singer fumbles for words. Repetitions and false starts have been omitted from the text.

1   Was the fourteenth day . . . . [1]
When the birds were sweetly singing,
This young man on his death-bed lay
For the love of Barbry Allen.

2   He sent his servant to the town
Where Barbry Allen were dwelling.

"My master said [to] bring both of you,[2]
  If your name be Barbry Allen."

3 Slowly she rose, slowly she turned,
     Slowly she came unto him,
   And when she looked upon his face,
     She said, "Young man, you're dying."

4 "Yes, I am sick and very sick,
     And death is in my dwelling,
   And only better I ever can't be
     If I don't get Barbry Allen."

5 "Don't you remember the other day
     While drinking at the tavern,
   You drank your health to the ladies around
     And slighted Barbry Allen?"

6 "Yes, I remember the other day
     While drinking at the tavern,
   I drank my health to the ladies around,
     Likewise to Barbry Allen."

7 She had not got three miles from town
     Before death-bells were ringing,
   And every tone did seem to say,
     "Hard-hearted Barbry Allen."

8 Saying, "Cursed be my name," says she,
     "Though cursed be my nature.
   I might have saved this young man's life
     By doing . . . . ."[3]

9 Sweet Will died today,
     And Barbry died tomorrow.
   One of them died from fear to live,
     And the other one died for sorrow.

10 They taken them both to the new church yard,
      And there they both were buried.
    A red rose sprang from one of the graves
      And a green briar from the other.

11 They grew as tall as the top of the church
      And scarce could grow any higher.
    They linked and they tied in a true love's knot,
      Both lived and died . . . . .[4]

1. Unclear.
2. Unclear, could be "drink health of you."
3. Unclear.
4. Unclear.

FF*

"Barbry Allen." Phonograph record (fiber base) made by Fred F. Knobloch, of Crozet, Va. Sung by Mrs. Edna Ethel McAlexander, of Meadows of Dan, Va. Patrick County. April 1, 1948. Text transcribed by P. C. Worthington. Tune noted by G. W. Williams and E. C. Mead.

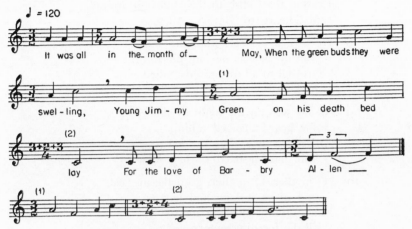

1 It was all in the month of May,
     When the greenbuds they were swelling,
   Young Jimmy Green on his death bed lay,
     For the love of Barbry Allen.

2 He sent his servant to a town,
     To the place where she was dwelling,
   "My master's sick and sends for you,
     Oh, haste ye, Barbry Allen."

3 Then slowly, slowly she got up,
     And slowly drew she nigh him,
   But all she said when she got there,
     "Young man, I think you're dying."

4 "Oh, yes, I'm sick, and very sick,
     And death is on me dwelling,
   No better, no better I'll ever shall be,
     If I can't have Barbry Allen."

5 "Oh, yes, you're sick and very sick,
     And death is on you dwellin',
   No better, no better you ever shall be,
     For you can't have Barbry Allen.

6 "Oh, don't you remember last Saturday night,
     When we were at the tavern together,

You drank a health to the ladies all around,
    And slighted Barbry Allen?"

7   "Oh, yes, I remember last Saturday night,
        When we were at the tavern together,
    I drank the health to the ladies all around,
        My heart to Barbry Allen."

8   He turned his face unto the wall,
        And death was on him dwellin',
    "Farewell to all my friends, adieu,
        And farewell to Barbry Allen."

9   As she was on the highway home,
        She heard the bell tollin',
    And every tone, they seemed to say,
        "Oh, hard-hearted Barbry Allen."

10 "O mother, O mother, go make my bed,
        And make it long and narrow,
    Young Jimmy died for me today,
        I'll die for him tomorrow."

11 They laid them in all side by side,
        And he was buried by her,
    And out his grave grew a red, red rose,
        And out of hers a brier.

12 They grew and they grew in the old churchyard,
        Till they could not grow any higher,
    They wrapped and they twined in a true love's knot,
        The rose grew around the brier.

GG*

"Barbry Allen." Phonograph record (aluminum) made by A. K. Davis, Jr. Sung by Mrs. Texas Gladden, of near Roanoke, Va. Roanoke County. August 7, 1932. Text transcribed by P. C. Worthington. Tune noted by G. W. Williams and E. C. Mead.

This text is very close to *TBVa* I, collected with music from Mrs. Gladden in 1917; the tunes, however, are distinctly different. (Cf. *TBVa*, pp. 318-19, 578.) Again, fifteen years and a new musical transcription (now verifiable) have noted a difference.

learn - ing, — I fell in love ____ with a nice lit - tle

girl, And her name was Bar - bry — Al - len. —

Var. (1) (2) or

1   A way down yonders in London town,
     That's where I got my learning,
     I fell in love with a nice little girl,
     And her name was Barbry Allen.

2   I courted her for seven long years,
     She said she would not marry.
     Sweet Willie went home and taken down sick,
     And sent for Barbry Allen.

3   She dressed so slow for she hated to go,
     "Go tell him I am coming."
     As she went walking through the room,
     She heard some death-bell ringing.

4   She walked up to Sweet Willie's bedside,
     "Young man I think you're dying."
     He turned his face to the cold, cold wall,
     And bursted out to crying.

5   "Do you remember the other day,
     Down at the tavern drinking?
     You drank your health to the ladies all round,
     And slighted Barbry Allen."

6   "Oh no, oh no, oh no," said he,
     "I think you are mistaking.
     I drank my health to the ladies all round,
     My love to Barbry Allen."

7   As she went walking up the road,
     She heard the birds a-singing,
     And every one it seemed to say,
     "Hard-hearted Barbry Allen."

8   She looked to the east, she looked to the west,
     And spied the corpse a-coming,
     "O bring him on and let him down,
     That I might look upon him."

9 The more she looked, the more she wept,
    She bursted out to crying,
    "I might have saved this young man's life,
    And kept him from hard dying.

10 "O mother, mother, go make my bed,
    Oh, make it long and narrow,
    For Willie died for the love of me,
    And I shall die for sorrow."

11 They buried Sweet Willie in the new church yard,
    And Barbry in a-tire,[1]
    On Willie's grave sprang a bright red rose,
    On Barbry Allen's a green briar.

12 They grew as tall as the new church top,
    They could not grow any higher,
    They wrapped and tied in a true bow knot,
    And the rose ran down the briar.

1. Unclear. Might be "retire," or possibly "choir."

HH*

"Barbra Allen." Collected by John Stone, of Paint Bank, Va. Sung by Miss Bonnie Reynolds, of Paint Bank, Va. Craig County. April 14, 1934. Tune noted by Mr. Stone.

1 In Scarlet town where I was born,
    There was a fair maid dwelling,
    Made every youth cry well-a-way,
    Her name was Barbra Allen.

26

LADY ALICE
(CHILD, No. 85)

Child, though he finally prints five versions of "Lady Alice"—
only two as his main entry and three in Additions and Corrections
—gives summary treatment to this ballad in one of his shortest
headnotes (only six lines). This is in marked contrast to his
elaborate discussion (sixteen double-column pages) of the very
closely related ballad of "Clerk Colvill" (Child, No. 42). The
explanation of the discrepancy is that Child was apparently unaware
of the "Johnny Collins" version of "Lady Alice," the version which
supplies the connecting link with "Clerk Colvill." Since he knew
only the "Giles Collins" or "Lady Alice" versions, he is to be for-
given for ignoring the "Clerk Colvill" relationship and finding
"Lady Alice" a sort of counterpart of "Lord Lovel," which, in its
shortened and simplified form of "George Collins" and the like, it is.

Some eight years after the publication of Child's last volume,
George B. Gardner, of Melrose, collected in Hampshire three partial
texts and tunes of a song called "George Collins" containing some
introductory stanzas introducing a second lady-love of a mermaid
or supernatural character, to whom Collins is apparently unfaithful
and who in requital causes his otherwise unexplained death, so
deeply mourned by his earthly lady who in turn dies of her love and
sorrow. Mr. Gardner published these (and other) Hampshire songs
in *JFSS*, III (1908-9), 299-302. The three not quite complete
texts seem to constitute the first appearance of what is now recognized as the "John Collins" or "Johnny Collins" version of the
ballad, the version that links "Lady Alice" so closely with "Clerk
Colvill" that at least two scholarly commentators have concluded
that the "Johnny Collins" version of the ballad represents an
older form of "Lady Alice" (Child, No. 85) and that all versions
of this ballad may quite possibly be versions or variants of "Clerk
Colvill" (Child, No. 42).

Miss Barbara M. C'raster, writing in the next volume of *JFSS*,
IV (1910-13), 106-9, identifies the three main incidents of Mr.
Gardner's texts as: (1) his [Collins'] meeting with a maiden by a
stream, the maiden being evidently of a supernatural nature; (2) his

return home and death as the result of the meeting; and (3) his true-love's realization of the tragedy through the sight of his coffin, and her own consequent death. Miss C'raster points out that all stock versions of the ballad omit incident (1) entirely, thus giving no reason for the man's death, while some are still further reduced, and contain only incident (3). She goes on to ask the question about Mr. Gardner's text, "Is this not more probably a survival of the original ballad from which both 'Clerk Colvill' and 'Giles Collins' are descended?" She bolsters her affirmative answer by reference to the three ballads and to their Scandinavian and Bretan analogues.

Meanwhile, variants of the "Johnny Collins" form began to appear from American tradition, often from sections populated by the Irish and with Dublin substituted for London in the ballad's geography. Cox's A, B, and E versions from West Virginia are of this type, as are *TBVa*'s A and B texts from Virginia and several of Samuel P. Bayard's collections in Pennsylvania and northern West Virginia. Other representative collections, such as Sharp-Karpeles, Brown, Barry, Randolph, etc., seem to lack this more interesting version entirely.

Samuel P. Bayard has provided the fullest scholarly discussion of the ballad and its relationship to "Clerk Colvill," in his article "The 'Johnny Collins' Version of *Lady Alice*" in *JAFL,* LVIII (April-June, 1945), 73-103. After examining all details and analogues of the ballads concerned, he concludes (p. 100) :

I believe that the foregoing comparison between these two ballads makes plain the fact that they tell the same story; and that it also shows the correspondence of the pieces in all the important details of that story to be amazingly close. Even more curious is the fact that the full *Lady Alice* version apparently outlines the events of a part of *Clerk Colvill* which has completely disappeared from the British form of that ballad.

All appearances, then, seem to argue not only similarity, but identity for these two pieces. They suggest strongly that *Lady Alice* must be simply another offshoot of the ancient *Clerk Colvill* ballad—abbreviated and obscured in most texts, but still having one version ("Johnny Collins") that tells the *entire ballad story,* as it is found nowhere else in English folksong. The obvious differences in rhythms and language between these ballads seem unimportant compared with their striking similarities in all other respects. No two ballads in English are more closely allied than the pair now under scrutiny.

Interesting and valuable as are these revelations of the interrelations, part proven, part still speculative, of the two ballads, we are not to conclude, I think, either that Child was wrong in his classification or that we must henceforth regard the several "Lady Alice" texts as a version or as versions of "Clerk Colvill." The exact degree of difference necessary to remove a given unusual version from its putative parent stock and constitute it a separate ballad in its own right is one of the subtlest and most difficult problems of ballad scholarship. It is hard to see how Child, who did not know the "Johnny Collins" type, could possibly have classified "Lady Alice" with "Clerk Colvill." Nor are we, who know the various "Johnny Collins" ballads, willing to concede more than that "Johnny Collins" is an extremely interesting intermediate type between Child, Nos. 42 and 85, suggesting the possibility that "Lady Alice" may have split off from the "Clerk Colvill" stock or from a common ancestor of the two. The facts are hidden in the dark backward and abysm of oral tradition. The typical "Lady Alice" or "George Collins" ballad, which has eliminated both the triangle and any clear suggestion of the supernatural, is certainly best regarded as a ballad distinct from "Clerk Colvill."

"George Collins," as distinct from "Johnny Collins," is fairly common in American tradition. *TBVa* printed six texts (not counting the two "Johnny Collins" texts) and five tunes from an available eighteen. Sharp-Karpeles (I, 196-99) print six texts or tunes. Cox (pp. 110-14) prints two (in addition to the three "Johnny Collins" texts). The Brown collection (II, 131-40, and IV, 69-74) prints or reports fifteen texts, many of them fragments, with nine tunes, but with no trace of "Johnny Collins." The Ozark collection (I, 139-40) gives only one text and tune, plus a parody. The ballad is missing from *British Ballads from Maine*. And so on. Except for the Gardner texts from Hampshire, mentioned above, the ballad does not seem to survive in recent British tradition, either in England or Scotland.

Since the ballad presents a fairly constant and standard text, the thirteen items more recently collected in Virginia may be adequately represented by the four texts and four tunes that follow. They follow Coffin's Story Type B or D, in which George Collins rides out one cold winter night, returns home, is taken sick, and dies. His sweetheart when she hears the news lays aside the silk on which she has been sewing, follows him to his grave, asks that the coffin be opened so that she may kiss his clay-cold lips. She answers her mother's efforts at consolation with a statement of her once happy but now inconsolable love for him.   The ballad concludes generally with the "turtle dove" or "lonesome road" stanza, sometimes with both.   The tunes are haunting and moving, but perhaps not musically distinguished.

The man's name is fairly constantly George Collins, but changes once to George Allen.   (The John or Johnny version is not represented here.)   The girl is generally Mary, but shifts to Mattie, Nellie, and Annie.   An omitted text calls itself "The Dying Hobo," and begins with a stanza from that otherwise unrelated comic song. It is perhaps not chance that this text comes from a small railroad junction in Amherst County.   Perhaps the deep emotion of the song invites the relief of parody, as in "Giles Scroggins."   See *TBVa*, pp. 352-53, and *Ozark Folksongs*, I, 140; also Coffin's fuller bibliography (p. 92).

Here is another instance where an old ballad has lost a supernatural content which has become confused and meaningless to more modern singers.   It has, indeed, lost most of its narrative element and become largely a "folk lyric" or an amatory lament.   Though it has somewhat changed character, it has not necessarily deteriorated or lost effectiveness.   Indeed, its condensation may well represent the artistic effort, conscious or unconscious, of some talented traditional re-creator whose product has commended itself to the perpetuation of the folk.

Since the ballads here printed all lack the supernatural element found in "Johnny Collins" and in "Clerk Colvill," we may dismiss with the briefest of mentions the discussions of the specific supernatural character of the fairy woman, whether she is a mermaid, a banshee, a "washer at the ford," or some other form of elf-woman. Bayard, in the article cited above, argues in favor of the banshee (pp. 98-100), but he is effectively answered by Harbison Parker, in *JAFL*, LX (July-September, 1947), 265 ff., who identifies the woman with Shetland-Orkney "silkie lore," and who questions the Irish tradition suggested by Bayard.   Whatever her exact character, is is clear that death is the penalty for a mortal's unfaithfulness to such a one.   More relevant to the "George Collins" variants given here is Child's mention (in another connection) of the old custom of a maid's making a shirt for her beloved.   "A man's asking a maid to sew him a shirt is equivalent to asking for her love, and her consent to sew the shirt to an acceptance of the suitor" (V, 284).

The usual second stanza of the ballad refers to this custom and indicates that the mourning mortal lady is betrothed to George Collins.

AA

"George Collins." Phonograph record (aluminum) made by A. K. Davis, Jr. Sung by Miss Eunice Yeatts, of Meadows of Dan, Va. Patrick County. August 10, 1932. Text transcribed by P. C. Worthington. Tune noted by G. W. Williams.

George Col - lins rode home one cold __ win - ter night, George Col - lins rode home so fine, __ George Col - lins rode home one cold __ win - ter night, Was tak - en sick __ and died. __

Var (1)

1 George Collins rode home one cold winter night,
   George Collins rode home so fine,
   George Collins rode home one cold winter night,
   Was taken sick and died.

2 His Mary dear in yonders hall
   Was sewing his silk so fine,
   And when she found that George was dead,
   She laid his silk aside.

3 She followed him up, she followed him down,
   She followed him to his grave,
   And there she fell on bended knee,
   She wept, she mourned, she prayed.

4 "Take off the lid, take off the lid,
   Lay back the linen so fine,
   And let me kiss his cold, cold, lips,
   For I'm sure they'll never kiss mine."

5 "Oh, Mary dear, why do you mourn?
   There's others that you'd enjoy."
   "No, Mother, George has won my heart,
   And now he's dead and gone.

6 "The happiest hour that ever I spent
    Was sitting by his side;
The saddest hour that ever I spent
    Was when sweet George had died.

7 "Oh, don't you see that turtle dove,
    A-mourning in yonders pine,
He's mourning for his own true love,
    Just like I mourn for mine."

BB

"George Collins." Collected by John Stone, of Paint Bank, Va. Sung by Mrs. J. H. Humphreys, of Paint Bank, Va. Craig County. September 30, 1932. Tune noted by Mr. Stone.

1 George Collins rode home one cold winter night,
    George Collins rode home so fine,
George Collins rode home one cold winter night
    And taken sick and died.

2 Little Mattie was sitting in George's room,
    A-sewing her silk so fine,
And when she heard that George was dead,
    She laid her silks aside.

3 She followed him up, she followed him down,
    She followed him to his grave,
And fell upon her bending knees,
    She wept, she mourned, she prayed.

4 "O daughter, O daughter, don't grieve and cry,
    There's other young men besides George."
"Mother, O Mother, George has my heart
    And now he's dead and gone.

5 "Lay the crown back of the coffin or the lid,
    Lay back the linen so fine,

And let me kiss his pale, cold cheek,
   For I know he'll never kiss mine.

6 "O don't you see that little turtle dove
   A-sitting on yonder's pine,
   A-mourning for its own true love
   Just like I mourn for mine?

7 "Look up, look down this lonesome road,
   Hang down your head and cry,
   For the best of friends must part some time,
   And why not George and I?"

CC

"George Collins." Collected by Miss Juliet Fauntleroy, of Altavista, Va. Sung by Mrs. Kit Williamson, of Yellow Branch, Va., who learned it from Mr. Kit Williamson who in turn learned it from Bessie Vandegrift, in North Carolina. Campbell County. August 26, 1933. Tune noted by Mrs. Paul Cheatham, of Lynchburg, Va.

1 George Collins rode home one cold winter night,
   George Collins rode home so fine,
   George Collins rode home one cold winter night,
   Was taken sick and died.

2 And oh! Sweet Mary in yonders hall,
   A-sewing her silks so fine,
   And when she heard that George was dead,
   She laid her silks aside.

3 She followed him up, she followed him down,
   She followed him to the grave,
   And there she knelt on her bended knees,
   She wept, she mourned, she prayed.

4 "Take down his coffin, take off the led,
   And lay back the linen so fine,

And let me kiss his cold, pale cheeks,
For I know he'll never kiss mine."

5 "Daughter, oh daughter, what makes you grieve so,
When there's more young men than George?"
"Oh Mother, oh Mother, George has my heart,
And now he's dead and gone.

6 "Don't you see them lonesome doves,
Seting on yonders pine,
A-weeping and a-mourning for her old true love,
Why can't I weep for mine?"

DD

No local title. Collected by Miss Juliet Fauntleroy, of Altavista. Sung by
Mrs. N. E. Clement, of Chatham, Va. Pittsylvania County. October
1931. Tune noted by Miss Fauntleroy.

1 "Don't you see that little turtle dove
Sitting in yonders pine,
A-mourning for its own true love,
Just like I mourn for mine, mine, mine,
Just like I mourn for mine?"

27

JELLON GRAME
(Child, No. 90)

"Jellon Grame" is one of the rarest ballads of the Virginia collection. Since the publication of Child's volumes, only two texts of this ballad have appeared from traditional sources: a three-stanza fragment from Scotland, and the present almost complete text from Virginia, penultimately from North Carolina.

The essentials of the story of the ballad are that a woman big with child is murdered by a man, either her favored or her rejected lover, who raises the child, a boy; when the boy grows up and learns of the murder of his mother, he avenges her death by killing the murderer.

The ballad is one of only two in Child's collection dealing with patricide, although this specific form of murder has been clearly retained in only one version (A). The other instance is the B version of "Edward" (Child, No. 13). For a discussion of domestic tragedy in ballads, see Gerould, *The Ballad of Tradition,* pp. 49 ff.

Child prints five versions of this ballad, four in Volume II and a fifth in Additions and Corrections in Volume V. Although the ballad first appeared in Scott's *Minstrelsy* in 1802, Scott undertook characteristically some "conjectural emendations" and apparently added four stanzas before the last two. Child therefore rejects Scott's version in favor of Mrs. Brown's maunscript copy as his A text, but with characteristic thoroughness lists in his notes all of Scott's emendations and additions. Since the story varies considerably in the several versions, we may briefly distinguish the five Child texts before examining the two more recent ones.

Child A, with twenty-two stanzas, is from Fraser Tytler's "Brown Manuscript." Jellon Grame sends a page to bring his love, Lillie Flower, to the Silver Wood. The page warns her that she may never return home, but she goes, nevertheless. Jellon accosts her, and she pleads for her life. She is carrying his child, and to see it weltering in her blood would be a piteous sight. Jellon replies that her father would hang him should he spare her life until their child is born. Although she offers to stay in the woods and raise the child there, Jellon slays her but takes pity on the surviving child, a "bonny boy" who is unnamed, and raises him, calling him his sister's son. One day as they ride through Silver Wood, the boy asks him why his mother never takes him home. Jellon points out the place beneath a nearby oak where he had murdered the boy's mother. Upon learning of his deed, the youth bends his bow and shoots an arrow through his father.

Child B, also twenty-two stanzas, from Motherwell's manuscript, tells a slightly different story. May Margerie learns that she must go to the green-wood and make her love a shirt. She is surprised, because not a month of the year has gone by that she had not made him three. Her mother warns her that someone seeks her life, but May Margerie leaves. In the green-wood Hind Henry accosts and kills her, because she loves Brown Robin rather than himself. The boy who led May Margerie's horse returns to her home, and her sister runs to the wood, secures the new-born babe, and raises him, calling the child Brown Robin. One day, as he is playing in the green-wood after school, he meets Hind Henry, and asks him if he knows why all the wood is growing grass with the exception of one spot. Hind Henry explains that that is the very spot where he killed the boy's mother. Brown Robin seizes Hind Henry's sword and kills him.

Child C, with forty stanzas, is from Buchan's *Ballads of the North of Scotland*. It relates nearly the same incidents as Child B, "diluted and vulgarized in almost twice as many verses" (II, 302). The unfortunate lady is May-a-Roe, and her murderer, Hind Henry; Brown Robin is Hind Henry's brother. The sister makes no appearance, and, as in Child A, the murderer raises the boy, but names him Robin Hood. On hearing how his mother met her death, the boy kills Hind Henry with an arrow.

Child D is a fragment of five stanzas from Cromek's *Remains of Nithsdale and Galloway Song*. The lady is Lady Margerie, as in Child B, and the murderer is simply Henry. Child's fifth text in Volume V is from the papers of Charles Kirkpatrick Sharpe. It has twenty-two stanzas and is a close variant of Child B, but the lady's name is May Young Ro, and the boy's own dagger is used instead of the murderer's sword.

The ballad seems to preserve some ancient mythology. Child writes (II, 303):

It is interesting to find an ancient and original trait preserved even in so extremely corrupted a version as C of the present ballad, a circum-

stance very far from unexampled. In stanza 18 we read that the child
who is to avenge his mother "grew as big in ae year auld as some boys
would in three," and we have a faint trace of the same extraordinary
thriving in B 15: "Of all the youths was at that school none could
with him compare." So in one of the Scandinavian ballads akin to
'Fause Food-rage,' and more remotely to 'Jellon Grame,' the corresponding child grows more in two months than other boys in eight
years . . . .

Other examples of precocious growth can be found in various litera-
tures; for example, in the French romance of Alexander, and in
Gargantua and *Pantagruel*. "Jellon Grame" resembles "Child
Maurice" (Child, No. 83) in its beginning, and Wimberly finds a
trace of the enchanted forest myth in the Silver Wood which appears in both:

Bearing . . . in mind the generally sacred character of the birch, we may
venture to see an Otherworld forest in the Silver Wood of *Child
Maurice* (83 A 1, G 1) and *Jellon Grame* (90 A 1, 5, 6, 17; D 5), for
there is a hint of myth in it.

Other touches of folklore may perhaps be seen in the implied close
relationship of a "sister's son" or in the poetic suggestion of a blood-
omen in "The red run's i the rain" or "The blood runs cold as rain."

As Child remarks, "Jellon Grame" may be considered a counterpart of "Fause Foodrage" (Child, No. 89). In all versions of
"Jellon Grame," except A, the woman has two lovers. The one
who is preferred is killed by the other in "Fause Foodrage," while
in "Jellon Grame" the woman herself is killed by the lover she
has rejected; in both ballads the woman's son takes vengeance on
the murderer before he (the son) reaches manhood.

Since the publication of Child's texts, as was stated above, only
two texts of this ballad seem to have been recovered: one Scottish
fragment, and the present excellent Virginia text. The Scottish
text, with its tune, was published in Greig's *Last Leaves of Traditional Ballads and Ballad Airs*, 1925, pp. 70-71. The text is a
somewhat confused fragment, which is related to Child A. Greig's
stanzas 1 and 2 are comparable to Child A 1 and 2, Greig's third
stanza to Child A 9. Greig's tune is especially valuable, since, although the Virginia version was apparently sung, its tune was not
recorded. Child mentions no tunes to "Jellon Grame" in manuscript
or published collections; thus it appears that Greig's tune, contributed earlier to the *Miscellanea* of the Rymour Club, has, as the editor

Alexander Keith states, the "interest of being, apparently, the only air yet noted for the ballad" (p. 71). He describes it as "in typical old ballad style, Aeolian and pentatonic."

In North America no texts seem to have been recovered, except that found in Virginia. The present text is the text of "Jellon Grame" listed in Reed Smith's census of ballad survivals in the *Southern Folklore Quarterly* for 1937, and in Coffin's bibliographical survey.

The Virginia text was contributed to the Virginia Folklore Society by R. E. Lee Smith, January 20, 1932, as it was sung by his brother, Thomas P. Smith, and himself. They learned it from M. A. Yarber, of Mast, North Carolina, January 16, 1914. A note on the manuscript by Mr. Smith reads: "M. A. Yarber heared it sang by his father John Yarber now it be 60 or more years ago. The Cox women also sang this song at least 50 years ago." Mr. Smith's text has twenty stanzas (of which two lack one line each), and like Greig's fragment it is related to Child A. It follows the story closely, but differs greatly in wording, as does the Greig fragment. Often the Virginia text and the Greig text both vary from Child A, and from each other.

For a detailed illustration of these verbal differences, see the article by Arthur Kyle Davis, Jr., and Paul Clayton Worthington, "Another New Traditional Ballad from Virginia: 'Jellon Grame' (Child, No. 90)," *SFQ*, XXII (December, 1958), 163-72, where this text was first printed with a detailed commentary. The Virginia text has lost all Scottish dialect and unusual words and is spoken in the natural language of rural Virginia or North Carolina. Instead of "His errand for to gang" of Child A, the Virginia text has "His errand for to go"; instead of " 'Win up, my bonny boy,' he says," it has " 'Hurry up, my little boy,' he said"; instead of "She lighted off her milk-white steed," the Virginia text has "jumped off"; instead of "Though I should never win hame," it has "If I never come back again"; instead of "As a hunting they did gay," it has "As they was hunting game"; and so on. Virginia's name for the unhappy lady, Rosy Flower, varies poetically the Lillie Flower of Child A and the May-a-Roe of Child C or the May Young Ro of Child's fifth version, Volume V.

Except for the numerous verbal differences, the Virginia text corresponds closely to Child A with the omission of Child A, stanzas 10 and 15, presenting an interesting sidelight on the oral "editing" of ballads. Child A 10 reads:

10 'Your bairn, that stirs between my sides,
      Maun shortly see the light;
    But to see it weltring in my blude
      Would be a piteous sight.'

This stanza is the one needed to indicate clearly that the babe is
Jellon Grame's. Although the Virginia text strongly implies such
a relationship, the fact is not openly stated: perhaps an unconscious
folk excision of a detail which makes the tragic action in the ballad
even more repugnant; it is a situation the folk have not cared to
sing of. The second stanza not found in the Virginia text reads
(Child A 15):

15   Up has he taen that bonny boy,
       Gien him to nurices nine,
     Three to wake, and three to sleep,
       And three to go between.

It adds little to the story, which is continued, "And he's brought up
that bonny boy," and even presents a slightly discordant picture of
Jellon Grame as somewhat more civilized than the half-wild creature
of the forest, such as the rest of the ballad suggests. The idea of
nine nurses for a single babe would hardly commend itself or be
credible to the American folk.

     To sum up, the present text, though without tune, is among
Virginia's rarer contributions to American folk-song. It is the only
non-fragmentary text of "Jellon Grame" recovered from oral tradition since Child's publication, and the only version of this ballad
to be found in North America. It is a fine text, and its "imper-
fections" seem only to vindicate its authenticity. What a pity it
lacks a tune! But it is wiser to be grateful for the salvage of a
unique text.

AA

"Jellon Grame." Collected by R. E. Lee Smith, of Palmyra, Va. Sung by
his brother, Thomas P. Smith, of Palmyra, Va., and himself. Fluvanna
County. January 20, 1932. Notes on the manuscript by Mr. Smith state:
"Sang by M. A. Yarber, Mast, N. C., Jan. 6, 1914. M. A. Yarber heard
it sang by his father, John Yarber, now it be 60 or more years ago. The
Cox women also sang this song at least 50 years ago." A few line divisions
are uncertain in the manuscript.

1   Jellon Grame was in the Greenwoods
      And he whistled and sang,
    And he called his little servant boy
      His errand for to go.

2   "Hurry up, my little boy," he said,
         "As quick as you ever can,
     For you must go for the Rosy Flower
         Before the break of day."

3   The boy buckled his belt on,
         And through the woods he run,
     Until he come to the lady's door
         Before the day dawned.

4   "Are you awake, Rosy Flower?
         The blood runs cold as rain."
     "I am awake," said she,
         "Who's that that calls my name?"

5   "You are called to come to Greenwood
         To meet Jellon Grame,
     And I fear it will be the last time
         You will meet Jellon Grame."

6   "I'll go to the Greenwood
         If I never come back again,
     For the man I most desire to see
         On earth is Jellon Grame."

7   She had not rode over three miles
     . . . .
     When she came to a new-made grave
         Beneath a large oak tree.

8   And up walked Jellon Grame
         Out of the woods close by,
     "Light down, light down, my Rosy Flower,
         For here is where you must die."

9   She jumped off her milk-white steed
         And pled upon her knee,
     "Oh, please have mercy, Jellon Grame,
         For I am not prepared to die."

10   "If I should spare your life," he said,
         "Until your child be borned,
     I know your cruel father would
         Have me hanged by morn."

11   "Oh, spare my life, dear Jellon,
         My father you need not dread.
     I will keep my child in the Greenwood
         And go and beg my bread."

12 He had no mercy on the fair lady,
       Though she for her life did pray;
    He stopped[1] her through the heart,
       And at his feet did lay.

13 He had no mercy for that lady,
       Although she was lying dead,
    But he had for the little child
       That was weltering in her blood.

14 And he raised up that little child
       And he called him his sister's son;
    He thought no one could ever find
       The cruel deed he had done.

15 But it fell one summertime
       As they was hunting game,
    They stopped to rest in Greenwoods
       Upon a pleasant day.

16 Then out spoke the little boy
       With tears in his eyes,
    "Please tell me the truth, Jellon Grame,
       And do not tell me a lie.

17 "What is the reason my mammy dear
       Does never take me home?
    To keep me in the woods all the time
       Is a cruel shame."

18 "I killed your mother dear
       . . . .
    And she lies buried beneath
       Yonder green oak tree."

19 The boy drew his bow,
       It was made very strong,
    And he pierced an arrow
       Through Jellon Grame's heart.

20 "Now lay there, Jellon Grame,
       You cruel murderous beast;
    The place my dear mammy lays buried
       Is too good for thee."

1. Probably for "stobbed," an older pronunciation of "stabbed."

28

LAMKIN
(CHILD, No. 93)

The highly unpleasant story told in this ballad is of a mason, Lamkin or Beaulampkins or some such name, who built a fine castle for a landlord but received no payment. The landlord warns his lady of possible trouble when he is away from home, but the lady reassures him, since the doors will be bolted and the windows barred. Beaulampkins rides up when the landlord is away and is admitted by the false nurse, who reveals that the lady is upstairs, and suggests sticking the baby full of needles and pins in order to bring the lady down. When she comes down, Beaulampkins seizes her. She pleads for her life, offering gold and even her daughter Betsy. But Beaulampkins is scornful and orders a silver basin to catch her heart's blood. Before her death, the mother warns her daughter to stay in her chamber until her father comes home. On his return, daughter Betsy reveals that Beaulampkins has killed her mother while he was away. Beaulampkins is hanged, and the false nurse is burned at the stake (or vice versa).

The essentials of the story remain fairly constant, but with a few significant variations. For instance, in several texts the wronged mason vanishes, sometimes to be replaced by a border ruffian, and it becomes necessary to find a new motive for the man's enmity and cruelty. In a few texts, the mason gains access to the house through a (false) window rather than by the help of the false nurse. Sometimes the baby is apparently killed; sometimes it is only hurt and made to cry. At least one text (*TBVa* B) suggests a previous love affair between Lamkin and the lady.

Child prints an astonishing total of twenty-six texts of the ballad, some fragmentary, including two from America, one from Virginia and one from North Carolina—the two states, incidentally, from which the present quite different version emanates. The Virginia reference is found among the Additions and Corrections at the end of Volume III (p. 515). By this time (1889) Child had been made aware of the traditional survival of these ballads in America, but he made no systematic effort to collect them. After all, his hands were full. (He left a rich harvest for later gleaners.) The North

Carolina reference is found among Additions and Corrections to Volume V (p. 296) and is dated 1895.

Since the time of Child, the ballad has been found in many geographical areas both in Britain and in America, but in a rather limited number of texts. In Britain, it has been reported from Surrey, Hampshire, Somerset, Cambridgeshire, and Aberdeenshire; in North America, from Newfoundland, Maine, Massachusetts, New York, Virginia, Kentucky, Tennessee, North Carolina, Arkansas, Indiana, and Michigan. As samples of the relative paucity of texts and tunes in major recent collections, Greig-Keith print one text and one tune; Cox no text or tune; Sharp-Karpeles, five texts and five tunes; Barry, two texts and one tune; Randolph, one text and one tune; Brown, two texts and four tunes; *TBVa*, four texts and one tune. Since *TBVa*, only a single text, without tune, has been added to the Virginia collection.

For more detailed bibliographical guidance, see Margaret Dean-Smith, p. 83; Coffin, p. 94; Brown, p. 140; and *JEFDSS*, I (December 1932), 17.

The fullest discussion of the ballad is found in an article, "Lamkin: A Study in Evolution," by Miss Anne Gilchrist in *JEFDSS*, I (December, 1932), 1-17. Surveying the known versions of the ballad and its tunes from its first printing by Herd in Scotland and Percy in England (in 1776 and 1775, respectively) up to the date of her article, she traces the development of its two streams of tradition, which she distinguishes as "Lambkin, the Wronged Mason," the Scottish form, and "Longkin, the Border Ruffian," the Northumbrian form. From the absence of foreign counterparts of the ballad, she suggests that the ballad is based upon a real event in British domestic history. She is unwilling to accept either of Child's explanations of the name Lamkin as "a soubriquet applied in derision of the meekness with which the builder had submitted to his injury" or "a simply ironical designation for the bloody mason, the terror of countless nurseries." Instead, she finds Lambkin a Flemish form of the name Lambert and she connects the name and the ballad with the fame of the Flemish builders and masons in Britain—certainly a possible, though still a speculative, inference. Her discussion of the ballad's tune is especially valuable.

The present Virginia text is very close indeed to the A text of the Brown collection from North Carolina. This is scarcely to be wondered at, since the texts emanate from the same locality and (apparently) from the same family of singers and the same family of collectors. Indeed, though the two brother collectors (who were also singers) attribute the song to two different singers of the same surname and locality (plus a third singer of a nearby town), and though a period of some fifteen or twenty years and a change of residence intervened between the two contributions, it seems quite possible that the two texts represent two transcriptions of essentially the same song, perhaps even the same song.

The North Carolina ballad was originally sent to C. Alphonso Smith, then Archivist of the Virginia Folklore Society, by Thomas P. Smith, then of Zionville, Watauga County, N. C., in March 1914, for the Virginia Collection. C. Alphonso Smith, being also a loyal North Carolinian, sent the ballad (and others from the same source) to his friend, Frank C. Brown, of Trinity College, N. C., from whose papers the ballad was published in the Brown Collection in 1952. Its headnote reads, "As sung by Mrs. Emma Smith and Mrs. Polly Rayfield, both of whom heard it when children, probably forty or fifty years ago" (in 1914).

Some time after 1914 and before the late twenties, the two Smith brothers, Thomas P. Smith, who was an accomplished singer as well as an intelligent collector of ballads and the better educated of the two, and R. E. Lee Smith, also a singer and collector but not of the class of his brother, moved to Virginia, bringing their songs with them, and eventually settled near Palmyra, in Fluvanna County. From there Thomas P. Smith wrote to the present editor, who was then Archivist of the Virginia collection, in succession to C. Alphonso Smith, offering to sing and to present the ballads he knew and had collected. Unhappily, the elder brother Thomas died before contact was made with him, but R. E. Lee Smith who also knew and (in a fashion) sang the songs and who had custody of his brother's or their joint collection, offered his help. This was the beginning of a very fruitful correspondence and association, including one or more personal visits, between R. E. Lee Smith and the present editor, some details of which have been told elsewhere.

On May 21, 1931, the Archivist received from Mr. Smith the present fifteen-stanza text of "Beaulampkins." On a corner of the clear penciled manuscript (now before me) is written, "Sung 30 years ago B. Smith, Zionville, N. C. M. A. Yarber, Mart, N. C." The singer of Brown A version, it will be recalled, was Miss Ellen Smith, and her tune, recorded as manuscript score in Zionville, Watauga County, in March, 1914, appears in Brown IV, 74-75.

Neither this tune, nor the B. Smith or Yarber one, reached the Virginia collection.

Close as the Virginia text is to its North Carolina parallel, there are many reasons why the Virginia text should be printed: (1) it has been long resident in Virginia; (2) it was contributed by each of the Smith brothers, who evidently wanted it to be a part of the Virginia collection; and (3) there are about twenty minor verbal variations, plus the dropping of two stanzas by the Virginia text, and a comparison of the two texts reveals what may happen to ballads of identical or near-identical stock in a few years.

The two missing stanzas are the sixth and ninth of Brown A, which would fall between stanzas 5 and 6, and 7 and 8, respectively, of the Virginia text. The first reads:

> "Where is his lady?
> Or is she within?"
> "She is upstairs sleeping,"
> Said the false nurse to him.

This stanza, parallel to the stanza preceding which inquires the whereabouts of the landlord, though a good example of incremental repetition, is hardly necessary to the narrative, especially as its essential information is repeated in stanza 7 of the Virginia text (stanza 8 in Brown). It may have been dropped (or forgotten) as non-essential.

The second missing stanza reads:

> Beaulampkins rocked hard
> And the false nurse she sung,
> While tears and red blood
> From the cradle did run.

This stanza merely reports the carrying out of the action proposed in the preceding stanza (Virginia 7, Brown 8), which may be taken more or less for granted. But it is more probable that the stanza was omitted because of the repulsive idea of blood and tears running from a baby's cradle. Neither text makes perfectly clear whether the baby was killed or only pricked hard enough to make it cry and bring the mother down. The North Carolina text is the bloodier of the two.

The verbal variations (about twenty) are so minor as scarcely to deserve collation. A few words are varied, a few added, a few omitted. Here are some examples: "My baby does cry" (Va.

10d) for "My *little* baby does cry" (N. C. 12d) ; "My *one* blooming flower" (Va. 11d) for "My *own* blooming flower" (N. C. 13d) ; "Oh, stay *upstairs,* daughter Betsy" (Va. 13a) for "Oh stay, *my* daughter Betsy" (N. C. 15a) ; "As he comes riding *hard* by (Va. 13d) for "As he comes riding by" (N. C. 15d) ; "While you were *away*" (Va. 14d) for "While you was *gone*" (N. C. 16d) ; and "While the false nurse burned / *At* a stake standing *close* by" (Va. 15c, d) for "While the false nurse *was* burned / *To* a stake standing by" (N. C. 17c, d). (Italics added to indicate variations.) It is possible, of course, that some of these changes may be due to the transcriber, either in Virginia or North Carolina. But the number of variants suggests at least the beginning of the process of oral tradition separating the two from some parent version. The Virginia text follows the Smith manuscript in every detail except punctuation.

The Virginia text follows Coffin's Story Type A, as does *TBVa* A, but verbally the two texts are far apart. There is no suggestion, as in *TBVa* B, of an earlier love affair between Lamkin and the lady (Coffin's Story Type D). The fact that the present version differs considerably from the texts of *TBVa* is another reason for its publication. It is clearly the "wronged mason" form of the ballad.

Beaulampkins is a rather obvious corruption or folk-etymological form of Bold Lamkin, or some similar form. To date no Virginia edifice, so far as I know, has laid claim to Beaulampkins as its builder, as have a number of old buildings in Scotland (see Child, II, 321).

AA

"Beaulampkins." Contributed by R. E. Lee Smith, of Palmyra, Va. Sung by his brother, Thomas P. Smith, of Palmyra, Va., and himself. Also sung by B. Smith, of Zionville, N. C., and M. A. Yarber, of Mast, N. C., from whom the Smith brothers apparently got the song "30 years ago." Fluvanna County. May 25, 1931.

1 Beaulampkins was as fine a mason
As ever laid stone,
He built a fine castle
And pay he got none.

2 Said the landlord to his lady,
"When I am from home,
Beware of Beaulampkins
Should he catch you alone."

3 "Oh, no," said his lady,
   "We need not fear him,
For our doors are fast bolted
   And our windows barred in."

4 Beaulampkins rode up
   When the landlord was away,
And seeing the false nurse
   At a window did say:

5 "Oh, where is the landlord,
   Or is he at home?"
"He's gone to merry England
   To visit his son."

6 "How will I enter?"
   Said Beaulampkins to her,
Then the false nurse arose
   And unbolted the door.

7 "If the lady is upstairs
   And how will we get her down?"
"We will stick the little baby
   Full of needles and pins."

8 The lady came downstairs,
   Not thinking of harm,
When Beaulampkins arose,
   And caught her in his arms.

9 "Oh, spare me, Beaulampkins,
   Oh, spare me one day,
You shall have as much gold
   As your horse can carry away.

10 "Oh, spare me, Beaulampkins,
   Oh, spare me awhile,
Don't you hear how mournful
   My baby does cry?

11 "Oh, spare me, Beaulampkins,
   Oh, spare me one hour,
You shall have my daughter Besty,
   My one blooming flower."

12 "You may keep your daughter Betsy
   To wade thru the flood,
Hold here that silver basin
   To catch your heart's blood."

13 "Oh, stay upstairs, daughter Betsy,
      In your chamber so high,
   Till you see your dear father
      As he comes riding hard by."

14 "Oh, father," said daughter Betsy,
      When the landlord came home,
   "Beaulampkins has killed my mother
      While you were away."

15 Beaulampkins was hanged
      To a gallows so high,
   While the false nurse burned
      At a stake standing close by.

29

THE MAID FREED FROM THE GALLOWS
(CHILD, No. 95)

The widespread European popularity of this ballad is emphasized by Child, who devotes most of his five-page headnote to a summary description of versions in the following languages: Sicilian, Spanish, Faröe, Icelandic, Swedish, Danish, German, Esthonian, Wendish, Russian, Little-Russian, and Slovenian.

The usual story of the ballad, both in northern and southern Europe, is thus summarized by Child: "A young woman has fallen into the hands of corsairs; father, mother, brother, sister, refuse to pay ransom, but her lover, in one case husband, stickles at no price which may be necessary to retrieve her." By comparison with these texts, Child finds the English versions "defective and distorted," and they are so in the sense that they seldom give any explanation for the maid's plight but present only the final conversational drama and its happy resolution, with the resulting release of tension. In any other sense, one would find Child's adjectives unduly harsh, in view of the known tendency of ballads to reduce antecedent action to a minimum and to concentrate on the crucial situation. Such simplification and concentration do not suggest inferiority. On the contrary, whether or not all of our curiosity about the situation is satisfied, the ballad is a superb example of ballad compression, dramatic presentation, objectivity of narrative method, and incremental repetition.

A few English and American texts do offer some explanation of the girl's plight: she has lost or stolen a golden ball, comb, key, or cup. Miss Lucy Broadwood and others following her have suggested that the golden ball represents virginity. See Coffin, pp. 96-99, for detailed references.

Since the time of Child, the ballad has been widely collected in many versions in England and the United States, but not in Scotland or in Canada. *TBVa* prints twenty-two of thirty-one available texts, and five tunes. More recently, four additional items, with two tunes, have been recovered from Virginia. All four and both tunes have been found worthy of inclusion here.

In a sampling of recent American collections, the ballad is represented as follows: Cox, seven texts and no tune; Barry, four texts and no tune; Sharp-Karpeles, ten texts (or partial texts) and ten tunes; Belden, one text and one tune; Randolph, six texts and four tunes; Brown, thirteen texts and eight tunes; and so on. Belden (p. 66) lists fourteen American states in which the ballad had been found before 1940, and Brown (II, 143) adds four more states recently heard from. Coffin (p. 96) gives an impressive list of references.

In America the somewhat ponderous Child title is more often "Hangman," "Hangman's Tree," "The Gallows Tree," or some such title. The sex of the victim is sometimes changed from a girl to a man, sometimes left in doubt. The "golden ball" form of the story or other explanation of the girl's predicament is rare. Occasionally, the ballad is acted as a play or used as a game, especially by Negroes, to whom the ballad's simple dramatic form and repetitive stanzaic pattern (the latter so closely akin to their own spirituals) seem to have appealed. In this connection, note Kittredge's use of a version of this ballad (incidentally, a version which was brought over to Virginia before the Revolution) to illustrate the possibility of a qualified form of so-called "communal composition," in his Introduction to the one-volume edition of Child (pp. xxv-xxvii). But let us not revive ancient controversy!

The ballad has been much written about, especially as to its currency among Negroes, who also make use of the story as a combination of ballad stanzas and interpolated narrative or folk tale closely related to the form known as *cante-fable*. (Several of Child's texts also approach the *cante-fable* form.) Chapter 8 of Reed Smith's *South Carolina Ballads* traces "Five Hundred Years of 'The Maid Freed from the Gallows' " (pp. 80-94). Miss Dorothy Scarborough writes delightfully and informatively of her encounters with this ballad in *On the Trail of Negro Folk-Songs* (pp. 35-43). Versions of the *cante-fable* form current among the Negroes of Jamaica and the Bahamas are given in Walter Jekyll's *Jamaican Song and Story* (pp. 35 ff.), by Elsie Clews Parsons in "Folk-Tales of Andros Island, Bahamas," *Memoirs of the American Folk Lore Society*, XIII (1918), 152-54, and by Miss Martha M. Beckwith in "The English Ballad in Jamaica," *PMLA*, XXXIX (June, 1924), 475-76. Miss Beckwith's *cante-fable* text from Jamaica is reprinted in *The Ballad Book* (1955) of MacEdward Leach as his version C (pp. 298-99), and also in *The Viking*

Book of Folk Ballads of the English Speaking World (1956) of Albert B. Friedman as his version C (pp. 134-36).

The four items here presented—three new texts and two new tunes—add something to the very full record of this ballad in *TBVa*. AA follows the usual pattern of the ballad in America in addressing the "hangman" rather than the "judge" usually found in British texts. It has an unusual final stanza, appropriate enough but obviously imported from a later song. BB is a recently recovered tune for a text which was printed in *TBVa* without tune. The full text (not here reproduced) reveals that the prisoner is a man. CC is an interesting fragment in which the compressed third stanza of the cycle of three is not spoken directly by the relative but is indirectly reported by the prisoner, who is apparently the speaker throughout the ballad.

DD adds a new type of version to the Virginia collection. It is called "Highway Man," and represents a crossing of the old ballad with a more recent badman ballad or convict song generally known as "Poor Boy," "Gambling Man," or "The Roving Gambler." The "maid" has become a highwayman who is saved from hanging by his girl. The first two stanzas and refrain of first-person emotive depression are imported from the more recent song, but with the third stanza the pattern of the old ballad takes charge, to continue through stanza 11. The final stanza with its "I love that highway man" reverts to the newer song. It is an interesting but not a unique patchwork version. Coffin cites three examples as his Story Type F, from Mississippi (Hudson), North Carolina (Henry), and Kentucky (Fuson). Henry (pp. 94-95) prints a long letter from Phillips Barry commenting on the ballad and rightly urging its printing as an actual version of the old ballad, not as an appendix. Since that time Alton Morris has presented a fragmentary text in *Folksongs of Florida* (1950), pp. 298-99, and the Brown Collection (1952) prints a seven-stanza text from North Carolina (pp. 148-49). The latter text is reprinted in Friedman's recent (1956) anthology, pp. 136-37. The present Virginia text of twelve stanzas plus refrain is the fullest text of this version so far recovered, and includes interesting verbal variations. Other versions include only the coming of the girl in addition to the emotive stanzas. In the Virginia text, mother, father, and girl appear, making nine stanzas from the old ballad as against four from the newer one. It will be noted that the prisoner's appeal is to "Mr. Judge" (the usual English form), not to the hangman.

To be added to the references of Coffin and others is an eight-stanza Louisiana text of "The Highway Man," published in Saxon-Dreyer-Tallant, *Gumbo Ya-Ya* (Cambridge, Mass., 1945), p. 444. There is no tune. The book is a collection of Lousiana folk tales and other folklore brought together by the Louisiana Writers' Project.

Barry's letter to Henry draws attention to the fact that "The Maid Freed from the Gallows" is also found in combination with two versions of "Mary Hamilton" printed by Child, "in which the heroine is not hanged in Edinburgh town, but is ransomed by her lover" (Henry, p. 94). This may be a more respectable liaison than that with the highwayman, but it represents the operation of the same process in oral tradition.

The two tunes here given seem relatively undistinguished but add something to the musical record of the ballad in America.

AA

"Hangman." Collected by John Stone, of Paint Bank, Va. Sung by Mrs. J. H. Humphreys, of Paint Bank, Va. Craig County. September 22, 1932. The final stanza is not usual with this ballad, and is an obvious importation from any one of a number of later love songs such as "The True Lover's Farewell." (See Sharp-Karpeles, II, 114.) Tune noted by Mr. Stone.

"Hang-man, hang-man, slack your rope, Please slack it for a while, Slack it till my moth-er comes, She's rid-ing man-y a long mile."

    1   "Hangman, hangman, slack your rope,
           Please slack it for a while,
        Slack it till my mother comes,
           She's riding many a long mile.

    2   "Mother, O Mother, did you bring me gold,
           Likewise to pay my fine,
        Or did you come for to see me hanged
           Way down on the gallows line?"

3 "No, O no, I brought you no gold,
   Likewise to pay your fine,
But I also come for see you hanged
   Way down on the gallows line."

4 "Hangman, hangman, slack your rope,
   Please slack it for a while,
Slack it till my father comes,
   He's riding many a long mile.

5 "Father, O Father, did you bring me gold,
   Likewise to pay my fine,
Or did you come for to see me hanged
   Way down on the gallows line?"

6 "No, O no, I brought you no gold,
   Likewise to pay your fine,
But I also come for see you hanged
   Way down on the gallows line."

7 "Hangman, hangman, slack your rope,
   Please slack it for a while,
Slack it till my brother comes,
   He's riding many a long mile.

8 "Brother, O Brother, did you bring me gold,
   Likewise to pay my fine,
Or did you come for to see me hanged
   Way down on the gallows line?"

9 "No, O no, I brought you no gold,
   Likewise to pay your fine,
But I also come for see you hanged
   Way down on the gallows line."

10 "Hangman, hangman, slack your rope,
   Please slack it for a while,
Slack it till my sister comes,
   She's riding many a long mile.

11 "Sister, O Sister, did you bring me gold,
   Likewise to pay my fine,
Or did you come for to see me hanged
   Way down on the gallows line?"

12 "No, O no, I brought you no gold,
   Likewise to pay your fine,
But I also come for see you hanged
   Way down on the gallows line."

13 "Hangman, hangman, slack your rope,
    Please slack it for a while,
    Slack it till my true love comes,
    He's riding many a long mile.

14 "True love, true love, did you bring me gold,
    Likewise to pay my fine,
    Or did you come for to see me hanged
    Way down on the gallows line?"

15 "Yes, O yes, I brought you gold,
    Likewise to pay your fine,
    But I did not come to see you hanged
    Way down on the gallows line."

16 "The blackest crow that ever flew
    Will surely turn white
    If ever I prove false to thee,
    Bright day shall turn to night."

BB

"The Gallows Tree." Collected by Miss Juliet Fauntleroy, of Altavista, Va. Sung by Mrs. Kit Williamson, of Yellow Branch, Va. Campbell County. March 15, 1934. Tune noted by Mrs. Paul Cheatham, of Lynchburg, Va. The text of Mrs. Williamson's song (she was then Mrs. Sprouse) has been printed earlier as *TBVa* H, without tune. The full text is therefore not reprinted here. (Cf. *TBVa*, pp. 370-71.) It will be noted that the "hangman" of the *TBVa* text has become "hangsman" in this more recent singing. Reference to the full text reveals that the sexes of the prisoner and rescuer are apparently reversed, since the replies to the prisoner's questions are "No, sir" up to the last stanza, and then "Yes, sir."

"Hangs - man, hangs - man, slack - en your rope_ And a
few more min - utes for me, I_ think I see my
fa - ther a - com - ing, He's com - ing for man - y a long mile."

1 "Hangsman, Hangsman, slacken your rope,
    And a few more minutes for me,
    I think I see my father a-coming,
    He's coming for many a long mile."

CC

"Hangsman's Tree." Collected by Fred F. Knobloch, of Crozet, Va. Sung by Mrs. Martha Elizabeth Gibson, of Crozet, Va. Albemarle County. May 29, 1931. Concerning the ballad, Mr. Knobloch notes on the manuscript: "The third stanza is given here exactly as the singer gave it. She insisted that this was the regular verse form, and not shortened at all." Of the later stanzas, Mr. Knobloch adds: "Unfortunately Mrs. Gibson does not recall the words to the last stanzas. She only remembers that the lover brought gold to set her lover free." The variant is a less literate fragment, but has some interesting points. See the general headnote to this ballad, above.

1 "Hangsman, hangsman, hold your rope,
   Just hold it for a while.
   I think I see my own dear father
   A-comin' a many long mile.

2 "Father, father, have you any gold,
   Have you any gold for me?
   Or have you came to see me hung
   Or came to set me free?

3 "He said he didn't have any gold,
   He came to see me hung."
   (*Then follow various brothers, sisters,
   mother, etc., until her lover comes.*)

DD

"Highway Man." Collected by Miss Virginia Cash, of New Glasgow, Va. Contributed by Luther Wright, of Monroe, Va. Amherst County. May, 1936. For detailed comment on this combination of Child, No. 95, and a later badman or convict song, see the general headnote to this ballad. Apparently the refrain was sung only after the first and second stanzas, before the Child, No. 95, portion of the ballad begins.

1 I went down to the old depot
   To see a train roll by,
   A train roll by with the woman I love;
   I hung my head and cried.

Refrain
No one knew my name,
   No one knew my name,
No one knew my name, my boy,
   No one knew my name.

2 The night was dark and stormy,
   And it sure did look like rain;
   Not a friend in this whole wide world,
   And no one knew my name.

Refrain

3 "Oh! Mr. Judge! Oh! Mr. Judge!
  Please wait a while;
  I think I see my mother coming,
  Who has walked many a mile.

4 "Dear Mother, have you brought me silver?
  Dear Mother, have you brought me gold?
  Have you walked this many many mile
  To take me from the hangman's pole?"

5 "Dear Boy, I've not brought silver,
  Dear Boy, I've not brought gold,
  Dear Boy, I've walked this many mile
  To see you hanged on the hangman's pole."

6 "Oh! Mr. Judge! Oh! Mr. Judge!
  Please wait a little while;
  I think I see my father coming,
  Who has walked many a mile.

7 "Dear Father, have you brought me silver?
  Dear Father, have you brought me gold?
  Dear Father, have you walked many a mile
  To see me hanged on the hangman's pole?"

8 "Dear Boy, I haven't brought silver,
  Dear Boy, I haven't brought gold,
  Dear Boy, I have come to see
  You hanged on the hangman's pole."

9 "Oh! Mr. Judge! Oh! Mr. Judge!
  Please wait a little while;
  I think I see my dear old girl,
  Who's walked a many mile.

10 "Dear girl, have you brought me silver?
   Dear girl, have you brought me gold?
   Oh, have you come to see me
   Hanged on the hangman's pole?"

11 "Oh! Boy, I've brought you silver.
   Oh! Boy, I've brought you gold,
   Oh! Boy, I've walked this many mile
   To take you from this hangman's pole."

12 She said, "I love that highway man,"
   She said, "I love that highway man."
   The tears rolled down that poor girl's cheek
   As she said, "I love that highway man."

30

SIR HUGH, or THE JEW'S DAUGHTER
(CHILD, No. 155)

TBVa prints thirteen of sixteen available texts of this ballad, plus seven tunes. Seven items, including four tunes, have been added more recently to the Virginia collection, of which four (or perhaps five, since two of the seven are overlapping items) are here presented, all four with tunes.

The primary theme of the ballad is the "ritual murder" of a Christian child by Jews. The blood of a Chirstian child was needed —or so medieval Christians alleged—for the rites of the Jewish Passover. A secondary theme, found only in older versions of the ballad, is the miracle of Mary, in which the dead child miraculously reveals his whereabouts, sometimes by singing the *Alma Redemptoris Mater,* as in Chaucer's literary utilization of the story in his "Prioress's Tale."

The actual episode upon which the ballad is based seems to be the death of Hugh of Lincoln in 1255. The story is recorded in several contemporary or near-contemporary chronicles: a 1255 entry in *The Annals of the Monastery of Waverley;* in the *Chronica Majora* of Matthew Paris (who died in 1259); and in the *Annals of Burton.* Child also mentions an Anglo-French ballad of ninety-two stanzas, which also appears to be contemporary with the event. No doubt the English ballad goes back in tradition very close to the original event, but the earliest surviving texts were recorded much later, in the eighteenth century.

The story of the ballad, simplified from the more elaborate chronicle forms, is briefly this: A boy, Hugh, is playing ball with his fellows and inadvertently tosses the ball into the Jew's garden. He is afraid to retrieve it, but is lured into the house by the Jew's daughter, who kills him. His body is then disposed of. In earlier versions, the body does miraculous works leading to its recovery by the mother, and is buried in Lincoln Cathedral. In later versions, the boy before his death gives directions for his burial and sends messages to his playmates, his mother, his true love. This somewhat commonplace ending is shared by most versions of "The Two Brothers" (Child, No. 49), from which it may have been borrowed.

Child prints twenty-one texts of "Sir Hugh," three of them from America. He devotes much of his elaborate eleven-page headnote to the condemnation of alleged instances of Jewish cruelty to Christian children and the savage Christian "reprisals." The number of recent reprisals, even before the time of Hitler and World War II, is appalling. It is interesting to note that even before our time instances are most numerous in Germany. But Belden (p. 69) mentions a charge of ritual murder in New York, as late as 1928. Although Friedman (pp. 62 ff.) still classifies this ballad among his "Religious Ballads," it seems clear that the song as sung today is scarcely a vehicle of racial hatred or religious intolerance but rather a tale of the pathetic death of a little schoolboy. Child reports no traditional counterparts of this ballad from Continental Europe.

Since the time of Child, versions have been collected in England in Hampshire, Lincolnshire, Somerset, and possibly another county or two. No recent version seems to have been found in Scotland. In the Western Hemisphere, texts have appeared in the Bahamas and Nova Scotia, and in the United States, in addition to the usual states of the Atlantic seaboard and the Southern Appalachians, survivals have been reported from Ohio, Indiana, Missouri, Michigan, and Wisconsin. The moderate popularity of the ballad in America is all the more surprising in that the story originally dealt with themes which are no longer of interest to the folk: the miracles of the Virgin and ritual murder by the Jews. But these themes have been blurred or omitted in most recent versions.

A sampling from a few representative American collections yields the following statistical results: Sharp-Karpeles, ten texts or partial texts and ten tunes; Cox, six texts printed of an available fourteen, with no tune; Barry, no text or tune; Brown, four texts and two tunes; Belden, three texts, no tune; Henry, two texts, one tune; Reed Smith, one text, one tune; Randolph, four texts, one tune; Eddy, one text, one tune; and so on.

In the present series, vestiges of the ritual murder theme may be recognized in such details as the decking of the victim, the description of the altar, the basin for the blood, and the imagery of the sacrificial animal. AA and CC preserve the reference to the well in which the body is concealed, "Our Lady's deep draw-well" of Child A—possibly also a vestige of the miracle of Our Lady theme.

The ballad's opening report of foul weather is fairly normal both in England and in America; the rain of AA, BB, and DD has

changed to snow in CC.   The presence of the boy's nurse in the
kitchen of the Jew's house (again in CC) seems odd.   Miss Broadwood suggests, in *JFSS*, V (1914-17), 256, that the boy actually
sees a vision of his nurse as a part of the enticement practiced by the
Jew's daughter.   CC has the rare "picking of a chicken" phrase
found also in a few English texts—also in a few other American
texts.   The "true love" of AA 12 seems inconsistent with the boy's
apparent age.

The two texts collected near Petersburg by Foster B. Gresham
and contributed to the Virginia collection (see *FSVa*, p. 25) are
not reproduced here because they were printed and discussed by Mr.
Gresham in *JAFL*, XLVII (October-December, 1934), 358-61.

The four tunes here presented are of considerable musical interest, especially the less usual tunes to CC and DD.   More detailed
comments will be found in the headnotes of the respective variants.

AA

"The Jew's Daughter." Collected by Fred F. Knobloch, John Powell, Hilton
Rufty, and A. K. Davis, Jr.   Sung by Mrs. Martha Elizabeth Gibson, of
Crozet, Va.   Albemarle County.   May 17, 1931.   Tune noted by Mr. Powell.
Ionian on C.   There is apparently some confusion of order as well as some
confused repetition between stanzas 4 and 8.   Note also "entoss" in stanza
3 but "entice" in stanza 7, "rement" for "lament" in stanza 9, and "For
were" in stanza 13.

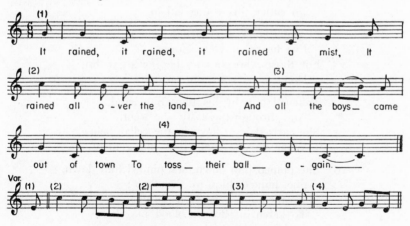

 I It rained, it rained, it rained a mist,
   It rained all over the land,
   And all the boys came out of town
    To toss their ball again.

2 First they tossed the ball too high,
   And again too low,
   And then over in the Jew's gar-din,
   Where none was dared to go.

3 He hankered fur, he hankered near,
   Till the Jew's daughter came down.
   When she came down she was dressed in swine,
   To entoss this young man in.

4 "I won't come in, I shan't come in,
   I've heard of you before,
   For those who goes in the Jew's gar-din,
   Don't never come out no more."

5 "Come in, come in, you nice young man,
   You shall have your ball again."
   . . . .
   . . . .

6 "I won't come in, I shan't come in,
   I've heard of you before,
   For those who goes in the Jew's gar-din,
   Don't never come out no more."

7 First she offered him a mellowed apple,
   And then a gay gold ring,
   Then a cherry as red as blood,
   To entice this young lad in.

8 "I won't come in, I shan't come in,
   I've heard of you before,
   For those who goes in the Jew's gar-din,
   Don't never come out no more."

9 Takened him by his lily-white hand,
   And through the castle she went,
   She carried him down in the cellar below
   Whar no one could hear him rement.

10 She pinned him down, she pinned him down,
   She pinned him to the floor;
   She called for a basin as bright as gold
   To ketch his heart's blood in.

11 "Pray lay my prayer book at my head,
   My Bible at my feet,
   If my school mates come call for me
   Just tell them that I'm asleep.

12 "Pray lay my prayer book at my feet,
    My Bible at my head,
  If my true love calls for me
    Pray tell her that I'm dead."

13 Some takened him by his yellow brown hair,
    Some by his hand and feet,
  They tossed him over in the wide water,
    For were both cold and deep.

BB

"The Jewish Lady." Phonograph record (aluminum) made by A. K. Davis, Jr. Sung by Miss Eunice Yeatts, of Meadows of Dan, Va. Patrick County. August 10, 1932. Text transcribed by P. C. Worthington. Tune noted by G. W. Williams. Ionian on C.

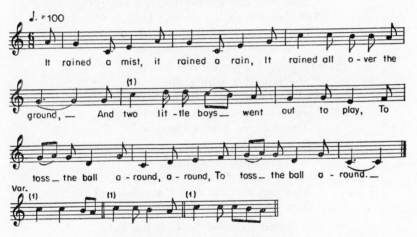

1 It rained a mist, it rained a rain,
    It rained all over the ground,
  And two little boys went out to play,
    To toss the ball around, around,
    To toss the ball around.

2 They tossed it 'round, they tossed it high,
    And then they tossed it low,
  They tossed it in[to] the Jewish yard,
    Where no one was allowed to go-o-o,
    Where no one was allowed to go.

3 The Jewish lady came to the door,
    She says, "You may have your ball."

"O, no, I can't, I won't come in,
　　Unless that my playmate comes too-oo-oo,
　　Unless that my playmate comes too."

4　First she showed him a golden apple,
　　　And then she showed him a ring,
　　And then she showed him a lily-white rose,
　　　To entice his little heart i-i-in,
　　　To entice his little heart in.

5　She took him by his little white hand,
　　　She led him through the hall,
　　She led him to a distant room,
　　　Where his playmate couldn't hear his ca-a-all,
　　　Where his playmate couldn't hear his call.

6　First she showed him the lily-white rose,
　　　And then she showed him the ring,
　　And then she took a carving knife,
　　　And carved his little heart i-i-in,
　　　And carved his little heart in.

7　She pinned a napkin o'er his face,
　　　She pinned it with a pin,
　　And then she says, "I've got a pan,
　　　To catch his heart's blood i-i-in,
　　　To catch his heart's blood in."

8　"Go bury my song-book at my feet,
　　　And my Bible at my head,
　　And when my playmate calls for me,
　　　You may tell him that I am de-e-ead,
　　　You many tell him that I am dead."

9　She buried the song book at his feet,
　　　And a Bible at his head,
　　And when his playmate called for him,
　　　She told him that he was dead, was dead,
　　　She told him that he was dead.

CC

"Little Boy and the Ball." Contributed by Miss Margaret Purcell, of Greenwood, Va. Sung by her mother, Elizabeth Ashton Garrett Purcell (Mrs.
S. H.) of Greenwood, in the early 1890's. May, 1934. Tune noted by
Winston Wilkinson. According to Mr. Wilkinson, stanzas 3, 4, 6, and 7 are
sung to the second half of the tune. E. C. Mead describes this as "an exceptionally fine Mixolydian tune," and points to its "simple rounded binary
form, expressive arch." The stanzaic divisions are peculiar, but seem to be
correct. See the note above, as to singing.

1   A little boy threw his ball so high,
    A little boy threw it so low,
    He threw it into a dusty garden
    Among some blades of snow.
    "Come hither, come hither, my sweet little boy,
    And you shall have your ball."
    "I'll neither come hither, I'll neither come there,
    Neither will I come for my ball."

2   She showed him an apple as yellow as gold,
    She showed him a bright gold ring,

She showed him a cherry as red as blood,
    And that enticed him in.
She enticed this little boy into the hall,
    She enticed him into the kitchen,
And there she met with his own dear nurse,
    Picking of a chicken.

3   "Pray spare my life, my own dear nurse,
        Pray spare my life or else never,
    And if ever I live to be a man,
        We'll spend our remains together."

4   "I'll neither spare your life, I'll neither spare my life,
        For I minded you but when a babe,
    I've been cleaning this basin,
        To catch your heart's blood in."

5   She sat him down on a golden chair,
        She fed him on sugar and sweet,
    She laid him down on a dusty board
        And stabbed him like a sheep.
    "Pray put my Bible at my head,
        My prayer book at my feet,
    And if any of my playmates should call for me,
        Pray tell them I'm dead and asleep."

6   Some take hold of locks of hair,
        And others the soles of his feet,
    And lower him down in a deep dry well,
        Fifteen fathoms deep.

7   Some take hold of locks of hair,
        And others the soles of his feet,
    And lower him down in a deep dry well,
        Where weary travelers sleep.

DD

"The Jewses' Daughter." Phonograph record (aluminum) made by A. K. Davis, Jr. Sung by Mrs. W. F. Starke, of Crozet, Va. Albemarle County. November 11, 1932. Text transcribed by P. C. Worthington. Tune noted by E. C. Mead, who comments upon the tune's "incredible fluidity of rhythm, almost defying scansion," and adds: "The rhythmic and pitch variation from stanza to stanza suggests a set of melodic variations." He also points to the tune's "very triadic major-minor character." Text and tune independently collected by Fred F. Knobloch. May 1, 1931. Significant variants are indicated in footnotes. Assuming that Mr. Knobloch's transcription of the text was correct at the time, note the changes that have taken place in the eighteen-months interval.

It rained all day and it rained all night, And it
rained so hard that all the boys who were in the town Came
out to toss their ball.____

Stanza 2

Stanza 3

Stanza 4

Stanza 5

Stanza 6

Stanza 7

1   It rained all day and it rained all night,
    And it rained so hard that all the boys
    Who were in the town
    Came out to toss their ball.

2   First they tossed too high,
    And then they tossed too low,
    And then into the Jewses' garden,
    Where none was dared to go.

3   Up came the Jewses' daughter
    All dressed in a suit of green,
    Saying, "Come in, come in, my little lad,
    You shall have your ball again."

4   She offered him a red, red rose
    To entice the little lad in,[1]
    She offered him a ring of gold
    To entice the little lad in,[2]
    She offered him a suit of clothes
    To entice the little lad in.

5   Gently[3] took him by his little white hand
    And led him to the cellar door,
    There she called for a basin as white as the snow[4]
    To catch his heart's blood in.

6   "Put a marble stone at my head,[5]
    And cold clay at my feet,
    And if my playmates call for me,
    Tell them that I'm asleep.

7   "But if my mother should call for me,
    Tell her that I'm dead.
    If my mother should call for me,
    Tell her that I'm dead."

1. MS. omits first two lines of this stanza.
2. MS. adds after this line: "She offered him some red ripe cherries."
3. MS. has: "Then she."
4. MS. omits: "as white as the snow."
5. MS. introduces this line: "He said,"

31

THE HUNTING OF THE CHEVIOT
(CHILD, No. 162)

The only but important addition of material pertaining to this extremely rare ballad since the publication of *TBVa* is the tune to the text there printed without tune. In view of the great rarity of traditional texts of the ballad, and even greater rarity of its traditional tunes, the ballad seems to deserve the space given to it here. Since *TBVa* is out of print, and since it is all-important to unite the text and tune, the *TBVa* text is here reprinted with its more recently contributed tune.

Ballad lovers and students of English literature will remember the glowing tributes paid to this ballad by Sir Philip Sidney, Ben Johnson, and Joseph Addison. All three appreciations are quoted in the *TBVa* headnote (and elsewhere), and need not be repeated here.

Two famous ballads, in a number of versions, deal with the hard-fought battle of Otterburn, one of the more serious border forays between the English and the Scots, fought on Wednesday, August 19, 1388, and described in detail by Froissart: "The Battle of Otterburn" (Child, No. 161) and "The Hunting of the Cheviot" (Child, No. 162). History records that the Scots had the better of the day of valorous combat on both sides, that Henry Percy was taken prisoner, and that James, Earl of Douglas, was killed. Though some versions follow the historical facts fairly closely, others color the narrative freely with their political or national sympathies, as ballads of history customarily do.

"The Battle of Otterburn" is the older of the two ballads, and follows history more closely. But "The Hunting of the Cheviot," more popularly known as "Chevy Chase," is the more widely known of the two and often has been reprinted on broadsides, from which it has renewed its traditional life. In the older ballad, Douglas invades Northumberland; in the later, Percy is the aggressor when he goes hunting in Scotland. In both, Douglas is slain. In the older ballad, as in history, Percy is taken prisoner; in the later, Percy, like Douglas, is killed. The fates of lesser combatants vary from version to version.

The present ballad is the later one, "The Hunting of the Cheviot." Of it Child prints two versions: A, from an Ashmolean manuscript of about 1555; and B, a more modern version of A found in many broadside collections since 1600, and widely known and sung since that time. Child B is the text which Addison so admired, and this is the version which is here presented from Virginia tradition.

Since the time of Child, traces of the ballad have been few. Margaret Dean-Smith reports only one twentieth-century printing of it in Great Britain: by W. G. Whittaker, in *North Countrie Ballads* (1921), which I have not seen. Greig-Keith report no trace of it from Scotland. In America, four early Massachusetts broadsides were reported in the collections of the Harvard College Library and the Boston Public Library, and in the Isaiah Thomas Collection of the American Antiquarian Society at Worcester, Mass. (See *TBVa* headnote.) In *JAFL*, XVIII (October-December, 1905), 294, Phillips Barry reported, in addition to one of the broadsides listed above, a Revolutionary anecdote mentioning the song, and a tune without words from a Newburyport, Mass., manuscript of 1790, source unidentified. The really significant year is 1929, when simultaneously, and without enough advance notice to take one another into account, there appeared two good but incomplete texts from traditional sources, in *British Ballads from Maine* and in *TBVa,* respectively, without tunes. Since that time, Coffin (p. 112) has unearthed from an unpublished Master's thesis only a two-stanza fragment from Cannon County, Tennessee, of "a brutal fight between two earls," which may well be a fragment of this ballad.

Both the Maine and the Virginia texts are variants, at some remove, of the Child B broadside version, and editors Barry and Davis have been at some pains to collate their respective texts with the Child B text. Each is considerably shorter than the 64-stanza text of Child B. The Maine text of 28 stanzas is fuller than the Virginia text of 12 stanzas, but since the Virginia contributor interpolates the story of the missing stanzas, somewhat after the fashion of the *cante-fable,* the Virginia text tells the fuller and more dramatic story. The chief omissions of the Virginia text as compared with the Maine are the daring of the young squire Withrington (Witheringhton in Child B) and the aftermath of confused general fighting. The Maine text entirely omits the death of Douglas by an English arrow, so tellingly described in the final Virginia stanza:

> With such vehement force and might
> It did his body gore,

The spear went through the other side
A good cloth yard or more.

This stanza corresponds to Child B 43. If the Maine text leaves Earl Douglas alive, the Virginia text reverses the order of the deaths in Child B. The Maine title, "The Battle of Shiver Chase," varies the more normal Virginia, "The Battle of Chevy Chase." Though Virginia may well envy the relative fullness of the Maine text, the Virginia text would seem to represent the more artistic working of the selective memory. It is good to have two such American texts from traditional sources, even if the influence of the broadside press is still apparent in both.

Detailed comparison is less profitable because of the fragmentation of both texts. It is possible, however, to indicate the stanzaic correspondences as follows: Va. 1 corresponds to Me. 1; Va. 2 corresponds to Me. 3; Va. 3 (lines 1, 2) correspond to Me. 4 (lines 1, 2); Va. 3 (lines 3, 4) correspond to Me. 2 (lines 3, 4); Va. 4 (lines 1, 2) correspond to Me. 2 (lines 1, 2); Va. 4 (lines 3, 4) correspond to Me. 4 (lines 3, 4); Va. 5 corresponds to Me. 5; Va. 6 corresponds to Me. 8; Va. 7 and 8 are missing in Me.; Va. 9 corresponds to Me. 17; Va. 10, 11, and 12 are missing in Me. But the Maine numbering is misleading, because the missing stanzas are also numbered, on what principle it is not clear. Of course the Virginia interpolated narrative sections are unnumbered. Leach's recent Ballad Book (pp. 446-63) reprints the Maine text as version C, following the two Child texts.

Miss Dean-Smith, basing her statements upon such earlier collectors as Ritson, Percy (via Rimbault), Chappell, Bruce, and Stockoe, finds three traditional tunes commonly associated with this ballad: one is the well-known air usually identified with "The Children in the Wood" or with the equally familiar "Oh, Ponder Well" of John Gay's eighteenth-century ballad opera, The Beggar's Opera; another is the tune generally known as "Peascod Time," which Rimbault in his Music to Percy's Reliques calls "the true Chevy Chace Melody"; the third is the tune known as "Flying Fame," given for this ballad by Ritson in his English Songs, III. Other ballads also associated with these tunes are "The Bitter Withy," "The Folkstone Murder," and "The Holly and the Ivy." A ballad's appropriation of the tune of another song is one of the most familiar phenomena of balladry. And whose tune is it? It belongs to both, perhaps in differing degrees.

The Virginia tune differs markedly from any of the three other tunes to which the ballad is traditionally sung, and is not inferior to them musically. Appropriately enough, its general character suggests a hunting song, and its ending, if not the whole tune, seems Scottish rather than English—as might be expected in a version in which Douglas slays Percy in personal combat and meets his end only later and from an English arrow or spear. The tune seems an important American contribution to the tradition of the ballad.

Of the three other tunes associated with the ballad, Friedman reproduces two in his *Viking Book of Folk Ballads,* p. 277: "In Peascod Time" and "Flying Fame." He apparently thinks "The Children in the Wood" too well known and easily accessible for reproduction. It may be found in the score of Gay's *The Beggar's Opera* as "Oh, Ponder Well." John Murray Gibbon prints both "In Peascod Time" and "Flying Fame" from earlier sources and presents the tunes as applied specifically to "The Hunting of the Cheviot" in his *Melody and the Lyric from Chaucer to the Cavaliers* (1930), pp. 22-24. Readers who want to make their own comparisons of the tunes may consult these or other sources.

AA

"The Battle of Chevy Chase." Contributed by Miss Martha M. Davis, of Harrisonburg, Va., in whose family the ballad is traditionally known and sung. Rockingham County. January 8, 1914. Tune noted by Miss Eunice Kettering, of Harrisonburg State Teachers College, Va., in 1931. Miss Davis' uncle, then resident in California, wrote down what he could remember of the song which, he says, he often sang with his Virginia mother. See *TBVa* for direct quotations from his and Miss Davis' letters. Miss Kettering seems to to have noted the tune directly from Miss Davis' singing. Miss Davis describes the ballad as "traditional with us" and as "mine by ordinary generation." The text is from *TBVa*, pp. 417-18, the tune new. Notations in italics are by Miss Davis' uncle.

God pros - per long   our   no - ble king,   Our lives   and   safe - ties   all! ___   A   woe - ful   hunt - ing once   there did   In   Chev - y   Chase   be - fall.

1   God prosper long our noble king,
       Our lives and safeties all,
    A woeful hunting once there did
       In Chevy Chase befall.

2   Earl Percy of Northumberland
       A vow to God did make
    His pleasure in the Scottish woods
       Two summer days to take,

3   The chiefest harts in Chevy Chase
       To kill and bear away.
    The child may rue that was unborn
       The hunting of that day.

A forgotten verse which tells about the men who were his followers.

4   To chase the dear with hound and horn
       Earl Percy took his way;
    Like tidings to Earl Douglas came
       In Scotland where he lay,

5   Who sent Earl Percy present word
       He would prevent his sport;
    The English Earl not fearing this
       Did to the woods resort.

6   And long before the noon they had
       A hundred fat bucks slain,
    And having dined the drovers went
       To rouse them up again.

7   Earl Percy to the quarry went
       To view the nimble deer.
    He says, "Earl Douglas promisèd
       This day to meet me here.

8   "And if I thought he would not come,
       No longer would I stay,
    For we now have plenty killed
       For us to bear away."

Just then Douglas and his clansmen come into view.

9   Earl Douglas on a milk-white steed,
       Most like a baron bold,
    Rode foremost of his company;
       His armor shone like gold.

*Another verse missing, hot words and a challenge from Douglas that
they two fight it out, while the men looked on. They fought with
swords. At last Douglas saw that Percy was weakening.*

10   "Yield, yield, Earl Percy," Douglas said,
  "For faith I will thee bring,
  And thou shalt high renownèd be
  By James our Scottish King."

11   "Nay, nay, Earl Douglas," Percy said,
  "Thy proffer do I scorn,
  I would not yield to any Scot
  That ever yet was born."

They fought on until Percy fell dead. Then an arrow from an English bow struck Douglas. The song says,

12   With such vehement force and might
  It did his body gore,
  The spear went through the other side
  A good cloth yard or more.

Then the fighting became general—a hand to hand fight—neither side would yield until night came when there were only a few left. These deeds of valor of the men with their names were given in the song, but I cannot recall any more of the verse.

32

MARY HAMILTON
(CHILD, No. 173)

In place of the final lyrical lament of Mary Hamilton, plus tune, of *TBVa*, a full text and tune are now available from phonographic recording, plus two additional fragments.

Child overran the alphabet from A to BB in printing twenty-eight texts or partial texts of the ballad from all the recognized Scottish sources—Sharpe, Motherwell, Scott, Buchan, Burns, Kinloch, and the rest, including nine unpublished texts from Scott's Abbotsford materials for his *Minstrelsy*. A single tune going back to the eighteenth century, in Child's "Ballad Airs from Manuscript" (V, 421), represented the only musical record of the ballad to that date (1898), except the 1884 air from the Perthshire highlands printed by Colin Brown in *The Thistle*, mentioned by Greig-Keith, p. 109.

Since the time of Child, no English text or tune seems to have appeared from tradition—understandably, since the ballad is essentially Scottish—but, surprisingly enough, only two fragmentary texts and two tunes have been recovered by Greig and Keith from Scottish sources (pp. 107-9).

In America, the garner has been only slightly better. Until the present publication, only one full text from tradition has been printed, by J. H. Combs in *Folk-Songs du Midi des États-Unis* (1925), pp. 141-43, from West Virginia. Barry finds no text from Maine, but with characteristic inclusiveness reaches across the border to New Brunswick for a fragmentary "secondary tradition" of the piece (pp. 258-64). (He also prints as his version B a Scottish fragment, and as his version C a single stanza of a poem by a Maine poet into which a stanza of "Mary Hamilton" has entered.) *TBVa* (pp. 421-22) mustered only two slightly varying fragments (from the same singer), plus tune. Randolph (p. 151) has only a less-than-two-stanza fragment from Missouri, no tune. And there the traditional record of the ballad in America seems to end. The appearance of the ballad in various song collections, such as J. P. McCaskey's *Franklin Square Song Collection* (New York, 1887) and Thomas A. Becket, Jr.'s *Scotch Songs* (Boston: Oliver Ditson;

Philadelphia: The W. F. Shaw Co., 1888), both listed by Coffin, must be set down to reprinting from other sources, as must also the text and tune in Reed Smith and Hilton Rufty's *American Anthology of Old World Ballads* (New York, 1937), pp. 42-43, which are reprinted, with permission and with acknowledgment, from *TBVa* (with some additions from an unidentified source).

The present fuller text and tune, from the son, daughter, and granddaughter of the Mrs. Chandler from whom the earlier Virginia version came, is especially welcome. Miss Peel has recorded that after she had taken down from her grandmother, who was then very old, the fragments of *TBVa* and sent them to the Archivist, her own memory of the song was refreshed by hearing it sung by her uncle, St. Lawrence Chandler, then of Chicago, Ill., when he was visiting in Virginia about 1924. The present editor, who took down the words and made the recording on August 9, 1932, is a witness to the familiarity also of Miss Peel's aunt, Miss Letha Chandler, of Salem, Va., with the words and tune of the song, to which she made some contribution. Though the recording was made by Miss Peel, the song had just previously been sung by Miss Chandler and Miss Peel, earlier (around 1924) by the uncle, Mr. Chandler, and earlier still by the grandmother, Mrs. Marion Chandler, who brought the song with her from Bristol, England. Mrs. Chandler learned the song from her father. We have here a direct family tradition of the ballad reaching back far into the nineteenth century and to the Old Country. Mrs. Chandler seems to have been of Scottish descent, since Miss Peel's letter (quoted in *TBVa*, pp. 421-22) records, "My grandmother's family all fought with the Stuarts."

In addition to the longer grandmaternal text and tune, Miss Peel is responsible for the recovery of two one-stanza fragments: a "little did my mother think" stanza from Amherst County, and a "four Marys" stanza from Roanoke County mentioning Mary Livingstone, one of the historic Marys of the Scottish court. Both are printed, as traces of this rare ballad in Virginia.

The historicity of the ballad presents some curious problems, and is still a matter of dispute. On its face, the ballad would seem to deal with an incident at the court of Mary Queen of Scots, in which Mary Hamilton, one of the Queen's ladies-in-waiting, is accused of murdering her newborn babe, perhaps fathered by Darnley, the Queen's husband. She is arraigned by the Queen and duly executed, after she has told her piteous story and made her lament. Scholars, including Child, have been troubled by the fact that there was no historical Mary Hamilton attendant on Queen Mary, that there was no recorded case of child-murder involving any of the real four Marys (Fleming, Livingston, Seton, and Beaton) and that the ballad itself was not known until Robert Burns in 1790 dropped a stanza of it into a personal letter and Walter Scott collected many versions of it from Scottish tradition and printed eight of them in his *Minstrelsy* in 1802. Scott himself thought that the ballad dealt with an incident recorded by John Knox concerning a French woman that served in the Queen's chamber and the Queen's own apothecary, both of whom were subsequently hanged in Edinburgh.

In 1824 C. K. Sharpe first called attention to the remarkable parallel of a case of child-murder and execution involving a real Mary Hamilton (or Hambleton), a Scottish lady-in-waiting to Queen Catherine at the court of Czar Peter the Great in Russia in 1718-19. Child, with less than his usual caution, at least for a time, gave his assent to the Russian story as the basis of the ballad, which he therefore attributes to the eighteenth century (III, 382-84), and his recantation, if it is a recantation (V, 298-99), is by no means clear-cut, nor does he present any satisfactory explanation of the ballad's history. In fairness it should be noted, however, that Child did not live to see through the press his final volume in which his later notes on the subject appear.

Child's recantation, if it is one, is the result of an article by Andrew Lang, "The Mystery of 'The Queen's Marie,'" in *Blackwood's Magazine* for September, 1895, pp. 381-90, in which he attacks Child's preference for the Russian origin and argues strongly for the ballad's Scottish origin and greater age than post-1718-19.

Albert H. Tolman, in an article on *"Mary Hamilton;* The Group Authorship of Ballads," in *PMLA,* XLII (June, 1927), 422-32, finds the dilemma of Scotch or Russian origin fallacious, and concludes soundly but rather cautiously, "Some versions are plainly a mixture of elements derived from both sources."

In the light of all the known facts, and in view of the known ways of ballads in oral tradition, the following seems the most likely account of the origin and life-history of "Mary Hamilton." The ballad is of sixteenth-century Scottish birth and originated, as Scott thought, in the French serving woman and Queen's apothecary incident at the court of Mary, Queen of Scots, in 1563. One of the versions not known to Child when he wrote his original headnote, but printed in a later volume (IV, 509-10), has a stanza identifying the man as an apothecary (Child U 13):

> 'My love he is a pottinger,
>   Mony drink he gae me,
> And a' to put back that bonnie babe!
>   But alas! it wad na do.'

It is significant that this version comes from the materials of Sir Walter Scott, who first put forward the apothecary incident as the ballad's origin, with substantiating quotations from John Knox. Since Darnley did not come to Scotland until 1565, the beginnings of the ballad can scarcely have concerned him. But given his known habit of philandering even with the Queen's attendants and John Knox's bitter denunciation of the morals of the court and of the Maries, specifically Mary Livingston (Child, III, 382), it is easy to see how the ballad might have moved to the higher levels of the court, to substitute a lady-in-waiting and "the highest Stuart of all," or Darnley, for the French woman and the apothecary. John Knox testifies that there were such ballads at the time: "What bruit the Maries and the rest of the dancers of the court had, the ballads of that age did witness, which we for modesty's sake omit" (quoted by Child from Knox's *History of the Reformation, ibid.,* footnote).

From this time until the early eighteenth century, we lose sight of the ballad, but no doubt it was known and sung in Scotland. What the name of the original "heroine" was, we do not know, but then comes the parallel incident at the Russian court involving a Scottish lady-in-waiting actually named Mary Hamilton, who was supposed to have had an intrigue not only with her officer but with the Czar, and who is tried and condemned to die. That the existing Scotch ballad should not have been influenced by this no-torious parallel is almost unthinkable, and it is possible that the name of Mary Hamilton attached itself to the existing ballad at this time. The condemned woman's address to the sailors and reference to her dying in a foreign land also point to the influence of the Russian story. But a still more conclusive argument for the impact of the Russian story on the existing tradition is that, from long obscurity, the ballad emerged into the great eighteenth-century popularity that resulted in the collection of so many variants by Scott and others by the end of the century. A clinching argument for the greater antiquity of the ballad is that no ballad of comparable quality has been known to originate in the eighteenth

century.   The concluding sentence of Child's headnote reads, "It
is remarkable that one of the very latest of the Scottish popular
ballads should be one of the best."   It is not one of the latest.   It
was, however, colored by the recent Russian affair, and the two
traditions became intermingled and confused as the ballad became
more popular in eighteenth-century Scotland.   Even if documentary
proof is lacking at certain points, the inferences seem to square with
the present state of our knowledge of the ballad and of ballads in
general.

After so large a venture in historical reconstruction, it is interesting to note that Professor Friedman's recent *Viking Book of
Ballads* (p. 183) classifies "Mary Hamilton" not among historical
ballads but under the head of "Tabloid Crime."   Yet that settles
nothing.

Of the two more or less complete American texts of the ballad,
the Combs text from West Virginia and the present Virginia text,
both are closer to Child A than to any other Child text.   Indeed,
the thirteen-stanza West Virginia text is very close to the eighteen-
stanza Child A.   The correspondence of its thirteen stanzas to the
stanzas of Child A, in order, is as follows: 1, 3, 4, 5, 7, 9, 10, first
half of 11 (last half = Child E 13), 12, 14, 15, 16, 17.   The only
significant variations (apart from omissions of stanzas 2, 6, half of
11, 13, and 18) are the presence of the lines

> Seek never grace of a graceless face,
> For that you will never see

found in Child E 13 and other texts, but not in Child A, and the
omission of the final "Last night there were four Maries" stanza.

The relationship of the Virginia text to Child A is far more
complicated by reason of the dislocation of stanzas and telescoping
of parts of different stanzas.   There is no mention of "the hichest
Stuart of a'" in the first stanza, nor of the bad omen, "The heel
cam aff her shee," of stanza 9, and the following stanzas are entirely
missing: 2, 5, 11, 16.   Parts of other stanzas are omitted or freely
telescoped without loss of sense.   The lines of the lament, present
in the Virginia text but not in Child A,

> "They'll tie a napkin 'round my eyes
> And ne'er let me see to dee"

are found only in the final Child fragment BB.   The repetition of
the "four Maries" stanza, without increment, as stanza 9 and as

the final stanza, is unknown to Child A or to any other Child variant. On the whole, verbally and otherwise, the Virginia text shows the operation of oral tradition more clearly than the West Virginia text. Compare the two lyrical fragments of *TBVa* from the same source.

AA

"Mary Hamilton." Phonograph record (aluminum) made by A. K. Davis, Jr. Sung by Miss Alfreda M. Peel, of Salem, Va., from her recollection of the singing of her grandmother, Mrs. Marion Chandler, of Bristol, England, and Salem, Va. Miss Peel's memory of the song was refreshed by hearing it sung by her uncle, St. Lawrence Chandler, of Chicago, Ill., when he was visiting Virginia about 1924. Roanoke County. August 9, 1932. Text transcribed by M. J. Bruccoli. Tune noted by E. C. Mead. On the same date when this recording was made, A. K. Davis, Jr., transcribed the text from the singing of Miss Peel and her aunt, Miss Letha Chandler, of Salem, Va.; this text differs only very slightly from that taken from the record. (Cf. *TBVa*, pp. 428, 590.)

1   Word has come from the kitchen,
    And word has come to me,
    That Mary Hamilton's slain her babe
    And thrown him in the sea.

2   Down came the old queen,
    Gold tassels in her hair.
    "O Mary Hamilton, where's your babe?
    I heard it greet so sair.

3   "Mary put on your robes of black,
    Or yet your robes of brown,
    That you can go with me today
    To see fair Edinburgh town."

4   She put on[1] her robe of black,
      Nor yet her robe of brown,
    But she put on her robe so white
      To see fair Edinburgh town.

5   When she went up the Canno' gate,
      The Canno' gate so free,
    Many a lady looked o'er her casement
      And wept for this ladye.

6   When she went up the Parliament stair
      A loud, loud laugh laughed she.
    But when she came down the Parliament stair,
      A tear was in her ee.

7   "O, bring to me the red, red wine,
      The best you bring to me,
    That I may drink to the jolly bold sailors
      That brought me o'er the sea.

8   "Little did my mother think,
      When first she cradled me,
    That I should die so far from home,
      So far o'er the salt, salt sea.

9   "Last night there were four Maries,
      Tonight there'll be but three;
    There was Mary Seaton and Mary Beaton
      And Mary Carmichael and me.

10 "Last night I washed the old queen's feet,
      And carried her to her bed;
    Today she gave me my reward,
      The gallows hard to tread.

11 "They'll tie a napkin 'round my eyes
      And ne'er let me see to dee;
    They'll ne'er let on to my father and mother
      That I'm far away o'er the sea.

12 "Last night there were four Maries,
      Tonight there'll be but three;
    There was Mary Beaton and Mary Seaton
      And Mary Carmichael and me."

1. MS. has "put not on," which the sense demands.

BB

No local title. Collected by Miss Alfreda M. Peel, of Salem, Va. Sung
by Mrs. William Horton, of Roanoke, Va., who learned it from her father,
Nathaniel Harden Roberts, of Albemarle County. Roanoke County. August

23, 1932. Of the Child texts, only one (F) mentions one of the Marys as Livingston(e), one of the historic Marys, unlike Mary Hamilton and Mary Carmichael. See the general headnote.

> 1   "Last night there were four Maries,
>   Tonight there'll be but three;
>   There was Mary Beaton, Mary Seaton
>   And Mary Livingstone and me."

CC

"Four Maries." Collected by Miss Alfreda M. Peel, of Salem, Va. Sung by Miss Margaret Voorhies, of Amherst, Va. Amherst County. June 27, 1935. The fragment is printed as another trace in Virginia of this rare ballad. It is this stanza (with minor variations) which Robert Burns copies into his letter to Mrs. Dunlop, January 25, 1790, with the remark, "I remember a stanza in an old Scottish ballad, which, notwithstanding its rude simplicity, speaks feelingly to the heart." This is the earliest known literary reference to the ballad.

> 1   "Oh, little did my mother think,
>   The day she cradled me,
>   The lands I was to travel in,
>   The death I was to dee."

33

THE GYPSY LADDIE
(CHILD, No. 200)

TBVa prints eight texts and three tunes of this ballad. Since then, nine new texts and two tunes have been recovered in Virginia. Of these, five texts and the two tunes are given here.

The history of gypsies or "Egyptians" in England and Scotland is a confused and contradictory one. They are alternately tolerated and persecuted. The name of Johnny Faa recurs in the early records as one of their leaders. As early as 1540 or earlier, a Johnne Faw's right and title as "lord and earl of Little Egypt" were recognized by King James V of Scotland, but in the next year Egyptians were ordered to quit the realm within thirty days on pain of death. The gypsies were expelled from Scotland by act of Parliament in 1609. Soon after this date there are several records of the execution of Johnny, or Willie, Faa and of other Egyptians, culminating in the execution of a notorious chieftain of that name in 1624. This seems to have impressed the popular mind and may well be the basis of the ballad. Later Scottish tradition and some of the ballads themselves have identified the lady as the wife of the mid-seventeenth-century Earl of Cassilis, apparently without any foundation whatever—except that the first line of some texts of the ballad have the gypsies come to the "castle-gate." The earliest extant copies of the ballad date from the early eighteenth century, and Child finds that the English ballad, though printed earlier (around 1720), was derived from the Scottish. He finds no European analogues.

Child briefly recounts the story of the earliest traditional Scottish version (Child A) as follows: "Gypsies sing so sweetly at our lord's gate as to entice his lady to come down; as soon as she shows herself, they cast the glamour on her. She gives herself over to the chief gypsy, Johny Faa by name, without reservation of any description. Her lord, upon returning and finding her gone, sets out to recover her, and captures and hangs fifteen gypsies."

The story has become both simpler and more complicated in the United States. Coffin lists nine different story types, though the variations are slight. The most common American version has the lady, charmed but not "glamourized," desert her husband willingly to follow the gypsy. The husband follows and finds her, but she will not return. Usually the husband demands the return of the shoes she wears, and the conclusion generally compares her former comfort to her present more rugged existence. The hanging of the gypsies does not occur in American texts, but occasionally the lady repents and returns home, or the gypsy casts her off, or there is a slightly more complicated ending. American texts seem generally to follow, with variations, the Child sequence H, I, J. Belden also mentions Child G, the earliest English broadside copy. The most common story lines are Coffin's Story Types A and H.

Child prints twelve texts or partial texts of the ballad, from England, Scotland, and America, with Scotland predominating. Miss Dean-Smith (p. 69) shows the ballad still vigorous in recent English tradition, especially in the West and South, in the counties of Somerset, Oxfordshire, Berkshire, and Shropshire. One of Cecil Sharp's Somerset versions known as "The Raggle Taggle Gipsies O" (see C. J. Sharp and C. L. Marson, *Folk Songs from Somerset,* First Series, pp. 18-19, and C. J. Sharp, *One Hundred English Folk Songs,* pp. 13-16) has become the most popular and widely sung version of the ballad in "non-folk" circles. The Scottish tradition appears even stronger. Gavin Greig and Alexander Keith (pp. 126-29) report eight versions falling into two distinct types. They print one example of each type and four tunes, under the general title of "The Three Gypsy Laddies," three being the number of gypsies involved in all the recent Scottish versions, elsewhere generally seven.

Back in 1917 Professor Kittredge warned (*JAFL,* XXX, 323) American collectors that the popular Sharp version of "The Raggle Taggle Gypsies" was apt to turn up in America and that collectors who ran across this song should scrutinize its pedigree very carefully. Two of the three texts and one tune printed by Cox in *Traditional Ballads Mainly from West Virginia,* pp. 33-35, are so close to the Sharp text and tune as to suggest a failure to heed Professor Kittredge's warning. Miss Eddy seems to have fallen into the same error in printing (pp. 67-68) a text and tune from Ohio which she herself declares to be "almost identical with Sharp's text and tune in *One Hundred English Folk-Songs.*"

The ballad is popular in the United States and has been found also in Newfoundland and Nova Scotia. A sampling of its appearance in representative American publications produced the fol-

lowing results: Cox, four texts and one tune (later added, one text
and tune, not counting the two suspect items mentioned above);
Sharp-Karpeles, eleven texts (or partial texts) and eleven tunes;
Barry, six texts and two tunes; Randolph, seven texts and three
tunes; Brown, seven texts and thirteen tunes; Belden, three texts,
no tune; Morris, two texts and two tunes; and so on.

The present Virginia texts contain no reference to Johnny Faa
or to the Earl of Cassilis. The hero varies from "Black Jack Davy"
in AA to "Black Cat Davy" in BB, to "The Gyps of Davy" in CC,
surprisingly to "Harvey Walker" in DD, to "Black-eyed Davey"
in EE. Texts not here reproduced have "Black Jack Daird," and
"Egyptian Davio" as variants. AA and BB, both with tunes from
records, represent the Coffin Story Type H, in which some stanzas
from the old English folk-song, "I'm Seventeen Come Sunday" or
"My Pretty Little Miss," have been introduced near the beginning
of the song. BB is a compressed version which omits the husband's
homecoming and pursuit. CC is without the intrusion of the
"seventeen [or sixteen] come Sunday" stanzas and tells the story
only from the point of the "landlord's" coming home. DD and
EE introduced the nonsense refrains found in many American texts
but lacking in AA, BB, and CC. DD, with its "Harvey Walker"
title and reference to Johnnie and to Jimmy Taylor, seems to have
picked up some local characters somewhere (cf. "Bill Harman,"
Cox D, p. 133). DD, like a number of versions of this ballad (see
JAFL, XXX, 323-24, and Belden, p. 75, for example), is definitely
moving toward nonsense and has fully arrived there in the last two
stanzas imported from a nonsense song, perhaps "Devilish Mary."
The curious fragment EE shows more verbal variation than any
other of these texts, but it tells a very confused story.

Three other texts long resident in Virginia and contributed directly to the Virginia Collection are not reproduced here because
they were sent also to the Brown Collection and are printed in full
there (see Brown, II, 162-65, and IV, 84-87).

It is probably to this ballad that John Randolph of Roanoke is re-
ferring when, in writing to his niece on February 20, 1822, he
asks: "Do you know a ballad that used to be sung to me when I
was a child by a mulatto servant girl of my cousin Patsy Banister,
called Patience, about a rich suitor offering 'His lands so broad' and
his golden store to a girl of spirit whose reply was somehow thus:

What care I for your golden treasures?
What care I for your house and land?
What care I for your costly pleasures?
So as I get but a handsome man.

I pry' thee get me that ballad. I can give you the tune." (See
William Cabell Bruce, *Life of John Randolph of Roanoke*, I, 38.)
If this is the ballad referred to, as seems most likely, the Virginia
tradition of "The Gypsy Laddie" is carried back to the later eighteenth century, John Randolph having been born in 1773. It is a
pleasure to recognize the distinguished Virginia statesman as a
lover, singer, and collector of ballads.

AA

"Black Jack Davy." Phonograph record (aluminum) made by A. K. Davis,
Jr. Sung by Misses Allie and Vergie Wallace, of Castle Craig, Va. Camp-
bell County. August 4, 1932. Text transcribed by P. C. Worthington.
Tune noted by G. W. Williams. Text independently collected by Miss
Juliet Fauntleroy, of Altavista, Va., as sung by Miss Allie Wallace, at
Castle Craig, Va. Campbell County. December 16, 1931. Between the
two texts there are no significant variations. Note that stanzas 2 and 3
are imported from the English folk-song, "My Pretty Little Miss" or "I'm
Seventeen Come Sunday." The tune is pentatonic.

Black Jack Da-vy came rid - ing thru the woods, Black Jack Da- vy came sing - ing,

Black Jack Da-vy came rid-ing thru the woods And he charmed the heart of   a   la - dy, He

charmed the heart   of   a   la - dy.

1   Black Jack Davy come riding through the woods,
    Black Jack Davy came singing,
    Black Jack Davy came riding through the woods,
    And he charmed the heart of a lady,
    He charmed the heart of a lady.

2   "How old are you, my pretty little Miss?
    How old are you, my honey?"

She answered him with a "Te-he-he,
   I'll be sixteen next Sunday,
   I'll be sixteen next Sunday."

3 "Come go with me, my pretty little Miss,
   Come go with me, my honey,
I'll take you across the deep blue sea,
   Where you never shall want for money,
   Where you never shall want for money."

4 She took off her high-heeled shoes,
   All made of Spanish leather,
She put on her low-heeled shoes,
   And they both rode off together,
   And they both rode off together.

5 That night when the landlord came,
   Inquiring for his lady,
He was informed by a pretty little Miss,
   "She's gone with Black Jack Davy,
   She's gone with Black Jack Davy."

6 "Go bridle, go saddle my big black mare,
   Go bridle, go saddle my pony;
I'll ride east and I'll ride west
   Till I overtake my honey,
   Till I overtake my honey."

7 He rode east and he rode west,
   He rode to the deep blue sea,
The tears were rollin' down his cheeks,
   And there he spied his honey,
   And there he spied his honey.

8 "Have you forsaken your house and land,
   Have you forsaken your baby?
Have you forsaken your husband dear
   And gone with Black Jack Davy,
   And gone with Black Jack Davy?"

9 "Yes I've forsaken my house and land,
   And I've forsaken my baby,
I've forsaken my husband dear,
   And gone with Black Jack Davy,
   And gone with Black Jack Davy."

10 "Last night you slept on a fine feather bed,
   By the side of your husband and baby,
Tonight you sleep in a wilderness,

With the wild beasts howlin' all around you,
With the wild beasts howlin' all around you."

11   "Last night I slept in a fine feather bed,
By the side of my husband and baby,
Tonight I'll sleep on the cold damp ground,
By the side of Black Jack Davy,
By the side of Black Jack Davy."

BB

"Black Cat Davy." Phonograph record (fiber base) made by Fred F. Knobloch, of Crozet, Va. Sung by Mrs. Eunice Yeatts McAlexander, of Meadows of Dan, Va. Patrick County. April 1, 1948. Text transcribed by P. C. Worthington. Tune noted by G. W. Williams. Note that, as in AA, stanzas 2 and 3 are imported from the English folk-song, "My Pretty Little Miss" or "I'm Seventeen Come Sunday." The tune is pentatonic.

1   Black Cat Davy came a-ridin' through the woods,
A-singing a song so gaily,
He made the hills around him ring,[1]
And he charmed the heart of Lady,
And he charmed the heart of Lady.

2   "How old are you, my pretty little Miss?
How old are you, my honey?"
She answered him with a sweet little kiss,
"I'll be sixteen next Sunday,
I'll be sixteen next Sunday."

3   "Come go with me, my pretty little Miss,
Come go with me, my honey.

I'll take you across the deep blue sea,
   Where you never shall want for money,
   Where you never shall want for money."

4 She pulled off her high-heeled shoes,
   All made of Spanish leather,
She put off her low-heeled shoes,
   And they both rode off together,
   And they both rode off together.

5 Last night she lay on a warm feather bed,
   Beside her husband and baby,
Tonight she lies on the cold, cold ground,
   Beside of Black Cat Davy,
   Beside of Black Cat Davy.

1. Could be "and mountains ring."

CC

"The Gyps of Davy." Collected by E. J. Sutherland, of Clintwood, Va. Contributed by Edgar Beverly, of Clinchco (Freeling), Va. Sung by Leonard Sutherland, of Haysi, Va. Dickenson County. March 12, 1932.

1 'Twas late that night when the landlord came,
   Inquiring for his lady.
The answer came a quick reply,
   "She's gone with the Gyps of Davy."

2 "Go saddle up my little black horse,
   The gray is not so speedy.
I'll ride all day, I'll ride all night,
   Or overtake my lady."

3 He rode all day, he rode all night,
   The water swift and muddy.
The tears did flow like the raindrops down,
   And there he spied his lady.

4 "Come back, come back, my pretty little dove,
   Come back, come back, my honey.
I'll swear by the sword that hangs by my side
   You shall never want for money.

5 "Come pull off your high-heel shoes
   That are made of Spanish leather,
And give to me your lily-white hand
   That we may live together."

6 "Yes, I'll pull off my high-heel shoes
   That are made of Spanish leather,

And I'll give to you my lily-white hand
That we may part forever.

7   "Last night I lay on a nice feather bed,
My arms about my baby;
Tonight I lie on the cold frozen earth,
So cold, so cold and dreary."

DD

"Harvey Walker." Collected by E. J. Sutherland, of Clintwood, Va. Contributed by Miss Nannie McConnell, of Dickenson Memorial School, Va. Received from Miss Goldia Salyer, who learned it from her grandmother, Mrs. Salyer, of Caney Ridge, Va. Dickenson County. April 4, 1932. The last two stanzas of this version are reminiscent of the folk-song "Devilish Mary," and clearly deviate into nonsense. The ballad seems to have taken on some local characters.

1   "Go saddle me up my milk-white horse,
And you may ride the brownie.
I'll ride all night and I'll ride all day
Till I overtake my Johnnie."

To my rattle daddle ding-ding dido,   } *Refrain*
To my rattle daddle ding-ding dido.   }

2   "Will you forsake your house and land,
Will you forsake your plunder,
Will you forsake your house and land,
To go with Harvey Walker?"
Refrain

3   "Yes, I'll forsake my house and land,
And go with Harvey Walker."
She pulled off the old coarse shoes
That Harvey Walker gave her,
And put on the fine cloth shoes
That Jimmie Taylor gave her.
Refrain

4   Last night she lay on a feather bed,
Jimmie Taylor behind her.
Tonight she goes through frost and snow,
With Harvey Walker by her.
Refrain

5   There were two fools all in our town,
Talking of their riches;
And all they had to talk about
Was a pair of linen britches.
Refrain

6 Johnny had a little calf;
  It was so devilish burry,
Johnny killed and eat his calf
  While I was courting Mary.

Refrain

EE

"A Neat Young Lady." Collected by Miss Alfreda M. Peel, of Salem, Va.
Sung by W. Palmer, of Salem, Va. Roanoke County. November 5, 1916.
The title and the first stanza suggest the intrusion of some later song. Perhaps that is why, according to the manuscript, the "chorus" or refrain is
picked up after the second stanza.

1 A neat young lady comes tripping downstairs
  With her shoes all laced in silver,
A bottle of wine all in her hands,
  A drinking to her danger.

2 "Saddle up, saddle up my little bay horse,
  My black is not so speedy;
I'll ride all night and I'll ride all day
  Till I overtake my lady."

Chorus: Come-a-riddle um-a-ding,
         Come-a-riddle um-a-ding,
         Come-a-riddle um-a-ding dum day-du.

3 The owner of the manor came home that night,
  Inquiring for his lady.
He inquired all through the town,
  "She's gone with the Black-eyed Davey."

4 "Oh, will you, my dear?
  Oh, will you, my honey?
I swear by the sword that hangs by my side,
  That I never will lack for money."

5 We rode and we rode to vine water side,
  That looked so deep and wavy.
The tears came trickly down my cheeks,
  There I beheld my lady.

34

GEORDIE

(CHILD, No. 209)

TBVa was able to print only one full text of this ballad, one text of medium length, and two fragments of two and three stanzas, respectively, the last of these with a previously unpublished tune presented by Cecil Sharp from his Virginia collecting. Since *TBVa,* only a single phonograph record has been added to the Virginia collection, but the text is a fairly full one and the tune an especially fine one. E. C. Mead urges that all variants be printed. See his comments in the last paragraph, below.

Child prints ten full texts and four fragments, all from Scotland. In addition he presents in an appendix two seventeenth-century English broadsides entitled "George Stoole" and "George of Oxford" which seem to be related in some fashion to the Scottish ballad, just how is uncertain. But it seems clear that the traditional and broadside forms have intermingled in more recent traditional texts.

The story of the traditional Scottish ballad is thus briefly summarized by Child: "Geordie Gordon is in prison, on a charge endangering his life. He sends a message to his wife to come to Edinburgh. She rides thither with the utmost haste, and finds Geordie in extremity. She is told that his life may be redeemed by the payment of a large sum of money. She raises a contribution on the spot, pays the ransom, and rides off with her husband." The "hero" of the ballad has been identified, without certainty, as George Gordon, fourth Earl of Huntly, who was involved in a somewhat similiar situation in 1554. Whereas the traditional copies end happily with the ransom of Geordie, both broadsides have Georgy confess to the theft of some horses and suffer the death penalty. Most of the later traditional texts, including the present one, follow the latter ending.

Since the time of Child, the ballad has been found with only fair frequency, both in Great Britain and in America. Though texts or traces of it have been found in eight English counties (Sussex, Somerset, Cambridgeshire, Lincolnshire, Norfolk, Suffolk, Surrey, and Dorset), from most counties only a single version has been forthcoming. From Scotland, where the ballad might be expected

to flourish more vigorously, Greig-Keith print only a single text
(of six recorded), with three tunes. Belden (p. 76) mentions two
variants in John Ord's *Bothy Songs and Ballads* (1930), also from
Scotland.

In America, the story is the same: fairly wide dispersal, but few
versions per locality. From Newfoundland, only a single text,
without tune. In the United States, the ballad has been found in ten
states (Vermont, Pennsylvania, Virginia, West Virginia, North
Carolina, Arkansas, Missouri, Indiana, Illinois, and Michigan), but
in either a single or in very few variants from each locality. Here are
some statistics from a sampling of representative collections: Barry,
no text or tune; Cox, one text, no tune; Sharp-Karpeles, six texts
(or partial texts), six tunes; Belden, one text, two fragments, no
tune; Randolph, two texts, two fragments, two tunes; Brown, one
text, no tune; and so on.

The present Virginia text follows Coffin's Story Type A very
closely. A man walking over London Bridge hears a woman asking
that Georgie's life be spared. She will ride to the castle to plead for
the life of Georgie, and she does so, riding all day and all night. She
produces a purse of gold and offers the lawyers whatever they want
to spare the life of Georgie. George states that he never killed anybody, but confesses that he stole sixteen of the king's white horses
and sold them in Goannie. The oldest lawyer feels sorry for George
since by his own confession he has condemned himself to die. George
bids farewell to many, but grieves to bid farewell to his true love.
George is hanged with a golden chain because he comes of a royal
race and courted a virtuous lady. The lady wishes that she was back
where George had kissed her and that she had a sword and pistol
with which to fight for the life of Georgie.

With a few verbal variations, the text is very close to *TBVa* A
and to Belden A. On the whole—and especially in its unhappy ending—it is closer to the two English broadsides, especially to "George
of Oxford," than to any of the Scottish traditional texts. Stanzas 1,
2, 4, and 5 correspond fairly closely to stanzas 1, 4, 7, and 15 of
"George of Oxford," while stanzas 5, 7, and 9 correspond equally
closely to stanzas 20, 6, and 13 of "George Stoole." But when all
possible identifications have been made, there remains a goodly re-
siduum (stanzas 3 and 6, especially) to be found in no known broadside, which must be identified with the traditional ballad of
"Geordie." Perhaps we should call the present text (and others like

it) a new traditional ballad produced by the intermingling in more recent oral tradition of both broadside and traditional elements.

For the controversy concerning the relations of the broadside and traditional types—whether the broadside represents a re-working of the traditional story-song, or vice versa—see Child IV, 126-27; Ebsworth, *Roxburghe Ballads,* VII, 67-73; Belden, p. 76; and Coffin, p. 127. In the state of the evidence, caution rather than advocacy seems called for.

Final emphasis here should be put upon the tune, which is pentatonic. The omission of the time signature is intentional, since the tune defies rhythmical (metrical) scansion. E. C. Mead points to its "beautiful flowing figured melodic line whose beauty lies largely in the 'non-harmonic notes of real melodic significance.' " All variants are printed.

AA

"London's Bridge." Phonograph record (aluminum) made by A. K. Davis, Jr. Sung by S. F. Russell, of Marion, Va. Smyth County. August 15, 1932. Text transcribed by M. J. Bruccoli. Tune noted by E. C. Mead. The close resemblance of the text to *TBVa* (but note verbal variants in about thirteen lines) may be partially accounted for by the fact that the two singers lived in neighboring counties in southwest Virginia and may well have known one another and one another's songs. For comment on the very beautiful tune, see the last paragraph of the headnote, above.

1 As I walked over London's bridge
     So early in the morning,
   I overheard some fair one say,
     "Lord, spare me the life of Georgie,"[1]
   I overheard some fair one say,
     "Lord, spare me the life of Georgie.

2 "Go bridle and saddle my milk-white steed,
     Go saddle and bridle him neatly,
   I'll ride away to the lone castle fair
     A-pleading for the life of Georgie,
   I'll ride away to the lone castle fair
     A-pleading for the life of Georgie."

3 She rode all day and she rode all night,
     Till she came wet and weary,
   A-combing back her long yellow locks,
     A-pleading for the life of Georgie,
   A-combing back her long yellow locks,
     A-pleading for the life of Georgie.

4 And out of her pocket drew a purse of gold,
     The like I never saw any,
   Saying, "Lawyers, lawyers, come fee yourselves,
     And spare me the life of Georgie,"
   Saying, "Lawyers, lawyers, come fee yourselves,
     And spare me the life of Georgie."

5 George he was a-standing by,
     Saying, "I never killed anybody,
   But I stole sixteen of the king's white steeds
     And sold them in Goannie,
   But I stole sixteen of the king's white steeds
     And sold them in Goannie."

6 The oldest lawyer at the bar,
     Saying, "George, I'm sorry for you,
   That your own confession has condemned you to die,
     May the Lord have mercy on you,
   That your own confession has condemned you to die,
     May the Lord have mercy on you."

7   As George was walking up through the streets,
   He bid farewell to many,
He bid farewell to his own true love,
   Which grieved him worse than any,
He bid farewell to his own true love,
   Which grieved him worse than any.

8   George was hung with a golden chain,
   The like I never saw any,
Because he came of the royal race
   And courted a virtuous lady,
Because he came of the royal race
   And courted a virtuous lady.

9   "I wish I was on yonders hill,
   Where kisses I've had many,
My sword and pistol all on my side,
   I'd fight for the life of Georgie."

1. E. C. Mead recalls that Mr. Russell sang the name "Geordie" in 1935, though this recording of 1932 has "Georgie."

35

BONNIE JAMES CAMPBELL
(Child, No. 210)

This ballad, new to the Virginia collection and extremely rare in tradition, is one of the briefest and poetically one of the most beautiful of all ballads. By a few compressed narrative details, plus sometimes a speech or two, the effect of a poignant lyrical lament is produced. Nor is the ballad, so far as is known, a fragment of a larger whole, like the final lament of Mary Hamilton. The Virginia text of six stanzas is as long as any known traditional version of the ballad.

Efforts to identify the hero of the ballad have been unavailing. Motherwell and Maidment, at cross purposes, with confidence point to two different Campbells, James and John, of the 1590's. But Child concludes (IV, 142), "Campbells enow were killed, in battle or feud, before and after 1590, to forbid a guess as to an individual James or George grounded upon the slight data afforded by the ballad."

Child prints four versions of the ballad, of four, three, six, and two stanzas, respectively, all from Scottish sources. Barry (pp. 281-83) uncovers a fifth basic text of four stanzas (printed as two), "evidently unknown to Child," from the first edition of Smith's *Scotish Minstrel* of about 1823 (V, 42). Barry's bold "reconstructed version . . . containing all the known lines of the little song" (p. 281) amounts to only eight stanzas (printed as four), and is of little value, of course of no value as tradition.

The ballad tells simply but movingly how bonny James (or George or John or Willie) Campbell rode out one day and how, though his horse came home, he never returned. His family (mother, wife, sometimes sisters) mourn him, his crops and possessions are uncared for, his babe is unborn. Gaily he has ridden forth, but only his bloody saddle and horse come home, never comes he.

No trace of the ballad in recent tradition seems to have been found in Great Britain, either in England or, more surprisingly, in Scotland. North American texts are very few—a total of six, to be exact. In *JAFL,* XVIII (October-December, 1905), 294, Barry printed a single tune, with the words of one stanza, taken down in

Vermont from the singing of a resident of Quebec. When he reprinted this tune as his version D in *British Ballads from Maine,* he dropped the words, for some reason. In 1925, Combs published two texts from West Virginia, one of four and one of three stanzas, in his *Folk-Songs du Midi des États-Unis,* pp. 144-45, without tunes. In 1929, Barry's *British Ballads from Maine,* pp. 279-80, presented two New Brunswick texts from the same person, one recited and one written down, both of four stanzas, without tunes. Next came the present Virginia text of six stanzas, without tune, collected in 1931, announced in *FSVa* in 1949, and now first printed. Records of the Federal Writers' Project indicate that a text and tune have been found in Boyd County, Kentucky, but these are still unpublished.

In sum, three of the published North American items come either immediately or ultimately from Canada, the three United States items from West Virginia or Virginia. The Virginia text traces back earlier (in 1912 and before) to North Carolina. If the Kentucky item is added, the ballad would seem to be resident chiefly in the Southern Appalachian region.

All the known texts of this ballad, Child's and the rest, seem closely related. They differ chiefly in the degree of fragmentation, the order of stanzas, the presence or absence of Scottish dialect, and in minor verbal variations. In length (six stanzas) and in the order and content of its stanzas, Virginia AA seems closest to Child C, but its hero is Willie, not George, Campbell, and every trace of Scottish dialect has been lost in the natural language of the Southern highlander.

AA

"Willie Campbell." Collected by R. E. Lee Smith, of Palmyra, Va. Sung by his brother, Thomas P. Smith, of Palmyra, Va., and himself. Fluvanna County. July 9, 1931. A note on the manuscript reads: "Sang by Mrs. Chany Smith of Zionville, N. C., 1912. This song has been sang in the Smith family for over 100 years."

1 High up in the mountains
   On the river Tay,
   Gallant Willie Campbell
   Rode out so gay.

2 He was saddled and bridled
   And boldly rode he,
   And home come his horse,
   But never comes he.

3 Out come his mother dear,
   Weeping and wringing her hands,
And out come his own wife,
   Tearing her hair.

4 The meadows lies green,
   And the corn is unshocked,
But gallant Willie Campbell
   Will never come back.

5 Saddled and bridled
   And boots on rode he,
A feather in his helmet
   And a sword at his knee.

6 But home come his saddle
   All bloody, you see,
And home come his horse,
   But never comes he.

36

JAMES HARRIS (THE DÆMON LOVER)
(CHILD, No. 243)

Both of the Child titles are misnomers as applied to the American versions of this ballad: James Harris is not mentioned in them, and, except in a very few texts, the seductive lover has completely lost his demonic character. In America the song takes its title from the deserted husband and is, with few exceptions, known as "The House Carpenter," a variant of the "ship's carpenter" occupation of the husband in British texts.

Students of traditional song often speak as if the broadside were "the villain of the piece," as if it were the source only of corruption and degradation, even extinction, to the true traditional ballad. This is by no means the case. Many a traditional piece has been preserved only because at a certain point it had the good fortune to be printed as a broadside. More often, broadside writers have salvaged at least certain stanzas that bear the marks of tradition. Occasionally, new printed ballads have preserved and renewed old and traditional tunes in the broadside's instructions, "To be sung to the tune of ——————," or in the actual notation of the tune. And finally, the origin of some excellent now traditional pieces can be traced only to the broadside press itself. (See Gerould's Chapter Nine, "Ballads and Broadsides," pp. 235-54.)

The present ballad illustrates several of the relationships just mentioned. In the first place, Child finds a broadside of 1685 (from the Pepys collection) to be the basis of all the traditional forms known to him, and he accordingly prints it as his A text (in smaller type, to signify its non-traditional character), and remarks: "Two or three stanzas of A are of the popular [meaning traditional] description, but it does not seem necessary to posit a tradition behind A." The heading of this broadside deserves full quotation; it suggests the wide gulf which, in spite of the closer relationships mentioned above, clearly separates these "ballads in print o' life" from the products of genuine tradition (*The Pepys Ballads*, IV, 101):

A Warning for Married Women, being an examination of Mrs. Jane Reynolds (a West-country woman), born near Plymouth, who, having plighted her troth to a Seaman, was afterwards married to a

Carpenter, and at last carried away by a Spirit, the manner how shall presently be recited. To a West-country tune called "The Fair Maid of Bristol," "Bateman," or "John True."

The full text would show even more clearly the distance that normally lies between the broadside and the ballad of tradition, and the vast superiority of the latter. One finds it hard indeed to subscribe to Child's suggestion of this broadside as the "basis" of the traditional ballad, despite the wonder-working power of tradition. Child's B version is also a broadside or garland, of about a hundred years later, called "The Distressed Ship-Carpenter," and it has definitely taken on the traditional quality. The rest of Child's eight texts are definitely from tradition, either directly or via manuscript or print, and all are Scottish.

The American ballad also has broadside connections. Though Child prints no American text, his headnote reports (IV, 361): "An Americanized version of this ballad was printed not very long ago at Philadelphia, under the title of 'The House-Carpenter.' I have been able to secure only two stanzas, which were cited in Graham's Magazine, September, 1858:

'I might have married the king's daughter dear;'
'You might have married her,' cried she,
'For I am married to a house-carpenter,
And a fine young man is he.'

'Oh dry up your tears, my own true love,
And cease your weeping,' cried he,
'For soon you'll see your own happy home,
On the banks of old Tennessee.'

The two stanzas are not consecutive. The obviously traditional character of these verses, and especially of the last line quoted, strongly suggests that the ballad had been in America for some time, and that the printed text came from tradition. The impression is reenforced by the full text of the broadside printed by Barry in *JAFL,* XVIII (July-September, 1905), 207-9, from a broadside of about 1860 published by H. deMarsan, of New York. Barry's text was transcribed from a copy in the collection of the American Antiquarian Society, Worcester, Mass. Professor Kittredge points out, in *JAFL,* XXX (July-September, 1917), 325, that the deMarsan broadside is a reissue of one published by J. Andrews, of New York (whom deMarsan succeeded in business) in 1857 or thereabouts, and that a copy of the Andrews broadside is in the

Harris Collection of Brown University. Identical or similar broad-side forms of the ballad, then, were printed in both New York and Philadelphia as early as 1857 or 1858. Since these texts are close to the best-known American versions, it seems likely both that they were taken down originally from American tradition and that they have subsequently returned to that tradition and influenced it. The similarity of many American texts of the ballad may be thus in part explained. To an extent these broadsides may also explain the widespread distribution and popularity of the ballad in America. As Belden puts it (p. 79), "There can be, I think, no question, in the case of this ballad, of the importance of print in spreading and perpetuating it."

In contrast to its present American circulation, the ballad is all but lacking in recent British tradition. Margaret Dean-Smith (p. 80) lists only two incomplete texts, one from Baring-Gould's *Songs of the West* (revised edition, 1905), and one in *JEFSS,* III (1908-1909), 84, both with tunes. Professor Kittridge in *JAFL,* XXX (July-September, 1917), 326, reports a long text from Devon in the Baring-Gould manuscripts at Harvard. And from Scotland, the home of the ballad's traditional form, Greig-Keith (pp. 196-97) print only a single fragmentary text and tune.

In America the ballad is found in something like a profusion of texts wherever ballads are sung (See Coffin, p. 138.) *TBVa* over-ran the alphabet in printing twenty-nine texts of an available fifty-two, with seven tunes. More recently, according to *FSVa,* twenty-five items, including eleven tunes, nine of them from phonographic recordings, have been added to the Virginia collection. Ten texts, all with tunes, are here presented.

Other representative American collections yield the following tabulation: Cox (1), twenty-one texts (not all printed) and one tune, plus Cox (2), four texts and three tunes; Barry, two texts and one tune; Sharp-Karpeles, twenty-two texts (or partial texts) and twenty-two tunes; Belden, nine texts (not all printed) and two tunes; Randolph, thirteen texts (or fragments) and five tunes; Brown, fourteen texts (not all printed) and nine tunes; Gardner-Chickering, three texts and three tunes, Henry, four texts and three tunes; and so on.

The Virginia texts in general are most closely related to Child B. Like Child B, they omit all antecedent action and plunge im-mediately into the conversation between the returned lover and the carpenter's wife; but unlike Child B, they do not end with the carpenter's mourning the news of his wife's death and pronouncing the curse on delusive mariners or sailors. The final curse stanza, when it appears, is spoken by someone else, apparently by the wife herself just before her death. There is no suggestion of the supernatural or demonic character in the returned lover—except, perhaps, in the very few texts which include the "hills of heaven and hell" stanza or stanzas (cf. *TBVa* A, M, N, Appendix A). In addition to the "purer" texts, a number of Virginia texts are marked by the intrusion of stanzas from ballads or songs of related theme, such as "The Lass of Roch Royal" (Child, No. 76), "The Mermaid" (Child, No. 289), and such later songs as "The False Young Man," "The True Lover's Farewell," "The Rejected Lover," "The Wagoner's Lad," "Cold Winter's Night," "Careless Love," and others. See the *TBVa* headnote, p. 440, and *TBVa* texts R-AA and appendices. See also Coffin's "corruption chart," p. 166.

The usual story in America and in Virginia is this: A seaman returns to find his old love married, apparently happily, to a house carpenter, by whom she has a child (or more). By persuasion and promises the lover induces the wife to desert husband and babe(s) and sail away with him. But soon she pines for the old ties, weeps for her sweet little babe, and (sometimes after she has had a vision of the torment in store for her—not found in Child B) the ship springs a leak and sinks to the bottom of the sea. There is often a final stanza voicing her contrition, her curse upon deceiving men, or a warning to other women. Most of the Virginia texts follow Coffin's Story Type A; a few of the more fragmentary ones follow Story Type E, in which the boat does not clearly sink. There is no text similar to the rare Story Type F, which is independent of "The House Carpenter" tradition and seems, along with the single Greig-Keith text, to hark back to the older traditional form of the ballad. See the unique copy in *BFSSNE*, VI, 9, and Coffin, p. 139.

Because of the multiplicity of texts in *TBVa* and because the later texts follow essentially the same pattern of variation described in the *TBVa* headnote, a policy of drastic exclusion has been followed: only texts with good tunes are presented here. This means that some of the fuller and better texts are omitted; but their like may be found in *TBVa*. Only one quaintly garbled version contains the vision stanza about the "banks of heaven." In this same text the woman weeps for her "sweet sugar babe," and there are two stanzas imported from "The Mermaid" (Child, No. 289) and a stanza interpolated from "The False Young Man" or a similar later song. Other excluded texts have the "shoe my foot" stanzas imported from "The Lass of Roch Royal" (Child, No. 76), or an unusual stanza here and there. But the loss is not great.

A distinctive feature of the ballad is the number of fine tunes recently added, most of them on phonograph records and therefore fully verifiable. Ten of the eleven tunes are printed, often with comments by E. C. Mead in the particular headnotes. If the texts are somewhat standardized and sometimes dull, the tunes are more interesting and varied. It is proper to put the emphasis here upon the series of excellent tunes.

Next to "Barbara Allan" in Virginia popularity in the first phase of collecting, "The House Carpenter" failed by only a single item to overtake the cruel lady in the second phase. Drastic editorial surgery has been practiced here upon both of these prolific specimens of the ballad art.

Since the twenty-seven texts of this ballad printed in *TBVa* overran the alphabet to include an *AA* text, an asterisk has been added to the *AA* text here, to distinguish it from *TBVa AA*.

AA*

"The House Carpenter." Phonograph record (aluminum) made by A. K. Davis, Jr. Sung by Mrs. Victoria Morris, of Mt. Fair, Va. Albemarle County. March 10, 1933. Text transcribed by P. C. Worthington. Tune noted by Winston Wilkinson. E. C. Mead comments: "Magnificent tune: irregular rhythmic phrases and very definite rhythm; beautiful pitch shape."

1 "We have met, we have met, my own true love,"
     "Well met, well met," said she.
   "I have late-lie returned from the salt water sea,
     And it's all for the sake of thee.

2 "I coulda married the king's daughter dear,
     And she woulda married me,
   But all the crowns of gold I refused,
     And it's all for the sake of thee."

3 "If you coulda married the king's daughter dear,
     I am sure you were to blame,
   For I am married to a house carpenter,
     And they say he's a fine young man."

4 "Will you forsake on your house carpenter,
     And go along with me?
   I will take you where the grass grows green,
     On the banks of Sweet Willie."

5 "What do you have to maintain me on,
     To keep me from starving?" said she.
   "I have a hundred ships on the ocean a-sailin',
     And a-sailin' for dry land,
   And a hundred and ten of the nicest waiting men,
     Shall be at your command."

6 She pick-ed up her tender little baby,
     And the kisses she did give it were three,

"Stay at home, stay at home, my tender little thing,
  And keep your papa's company."

7 She hadn't been a-sailing on the sea two weeks,
     I'm sure it were not three,
   Before this poor damsel begin for to weep,
     And she wept most bitterly.

8 "Are you a-weepin' for my silver?" says he,
     "Or are you weepin' for my gold?
   Or are you a-weepin' for your house carpenter,
     For you'll never see no more?"

9 "I'm not a-weepin' for your silver," said she,
     "Nor neither for your gold.
   I am weeping for my tender little baby,
     That I'll never see no more."

10 She hadn't been a-sailin' on the sea three weeks,
      I'm sure it were not four,
    Before this vessel sprung a leakin' floor,
      And it sank to rise no more.

BB

"The House Carpenter." Phonograph record (aluminum) made by A. K.
Davis, Jr. Sung by S. F. Russell, of Marion, Va. Smyth County. August
15, 1932. Text transcribed by P. C. Worthington. Tune noted by E. C.
Mead, who comments: "Rhythmically fine, variety of rhythmic phrases, with
at the same time definite rhythm."

1   "I've just returned, my own true love,
     I have just returned," said he.
   "I have just returned from the salt, salt sea,
     And 'tis all for the sake of thee.
   I have just returned from the salt, salt sea,
     And 'tis all for the sake of thee.

2   "I could have married the king's daughter,
     And she would have married me,
   But I refused the crowns of gold,
     And 'twas all for the sake of thee."

3   "If you coulda married the king's daughter,
     I'm sure she was the one,
   For I have married a house carpenter,
     And I think he's a nice young man."

4   "If you'll forsake your house carpenter,
     And go along with me,
   I'll take you to where the grass grows green,
     On the banks of Sweet Willy."

5   "If I forsake my house carpenter,
     And go along with thee,
   What have you got to maintain me upon,
     To keep me from slavery?"

6   "I have ten boats all sailing on sea,
     All sailing for dry land,
   Two hundred and twenty jolly sailor boys,
     And they shall be at your command."

7   She picked up her sweet little babe,
     And kisses give hit three,
   Saying, "Stay you here, my sweet little babe,
     And keep your paw company."

8 She hadn't been on board but about three weeks,
   I'm sure it was not four,
   Till she began to weep and to moan,
   And the like I never saw before.

9 "Are you weeping for your house carpenter?
   Are you weeping for my store?
   Are you weeping for that sweet little babe,
   Whose face you will see no more?"

10 "I'm not weeping for my house carpenter,
   I'm not weeping for your store,
   I'm a-weeping for that sweet little babe,
   Whose face I'll see no more,
   I'm a-weeping for my sweet little babe,
   Whose face I will see no more."

CC

"The House Carpenter." Phonograph record (aluminum) made by A. K. Davis, Jr. Sung by Mrs. Lucy Perrin Gibbs, of Orange, Va. Orange County. November 14, 1932. Text transcribed by P. C. Worthington. Tune noted by Winston Wilkinson.

1 "Oh, I could have married the king's daughter dear,
   And she would have married me,
   But all the crowns of gold I refused,
   For the sake of marrying thee.
   But all the crowns of gold I refused,
   For the sake of marrying thee."

2 "If you could have married the king's daughter dear,
      Then I'm sure you are to blame,
   For I am engaged to a house carpenter,
      And he's a nice young man."

3 "If you will forsake your house carpenter,
      And go along with me,
   I'll take you where the grass grows green,
      On the banks of Sweet Scotly."

4 "If I will forsake my house carpenter,
      And go along with thee,
   Oh, what hast thou to support me upon,
      To save me from poverty?"

5 "I have a hundred ships out sailing on the sea,
      All sailing for dry land,
   And a hundred and ten of the finest of men,
      To be ready at your command."

6 They had not been sailing on the sea two weeks,
      I'm sure it was not three,
   Before that there damsel began to weep,
      And she wept most bitterly.

7 "Are you a-weeping for my gold?" says he,
      "Or is it for my store?
   Oh, are you a-weeping for your house carpenter,
      Whom you never shall see any more?"

8 Says, "I'm not a-weeping for my gold," says she,
      "Or is it for my store,
   But I am a-weeping for my house carpenter,
      Whom I never shall see any more."

9 They had not been sailing on that sea three weeks,
      I'm sure it was not four,
   Before the vessel sprang a leak,
      And she sunk for to rise no more.

DD

"The Salt Sea." Phonograph record (aluminum) made by A. K. Davis, Jr. Sung by Mrs. Molly Stinnett Whitehead, of Agricola, Va. Amherst County. August 8, 1935. Text transcribed by P. C. Worthington. Tune noted by E. C. Mead. Mrs. Whitehead's tune is very close to the tune to which she sings her version of "Young Hunting" (Child, No. 68), printed above as AA of that ballad. The second and ninth stanzas are sung as four-line stanzas, unlike the others.

"Oh met, oh met, my old true love, Oh met, oh met," said he, "I've just re-turned from that salt, salt sea, And it's all for the sake of thee. I've just returned from that salt, salt sea, And it's all for the sake of thee."

Var.

1   "Oh met, oh met, my old true love,
      Oh met, oh met," said he,
    "I have just returned from the salt, salt sea,
      And it's all for the sake of thee.
    I've just returned from the salt, salt sea,
      And it's all for the sake of thee.

2   "Oh, I could have married the king's daughter dear,
      I'm sure she'd have married me,
    But I've just returned from the salt salt sea,
      And it's all for the sake of thee."

3   "If you could have married the king's daughter dear,
      I'm sure you are to blame,
    For I am married to a house carpenter,
      And he is a nice young man.
    For I am married to a house carpenter,
      And he is a nice young man."

4   "Oh, won't you leave your house carpenter
      And come and go with me?
    I will take you where the grass grows green
      On the side of the salt, salt sea.

I will take you where the grass grows green
   On the side of the salt, salt sea."

5   Oh, she picked up her sweet little babe,
      And the kisses was one, two, three,
   Saying, "Stay at home, my sweet little babe,
      Keep your papa's company,"
   Saying, "Stay at home, my sweet little babe,
      Keep your papa's company."

6   Oh, she had not been on the sea two weeks,
      I'm sure it was not three,
   Before she wept, she began to weep,
      And she wept most bitterly,
   Before she wept, she began for to weep,
      And she wept most bitterly.

7   "Oh, it's are you weeping for my gold,
      Or weeping for my store?
   Oh, it's are you weeping for your house carpenter,
      Whose face you will see no more?
   Oh, it's are you weeping for your house carpenter,
      Whose face you will see no more?"

8   "I'm not a-weeping for your gold,
      Nor neither for your store,
   But I'm weeping for my sweet little babe,
      Whose face I will see no more,
   But I'm weeping for my sweet little babe,
      Whose face I will see no more."

9   She had not been on the sea three weeks,
      I'm sure it was not four,
   Before the ship it sprang a leak,
      And it sunk for to rise no more.

EE

"The House Carpenter." Phonograph record (aluminum) made by A. K. Davis, Jr. Sung by Mrs. Texas Gladden, of near Roanoke, Va. Roanoke County. August 7, 1932. Text transcribed by P. C. Worthington. Tune noted by Winston Wilkinson. Again, a beautiful tune, well sung.

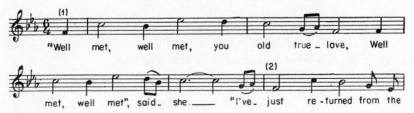

(1) "Well met, well met, you old true – love, Well
met, well met", said– she.—— "I've– just re -turned from the

sea   shore sea, From the   land where the grass grows   green."____

Var   (1) Mrs. Gladden varies it thus: etc.

(1) and: (2)   (2)   2

(2) ┌ 2 ┐   2   (3)   (4)   (4) ┌ 2 ┐   2

(4)   (4)

1 "Well met, well met, you old true love,"
   "Well met, well met," said she.
   "I've just returned from the sea shore sea,
   From the land where the grass grows green.

2 "Well, I could have married a king's daughter there,
   She would have married me;
   But I refused the golden crown,
   All for the sake of thee."

3 "If you could have married a king's daughter there,
   I'm sure you are to blame,
   For now I'm married to a house carpenter,
   And I think he's a nice young man."

4 "If you'll forsake your house carpenter,
   And come and go with me,
   I'll take you where the grass grows green,
   To the land on the banks of the sea."

5 She went, she took her sweet little babe,
   And kissed it one, two, three,
   Saying, "Stay at home with your papa dear,
   And keep him good company."

6 She went and dressed in her very best,
   And everyone could see,
   She glistened and glittered, and proudly she walked
   The streets on the banks of the sea.

7   She hadn't been sailing but about three weeks,
        I'm sure it was not four,
    Till this young lady began to weep,
        And her weeping never ceased anymore.

8   "Are you mourning for your house carpenter?
        Are you mourning for your store?"
    "No, I'm mourning for my sweet little babe,
        I never will see any more."

FF

"Sweet Wildee." Phonograph record (aluminum) made by A. K. Davis, Jr. Sung by Abner Keesee, of Altavista, Va. Campbell County. August 4, 1932. Text transcribed by P. C. Worthington. Tune noted by Winston Wilkinson. As to the tune, E. C. Mead comments: "Very beautiful; varied melodic line, fine ornamentation." As usual, Mr. Keesee's version, though compressed, is an artistic condensation of the essential story.

1 "Cheer up, cheer up, my pretty fair miss,
   Come go along with me,
And I will take you where the grass grows green,
   To the banks of the Sweet Wildee.
And I will take you where the grass grows green,
   To the banks of the Sweet Wildee."

2 She picked her babe up in her arms,
   And give it kisses three,
"Stay here, stay here, my poor little babe,
   And keep your father's company."

3 She hadn't been gone more than two long weeks,
   I am sure that it was not three,
Before she began to weep,
   And she wept most bitterly.

4 "You need not to weep for your house nor your land,
   Nor you need not to weep for your store,
And you need not to weep for your house carpenter,
   That you never shall see no more."

5 "I am not a-weepin' for my house nor my land,
   Nor I'm not a-weepin' for my store,
I am only a-weepin' for my poor little babe,
   That I never shall see no more."

6 She hadn't been gone more than three long weeks,
   I am sure that it was not four,
The ship sprung a leak and it did sink,
   And it sank to rise no more.

GG

"On the Banks of the Sweet Willie." Phonograph record (aluminum) made by A. K. Davis, Jr. Sung by Mrs. Merkley Keesee Lewis, of Castle Craig, Va. Campbell County. August 4, 1932. Text transcribed by P. C. Worthington. Tune noted by Winston Wilkinson. Another satisfactory condensed version from the same neighborhood as Mr. Keesee's (FF).

1   "Cheer up, cheer up, my pretty fair maid,
        Come go along with me,
    And I will take you where the grass grows green,
        To the banks of the Sweet Willie.
    And I will take you where the grass grows green,
        To the banks of the Sweet Willie."

2   She picked her babe up in her arms,
        And gave it kisses three,
    "Stay here, stay here, my poor little babe,
        And keep your father's company."

3   She dressed herself in silk so fine,
        And she walked off so bold,
    And every city that she went through,
        She shone like glittering gold.

4   She hadn't been gone more than two long weeks,
        I'm sure it was not three,
    Before, oh, oh, she begun to weep,
        And she wept most bitterly.

5   She hadn't been gone more than three long weeks,
        I'm sure it was not four,
    When the ship sprung a leak and it did sink,
        It sunk to rise no more.

HH

"The House Carpenter." Phonograph record (aluminum), made by A. K. Davis, Jr. Sung by Mrs. John Webb, of Lynch Station, Va. Campbell

County.   August 4, 1932.   Text transcribed by P. C. Worthington.   Tune noted by Winston Wilkinson.   Cf. *TBVa* V (pp. 469, 594) for the text and tune sung by Mrs. Webb, then Miss Callie Hogan, and her brother in February, 1914.   The text is essentially the same, the tune shows certain changes, which are now verifiable, and variants not previously recorded. Note that the first stanza and half the second are imported from "The False Young Man."

1   "Come in, come in, my own true love,
    Come in, come in," said she,
    "I haven't spoken a word to my own true love
    In five or seven years.
    I haven't spoken a word to my own true love,
    In five or seven years."

2   "I can't come in, I can't stay here,
    For I have not a moment of time,
    For I heard you was married to a house carpenter,
    And your heart is no more mine.

3   "If you will leave your house carpenter,
    And go along with me,

Oh, I'll carry you where the grass grows green,
   On the banks of Sweet Willy."

4 She picked her babe up in her arms,
      And kissed it one, two, three,
   Saying, "Stay at home, my sweet little babe,
      And keep your father's company."

II

"Salt Water Sea." Collected by Miss Alfreda M. Peel and Miss Caroline Melbard, of Salem, Va. Contributed and sung by Minter Grubb, of Back Creek, Va. Roanoke County. August 26, 1932. Tune noted by Miss Eloise Kelly, of Marion, Va. Miss Caroline Melbard, a friend of Miss Peel, copied the song from a manuscript as Mr. Grubb had written it on March 10, 1891. The minor differences between the full text and the text printed with the music are due to the fact that Miss Kelly noted the words from Mr. Grubb's later singing. As is not unusual in Mr. Grubb's versions, the text shows a few quaintnesses of phrase.

1 "We will meet, we will meet, my old true love,
      We will, we will meet," said he.
   "I have just returned from the salt water sea
      And it's all for the love of thee.

2 "I could have married a king's daughter, dear,
      And she would have married me.
   But I refused a crown of her gold
      And it's all for the love of thee."

3 "If you could have married a king's daughter, dear,
      I am sure you are not too,
   For I have married a house carpenter
      And I think he is a nice young man."

4 "If you will forsake your house carpenter
   And go along with me,
   I will take you where the grass grows so green
   On the banks of Sweet Willie."

5 "If I was to forsake my house carpenter
   And go along with you,
   What would you have to maintain me
   Or to keep me from severe?"

6 "I have seven old ships all on board
   A-sailing for dry land.
   Four hundred and ten jolly men
   Shall be at your command."

7 She picked up her sweet little babe
   The kisses she gave it three,
   Saying, "Stay here, my sweet little babe,
   And keep your Pa's company."

8 She dressed herself all in red,
   . . . .
   And as she marched along
   She looked like glittering gold.

9 She had not been on sea two weeks,
   It was not three, I am sure,
   Till she began to weep
   And wept most bitterly.

10 "Is it for my gold you weep,
    Or is it my store?
    Or is it for your house carpenter
    That you never shall see any more?"

11 "It's neither for your gold I weep,
    It's neither for your store,
    I am weeping for my sweet little babe
    That I never shall see any more."

12 She had not been on sea three weeks,
    I am sure it was not four,
    Till the ship it sprang a leap
    And sank to rise no more.

13 "A curse, a curse, to all sea men,
    A curse to the sailor.
    You have rallied me off from my house carpenter
    And it's taken away my life."

JJ

"The House Carpenter." Collected by Miss Juliet Fauntleroy, of Altavista, Va. Sung by Mrs. Kit Williamson, of Yellow Branch, Va. Campbell County. March 15, 1934. Tune noted by Mrs. Paul Cheatham, of Lynchburg, Va. The eleven-stanza text of Mrs. Williamson's song has been printed earlier as *TBVa* T, without tune. The full text is therefore not reprinted here. The first two stanzas of Mrs. Williamson's text, like the first two of HH above, belong to "The False Young Man." (Cf. *TBVa*, pp. 466-67.)

"Come in, come in, my old true love, And sit you down by me, For it's been over three quarters of a year, Since I spoke one word to thee."

1   "Come in, come in, my old true love,
    And sit you down by me,
    For it's been over three quarters of a year,
    Since I spoke one word to thee."

37

HENRY MARTYN
(CHILD, No. 250)

This is a new ballad in Virginia. *TBVa* did not have it; *FSVa* reports one text, without tune, given here.

There is also a major controversy about the ballad: whether it is a version of "Sir Andrew Barton" (Child, No. 167) or whether it is a separate but related ballad. Child obviously took the latter view, since he gave it a separate number, but in his comment, "The ballad must have sprung from the ashes of 'Andrew Barton,' of which the name Henry Martyn would be no extraordinary corruption," he opened the door slightly for those who have chosen to regard the two ballads as one. That the two deal with a somewhat similar story is quite true, but they deal with it quite differently, That some versions may represent crossing or intermingling of the two further complicates the problem. Two eminent English authorities take a different view of the relationship from Child's, while insisting even more strongly on the separateness of the two ballads, and feel that the traditional "Henry Martyn" is the older of the two. Cecil Sharp, in his *One Hundred English Folk Songs*, p. xvii, writes: "In Percy's *Reliques* there is a long and much edited ballad, called 'Sir Andrew Barton,' with which, however, the traditional versions have nothing in common." After quoting Child's remark about the relations of the two, he resumes: "The Rev. S. Baring Gould, in his note to the ballad in *Songs of the West*, differs from this view and contends that the Percy version is the ballad 'as recomposed in the reign of James I, when there was a perfect rage for rewriting the old historical ballads.' I am inclined to agree that the two versions are quite distinct. 'Sir Andrew Barton' deals with the final encounter between Barton and the King's ships, in which Andrew Barton's ship is sunk and he himself killed; whereas the traditional versions are concerned with a piratical raid made by Henry Martyn upon an English merchantman." Sharp further notes Baring-Gould's belief, not only that "Sir Andrew Barton" was a recomposition of earlier versions of the present day "Henry Martin," but also that the present Martyn "form of the ballad is probably earlier, but it is incomplete." Of course, neither Child, Sharp, nor Baring-

Gould were familiar with certain recent American texts upon which
the argument for one ballad rather than two is partly based. The
problem of classification is further complicated by the fact that
many texts of this ballad have taken over the ending of "Captain
Ward and the Rainbow" (Child, No. 287).

Before going further into these controversies, perhaps the present editor should say that he is convinced of the distinctness of the
ballads, despite some mixed versions, and that the present Virginia
ballad is a version of "Henry Martyn" and not of "Sir Andrew
Barton." He also finds Baring-Gould's theory of their relationship
more appealing than Child's, though it is perhaps unnecessary that
he commit himself on this hardly provable issue.

As background for summary consideration of the controversy,
let us briefly review Child's versions of both ballads, before we move
on to recently recovered texts and to the present unique Virginia
text.

Child prints three versions of "Sir Andrew Barton" (Child, No.
167). Child A, from the Percy MS., has eighty-two stanzas. Child
B, with sixty-four stanzas, tells essentially the same story as A.
Child collates a number of printed variants and gives in full a Scottish manuscript copy. A third text, which he might have labeled C
but did not, is given in Additions and Corrections, IV, 502-7, from
a manuscript written in a sixteenth-century hand and now in York
Minster Library, and runs to eighty-one stanzas. Child traces this
ballad of piracy through chronicles to historical events of June, 1511.

The ballad story in Child A, roughly followed in the other two
texts, is as follows: King Henry VIII, hearing of the piracy of the
Scot, Andrew Barton, asks for a lord to rid him of the traitor. Lord
Charles Howard volunteers, and others sail with him to track down
Barton. On the third day they meet a ship commanded by Henry
Hunt, who has just recently been robbed by Barton and who tells
them where they may find him. Howard takes Barton by surprise,
and after a long fight recounted in great detail, Barton is given a
death wound. Until he dies, Barton blows his whistle and urges his
men to fight on. After his death his men give o'er. Howard severs
Barton's head and throws the body overboard. The head is presented to King Henry and he rewards Howard and his men. To
Barton's men, in honor of their valor, he gives enough money to
get them to their Scottish homes.

The ballad is extremely long and very detailed. The outstanding features are three: the plea of the merchants to King Henry and

his subsequent action; the central core of the chase with the vividly detailed and involved battle with which most of the ballad is concerned; and the triumphant return of Howard to England after Barton's death.

"Henry Martyn" (Child, No. 250) is a much shorter ballad which in content might conceivably once have served as an introduction to the longer one. Child prints four versions as his main entry and a fifth important version, E, in Additions and Corrections, V, 302-3. Child A (ten stanzas) was taken down from recitation by the Reverend S. Baring-Gould. Child B (eight stanzas) has three sources: a broadside, and two traditional pieces collected by Kidson from oral tradition. Child C (seven stanzas) is from Motherwell's MS. Child D (two stanzas) and E (thirteen stanzas) are both American versions from oral tradition, from New Hampshire and South Carolina, respectively. All of these texts, it will be noticed, are of much more recent date than the texts of "Sir Andrew Barton."

The essential story of the ballad is perhaps most clearly and simply told in Child B. Three brothers in merry Scotland cast lots to see which of them should turn pirate. The lot falls to the youngest one, Henry Martyn, who turns robber on the salt sea to maintain his brothers and himself. He spies a rich merchant ship, refuses to let her pass by, and commences battle. At last Henry Martyn gives her a death wound and down to the bottom goes she. The bad news reaches England, of the loss of the merchant ship and the drowning of most of her merry men.

There are a few significant variations in Child's other texts. Child A, though it has the merchant ship sunk, has the pirate die, as in the longer ballad. But this is probably only a verbal change by which the pirate receives rather than gives the death wound. That the pirate's name changes to Robin Hood in Child C is unimportant. Child D, with its pirate named Andrew Bodee, is too fragmentary to offer much help. The essentials of the story of Child B—the lot-casting, the successful sinking of the merchant ship, the pirate victorious, and the bad news carried to England— certainly differentiate this ballad from "Sir Andrew Barton." This form of the story, best exemplified in Child B, will henceforth be referred to as the Martyn type of the ballad, even if by verbal confusion, as in Child A, the pirate is supposedly killed.

Child E is a different version, somewhat closer to "Sir Andrew Barton," but still properly classified under Child, No. 250. The story is more complicated. The brothers cast lots, Andrew Bartin goes to sea, a merchant ship is robbed, news reaches England, and stout ship is prepared, under the command of Captain Charles Stewart, for the pursuit of Bartin. Stewart's ship meets Bartin's, Stewart gives over, and Bartin sends by him his boastful message to the king (George) that the king may reign on dry land but that he, Bartin, will be king of the sea. This is getting a little closer to "Sir Andrew Barton," not only in the name of the hero but in some of the complications of the story. But the opening lot-casting, the sinking of the merchant ship, and the pirate victory all point to Child, No. 250. A further complication is that two stanzas—the "brass and steel" of stanza 11 and the final boastful stanza—are imported from another ballad, "Captain Ward and the Rainbow" (Child, No. 287). Child is certainly right in classifying this E text under 250 and not under 167. The form of the story exemplified in Child E will henceforth be referred to as the Ward type of the ballad.

Since the Virginia text belongs to the Ward type, we might perhaps drop this discussion here except that to do so would be to drop without an attempt at solution a fascinating and hitherto unsatisfactorily resolved problem in ballad scholarship and ballad relationships. To continue, then:

No texts of the Ward type or of a third type (yet to be discussed) still closer to the original story of "Sir Andrew Barton" seem to survive in recent British tradition. Texts of the Martyn type are fairly prevalent in England and have been recovered by Sharp, Baring-Gould, Broadwood, and Alfred Williams, among others. In addition to Miss Dean-Smith's listings, references are supplied by Kittredge in *JAFL,* XXX (July-September, 1917), 327, and by Belden, p. 87. A possible source of weakness in the testimony of Sharp and Baring-Gould as to the ballad's classification, as has been intimated before, is that they were unfamiliar with certain of the ballad's versions, recently recovered in America. But even in the light of the new evidence their conclusion seems to stand. Greig-Keith present no text or tune of "Henry Martyn" (Child, No. 250) from recent Scottish tradition. And no trace of the much longer ballad of "Sir Andrew Barton" (Child, No. 167) has been found in recent tradition, British or American, unless one accepts the theory that the two ballads are one.

The appearance of certain twentieth-century American texts and tunes has further complicated the problem of classification and precipitated controversy—and, be it admitted, some confusion, which it is the effort of this rather elaborate headnote to clear up if it can. Much of the confusion has resulted from Barry's determination to regard "Sir Andrew Barton" and "Henry Martyn" not as two ballads, but one, and to refer all American texts of "Henry Martyn" "without hesitation" to the tradition of "Sir Andrew Barton." His elaborate discussion (pp. 248-58) cannot (and need not) be summarized here. Further confusion has arisen from the fact that Coffin, following Barry, discusses North American texts of this ballad under Child, No. 167, as "Sir Andrew Barton (including 250, Henry Martyn)." Coffin has also made the American record of this ballad appear larger than it is by duplicate references and by listing a number of reprintings in America of well-known British texts.

Barry draws the strongest support for his argument from a Missouri text entitled "Andy Bardan," originally collected by Belden in 1911 and published by him in *JAFL,* XXV (April-June, 1912), 171-73, reprinted by Barry (pp. 252-53) as his version C, and again (later) printed by Belden in his *Missouri Ballads and Songs,* 1940, pp. 87-89. This thirteen-stanza version is indeed the closest of all texts of "Henry Martyn" to the "Sir Andrew Barton" story. Andy Bardan is the pirate, Captain Charles Stewart his pursuer, and the king, as in "Sir Andrew Barton," is Henry, not George. Lots are cast, Bardan takes to sea and robs a merchantman. News comes to the king, who gives orders for the building of a ship, warning that Bardan be taken on pain of death. Captain Charles Stewart challenges the robbers and will not let them pass by. The fight is joined, Stewart captures Bardan and takes him to England, where he (Bardan) makes a sad speech before he is to be hanged. Barry points out the several parallels to "Sir Andrew Barton," but of course notes that "the pirate, instead of meeting death in a sea-fight, is taken to England, a prisoner, and hanged." Barry continues: "It seems at least probable that the group of American texts, represented by 'Andy Bardan,' should be reckoned as of an older tradition than that of 'Henry Martyn,'" and in conclusion he states as his thesis "that 'Sir Andrew Barton,' a ballad extinct in English tradition, has survived in America." Hardly; only a version of "Henry Martyn" somewhat closer to "Sir Andrew Barton." This third form of the story of Child, No. 250, best exemplified in Belden's Missouri text, will henceforth be referred to as the Bardan type of the ballad.

Barry's contention ignores too much: the relative brevity of all the "Henry Martyn" texts, the standard opening of the brothers casting lots, the sinking of the merchantman, the usually but not always triumphant pirate. The best answer to Barry is given by Belden, the finder of the disputed text, who classifies it under "Henry Martyn" (Child, No. 250). He reviews Barry's arguments, then replies: "On the other hand, all the texts given by Child under *Henry Martyn* and all those recorded from tradition since Child's time—whether the hero is called Bardun or Battam or Bodee or Martin—have a formal likeness that alone is enough to warrant classing them together as a distinct ballad: they all begin with three brothers of old Scotland casting lots to see which of them shall go robbing all on the salt sea to maintain the family. Most of them, too, represent the pirate as triumphing over his foes. But form is a more trustworthy mark of identity than particulars of plot" (p. 87).

Barry's ingenious but rather far-fetched effort to identify the Captain Charles Stewart of the ballad as an American naval hero of that name (1778-1869) has been called in question by Miss Pound's Nebraska text brought from Ireland, in which the pursuer is Captain Joe Stuart. (*SFLQ*, II, 205-6.)

The conclusion as to classification is that in consideration of structure, details of plot, language, etc., the traditional ballads called "Henry Martyn" or some such approximate title, whether Martyn type, Ward type, or Bardan type, should be classed together under Child, No. 250, even though we recognize the fairly close relationship of some texts of this ballad to "Sir Andrew Barton" (Child, No. 167). It is a pity that recent American texts have been confusedly classified.

All of Coffin's American references (p. 113) should, in my opinion, be transferred from "Sir Andrew Barton" (Child, No. 167) to "Henry Martyn" (Child, No. 250). A few other editors have followed Barry and Coffin in their classification, and have furthered the confusion. To Coffin's references should be added the following more recent texts: a Ward-type text printed by Russell M. Harrison in *Western Folklore*, XI, 180-81, under Child, No. 167; a Ward-type text printed by Lester Hubbard and LeRoy J. Robertson in *JAFL*, LXIV (January-March, 1951), 49-50, under Child, No. 250; two Bardan-type texts printed by Flanders in *Ballads Migrant in New England*, pp. 72-74 and 201-3. And the present Virginia text, the Ward type.

Some twenty-odd texts and about half as many tunes of the ballad have been recovered from recent North American tradition. In addition to Newfoundland, at least the following states have produced variants: Maine, New Hampshire, Vermont, Connecticut, New York, West Virginia, Virginia, South Carolina, Arkansas, Ohio, Michigan, Missouri, Kansas, Nebraska, Minnesota, Utah, Oregon. The nautical theme of the ballad might have a bearing on its currency in the Northeast. More surprising is its wide circulation in the Middle West and West. Surprising, too, is its almost total absence from the ballad-singing regions of the South. Since Reed Smith's South Carolina text and tune (pp. 156-58) are only reprints of Child E, the present Virginia text appears to be a unique post-Child Southern text. Neither Sharp-Karpeles nor Brown nor any other Southern collection has it.

By the use of Coffin's references and those which have been added here, a summary classification by types may be made of the published American texts. Equality signs between texts indicate that these references are to one text which has been reprinted two or more times. The two American texts printed by Child are included. Texts of the Martyn type are three in number (Eddy A; Karpeles; *JAFL,* XVIII, 135*). Ward texts are eleven in number including the present Virginia text (*Adventure,* 1923; Barry A; Child E = Reed Smith; Cox; Garner and Chickering A and B; Randolph; Flanders, *Country Songs of Vermont; Western Folklore,* XI, 1952; *JAFL,* LXIV, 1951; Virginia text). Texts of the Bardan type are seven in number (Barry B = *JAFL,* XVIII, 302 = Gray; *JAFL,* XXV, 171 = Belden = Barry C; Eddy B; *SFLQ,* II, 205; Thompson; Flanders, *Ballads Migrant in New England,* 1953, pp. 72-74 and 201-3). Two more North American texts, that of Mackenzie from Novia Scotia and Child D from New Hampshire, seem too fragmentary for accurate classification, but they too seem to point toward the Ward type, which is clearly the most numerous type in American oral tradition. The total number of distinct American texts involved in this tabulation is twenty-three.

The Virginia Ward-type text of ten stanzas has the robber named Ronald Barton, his pursuer William Stewart, the king Henry, not George. Ronald Barton of the North Countree becomes a pirate of the Northern seas because he and his brothers "could not make a living." Dice are cast, and the youngest, Ronald Barton,

* This text is of the "Henry Martyn" form, but as in Child Aa the robber is killed. It does not relate structurally to the "Bardan" type.

goes to sea. No single encounter with a merchant ship is recited, but "he sunk and robbed a hundred ships to support himself and brothers on the Northern seas." William Stewart in a unique oath swears to bring Barton back "dead or alive" to London town. He gets "the best ship of England," and sails away. Sighting Barton's ship, he orders him not to pass by. Barton says he will die rather than give in. After a three-hour battle it is Stewart who gives in. Barton sends him back to England to deliver a message to King Henry that the King can rule over dry land, but Barton is king of the sea. The version ends with a stanza not found in any other text, telling how after the battle Ronald Barton set sail and was never seen any more; he never returned again to the Northern seas. Baring-Gould felt that another stanza was needed after the pirate's boastful taunt, and wrote one himself, a very different one, as follows (*Songs of the West,* Revised edition, 1905, p. 115):

> O had I a twisted rope of hemp,
>   A bowstring strong though thin;
> I'd soon hang him up to his middle yard arm
>   And have done with Henry Martyn.

The Virginia text supplies such a stanza, and a much better stanza, from oral tradition.

The genuine antique flavor of the text is apparent. It has required some editorial attention to line and stanza divisions, but is otherwise untouched. See the more specific headnote, below.

One final word may be in order on the problem of the relationship of "Henry Martyn" to "Andrew Barton," which has received so much attention in this headnote. What degree of difference distinguishes a separate ballad from a somewhat distant version of the same ballad is an extremely delicate and difficult question. It is by no means a "yes-or-no" question, but often a matter of agonized decision, the essential problem being just where the line may best be drawn. The habit of ballad intermixture and contamination further complicates the issue. But in the case of these apparently somewhat related ballads of piracy at sea, both the degree of difference and the nature of the differences point to the conclusions that the ballads are two and not one, and to the identification of all three types from recent tradition as belonging with "Henry Martyn" and not with "Sir Andrew Barton."

AA

"Ronald Barton." Collected by R. E. Lee Smith, of Palmyra, Va. Sung by his brother, Thomas P. Smith, and himself. Fluvanna County. October 28, 1932. Mr. Smith writes on the manuscript: "Sang partly by Bennett Smith, June 10, 1910; he heard it over 40 years before that date. Mrs. Polly J. Rayfield, of Zionville, N. C. quoted over the balance, Jan. 18, 1914 to R. E. L. Smith." Thus it will be seen that this is actually a composite version, a fact which may account for some of the irregularities of this text, which presents some metrical difficulties as well as problems of line and stanza divisions. Mr. Smith's manuscript has been presented with only the barest minimum of editorial liberty. Many British and American singers of the "Martyn" song put the accent on the last syllable of the proper name. Since there is no tune, it is not known whether the Smith family sang the song in this fashion. "Ronald Barton" seems to be a unique title for the ballad, as does the name William Stewart as his pursuer. Henry rather than George as the name of the king points back to earlier texts of the ballad. The final stanza is without known parallel. See the general headnote, above. Note that at least a part of the ballad was recited and not sung.

1   There was three brothers
    Who lived in the North Countree;
  They could not make a living,
    These brothers three.

2   So they cast their dice to see
    Which one would a pirate be
  To make a living
    For the brothers three.

3   The lot fell on the youngest one
    To become a pirate of the Northern[1] seas.
  No bolder pirate could ever be
    Than young Ronald Barton of Northern seas.

4   He sunk and robbed
    A hundred ships
  To support himself
    And brothers on the Northern seas.

5   William Stewart swore he would bring this pirate
    Dead or alive to London town
  Insight [sic] of a week
    Or else go down.

6   He got the best ship of England
    All trimmed and sailed away.
  He saw young Ronald Barton's ship
    About two hours after day

And ordered young Barton's ship
  To not pass by.

7 "Before I will give in
    I will die,"
  Was the answer young Barton
    Gave William Stewart alright.

8 Then the battle commenced
    And lasted over three hours
  Before William Stewart give in.

9 "Now carry this message
    To the King of old England:
  'King Henry can rule over dry land,
    But Ronald Barton is the King of the sea.' "

10 Ronald Barton after the battle set sail
    And was never seen any more;
  He sailed away and never returned
    Again to the Northern seas.

1. Here, but not elsewhere in the MS., spelled "Nothern."

38

OUR GOODMAN
(Child, No. 274)

Until better versions of this down-to-earth bit of folk humor show up from traditional sources—with or without the "indecorous extensions" spoken of by Kittredge in *JAFL*, XXX (July-September, 1917), 328—the ballad can be given fairly summary treatment.

TBVa mustered eight items: five texts and five tunes (two not overlapping), plus a Scottish dialect text via West Virginia printed as an appendix. The seven new items of *FSVa* have very little new to offer, except the tunes from phonograph records. Only the two texts and two tunes from records are given here.

Child prints only two versions of the ballad, from Herd's MSS. and from a London broadside, respectively, the second being of considerably more interest than the first. *TBVa* A and B resemble Child A and B, respectively. *TBVa* B, in which the woman is entertaining three lovers, is an unusual text in America. The present Virginia texts follow Child A rather than B, but actually are to be classified with the more recent and usual American form generally known as "Three Nights' Experience," in which the action is represented as taking place on consecutive nights. This is Coffin's Story Type C.

Child has indicated the wide range of the ballad in other languages and on the Continent: in Gaelic, Flemish, German, Danish, Norwegian, Swedish, Magyar, French, Italian, and Catalan.

Apparently the jocular treatment of marital infidelity has a wide human appeal. A husband returns home—in some versions, drunk and on successive nights—to find objects which arouse his suspicion that his wife is entertaining a lover (or lovers). He questions her, but she ingeniously explains that the horse is a milk cow, the coat is a bed quilt, the man's head a cabbage head, or the like. The husband, apparently not satisfied with these answers, protests that he never saw a saddle on a milk cow, pockets on a bed quilt, a mustache on a cabbage head, and the like. But no tragedy ensues. The ballad maintains its lightness of tone and ends as a humorous ballad of situation—one of not too many humorous ballads admitted by Child within his portals.

The song has not been widely found in recent British tradition. S. Baring-Gould reports texts from the West of England (Devonshire and Cornwall); Alfred Williams finds it well known in the Thames Valley, especially in Berkshire; Elsie Clews Parsons has collected it in the Bahamas; from Aberdeenshire, Greig-Keith report the collecting of two versions and two tunes. Their very full printed version in Scottish dialect has a "Jacobite touch," like the piece printed in Smith's *Scotish Minstrel* and the *TBVa* Appendix.

In America the ballad is considerably more popular and widely dispersed, even if one suspects that some of the texts and tunes are not so far removed from song-books or records. In addition to Nova Scotia, the following American states have it: Maine, Massachusetts, Virginia, West Virginia, Kentucky, Tennessee, North Carolina, South Carolina, Mississippi, Florida, Ohio, Michigan, Indiana, Iowa, Kansas. If ribald versions were collected and printed, no doubt every state would be represented!

In spite of this wide distribution, a glance at representative collections reveals surprisingly few published texts. Here are some counts: Cox, three texts, no tunes; Barry, two texts and one tune; Sharp-Karpeles, five texts (or partial texts) and five tunes; Belden, two texts, no tune; Randolph, two texts, two tunes; Hudson, one text (expurgated), no tune; Brown, four texts, ten tunes; Reed Smith, one text (expurgated), one tune; and so on. Probably other texts than Reed Smith's and Hudson's are expurgated, but by exclusion rather than by substitution, and the expurgation is not so apparent. Perhaps the indelicacy or obscenity of many versions has reduced the number of texts that reach collectors, certainly the number of published texts. Since some of these more free-spoken texts and their tunes may be among the best ballad versions, there is need of a serious scholarly project which will reduce such squeamishness to a minimum. News has recently come of such a project undertaken by a scholar now resident in France. It deserves support.

It may be admitted that neither the texts nor the tunes of this ballad are among the most exciting of the recent phase of Virginia collecting, but the two recorded texts and tunes given below seem to merit publication, perhaps more for the sake of their tunes than for their texts.

Students of ballad style will note how the ballad is built by incremental repetition upon the stanzaic frame.

AA

No local title. Phonograph record (aluminum) made by A. K. Davis, Jr.
Sung by Miss Eleanor Christian, of New Glasgow, Va. Amherst County.
May, 1936. Text transcribed by M. J. Bruccoli. Tune noted by G. W.
Williams and E. C. Mead. Miss Christian learned the song from Miss
Irene Bowling, of New Glasgow, and copied down from her the words of
the text. Note that the song is sung here and in BB by young women
who may not even know of the less polite versions but who no doubt enjoy
the triumph of female wit over the gullible husband.

1   I came in the first night drunk as I could be,
    Found a horse in my horse stall where my horse ought to be.
    "Say come here, little wife, and 'splain this thing to me,
    What's a horse doin' in my horse stall where my horse ought to be?"
    "Cryin' fool, blind fool, can't you never see?
    It's only a milk cow your granny sent to me."
    "Oh, I've travelled this wide world more times than three,
    But a saddle on a milk cow never before did I see."

2 I come in the second night drunk as I could be,
Found a coat on my coat rack where my coat ought to be.
"Say come here, little wifie, and 'splain this thing to me,
What's a coat doin' on my coat rack where my coat ought to be?"
"Cryin' fool, blind fool, can't you never see?
It's only a bed quilt your granny sent to me."
"Oh, I've travelled this wide world more times than three,
But pockets on a bed quilt never before did I see."

3 I come in the third night drunk as I could be,
Found a head on my pillow where my head ought to be.
"Say come here, little wifie, and 'splain this thing to me,
What's a head doin' on my pillow where my head ought to be?"
"Cryin' fool, blind fool, can't you never see?
It's only a cabbage head your granny sent to me."
"Oh, I've travelled this wide world more times than three,
But a mustache on a cabbage head never before did I see."

BB

"Three Nights' Experience." Phonograph record (aluminum) made by A.
K. Davis, Jr. Sung by Misses Virginia and Mary Howdyshell, of Crozet,
Va. Albemarle County. November 11, 1932. Text transcribed by P. C.
Worthington. Tune noted by G. W. Williams. Text independently collected by Fred F. Knobloch, who adds: "The girls learned the song from
their mother, Mrs. Richard Howdyshell, who . . . learned the song when
she was a little girl. This song is also sung to the tune of 'The Rovin'
Gambler.'" Again the song is sung with relish and without offense by
young women. The tune has been slightly abbreviated, in view of its likeness to AA.

1   First night when I came home as drunk as I could be,
     I found a horse in the stable where my horse ought to be.
     "Come here, my little wifie, and explain this thing to me.
     How come a horse in the stable where my horse ought to be?"
     "Shoo fly! Can't you never see?
     It's nothing but a milk cow your granny sent to me."
     "Travelled this world over for a thousand miles or more,
     But a saddle upon a milk cow's back I never did see before."

2   The second night when I come home as drunk as I could be,
     Found a coat a-hanging on the rack where my coat ought to be.
     ["Come here, my little wifie, and 'plain this thing to me.
     How come this coat a-hanging on the rack where my own coat
             ought to be?"]¹
     "Shoo fly! Can't you never see?
     It's nothing but a bed quilt your granny sent to me."
     "Travelled this world over for a thousand miles or more,
     Pockets upon a bed quilt I never did see before."

3   The third night when I came home as drunk as I could be,
     I found a head a-layin' on the pillow where my head ought to be.
     "Come here, my little wifie, and explain this thing to me.
     How come a head a-layin' on the pillow where my head ought
             to be?"
     "Shoo fly! Can't you never see?
     It's nothing but a cabbage head your granny sent to me."
     "I've travelled this world over for a thousand miles or more,
     Mustache on a cabbage head I never did see before."

    1. The lines within brackets are lacking on the record, but they appear in the
MS. Their omission is clearly an inadvertence on the part of the singers.

39

THE WIFE WRAPT IN WETHER'S SKIN
(CHILD, No. 277)

The title seems to have been adapted by Child from the old tale which he supposes to be the source of the ballad, about "the wife lapped in Morrell's skin," Morrell being the husband's old horse flayed to excuse the wife-beating. The title does not appear as a local title in any of Child's versions. "Sweet Robin," "The Cooper of Fife," and first lines are the only titles found there.

As main entry for this ballad Child prints five texts (A-E), all from Scottish sources, and summarizes the story in this fashion (V, 104) : "Robin has married a wife of too high kin to bake or brew, wash or wring. He strips off a wether's skin and lays it on her back, or prins [that is, pins] her in it. He dares not beat her, for her proud kin, but he may beat the wether's skin, and does. This makes an ill wife good."

Not one of these Scottish texts, despite the general outline of their story, bears much formal or verbal resemblance to the well-known American versions. It is therefore a relief to find in the final Additions and Corrections (V, 304-5) two additional texts, one from Massachusetts, with a "Gentle Jenny cried rosemaree" refrain, and one from Suffolk, England, beginning, "There was a man lived in the West" and with a "clashmo" refrain, which immediately suggest two of the types of the ballad found in America, including several of those here printed.

Although the ballad is apparently not known on the Continent or in other languages, it survives in more recent British tradition, but hardly vigorously. It has been found in the English counties of Somerset and Lancashire, in addition to Suffolk (see above); and Greig-Keith (pp. 218-19) print one text and three tunes and report no others as collected but refer in their headnote to "this exceedingly popular song"—as, indeed, one would expect "The Cooper of Fife" to be in Scotland. But the evidence of Old Country popularity is lacking.

The ballad seems to have achieved a somewhat wider distribution in America, but still there is no multiplicity of published texts or tunes. Here are the statistics of some representative collections:

Cox (1), five texts, no tune, plus Cox (2), three texts and one tune; Barry, two texts, one tune; *TBVa*, twelve texts, two tunes; Sharp-Karpeles, five texts, five tunes; Belden, two texts, one tune; Randolph, one text, one tune; Henry, one text, no tune; Hudson, one text, no tune; Morris, one text, one tune; Brown, four texts, four tunes; Eddy, no text or tune; Gardner-Chickering, no text or tune; and so on. As to geographical distribution, the ballad has been collected in the following states: Maine, Vermont, Connecticut, Virginia, West Virginia, Kentucky, North Carolina, Tennessee, Mississippi, Florida, Indiana, Missouri, Nebraska. There are a good many gaps in the list.

Belden (p. 92) has suggested the grouping of texts, roughly, by refrains, as follows: (1) the "Cooper of Fife" form, exemplified by Child C and D, the Lancashire, Aberdeenshire, and Connecticut texts; (2) the "clish-a-ma-clingo" form, exemplified by Child's Suffolk version and *TBVa* A; (3) the "Iero" form, exemplified only by Sharp's Somerset version; (4) the "Dandoo" form, exemplified by most of the *TBVa* texts except A and by most of the other Southern and Midwestern texts; and (5) the "rosemary" form, exemplified by Barry A and B and by most of the other New England texts.

Though we shall undertake no accurate count, it seems obvious that the "Dandoo" form is most common in America, the "rosemary" next, the "clish-a-ma-clingo" third, the "Cooper of Fife" fourth, and the "Iero" so far unknown. The regional preferences are also of interest, especially New England's preference for the "rosemary" form, and the South's preference for the "Dandoo" form, with the "clish-a-ma-clingo" next.

Most of these refrains appear to be, so far as is known, mere nonsense refrains, or rather, sound rather than sense refrains. Some of them (see below) are elaborately interwoven with the meager two-line text, piling up the jargon at the end for sound effect. There is, however, one exception: the "rosemary" refrain, with its varying forms approximating the "Jenny for gentle Rose Marie" of AA, below. This refrain, incidentally, may be borrowed from "The Elfin Knight" (Child, No. 2; *MTBVa*, No. 2, which see) or the two ballads share the refrain. Though the singers seem to understand the line as a combination of proper names and adjectives, it is likely that the original line (preserved in some variants) was "juniper, gentian, and rosemary," a plant-burden which the superstitious supposed would keep off the devil. Miss Broadwood

(JEFSS, II, 12-15) suggests that when a demon disappeared from a song, the plant-burden remained. Barry (pp. 324-25) further suggests that "the ungentle wife may have been regarded as possessed of an evil spirit, so that not only the plant-burden, but also the beating would be part of an exorcising ceremony." But this seems to read too much into the ballad before us in the effort to explain its burden.

Of the twelve Virginia texts previously published in *TBVa,* eight have the "Dandoo" refrain, one the "clish-a-ma-clingo," two are mixed or irregular, and one is without refrain. Of course, all the "Dandoo" texts have some approximation to the "clish-a-ma-clingo" line following the first repetition of the first line of each stanza. The longer refrains following the final lines are extremely varied and extremely nonsensical. Of the seven additional Virginia texts listed in *FSVa,* one has the "rosemary" refrain, two have new refrains of "Kitty Lorn" or a mixture of "Kitty alone" and "Lorum dan dorum," the rest have "Dandoo."

Of the five Virginia texts and two tunes here printed, AA is especially interesting, not only as the only "rosemary" text so far found in Virginia, but because it is the only Virginia text which makes clear the wife's reformation. It is closest to the Child, V, 304, text from Massachusetts and to Barry A, and is the sole representative here of Coffin's Story Type A. BB, from a member of a famous fiddling and singing family, is of the "Dandoo" type, with a good tune. CC, with an exceptionally fine tune, shifts the refrain lines completely in the third stanza, from the "Lorum, dan do-rum" sequence to the "Kitty alone" sequence. DD, from the same neighborhood and probably representing the same version, has the "Kitty Lorn" sequence throughout. It is given especially for comparison with CC. EE is a later-collected and somewhat shortened form of the version from the same family printed as Brown A (II, 186). It is given especially for comparison with Brown A. Note that all the below texts except AA end directly with the husband's jesting or defensive reply about tanning his old wether's skin and do not suggest that the wife has reformed. Coffin, rather unaccountably, does not provide for this story type, which is the usual one for the "Dandoo" texts. See the individual headnotes, below.

Because of minor variations in repeated lines and in refrain lines, the texts are given in full, not in compressed form. See especially CC.

For further discussion concerning this ballad and its sub-divisions, see the article by William H. Jansen in the *Hoosier Folklore Bulletin,* IV (September, 1945), 41.

AA

No local title.   Collected by Miss Alfreda M. Peel, of Salem, Va.   Contributed by Mrs. Orpha Pedneau, Radford State College, Va.   Montgomery County.   February 11, 1932.   This text marks the first appearance of the "rosemary" refrain type in Virginia.   Mrs. Pedneau, though a resident of southwest Virginia, has a New England background.

1   Sweet William went to get him a wife,
      Jenny for gentle Rose Marie,
   To be the pride and joy of his life,
      As the dew flies over the green Vallee.

2   Jenny can' knit, and Jenny can' sew,
      Jenny for gentle Rose Marie,
   So I think I had better have let her go,
      As the dew flies over the green Vallee.

3   One day Sweet William came home from the plow,
      Jenny for gentle Rose Marie,
   Saying, "My dear wife, is my dinner done now?"
      As the dew flies over the green Vallee.

4   Jenny got up and called him a whelp,
      Jenny for gentle Rose Marie,
   "If want any dinner, why, get it yourself,"
      As the dew flies over the green Vallee.

5   Sweet William went straightway to the barn,
      Jenny for gentle Rose Marie,
   And he brought a wether skin under his arm,
      As the dew flies over the green Vallee.

6   He tried it on his little wife's back,
      Jenny for gentle Rose Marie,
   And with two sticks went whickety-whack,
      As the dew flies over the green Vallee.

7   Next day Sweet William came home from the plow,
      Jenny for gentle Rose Marie,
   Saying, "My dear wife, is my dinner done now?"
      As the dew flies over the green Vallee.

8   There stood the table all nice and neat,
      Jenny for gentle Rose Marie,
   "Oh, yes, my dear husband, sit right down and eat,"
      As the dew flies over the green Vallee.

BB

"Dandoo." Phonograph record (aluminum) made by A. K. Davis, Jr. Sung by J. H. Chisholm, of Greenwood, Va. Albemarle County. November 11, 1932. Text transcribed by P. C. Worthington. Tune noted by G. W. Williams. This version is quite close, as might be expected, to one collected with music by Cecil J. Sharp and Maud Karpeles in 1916 from Mr. Chisholm's brother, N. B. Chisholm, of Woodridge, Va. (Cf. *TBVa*, pp. 499-500, 597; Campbell and Sharp, No. 33A.) "Uncle Jim" Chisholm, though well advanced in years when this record was made, was still an expert fiddler and clogdancer as well as a singer. His sister, the late Mrs. Betty ("Aunt Betty") Smith, of Charlottesville, was also a fine singer, well represented in Cecil Sharp's Southern Appalachian collection. A great-niece now carries on the tradition and also sings in a church choir.

1   There was an old man who had a wife,
        Dandoo, dandoo,
    There was an old man who had a wife,
        Clim a clam a clearo,
    There was an old man who had a wife,
    And she plagued him out of his life,
        To mark a lam slam dang clero jomingo.

2   The old man strolled in from his plow,
        Dandoo, dandoo,
    The old man coming from his plow,
        Clim a clam a clearo,
    The old man coming from his plow,
    Saying, "Is my breakfast ready now?"
        To mark a lam slam dang clero jomingo.

3   She says, "There's a piece of bread upon the shelf,"
        Dandoo, dandoo,

"There's a piece of bread upon the shelf,"
      Clim a clam a clearo,
"There's a piece of bread upon the shelf,
If that won't do go bake it yourself,"
      To mark a lam slam dang clero jomingo.

4   This old man went unto his sheep pen,
        Dandoo, dandoo,
     He went unto his sheep pen,
        Clim a clam a clearo,
     He went unto his sheep pen,
     And seen that awful wether skin,
        To mark a lam slam dang clero jomingo.

5   He placed it on his wife's back,
        Dandoo, dandoo,
     He placed it on his wife's back,
        Clim a clam a clearo,
     He placed it on his wife's back,
     And with two sticks went whickety-whack,
        To mark a lam slam dang clero jomingo.

6   "I'll tell your daddy, and mammy and all your friends,"
        Dandoo, dandoo,
     "Tell your mammy and daddy and all your friends,"
        Clim a clam a clearo,
     "Tell your mammy and daddy and all your friends,
     Just how I tanned my wether skin,"
        To mark a lam slam dang clero jomingo.

CC

"The Old Man That Lived in the West." Phonograph record (aluminum) made by A. K. Davis, Jr. Sung by Abner Keesee, of Altavista, Va. Campbell County. August 4, 1932. Text transcribed by P. C. Worthington. Tune noted by Winston Wilkinson. Text independently collected from Mr. Keesee by Miss Juliet Fauntleroy, who adds that Mr. Keesee learned it from Pomp Tuck. Note the change in all three refrain lines after the second stanza, and compare the shorter but more regular refrains in DD from the same locality. Shifts in refrain lines notwithstanding, it is a fine tune, well sung.

Once there was an old man that lived in the West, Lo-rum dan-do-rum, Once there was an old man that lived in the West, Clim-a-

clish-ay am-a-cling-o, Once there was an old man that

lived in the West, He had a wife, she was none of the best,

Just like la-rum clo-ro, Mal-um gal-um, hal-um a lin-go.

Var. (1)

3. "There is a piece of bread lies on the shelf, Kit-ty 'lone,

Kit-ty 'lone, There is a piece of bread lies on the shelf,

Kit ty 'lone and I. There is a piece of bread lies

on the shelf, If you want an-y bet-ter, you may get it your-self,

Jack-a-ma-gees and Kit-ty 'lone, Kit-ty 'lone and I."

Var. (1) (2) (2) (3) (3)

(4) (5) (6)

(6) (6) (6) (6) (6)

1   Once there was an old man that lived in the West,
        Lo-rum, dan do-rum,
    Once there was an old man that lived in the West,
        Clim-a clish-ay, an' a clingo,
    Once there was an old man that lived in the West,
    He had a wife she was none of the best,
        Just like the la-rum clo-ro, ma-lum, ga-lum, ha-lum a lingo.

2   He come whistling from his plow,
        Lo-rum, dan do-rum,
    He come whistling from his plow,
        Clim-a clish-ay, an' a clingo,
    He come whistling from his plow,
    "Wife is breakfast ready now?"
        Just like the la-rum clo-ro, ma-lum, ga-lum, ha-lum a lingo.

3   "There is a piece of bread lies on the shelf,"
        Kitty alone, Kitty alone,
    "There is a piece of bread lies on the shelf,"
        Kitty alone and I,
    "There is a piece of bread lies on the shelf,
    If you want any better you can get it yourself,"
        Jack a-Ma-Gees sang Kitty alone, Kitty alone and I.

4   Took his wife to his sheep pen,
        Kitty alone, Kitty alone,
    He took his wife to his sheep pen,
        Kitty alone and I,
    He took his wife to his sheep pen,
    And soon whacked off an old sheep skin,
        Jack a-Ma-Gees sang Kitty alone, Kitty alone and I.

5   He throwed this skin on his wife's back,
        Kitty alone, Kitty alone,
    He throwed this skin on his wife's back,
        Kitty alone and I,
    He throwed this skin on his wife's back,
    And two little hickories went whickety-whack,
        Jack a-Ma-Gees sang Kitty alone, Kitty alone and I.

6   "I'll tell my father and mother too,"
        Kitty alone, Kitty alone,
    "I'll tell my father and mother too,"
        Kitty alone and I,
    "I'll tell my father and mother too,
    How I've been abused by you,"
        Jack a-Ma-Gees sang Kitty alone, Kitty alone and I.

7 "Go tell your mother and all o' your kin,"
     Kitty alone, Kitty alone,
   "Go tell your mother and all o' your kin,"
     Kitty alone and I,
   "Go tell your mother and all o' your kin,
   And then I'll whip my old sheep skin,"
     Jack a-Ma-Gees sang Kitty alone, Kitty alone and I.

DD

"Kitty Lorn." Collected by Miss Juliet Fauntleroy, of Altavista, Va. Contributed by Mrs. Merkley Keesee Lewis, near Castle Craig, Va. Campbell
County. September 26, 1931. Mrs. Lewis learned it from her father,
Meekin Keesee. This text is quite close to CC, except that Abner Keesee
uses the "lorum dan dorum" refrain in the first two stanzas, and then shifts
to the "Kitty lone" refrain for the rest of the ballad. CC is two stanzas
longer than DD. The text is printed especially for comparison with CC,
from the same locality but with the shifting refrain lines.

1 He come whistling from his plow,
     Kitty Lorn, Kitty Lorn,
   He come whistling from his plow,
     Kitty Lorn and I,
   He come whistling from his plow,
   "Wife, is breakfast ready now?"
     Jack-a-Magees and Kitty Lorn,
     Kitty Lorn and I.

2 "There's a piece of bread lies on the shelf,"
     Kitty Lorn, Kitty Lorn,
   "There's a piece of bread lies on the shelf,"
     Kitty Lorn and I,
   "There's a piece of bread lies on the shelf,
   If you want any better you can get it yourself,"
     Jack-a-Magees and Kitty Lorn,
     Kitty Lorn and I.

3 He throwed the skin on his wife's back,
     Kitty Lorn, Kitty Lorn,
   He throwed the skin on his wife's back,
     Kitty Lorn and I,
   He throwed the skin on his wife's back,
   And two little hickories went whickety-whack,
     Jack-a-Magees and Kitty Lorn,
     Kitty Lorn and I.

4 "I'll tell my mammy and daddy too,"
     Kitty Lorn, Kitty Lorn,

"I'll tell my mammy and daddy too,"
Kitty Lorn and I,
"I'll tell my mammy and daddy too,
The way I've been abused by you,"
Jack-a-Magees and Kitty Lorn,
Kitty Lorn and I.

5 "Go tell your mammy and all your kin,"
Kitty Lorn, Kitty Lorn,
"Go tell your mammy and all your kin,"
Kitty Lorn and I,
"Go tell your mammy and all your kin,
And then I'll whip your wether's skin,"
Jack-a-Magees and Kitty Lorn,
Kitty Lorn and I.

EE

"Dan-you." Collected by R. E. Lee Smith, of Palmyra, Va. Sung by himself. Fluvanna County. September 10, 1932. With this compare Brown A (II, 186), a seven-stanza text which was also contributed to the Virginia collection, but is not reported here. The five stanzas seem to be all that R. E. Lee Smith remembers. The two additional stanzas, 4 and 5 of Brown A, belong between stanzas 3 and 4 here, as follows:

4 He jumped into his sheep pen
And downed with a wether and took off its skin.

5 He tooked the sheepskin to his wife's back
And the way he made the hickory crack!

There are a number of variations between the two texts: Brown A has only one "Dan-you" after the first line and no repetition of it after the second; its final refrain line is "Um to diddle to Dan-you." The dissimilarities are therefore considerable.

1 There was an old man that lived in the West,
Dan-you, Dan-you,
There was an old man that lived in the West,
Dan-you, Dan-you,
And he had him a wife that was none of the best.
Gimme gimme gilly dimpty dillerm Dan-you.

2 One morning this old man come in from the plough,
Dan-you, Dan-you,
One morning this old man come in from the plough,
Dan-you, Dan-you,
Saying, "Wife, is breakfast ready now?"
Gimme gimme gilly dimpty dillerm Dan-you.

3 "There's a piece of bread laying on the shelf,"
      Dan-you, Dan-you,
   "There's a little piece of bread laying on the shelf,"
      Dan-you, Dan-you.
   "And if you want any more, go get it yourself."
   Gimme gimme gilly dimpty dillerm Dan-you.

4 "I will tell my father and brothers three,"
      Dan-you, Dan-you,
   "I'll tell my father and brothers three,"
      Dan-you, Dan-you,
   "Just what a whipping you give me."
   Gimme gimme gilly dimpty dillerm Dan-you.

5 "I don't care if you tell your father and all your kin,"
      Dan-you, Dan-you,
   "I don't care if you tell your father and all your kin,"
      Dan-you, Dan-you,
   "Just how I tanned my mutton skin."
   Gimme gimme gilly dimpty dillerm Dan-you.

40

THE FARMER'S CURST WIFE
(CHILD, No. 278)

Of the group of ballads concerned with the humorous treatment of married life, "The Farmer's Curst Wife" appears to be the most popular. "Our Goodman" treats marital infidelity lightly; "Get Up and Bar the Door" (not represented in this volume, but found in *TBVa*) depicts comically a domestic battle of wits; "The Wife Wrapt in Wether's Skin" jestingly suggests a safe method of wife taming; and now "The Farmer's Curst Wife" comments in amusing hyperbole upon a wife's invincible shrewishness.

A farmer who has a bad wife is glad to have the Devil take her, rather than his eldest son (oxen, himself), away to hell. But in hell she is as incorrigible as ever, kicking or murdering young imps until one of them urges the Devil to take her back to her husband before she murders them all. This he does, and philosophic remarks about the nature of women often end the ballad. Child prints only two versions, one English (A) and one Scottish (B), to much the same effect, except that A has "a chorus of whistlers" instead of the nonsense refrains of B, and B has a final stanza in which the woman on her return asks for the food she had left cooking when she went away years before. Child calls attention to a similar ballad composed by Robert Burns "from the old traditional version," but does not print the composed version, though it may be partly traditional. Child prints a traditional tune for B (V, 423).

The ballad seems to be extremely rare in recent British tradition. Only three English counties seem to have reported it: Sussex, Dorsetshire, and Wiltshire. See *JEFSS,* II (1905-6), 184-85; III (1908-9), 131-32; and Alfred Williams, *Folk Songs of the Upper Thames,* 1923, p. 211. Alfred Williams gives as the title of his Wiltshire text without tune, "There Was an Old Farmer in Sussex Did Dwell," its first line, and adds a note, "This is called the 'Sussex Whistling Song,' but whether it originated in Sussex, or elsewhere, it was very popular in the Thames Valley eighty years ago" (in 1923). The text is practically identical with Child A, which, under the title of "The Farmer's Old Wife," was taken from Dixon's *Ancient Poems, Ballads, and Songs of the Peasantry of England,*

1846. Twentieth-century Scotland seems to muster only a single tune, without words, of this ballad (Greig-Keith, p. 220).

Miss Broadwood has an extremely interesting note on whistling refrains in general and on this ballad in particular in *JEFSS*, V (1914-17), 208-9. "I think . . . that it has not yet been pointed out by any one that in songs where the devil is openly mentioned there is usually a rude nonsense-refrain, and in some cases the company whistles after each verse. Whistling is, of course, intimately connected with magic, and to whistle is to keep away, or put oneself on a comfortable footing with, the dreaded power . . . . I venture, therefore, to think that in the very old song of 'The Farmer's Old Wife' or 'The Devil and the Ploughman,' still so popular throughout our Islands, the whistling after each verse was intended to keep Satan at a distance." For the lore about whistling and nonsense-refrains we are most grateful, but "still so popular throughout our Islands"? The published record scarcely sustains this statement.

In America both texts and tunes are far more abundant and widely scattered. *TBVa* printed thirteen texts (of fifteen available) and six tunes. *FSVa* describes eight items more recently added, with five tunes. In addition to Virginia, the following states have been heard from, usually with a number of versions: Maine, Vermont, Massachusetts, West Virginia, Kentucky, Tennessee, North Carolina, Mississippi, Florida, Texas, Arkansas, Missouri, Michigan, Indiana, Nebraska. The ballad has also been found in Nova Scotia. Sampling of a few representative collections yields the following result—rather less impressive than one would have expected: Barry, five texts and one tune; Cox, one text, no tune; Sharp-Karpeles, seven texts, seven tunes; Belden, two texts, no tune; Randolph, two texts, one tune; Brown, two texts, four tunes; Eddy, no text or tune; Gardner-Chickering, five texts, two tunes; and so on.

The American texts and tunes of this ballad are so extremely complicated, by multiplicity and variation, that any effort to classify them would be a major undertaking and of doubtful validity. Barry (p. 332) has taken the trouble to piece together the story of the five Maine texts, but the result is of little value as to the Maine texts, and of less value outside them. Barry also tells a good anecdote somewhat paralleling the ballad story. He also would wish to make more of the demonological implications of the ballad. Comparing it to the former "The Wife Wrapt in Wether's Skin," he comments, "In the former the demon is exorcised; in the latter, he meets his match in the person of the cursed wife herself." And as to the present ballad, he concludes: "The cursed wife may be regarded as a stock character of medieval stories; but this particular ballad is probably steeped more deeply in demonology than appears from the fragments we have left of the tale." Yes, but we have a superb song left, with or without demonological implications. And America is preserving it, in the usual fashion of varying it by oral circulation, in many out-of-the-way places. Belden (p. 95), on the basis of two or three American texts which have the little devils "dancing on a wire," suggests a relationship to old mystery plays. But the expression does not occur in the Virginia texts.

The present eight versions or variants are essentially an extension of the *TBVa* material, but with five good tunes (AA-EE), especially the three (AA-CC) transcribed from phonograph records, and with many varying details, refrains, and wordings. No whistling refrains have been added, like those in Child A and in *TBVa* C, D, F, and L. In general, the texts look to Child A (except for its chorus of whistlers) rather than B, but occasional details point rather toward B. Naturally, the resemblance to American texts is closer, but not too close. None of the more recent texts has the detail found in Child B and in *TBVa* A, in which the returned wife asks for the food she has left cooking long ago. BB (stanza 11) seems to be the only text in which the returned wife beats her sick husband (Coffin's Story Type F). Coffin's Story Type A would cover most of these versions, with occasional glances at other types. The old man's plowing with cattle or pigs (Coffin's Story Type C) appears in AA, CC, HH, but the pact between the devil and the man is seldom made clear. The individual headnotes call attention to some specific points of interest. In general, the variation concerns the beginning and the ending, and, of course, the refrains, no two of which are alike. The final moral, whether or not a part of the original ballad, is infinitely varied and always amusing. All told, this ballad seems to be one of the better examples of ballad variation.

AA

"Two Little Devils." Phonograph record (aluminum) made by A. K. Davis, Jr. Sung by Mrs. Texas Gladden, of near Roanoke, Va. Roanoke County. August 7, 1932. Text transcribed by P. C. Worthington. Tune noted by G. W. Williams. Mrs. Gladden's strong, accurate, melodious voice does full justice to the lilting rhythms of the jolly song.

♩. = 80

There was an old man who owned a large farm, Fi do, fi
did-dle, fi dum, There was an old man who owned a large farm, He
had no hor-ses to plow his land, With his twice fi do, fi
do, fi did-dle, fi dum.

1 There was an old man who owned a large farm,
      Fi do, fi diddle, fi dum,
   There was an old man who owned a large farm,
   He had no horses to plow his land,
      With his twice fi do, fi do, fi diddle, fi dum.

2 Then he hooked up the sow and the cow to the plow,
      Fi do, fi diddle, fi dum,
   Then he hooked up the sow and the cow to the plow,
   And turned the sod the devil knows how,
      With his twice fi do, fi do, fi diddle, fi dum.

3 Then the devil came to the old man one day,
      Fi do, fi diddle, fi dum,
   Then the devil came to the old man one day,
   Says, "One of your family I'll sure take away,"
      With my twice fi do, fi do, fi diddle, fi dum.

4 Then said the old man, "Now surely I'm done,"
      Fi do, fi diddle, fi dum,
   Then said the old man, "Now surely I'm done,
   For the devil's done come for my oldest son,"
      With his twice fi do, fi do, fi diddle, fi dum.

5 "It's not your oldest son I crave,"
      Fi do, fi diddle, fi dum,
   "It's not your oldest son I crave,
   But your old scolding wife I'll sure take away,"
      With my twice fi do, fi do, fi diddle, fi dum.

6 "Then take her away with all o' your heart,"
      Fi do, fi diddle, fi dum,

"Then take her away with all o' your heart,
I hope from hell she never does part,"
    With a twice fi do, fi do, fi diddle, fi dum.

7   Then he shouldered her up all on his back,
        Fi do, fi diddle, fi dum,
    Then he shouldered her up all on his back,
    And off to hell he went clickety clack,
        With his twice fi do, fi do, fi diddle, fi dum.

8   He set her down at old hell's gate,
        Fi do, fi diddle, fi dum,
    He set her down at old hell's gate,
    And there he made the old gal walk straight,
        With his twice fi do, fi do, fi diddle, fi dum.

9   Then two little devils come rattlin' their chains,
        Fi do, fi diddle, fi dum,
    Two little devils come rattlin' their chains,
    She off with her slipper and knocked out their brains,
        With a twice fi do, fi do, fi diddle, fi dum.

10 Then two little devils peeped over the wall,
        Fi do, fi diddle, fi dum,
    Then two little devils peeped over the wall,
    Says, "Take her back, daddy, she'll murder us all,"
        With a twice fi do, fi do, fi diddle, fi dum.

11 Then he shouldered her up all on his back,
        Fi do, fi diddle, fi dum,
    Then he shouldered her up all on his back,
    Like an old fool he went luggin' her back,
        With his twice fi do, fi do, fi diddle, fi dum.

12 Then said the old man, "We're bound for a curse,"
        Fi do, fi diddle, fi dum,
    Then said the old man, "We're bound for a curse,
    For she's been to hell and she's ten times worse,"
        With a twice fi do, fi do, fi diddle, fi dum.

13 Then surely the women are worse than the men,
        Fi do, fi diddle, fi dum,
    Then surely the women are worse than the men,
    For they've been to hell and come back again,
        With a twice fi do, fi do, fi diddle, fi dum.

BB

"The Farmer's Curst Wife." Phonograph record (aluminum) made by A. K. Davis, Jr. Sung by Horton Barker, of near Chilhowie, Va. Washington

County. August 5, 1932. Text transcribed by P. C. Worthington. Tune noted by E. C. Mead. The song is magnificently sung, with Mr. Barker's usual verve and richness of tone. Mr. Barker's text and tune appear in Brown, IV, 116-17, from a recording of W. A. Abrams, of Boone, N. C. No address for Mr. Barker is given, and no date for the recording. The latter is presumably August 8, 1940, when Mr. Abrams made the recording of Mrs. Timmons and Mrs. York, at Boone (see Brown, IV, 118-19). Since Mr. Barker is a Southwest Virginian, and since the present recording was made on August 5, 1932, and since it was announced and described in *FSVa* (p. 34), published in 1949, whereas Brown, IV, appeared only in 1957, the priority of the Virginia claim is fully established. But perhaps the dual publication is a blessing, since it gives the opportunity to compare two variants of the same song sung by the same singer at an interval of (presumably) eight years.

The tunes are essentially the same, but E. C. Mead's transcription from the Virginia record gives six variants introduced in subsequent stanzas. No variants are recorded in the Schinhan notation. The prior Virginia text is two stanzas shorter than the Brown text: it omits stanzas 4 and 5 of Brown, which read as follows:

> 4 'Then,' said the old man, 'I am outdone,
> For I'm afraid you've come for my oldest one.'

> 5 'It's neither your son nor your daughter I crave,
> But your old scolding woman I now must have.'

In place of Virginia stanza 5, Brown 7 reads:

> 7 The devil put her in a sack,
> And he slung her up across his back.

The stanzas correspond, with minor variations, until the last two, where the order of the stanzas is reversed. The penultimate Virginia stanza:

> 12 Now this is what a woman can do,
> She can outdo the devil and her old man too.

reads in the final North Carolina stanza:

> 15 There's one advantage women have over men,
> They can go to hell and come back again.

Both texts have the rather rare stanza (Virginia 11, North Carolina 13) in which the returned wife beats her sick husband (cf. Coffin's Story Type F).

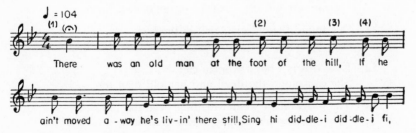

did - dle - i   did - dle - i   day.

1   There was an old man at the foot of the hill,
    If he ain't moved away he's livin' there still,
        Sing hi diddle-i diddle-i fi, diddle-i diddle-i day.

2   He hitched up his horse and he went out to plow,
    But how he got around he didn't know how.

3   The devil came to his house one day,
    Says, "One of your family I'm a-gonna take away."

4   "Take her on, take her on, with a joy in my heart,
    I hope by golly you'll never part."

5   When the old devil got her on his back,
    The old man says, "Now ball the jack."

6   When the old devil got her to the fork of the road,
    He says, "Old lady, you're a terrible load."

7   When the devil got her to the gates of hell,
    He says, "Punch up the fire, we're wanta scorch her well."

8   In come a little devil a-draggin' a chain,
    She up with a hatchet and split out his brains.

9   Another little devil went climbing the wall,
    Says, "Take her back daddy, she's a-murderin' us all!"

10 The old man was a-peepin' out of the crack,
    He saw the old devil come a-waggin' her back.

11 She found the old man sick in the bed,
    And up with the butterstick and paddled his head.

12 Now this is what a woman can do,
    She can outdo the devil and her old man too.

13 The old woman went whistling over the hill,
    "The devil wouldn't have me so I wonder who will?"

CC

"The Old Man That Went Out to Plow." Phonograph record (aluminum) made by A. K. Davis, Jr. Sung by Mrs. Nannie Harrison Ware, of Amherst, Va. Amherst County. May, 1936. Text transcribed by M. J. Bruccoli. Tune noted by G. W. Williams and E. C. Mead. An interesting text and tune, with some confusions. There is more than usual antecedent detail in the first four stanzas. Apparently the devil came for the steer, but took the wife instead. In stanza 4, "white" is sung in the first line, omitted in the repetitions; "him" should read "her" or "my wife," to make sense. The final stanza has an extra line apparently belonging to another stanza, but the singer manages by repetition to get the addition into the stanzaic pattern. The full stanza is given as sung. In stanza 6 it is the devil, not her husband, that the old woman beats. The refrain lines are unusual.

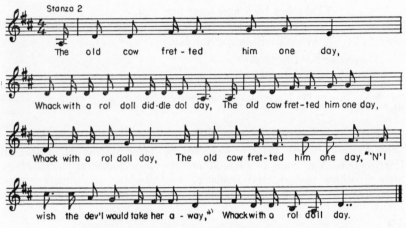

1   There was an old man who learned how to plow,
      Whack with a rol dol diddle dol day,
   There was an old man who learned how to plow,
      Whack with a rol dol day.
   There was an old man who learned how to plow,
      Whack with a rol dol diddle dol day,
   He plowed six steers and one old cow,
      Whack with a rol dol day.

2   The old cow fretted him one day,
     " 'N I wish the devil would take her away."

3   One day it come for the devil to appear,
     "My[1] old man, I want my steer."

4   "Go to the [white] house and take him away,
     For she cursed[2] me every day of my life."[3]

5   He picked her up upon his back,
     Like a peddler with his pack.

6 When he got to hell's big gate,
   She upped the shovel and knocked him on the pate.

7 The little young devils jumped on the wall,
   "Take her back, she'll kill us all."

8 He picked her up upon his back,
   Like a peddler with his pack.

9 "Here, old man, I've brought her back,
   Take her back and treat her well,"
        Whack with a rol dol diddle dol day,
   "Take her back and treat her well,"
        Whack with a rol dol day,
   "Take her back and treat her well,
   She's too mean for heaven and she can't stay in hell,"
        Whack with a rol dol day.

1. Uncertain: could be "Now."
2. Uncertain: could be "fussed."
3. The sense and rhyme in this stanza require mention of the wife. An omitted text has: "Go to the house and get my wife, / She frets me every day of my life."

DD

"The Farmer's Curst Wife." Collected by Miss Martha M. Davis, of Harrisonburg, Va. Sung by Miss Minnie Baylor, a student at Harrisonburg State Teachers College, Harrisonburg, Va. Rockingham County. 1931. Tune noted by Miss Baylor. A compressed but verbally unusual version, with a simple but satisfactory tune. The devil has become "Old Satan."

1 There was an old man lived under the hill,
      Tra la la la la la,
   And if he's not dead he's living there still,
      Tra la la la la la.

2 Old Satan came to him one day to his plow,
   Saying, "One of your family I must have now.

3   "It is not your oldest son I crave,
    But your old scolding wife, and she I must have."

4   "Take her, O Satan, with all my heart,
    That she and you may never part."

5   He took her to his journey's end,
    And made her the mistress of his old den.

6   Seven little imps came crawling the wall,
    She picked up a stick and knocked out their brains.

7   Three more little imps came crawling the wall,
    Saying, "Take her, old dad, she'll kill us all."

8   He took her upon his back,
    And took her back to the old man at last.

9   Saying, "I've been a Satan all the days of my life,
    But never knew torment till I got me a wife."

10 O what will become of the women, pray tell?
    They won't have them in heaven, they get kicked out of hell.

EE

"The Farmer's Curst Wife." Collected by Miss Juliet Fauntleroy, of Altavista, Va. Sung by Mrs. Kit Williamson, of Yellow Branch, Va. Campbell County. March 15, 1934. Tune noted by Mrs. Paul Cheatham, of
Lynchburg, Va. This fragment is the first stanza of *TBVa* H, collected
with music in 1915 from Mrs. Williamson (then Mrs. James Sprouse).
The present tune offers some interesting variants of the earlier tune. (Cf.
TBVa, pp. 512, 600.)

1   Up came the devil to the farmer one day,
        Oh me, sing tu, le la lu,
    Said, "One of your family I'm going to take away,"
        Sing tu, le la, lu le la, lu.

FF

"The Farmer's Curst Wife." Collected by John Stone, of Paint Bank, Va. Sung by T. H. Smith, of Alleghany, Va. Alleghany County. July 7, 1932.

1   There was an old man hired a farm,
    Fi-la-fi-liddle-fi-la,
He had no oxen to carry it on,
    To my twice fi-liddle fi-la-go-down.

Stanza missing.

2   "Now," said the old man, "I am undone,
For the devil has come for my oldest son."

3   "It's not your oldest son I crave,
It's your old scolding wife I'm determined to have."

4   He took her down to hell's own door,
Says, "Go in there and scold no more."

5   And she seen the little devils preparing their chains,
She up with her foot and kicked out their brains.

6   "Now," said the old devil, "we must cast her up higher,"
And she up with her foot and kicked nine in the fire.

7   "Now," says the old devil, "we must carry her back,
For I believe to my soul she will destroy the whole pack."

8   There are three things the devil can't drive,
A hog, a woman, and an old bee hive.

GG

"The Farmer's Wife." Collected by Miss Juliet Fauntleroy, of Altavista, Va. Sung by Mrs. S. A. Goin, near Castle Craig, Va. Campbell County. August 17, 1931.

1   The farmer was guiding his plow one day,
    Tra la la la la la la,
He wished the devil would come and take his wife away,
    Tra la la la la la la,
Six months later he looked up the lane,
    Tra la la la la la la,
And saw the devil coming with a hickory cane,
    Tra la la la la la la.

2   "You may have my oldest son,
If he won't do, you may take two for one."
"Tain't your oldest son I crave,
But your fetch-ed old wife I intend to have."

3   There he taken her in his sack,
    First on his shoulder, then on his back;
    He taken her down to the devil's den,
    The demons said, "Good lady, won't you come in?"

4   "No, no, I'm afraid of your fires and your mud."
    . . . .
    This is to prove that women are meaner than men,
    You send them to the devil and they'll come back again.

HH

"The Farmer's Wife." Collected by E. J. Sutherland, of Clintwood, Va. Sung by Mrs. Lucile G. Johnson, of Clinchco, Va. Dickenson County. May 5, 1932. Mrs. Johnson learned the ballad from her father, T. N. Greiner, who learned it in Wood County, W. Va.

1   There was an old man who had an old steer,
    Whack, with a rol-dol diddle dol dey,
    There was an old man who had an old steer,
    Whack, with a rol-dol-dey,
    There was an old man who had an old steer,
    One old steer and one old cow,
    Adam, Kal-Adam, a-lingo.

2   That old steer fretted him one day,
    Till he wished for the devil to take it away.

3   The day did come for the devil to appear,
    "Now, old man, where is that steer?"

4   "No, old devil, take my wife,
    She frets me every day of my life."

5   He picked her up upon his back,
    Like a peddler with his pack.

6   He got her as far as hell's gate,
    She picked up a shovel and laid him straight.

7   All the little devils jumped on the wall,
    "Take her away, or she'll kill us all."

8   So he picked her up upon his back,
    And like an old fool went packing her back.

9   "Here, old man, here is your wife,
    I wouldn't have her to save your life."

41

THE JOLLY BEGGAR
(CHILD, NO. 279)

Since only a single stanza of this ballad, plus a three-line chorus or refrain, have been found in Virginia, an elaborate headnote might seem unnecessary. But since the ballad is new to the Virginia collection, and since it is one of the very rarest of old ballads still known to survive traditionally, a somewhat fuller background discussion may not be disproportionate.

The two full versions of this ballad which Child prints tell a similar story. A seemingly arrogant beggar stops at a lodging house and demands a fine dinner and bed, although he claims to be penniless. In the middle of the night, he appears naked to the daughter of the household and seduces her, apparently with little or no difficulty or contention from her. Later, when she finds he is the beggar and not a gentleman as she has supposed, she is loud in her misgivings and reproaches. Upon hearing her words, he summons his waiting men by a blast of his horn, and lets his "duddies" fall, revealing his fine clothes beneath. He pays well for his lodging and for the nurse's fee, but leaves the girl, saying in A that if she had been a good woman he would have made her lady of castles eight or nine, in B merely exulting in his cleverness and the excellence of his entertainment.

Considering the mores of the time (1904), it is easy to see why this should be one of five ballads omitted by Sargent and Kittredge from the more popular one-volume Cambridge edition of *The English and Scottish Popular Ballads*. (The four others omitted are Nos. 33, 281, 290, and 299.) Two recent scholarly compilers of ballad books for popular consumption, Professors Leach and Friedman, have followed the example of Sargent and Kittredge. But Child was dedicated to a different task. In a footnote (V, 109), he supposes that the ballad "may have been omitted by Ramsay because he 'kept out all ribaldry' from the Tea-Table Miscellany. This is not a Tea-Table Miscellany, and I have no discretion." Nor has the present editor, who really has no problem of this sort. For the most recent discussion of the whole problem of ribaldry and expurgation of ballads, especially as it concerned Cecil Sharp, see

James Reeves, *The Idiom of the People* (The Macmillan Company, New York, 1958), particularly the section of the Introduction headed "The Revision of Folk Song Words," pp. 8-16. Sharp's amusingly innocuous courtship-conversation song, "O No John," was as originally collected a very realistic sex song of adulterous seduction! See Reeves, pp. 162-63.

Child's two full versions of the ballad are both Scottish: A, with twenty-six stanzas from the "Old Lady's Collection" (see his description of the manuscript sources of the texts, V, 398); and B, with fourteen stanzas from Herd's *The Ancient and Modern Scots Songs,* 1769 edition. To the B version he appends an editorialized text b, and two fragmentary texts, c and d, both recited by Miss Jane Webster of Crossmichael who learned the two versions from different sources. He also prints the ballad as it appears in an English broadside of the second half of the seventeenth century, "The Pollitick Begger-Man," from the Pepys collection, which he suggests may have been the foundation of the ballad, "but the Scottish ballad is a far superior piece of work" (V, 110).

Both A and B are composed of two-line stanzas, A without a refrain, and B with a "fa la la" refrain. This nonsense refrain was changed in Herd's second edition, 1776. "In this we have," Child records (V, 109), "instead of the Fa la la burden, the following, presumably later (see Herd's MSS., I, 5):

> And we'll gang nae mair a roving,
> Sae late into the night,
> And we'll gang nae mair a roving, boys,
> Let the moon shine neer sae bright,
> And we'll gang nae mair a roving."

Bryon had evidently known this old Scottish song when he wrote his quite similar "So We'll Go No More A-Roving" (composed 1817, published 1830). This "gang nae mair" chorus is important in the study of this ballad, because the 1776 version was widely reprinted by songsters (of which Child gives a partial listing, V, 109), and it may have acted as a reviving impetus for this ballad, much as did the broadsides. If so, texts recovered from oral tradition with this "gang nae mair" chorus are apt to be of a more recent tradition than texts with a nonsense chorus or none at all.

Outside of the garlands and song-books cited by Child and others, this ballad has seldom been found in Britain. The Rev. Sabine Baring-Gould secured a copy from the singing of a laborer on Dartmoor in 1889 and informed Child that the ballad which he took down "is sung throughout Cornwall and Devon." The version he collected, however, was a variant of Bb, an inferior editorialized text found in *The Forsaken Lover's Garland,* and its variations "are not the accidents of tradition, but deliberate alterations," according to Child (V, 109).

There are no references to this ballad in Margaret Dean-Smith, nor have any recent English versions of it been found. This would seem to mean that the ballad is extinct, or all but extinct, in recent English tradition. Not so in Scotland. Greig-Keith (pp. 220-23) report six versions or fragments collected from Aberdeenshire, with seven tunes, only two of them overlapping with the texts. Of the texts, the headnote reports, "None of the six wanders far from any of the Child texts," and of the tunes, "None of our airs for this ballad shows any approach to the tune usually associated with the piece." Only one incomplete eleven-stanza text is printed in full; except for omissions, it is very close to Child B. It has a nonsense refrain between the first two lines and another after the second line. One "We'll gang nae mair" verse is reported among the other five texts.

As a transition from the Old World to the New, Barry made the first report of the ballad in America by printing a tune without words in *JAFL,* XXII (January-March, 1909), 79, as "From S. C., Boston, Mass." (Several scholars, including Cox, Randolph, and Coffin, seem to be in error in attributing this text to New Hampshire.) Though sung in Boston, this version comes from County Tyrone, Ireland, and its unpublished text of three stanzas is now in the Manuscript Collection of Phillips Barry in the Harvard University Library, where it has been examined for this headnote. Its stanzas one and three and its nonsense refrain relate it to Child B, and its second stanza corresponds most closely to Child Bb 12, to a lesser extent to Child A 26: "If ye had been an honest girl," and so on. "S. C." is revealed as Mrs. Sarah Carson, Boston, Mass., and the date of the singing as April 4, 1908. This is the first American, Irish-American, record of the song.

Three of the texts listed by Coffin must be recognized as songster texts or texts directly from printed sources. Barry (pp. 475-76) reprints the version from the *Goose Hangs High Songster* (deWitt, Philadelphia, 1866), a seven-stanza text close to Child B, fully expurgated, and with a "gang nae mair a-roving" refrain. The John

Templeton-Oliver Ditson item is obviously a commercial republica-
tion.   The seven-stanza fragment in Cox's *Traditional Ballads
Mainly from West Virginia* (pp. 50-51) is almost identical with
the Barry songster text except for two varying stanzas, and with the
same refrain.   According to Cox, it was contributed by James Main
Dixon, of the University of Southern California, July, 1929.   Says
Cox (p. 100) : "He refers the song to *Lyric Gems of Scotland,* with
music, Sol Fa Edition, Glasgow : John Cameron, 83 Dunlop Street.
No date."   Obviously this fragmentary text is directly from print
and notation—another songster text.

Except for the Virginia fragment, only one other traditional text,
also a fragment, but of three stanzas and with tune, seems to have
been found in America.   Randolph (p. 194) gives it as sung by
Fred Terry, Joplin, Mo., January 30, 1933.   "Mr. Terry says that
it was originally a very long ballad, which he heard sung by a man
named Burkes in Argenta, Ark., about 1905."   Its three stanzas are
parallel to Child B, stanzas 1, 12, 13, but with the more American
"Looney Town" in place of Child B's "landart town" in stanza 1.
It is without the "gang nae mair" chorus or any other refrain, which
suggests an earlier text than those which have been influenced by
songsters.

The Virginia version is the meagerest of fragments : only one
stanza and nonsense chorus of three lines, without tune.   Like the
other recovered fragments, it is most closely related to Child B.
In form it agrees with Child Ba or Child Bc, since the nonsense refrain follows the stanza and is not interpolated.   As in the Randolph fragments, all trace of Scottish dialect has disapppeared.   This
fact seems to indicate an authentic American tradition of the song,
or at least one which shows no influence of the songsters, with
their typical "gang nae mair" chorus.   The Virginia nonsense chorus
is not similar to any other refrain for this ballad.   Mere fragment as
it is, it is a significant trace of a very rare ballad.

AA

"Fragment."   Contributed by R. E. Lee Smith, of Palmyra, Va.   Sung by
his brother, Thomas P. Smith, of Palmyra, Va., and himself.   Fluvanna
County.   July 5, 1931.   A note on the manuscript reads : "Fragments of
songs sang by B. Smith, Zionville, N. C.   He heard these sang 50 or more
years ago."

     1   There was a certain beggar
          That travelled up and down the road;

He called at a tavern
He had never called before.

Chorus

A hoo tho rolly,
A hoo tho rolly,
Hoo tho rolly day.

42

THE GABERLUNYIE-MAN
(CHILD, No. 279, APPENDIX)

Three adjacent ballads in Child, "The Jolly Beggar," "The Gaberlunyie-Man," and "The Beggar-Laddie" (Child, No. 280), are closely related to one another. "The Jolly Beggar," with its seduction and the seducer leaving the girl after revealing himself as a man of rank and property, is the most realistic and ribald of the three; "The Gaberlunyie-Man," with a similar beginning, is rather a romantic elopement with a happy ending; "The Beggar-Laddie," not represented here, is an even more romantic love story, in which the girl voluntarily follows the beggar, to discover that he is a man of property and to become his bride. The problem of classification is a nice one, since "The Gaberlunyie-Man" is almost if not quite as close to "The Beggar-Laddie" as it is to "The Jolly Beggar." Child chooses to print "The Gaberlunyie-Man" as an appendix to "The Jolly Beggar," which it resembles in initial situation but not in outcome or in tone. All points considered, it would seem to the present editor sounder to treat these three beggar songs as separate but related ballads, with "The Gaberlunyie-Man" the middle term equidistant from the other two. Literally, the Scottish term "gaberlunyie" or "gaberlunzie" means beggar's wallet, but by synecdoche it means the beggar himself. Hence the three titles are very close.

Child apparently printed "The Gaberlunyie-Man" as an appendix also in part because the text which he gives from Ramsay's *Tea-Table Miscellany,* 1724, and subsequent reprints, had been subjected to a good deal of editorial revision—enough, he may have thought, to bring its traditional character into question. But Child knew that the ballad was in oral tradition because he refers to "recited copies, as the 'Old Lady's Collection,' No. 13 (Skene MS., p. 65), and Motherwell's MS., p. 31" (V, 115). The fact that Child A of "The Jolly Beggar" comes from "The Old Lady's Collection," and that she knew "The Gaberlunyie-Man" as well, indicates that both ballads had some form of life as distinct and separate ballads in the mind of one singer or reciter. Why Child failed to present the two traditional or "recited" texts available to him and to give them precedence over Ramsay's revised text, as would be customary, he fails to explain.   Nor does he attempt to justify his presentation of the ballad as an appendix.   He simply states (V, 110): " 'The Gaberlunyie-Man' is given as an appendix."   Elsewhere (V, 109) he seems to support Percy in taking to task Horace Walpole for his confounding of this ballad with "The Jolly Beggar."

Can it be that the great Child was guilty of two errors with respect to "The Gaberlunyie-Man": (1) in relegating it to a position of dependency upon "The Jolly Beggar" and not acording it full status as an independent ballad; and (2) in failing to recognize its genuine traditional character, now widely accepted by scholars?   It would seem so.

The traditional claim that King James V of Scotland (1512-42) was the author of both "The Jolly Beggar" and "The Gaberlunyie-Man" is summarily disposed of by both Child (V, 109) and Greig-Keith (pp. 220, 223).   This would tend to dispose also of the traditional claim that the ballad chronicles one of King James's adventures in the guise of "the goodman of Ballangeich" (Greig-Keith, p. 223; Ord, p. 377).

The story as given in Ramsay's text is briefly this: An old poor man seeks lodging at a home, and immediately shows much attention to the daughter.   He tells her that were she black as her father's hat he would desire to take her with him; she replies that were she as white as the snow, she would go with him.   They form a plot, and while the mother sleeps, they flee together.   When the beggar's absence is discovered next morning, the mother fears that something may be stolen, but is relieved to find nothing gone.   She calls for the regular work to commence, and then discovers that her daughter is missing.   She sends out searchers, but they are apparently unsuccessful.   The daughter is happy with her lover, he with her, and in the concluding stanzas he describes how he will win their living and merrily "carry the gaberlunyie on."   Ramsay's text ends here, but Child (V, 115) refers to recited copies in which "the girl is made to come back again to see her mother (or the gaberlunyieman brings her) 'wi a bairn in her arms and ane in her wamb;' but for all that a fine lady, 'wi men- and maid-servants at her command.' "   The ribaldry of "The Jolly Beggar" is completely lacking.

"The Gaberlunyie-Man" has not often appeared in recent times, except possibly in Scotland.   Margaret Dean-Smith reports no texts in England, and none seem to have been reported from England since her date of publication.   In Scotland, however, both Greig-Keith and Ord find the ballad fairly popular in Aberdeenshire.   All recovered texts, including the two North American ones, can be traced directly back to Scottish sources.

Greig-Keith (pp. 223-26 and 276-77) print only one text in full, a version the equivalent of twenty four-line stanzas, out of a total of seven versions and fragments collected. They also print five of a total of twelve tunes collected. Four of the five collated texts "have a happy conclusion, relating the daughter's triumphant return with the gaberlunzie man and a 'quiver' fast becoming full" (pp. 223-24). This feature is in accord with the recited texts known to Child.

The only other British text to come to light is that published by John Ord in *The Bothy Songs and Ballads of Aberdeen, Banff, and Moray, Angus and the Mearns,* Paisley, 1930, pp. 375-77. The single text, with tune, is called "The Beggar Man," and consists of eighteen four-line stanzas, each followed by a nonsense refrain. The ending is the triumphant return of the beggar and daughter to the girl's mother. Of the ballad Ord writes (p. 377): "There are several versions of this well-known ballad, but the one here printed is the most common in the bothies and farm kitchens in the North of Scotland. I have given it preference to the others, as the words are specially adapted to the old bothy air, to which they are set. I heard the song first sung to this air at a Sunday school soiree in the parish of New Byth, Aberdeenshire, upwards of forty years ago."

Only two texts of this ballad seem to have been recovered from North America, a text published by Barry in *British Ballads from Maine,* pp. 333-35, and the present Virginia text. Without comment Barry gives his text full footing with the other Child ballads under the title "The Gaberlunyie-Man (Child 279, Appendix)." Its local title is "The Beggar's Bride," and the text was written down by Mrs. James McGill of Chamcook, New Brunswick, who was born in Scotland. Her air, which Barry publishes, was noted by George Herzog. The text has thirteen four-line stanzas, each followed by a nonsense line. The similarity of the Barry and Ord texts in placing near the beginning several stanzas which Ramsay places toward the end may indicate that their traditional place was at the beginning and that Ramsay replaced them at the end, perhaps in preference to the traditional happy conclusion.

The Virginia text was contributed by Miss Ruth K. Anderson, of Arrington, Virginia, as sung for her by Mrs. Jay P. Eaton, of Lansing, Michigan, who was born in Scotland. Mrs. Eaton seems to have visited Virginia in the summer of 1935, when the song was collected. "The Beggar Man," as its local title calls it, has fifteen four-line stanzas, each followed by a nonsense line, and is thus the longest text recovered in North America. Since Barry's informant, Mrs. McGill, was a resident of New Brunswick, the Virginia text seems to be the only instance of the recovery of this ballad in the United States. Miss Anderson writes of Mrs. Eaton, the singer: "Mrs. Eaton was born in Scotland. She was one of a family of fourteen children. Her parents with their children came to the United States when Mrs. Eaton was about sixteen years old. When I heard her sing this and asked for a copy, she said she had never had a copy, that it was a song she learned in the old country."

The Virginia text does not differ greatly from Barry or Ord, except that it adds more to the conclusion when the beggar returns with the daughter. Virginia 1 and 2 parallel Ramsay, Barry, Ord and Greig 1 and 2. Virginia 3 and 4 parallel Ramsay and Greig 5 and 6. The Virginia text lacks the stanzas which Barry and Ord give near the beginning but which Ramsay places near the end. Virginia 5 parallels Ramsay 7: the two make up a plot. Virginia 6 combines Ramsay 8 and 9: the old wife rises and misses the beggar all in one stanza. Virginia 7 parallels Ramsay 10: a check is made to see if the beggar has taken anything. Virginia 8 and 9 parallel Ramsay 11 and 12: the daughter is sent for, but it is "the auld man" who goes for her, rather than the servant girl as in Ramsay. Virginia 10 parallels Ramsay 14: a search is made for the beggar. Virginia 10 differs from Ramsay 14, however, in that it leads directly into the happy conclusion. Then follow Virginia stanzas 11 to 15, concluding the ballad with the return of the daughter "with servants one at every hand." A feature of the Virginia text is that when the beggar reappears, he asks what the mother would give to see her daughter again, and she recognizes him:

"Oh," quay the auld wife, "I little doubt it's ye,
An' I wish I had ye slain."

The daughter then appears with silks and satins such that no other lady in the land can compare with her and blesses the hour when she went away with the beggar man.

There are many changes of language and expression as between the several versions, even when their stanzas closely parallel each other as to action. The Virginia text supplies its quota of new and interesting variants.

Though Virginia cannot claim much of this ballad except its brief residence in the state and the honor of collecting it and adding it to the Virginia archives—and now of publishing it—the ballad is presented here, without apology, in the full panoply of its very un-Virginian Scottish dialect!

AA

"The Beggar Man." Contributed by Miss Ruth K. Anderson, of Arrington, Va. Sung by Mrs. Jay P. Eaton, of Lansing, Mich. Nelson County. Summer, 1935.

1 A beggar man com' o'er yon lea,
    Seeking haulp for charitee,
    He wa' seeking haulp for charitee,
    "Could ye lodge a beggar man?"
      Lau de lee au tau rau ray.

2 The night wa' cold and somewhat wet,
    Dauwn by the fireside the ault creeter crapt,
    He flung his meal pock off his back,
    As he lulted and sang.
      Lau de lee au tau rau ray.

3 "Lassie, oh lassie, if ye wa' as black,
    As black as the crauwn o' your dady's hat,
    I wauld tie my meal pock on your back
    And awa' wi me ye would gang."
      Lau de lee au tau rau ray.

4 "Laddie, oh laddie, if I wa' as white,
    As white as the snauw that lies on yon dyke,
    I would dress myself so lady-like
    And awa' wi ye I would gang."
      Lau de lee au tau rau ray.

5 An' then the twa made up the plot
    To rise in the morning ere the folk wa' up,
    To rise in the morning ere the folk wa' up,
    And out of the house they would gang.
      Lau de lee au tau rau ray.

6 Right early in the morning the old wife rose,
    She missed the beggar and his clothes,
    She missed the beggar and his clothes,
    "Hurley who," the old wife cried, "Yon beggar man's awa'."
      Lau de lee au tau rau ray.

7 Some ran to cupboard, some ran to kest,
    "There's nothing aw' that we can miss,"
    Saying quay the old wife, "We are happy blest,

There's none o' our good gear gang."
Lau de lee au tau rau ray.

8 "Go bin, auld man, and waken the bairn,
The kurns to kurn and the clauthes's to iron,
The kurns to kurn and the clauthes's to iron,
Bid her come speedily bin."
Lau de lee au tau rau ray.

9 The auld man bin where the darter lay,
The sheets wa' cold and she wa' awa',
The sheets wa' cold and she wa' awa',
They didn't know how nor when.
Lau de lee au tau rau ray.

10 Some rode horseback and some ran afoot,
The auld wife liken to lost her wits,
But never a sight o' the beggar wa' saw
Till seven long years wa' gang.
Lau de lee au tau rau ray.

11 When seven long years had passed and gang,
The beggar man come seeking haulp for charitee,
He wa' seeking haulp for charitee,
"Could ye lodge a beggar man?"
Lau de lee au tau rau ray.

12 "Oh beggars, beggars, we dinna like them,
We had one darter, we had but one,
And awa' wi' a beggar she did gang,
We knew not when nor where."
Lau de lee au tau rau ray.

13 "Auld wife, auld wife, what would ye gi'
If a sight o' your darter I let ye see?"
"Oh," quay the auld wife, "I little doubt it's ye,
An' I wish I had ye slain."
Lau de lee au tau rau ray.

14 "Oh, yonder she's a-coming up yon sand
With servants one at every hand,
And there's no lady in all the land
That can compare with Jean."
Lau de lee au tau rau ray.

15 Yonder she's a-coming up the bower
With silks and satins in a flower,
Now she holds up her hand and blesses the hour
That she went wi' the beggar man.
Lau de lee au tau rau ray.

43

THE SWEET TRINITY (THE GOLDEN VANITY)
(CHILD, No. 286)

Drastic excision has been practiced here, in printing only a single good text with its excellent tune from phonographic recording.

Child printed only three versions of the ballad, plus two tunes, but listed or collated many variants of the texts. He first suggested that traditional copies, such as his B and C versions (which are found also on later broadsides), probably derived from his A text, a late seventeenth-century Pepysian broadside entitled "Sir Walter Raleigh Sailing in the Low-Lands." He finds the conclusion of the older broadside so inadequate as "to impel almost any singer to attempt an improvement" (V, 136). He admits the possibility, however, that "the ultimate source of the traditional copies may be as old as the broadside." No attempt is made to establish an historical event as the source of the ballad.

The usual story of the ballad runs about as follows: Two ships meet in the Lowlands. The cabin-boy of The Golden Vanity (or other such name) offers to sink the hostile ship, The Turkish Revelee (or other such name), in return for land, fee, and the captain's daughter in marriage. He swims to the other ship and sinks it by boring holes with an auger, then returns to his own ship to claim his reward. Conclusions vary. In Child A, the captain will give gold and fee but not his daughter, and the ship-boy says farewell—a very lame conclusion. In B, the cabin-boy has to threaten to sink his own ship before his shipmates take him on board and prove better than their word. In C, after the captain's refusal to take the boy aboard, he is taken up by his messmates and dies on deck, whereupon his body is sewed in a cowhide and thrown overboard. The boy's refusal to sink his own ship because of the love he bears his shipmates (see TBVa C, D) seems to appear only in certain American texts. In Belden A the boy's ghost appears to the captain months later; in Belden C the captain and his crew go down with the cabin-boy. And so on. The names and nationalities of the ships are constantly varied.

Though the ballad appears to be unknown in other lands and languages, it has been scattered far and wide and collected near and far in English-speaking countries. In England in recent times, texts or tunes or both have been recovered from Sussex, Lancashire, Cornwall, Wiltshire, and possibly another county or two. In Scotland the tradition appears to be fading somewhat: Greig-Keith (pp. 238-39) report only a single text (with a happy ending) and a single tune from Aberdeenshire; but Ord (pp. 450-51) adds another record from the North Country. After all, the ballad is of English origin.

North America has been strongly heard from. In Canada the ballad has been found in New Brunswick, Nova Scotia, and Newfoundland. In the United States it has been reported from the following states: Maine, Vermont, Massachusetts, Pennsylvania, Virginia, West Virginia, Kentucky, Tennessee, North Carolina, Mississippi, Florida, Arkansas, Indiana, Illinois, Michigan, Wisconsin, and Nebraska—often in multiple versions or variants.

Barry (p. 347), noting that copies of this song are found about equally in New England and in the Southern Appalachians, argues overboldly: "One could hardly have better evidence of the date when it came to America. 'With the very first emigrants,' is the only answer." The argument is far from conclusive. Besides, there are regional differences in the texts: there is no "happy ending" in his Maine texts, nor do the New England versions include the cabin-boy's gallant refusal to sink his captain's ship—a detail found only in the South and Midwest. One would not undertake to prove that the ballad was not brought over with the earliest colonists, but it might be well to remember that Child's earliest known text is a broadside of 1682-85.

A sampling of some representative American collections produces the following results: *TBVa*, six texts and one tune; *FSVa*, four texts and two tunes; Cox (1), three texts, no tune, plus Cox (2), three texts, one tune; Barry, six texts, two tunes; Sharp-Karpeles, eleven texts, eleven tunes; Henry, three texts, one tune; Belden, three texts, no tune; Randolph, five texts, three tunes; Brown, six texts, six tunes; Eddy, no text or tune; Gardner-Chickering, one text, one tune; and so on.

The omission of three texts and one additional tune described in *FSVa* puts the proper emphasis here where it should be, on Mr. Barker's fine text and finer, more varied tune. Certain facts have made the omission of the three of four items easier. The R. E.

Lee text of fourteen stanzas and chorus has been published in the Brown Collection as version A (Brown, II, 191-92).   Only the tune would have been added to Mrs. Plummer's five-stanza text published in *TBVa,* pp. 518-19, and since there is reason for a slight suspicion of Mr. Stone's notation, the tune is omitted.   The six-stanza text of Mr. Austin (aged 86) is of some interest, but it is garbled at some points and represents much the same version as Mr. Barker's, below but with variations.   Mr. Austin's first stanza giving the names of both ships is unusual:

> There was a ship sailing on the sea,
> It went by the name of the Turkish Revelrie.
> There was another that sailed on the sea,
> It went by the name of the Golden Willow Tree.

The captain offers to give the boy "my daughter and twenty-four pounds" if he will sink the ship "before she makes her round." Then follows this probably telescoped stanza:

> Out jumps he with a tool for the use,
> To cut eleven notches and let in the juice.
> Some ran with their hats, while others their caps,
> Trying to stop up the salt water gaps.

The ballad ends with the boy's noble refusal to sink the ship because of his respect for the crew, his farewell, and his own sinking "in the lowland, lonesome, so low."   These details and wordings should be compared with the fuller version below, from another southwest Virginia county.

The present Virginia text differs in important particulars from all three of the Child texts.   It obviously belongs with the more usual American texts, especially the Southern and Midwestern ones, represented by Coffin's Story Type A, in which the boy dies of drowning after making his gesture of abnegation.   He is not brought aboard to die on deck and have his body sewn in a sack and thrown overboard, as in Child C and Barry A.   Since the refrain lines are considerably varied, it is necessary to repeat the printing of them after every stanza.

The varied and beautifully sung pentatonic tune has been much admired.

AA

"The Turkish Revelee."   Phonograph record (aluminum) made by A. K. Davis, Jr.   Sung by Horton Barker, of near Chilhowie, Va.   Washington

County. August 15, 1932. Text transcribed by P. C. Worthington. Tune noted by E. C. Mead, who comments upon its "very fine sinuous line" and "figured style."

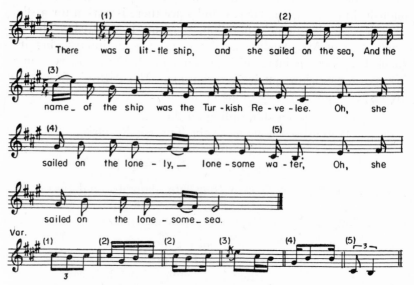

There was a lit-tle ship, and she sailed on the sea, And the name of the ship was the Tur-kish Re-ve-lee. Oh, she sailed on the lone-ly, — lone-some wa-ter, Oh, she sailed on the lone-some sea.

1   There was a little ship, and she sailed on the sea,
    And the name of the ship was the Turkish Revelee.
        Oh, she sailed on the lonely, lonesome water,
        Oh, she sailed on the lonesome sea.

2   Up stepped a little sailor saying, "What'll you give to me
    To sink that ship in the bottom of the sea,
        If I'll sink her in the lonely, lonesome water,
        If I'll sink her in the lonesome sea?"

3   "I have a house and I have land,
    And I have a daughter that shall be at your command,
        If you'll sink her in the lonely, lonesome water,
        If you'll sink her in the lonesome sea."

4   He bowed on his breast and away swum he,
    He swum till he came to the Turkish Revelee,
        And he sunk her in the lonely, lonesome water,
        Oh, he sunk her in the lonesome sea.

5   He had a little auger, all fit for to bore,
    He bored nine holes in the bottom of the floor,
        Oh, he sunk her in the lonely, lonesome water,
        Oh, he sunk her in the lonesome sea.

6 He bowed on his breast and away swum he,
   He swum till he came to the Golden Willow Tree,
      As she sunk in the lonely, lonesome water,
      Oh, she sunk in the lonesome sea.

7 "Captain, will you be as good as your word,
   Or either will you take me in on board?
      For I've sunk her in the lonely, lonesome water,
      Oh, I've sunk her in the lonesome sea."

8 "No, I won't be as good as my word,
   And neither will I take you in on board,
      Oh, you've sunk her in the lonely, lonesome water,
      Oh, you've sunk her in the lonesome sea."

9 "If it were not for the love I have for your men,
   I'd do unto you just as I've done unto them,
      I'd sink you in the lonely, lonesome water,
      Oh, I'd sink you in the lonesome sea."

10 He bowed on his breast and down sunk he,
   A-bidding farewell to the Golden Willow Tree,
      Oh, he sunk in the lonely, lonesome water,
      Oh, he sunk in the lonesome sea.

44

THE MERMAID
(CHILD, No. 289)

The folklore of the mermaid is extensive. Wimberly's index
(p. 457) lists seventeen references. She can be at will a lady on
land or a fish in the sea; she has the power to transform others; a
mortal's infidelity to her is punished by death, and so on. Her ac-
tivities are mainly malicious, and nothing is surer than that the appearance of a mermaid at sea forebodes disaster and shipwreck.
Such an appearance, followed by the despairing speeches of the ship's
company (captain, mate, cabin-boy, cook) and the sinking of the
ship, is the matter of this ballad.

A similar detail marks certain versions of "Sir Patrick Spens"
(Child, No. 58). Child's headnote remarks (II, 19): "A mermaid
appears to the navigators . . . and informs them . . . that they will
never see dry land, or are not far from land . . . which, coming from
a mermaid, they are good seamen enough to know means the same
thing. . . . If nothing worse, mermaids at least bode rough weather,
and sailors do not like to see them. . . . They have a reputation for
treachery: there is in a Danish ballad . . . one who has betrayed
seven ships." Wimberly (p. 287) mentions a Norse ballad in which
"the mermaid's magic is counteracted by the power of runes, which
the hero knows how to write." But the captain in the present bal-
land, who has also set sail on Friday in defiance of the omens, is
no such hero or master of rune-lore, and his ship goes down.

Child prints six texts of the ballad, part English, part Scottish,
at least two from broadside or garland, four from manuscript or
tradition. His oldest and longest text, A, has fourteen stanzas and
is from a garland of about 1765. The longest of the other five texts
runs to only six stanzas, and all five tell much the same story, slightly less detailed than A.

Both British and American texts of the song are quite recent as
ballad texts go and many versions show the influence of broadside or
songster publication. Kittredge gives an impressive list of such
publication of this ballad in *JAFL*, XXX (July-September, 1917),
333, and Coffin's references (p. 157) add to the list. Barry, among
others, is quite shameless in admitting songster texts to full status.

He prints as his D text the version from *The Forget-Me-Not Songster,* and his B text was learned "from a good old songster." Since
one of his five texts is only a three-line trace, since one comes from
New Brunswick and another from Prince Edward Island, we are
left with only a single apparently traditional text from Maine—itself
very close to the songster texts. No wonder he concludes (p. 368),
"No ballad has less interest to the student than this." There is
some general truth in the remark, and the fact is largely due to songster infiltration. When a song has appeared on so many broadsides
and in so many songsters, it behooves the folk collector and editor
to handle it with care.

The ballad persists in recent English and Scottish tradition.
Versions have been collected from the English counties of Cheshire,
Devonshire, Dorsetshire, Hampshire, and Oxfordshire, perhaps
another one or two. Greig-Keith (pp. 242-43) report five frag-
ments from Aberdeenshire, but print only one, with three tunes.
Ord (pp. 333-34) reports a version from the North of Scotland.

Canadian records of the ballad have come from New Brunswick,
Prince Edward Island, and Nova Scotia. The roster of American
states in which the ballad has been found includes Maine, Vermont,
Massachusetts, Virginia, West Virginia, Kentucky, Tennessee,
North Carolina, Mississippi, Florida, Texas, Arkansas, Missouri,
Illinois, Iowa, and Wyoming. In America especially, as suggested
above, the ballad owes some of its currency to its appearance on
broadsides, in popular songsters, and in college song-books, among
them at least three editions of *The Forget-Me-Not Songster, Uncle
Sam's Naval and Patriotic Songster, The American College Song-
ster,* and the widely distributed *Heart Songs.* In America, as in
Child E, the ballad sometimes takes a burlesque turn.

The statistical record in America would seem to indicate that
some folk collectors had been a bit chary about a ballad so well
known in print (as well they might be): *TBVa,* thirteen texts, two
tunes; *FSVa,* three texts, one tune; Barry (see above); Cox (1),
one text, no tune, with no text or tune in Cox (2); Sharp-Karpeles,
four texts, four tunes; Randolph, three texts, two tunes; Morris,
one text, no tune; Eddy, no text or tune; Henry, one text, no tune;
Gardner-Chickering, no text or tune; Brown, two texts, one tune;
Chappell, one text, one tune; and so on.

Of the three Virginia versions given below, AA is a full text of
seven stanzas and is unusual in several ways: it is straightforward
narrative, without chorus or refrain; it has four spokesmen: captain,

mate, cabin-boy, and (unusually) ship's doctor, who reports a dream of mermaids; the name of the ship is given as "The White-swan"; and the final stanza records the count of the ship's company and of those saved:

> The Whiteswan had four hundred sixty men,
>   And only nine was saved,
> The rest went down, down to the bottom of the sea,
>   Where the mermaid do stay.

Several of these details, the first and last particularly, connect the text with the longer Child A text, where the corresponding stanza from the middle of the ballad reads:

> In all, the number that was on board
>   Was five hundred and sixty-four,
> And all that ever came alive on shore
>   There was but poor ninety-five.

American texts that point toward Child A are extremely rare and seem not to have found entrance to the song-books, where the chorus and refrain versions are preferred. Most American texts, like BB below, are shortened forms of the story and tend to follow the Child sequence B-C-D. The tune to BB is a fairly usual one, not unlike certain songster tunes but not known to trace back to any songster. CC, with its unusual avaricious speech of the captain, and the almost comical speech of the "dirty old dishrag" of a cook, has definitely taken a turn to burlesque, like Child E. It is a pity Mrs. Tyler did not write out the rest of the stanzas. In the three items given below we have a sort of microcosm of the three Child types of the ballad, perhaps of the three American types as well. There is wide variation in the order of stanzas and in the position of the chorus, as here.

AA

"Doom Ship" or "Mermaid." Contributed by R. E. Lee Smith, of Palmyra, Va. Sung by his brother, Thomas P. Smith, of Palmyra, Va., and himself. Fluvanna County. May 19, 1931. Mr. Smith writes that this song was sung "by Mrs. Chaney Smith, of Zionville, N. C., 30 years ago. She was my grandmother. She said she had heard it when a child. She died at 85." A very unusual text. See the general headnote, above. Since the ballad mentions London and Exeter, the Richmond Town is probably the English, not the Virginian city. But in a Florida text (Morris, pp. 328-29), the captain has a wife "in the forest of New York," and "the man of the ship" has a wife "in old Virginia state."

1 One early morn our ship sailed,
   And we was not a hundred miles from land,
When we saw a handsome maid
   With a comb and glass in her hand.

2 Then up spoke the captain of our good ship,
   And a noble man was he,
"I've a wife in London Town,
   And a widow she soon will be."

3 And up ran the mate of our good ship,
   And a fine man was he,
"I've a daughter in Exeter Town,
   And a orphan she soon will be."

4 Then up walked the little cabin-boy,
   A nice pretty boy was he,
"I have a mother in Richmond Town,
   And she will mourn for me."

5 Then up come the ship's doctor,
   A lively man was he,
"Last night I dreamed I was down the bottom of the sea,
   With two pretty mermaids setting me."

6 Then round about, then round about,
   And round about once more,
Then down, down went our good ship
   To never rise any more.

7 The Whiteswan had four hundred sixty men,
   And only nine was saved,
The rest went down, down to the bottom of the sea,
   Where the mermaid do stay.

BB

"The Gallant Ship." Contributed by Miss Margaret Purcell, of Greenwood, Va. Sung by her mother, Elizabeth Ashton Garrett Purcell (Mrs. S. H.), of Greenwood, Va., in the early 1890's. May, 1934. Tune noted by Winston Wilkinson. Unlike most of Mrs. Purcell's songs, text and tune seem relatively undistinguished but are worth preserving.

lands-men are ly-ing down be-low, down be-low, while the

lands-men are ly-ing down be-low. 1. Out spoke the captain of

our _ gal-lant ship, And a fine spok-en man was he: "I've a

wife and chil-dren, too, _ at home, Who_ this night are look-ing out for

me, out for me, who this night are look-ing out for me."

(1) actually:

Chorus

And the stormy winds do blow, blow, blow,
  And the raging seas do flow.
And we poor sailors are toiling at the top,
  While the landsmen are lying down below, down below,
  While the landsmen are lying down below.

1 Out spoke the captain of our gallant ship,
     And a fine spoken man was he,
   "I've a wife and children too at home,
     Who this night are looking out for me, out for me,
     Who this night are looking out for me."

Chorus

2 Out spoke a sailor on our gallant ship,
     And a fine spoken man was he,
   "I've a father and a mother too at home,
     Who this night are looking out for me, out for me,
     Who this night are looking out for me."

Chorus

3 Three times around went our gallant ship,
     And three times around went she,

And as she was going the third time around
She sank to the bottom of the sea, of the sea,
She sank to the bottom of the sea.

Chorus

CC

No local title. Contributed by Mrs. Royal Holt Tyler, of Madison Heights, Va. Sung by her mother years ago in Mexico. Amherst County. February 15, 1932. Like Child E and some American texts, this version definitely takes a burlesque turn. See the general headnote, above.

1 Up stepped the captain of our gallant ship,
   A very brave man was he.
   Said he, "I care more for my coffers and my gold
   Than I do for the whole companie."

Chorus

Oh, the stormy winds may blow, blow, blow,
And the raging seas overflow, flow, flow,
And we poor sailors are a toiling at the ropes,
And the landsmen are lying down below.

2 Up stepped the cook of our gallant ship,
   A dirty old dishrag was he.
   Said he, "I care more for my pots and my pans
   Than I do for the whole companie."

And so on through the list of the crew.

45

JOHN OF HAZELGREEN
(CHILD, No. 293)

Back in 1929 when *TBVa* printed ten texts and three tunes of this ballad, the editor (who is also the present editor) stated that they appeared to be the only traditional copies to be printed from American sources up to that time. The statement was correct. But in the thirty-year interval the situation has changed somewhat. Yet "John of Hazelgreen" is still an uncommon ballad. Here added to the Virginia record of the ballad is a single good text with a tune from a phonographic recording.

Child prints five texts of the ballad, all apparently from Scottish sources or collectors. The first four tell much the same story, with slightly varying details; the fifth, Child E, is a two-stanza fragment of the traditional song upon which Sir Walter Scott is alleged to have built his "Jock of Hazeldean," first printed in 1816. Since later texts often omit some details, it will be well to have in mind Child's summary of his A text: "A gentleman overhears a damsel making a moan for Sir John of Hazelgreen. After some compliment on his part, and some slight information on hers, he tells her that Hazelgreen is married; then there is nothing for her to do, she says, but to hold her peace and die for him. The gentleman proposes that she shall let Hazelgreen go, marry his eldest son, and be made a lady gay; she is too mean a maid for that, and, anyway, had rather die for the object of her affection. Still she allows the gentleman to take her up behind him on his horse, and to buy clothes for her at Biggar, though all the time dropping tears for Hazelgreen. After the shopping they mount again, and at last they come to the gentleman's place, when the son runs out to welcome his father. The son is young Hazelgreen, who takes the maid in his arms and kisses off the still-falling tears. The father declares that the two shall be married the next day, and the young man have the family lands." Child B, C, and D have the shopping done in Edinburgh, and D adds the detail that the young people have seen each other only in dreams. The two-stanza Child E consists of the conversational exchange between the man and the girl, with the refrain lines:

But [or And] aye she loot the tears down fa
For John o Hazelgreen.

It is essentially a lyrical lament, without conclusion.

Since the time of Child, no traditional trace of the ballad seems to have been found in England. From Scotland (Aberdeenshire) Greig-Keith (pp. 244-45) report only "a most imperfect fragment" of ten lines, in which the weeping lady describes Hazelgreen. The editors note the preservation of "a stanza about his hair which does not appear elsewhere and seems to be a survival from an older version or a transference from another ballad." No tune is given, but it is noted that tunes are given by two earlier Scottish collectors, Kinloch and Christie.

The next chapter in the ballad's recorded history is the recovery, in the teens and early twenties of the present century, of the ten traditional texts and three tunes from Virginia, published in *TBVa*, pp. 529-36 and 604. Of these, the first nine texts, A-I, bear no very close resemblance to any Child text and may well represent a different version of the ballad as old as, perhaps older than, any of the late eighteenth- and early nineteenth-century texts in Child. This is the most usual form of the ballad in America, and we may hereafter refer to it as the normal American text. One text, *TBVa* J, is close to Child E and to the "Jock of Hazeldean" which Sir Walter Scott is supposed to have built upon the first stanza of the traditional song. It is possible that Scott did not write as much of the song as he has been credited with.

On this point, Maurice W. Kelley contributes a brief article to *Modern Language Notes*, XLVI (May, 1931), 304-6, in which he compares Scott's poem with Child E and with Virginia J. Confronted with the alternatives "that either Virginia *J* is derived from Scott and entered popular balladry from literary sources, or that Scott wrote less of *Jock of Hazeldean* than is usually thought," he gives the latter as his verdict, largely on the basis of the Virginia text's retention of the traditional name John of Hazelgreen, as in Child E, and the limitation of both these texts to two stanzas as compared to Scott's four. "Is it not possible," concludes Mr. Kelley, "that Scott, annotating the poem at least four years after its composition, had forgotten just how much of it he took from popular sources? If such be the case, Child and the editors of Scott were misled in assuming that *Jock of Hazeldean* derived only one stanza from popular balladry; and in the composition of his poem, Scott used some other version nearer to Virginia *J* than to Child *E*." The present editor inclines to agree. But the recent appearance of a one-stanza Florida text (Morris, p. 330) with the title and name of the hero as "Jock o'Hazeldean" and otherwise very close to Scott's stanza, suggests that both processes may have been at work: that *TBVa* J and similar "John of Hazelgreen" forms represent the survival of a tradition older than Scott, though not necessarily un-influenced by Scott, whereas the Florida text and other "Jock of Hazeldean" forms in all probability represent the appearance of Scott's poem in more or less—probably less—traditional forms.

Barry (pp. 369-71) gives a seven-stanza text and tune from New Brunswick, collected in 1929 and published late in that year. It is close to the normal American text, except for its unique title, "Willie of Hazel Green," and a stanza, probably imported from another ballad, in which the man is mounted upon a milk-white steed and the girl upon a bay. Barry describes the tune as "a lilting Irish melody of the modified come-all-ye type." He concludes his note as follows (p. 371): "Our version is the first to be recorded in the North. The only American versions previously taken down are from Virginia."

In *BFSSNE*, No. 3 (1931), pp. 9-10, Barry presents a slightly over-three-stanza text, also from New Brunswick, with a tune noted by George Herzog. Barry accurately describes the version as "an oddly *zersungen* variant, as to text and air, of Scott's 'Jock of Hazeldean.'" There is no doubt that Scott's poem has begun to enter, or to contaminate, the tradition.

Though Campbell and Sharp missed the ballad in their 1917 publication from the Southern Appalachians, Sharpe-Karpeles (I, 294) print a single text and tune from Nash, Va., collected in 1918. It is a normal American text of six stanzas.

Dorothy Scarborough in *A Song Catcher in Southern Mountains,* pp. 225-27 and 415-16, gives two fragmentary texts and tunes from Roach's Run and Yellow Branch, Va., respectively. Both are called "John over the Hazel Green" and are normal Ameri-can texts with variations and differing degrees of fragmentation. Both places are in the Blue Ridge Mountains of Virginia, where the tradition of the ballad appears to be strong.

Two single-stanza fragments collected in Florida complete the American roster of the ballad. One was collected by E. C. Kirkland from a University of Florida summer school student in 1949, print-ed by him, with some misgivings, in *SFLQ,* XIII (December,

1949), 173, with tune. Morris's text (p. 330) has been discussed above. Both are very close indeed, but Kirkland's closer, to Scott's first stanza and both have the title and name "Jock o'Hazeldean." The value of these texts, certainly of Kirkland's, as traditional material is subject to some question. Morris's text bears, as he says, some marks of oral transmission, if very slight ones.

With the present Virginia text and tune, we are back to the normal American version, with variations. It is time now to distinguish between it and the Child A-D texts. In Virginia a walker by the greenwood encounters a maid lamenting. He offers her his oldest son. She will have none but John of Hazelgreen, yet she rides away with the stranger and encounters John of Hazelgreen, who is glowingly described. He greets her affectionately and vows eternal fidelity or they do. The chief differences between the Virginia text and Child A—apart from the order of stanzas—are that the man makes no suggestion to the girl that Hazelgreen is married, that he does not take her up behind him or buy clothes for her, nor do they arrive at the man's house and reveal him as young Hazelgreen's father, nor is it clearly stated that the lovers are to be married. But the differences are largely omissions rather than overt changes in the story.

With the present text and tune added to those of *TBVa* and to the Virginia texts and tunes of Sharp-Karpeles and Dorothy Scarborough, this ballad appears to survive rather vigorously in Virginia, if not elsewhere in British or American tradition.

AA

"John of the Hazelgreen." Phonograph record (aluminum) made by A. K. Davis, Jr. Sung by Mrs. Victoria Morris, of Mt. Fair, Va. Albemarle County. March 10, 1933. Text transcribed by P. C. Worthington. Tune noted by Winston Wilkinson. See headnote, above. In addition, note "ink black road," not found elsewhere. Note also the record's uncertain ending. It is possible that the title should be "John over the Hazelgreen," as in stanzas 3 and 5.

As I was walking one fair May morning, All down by the Greenwood side, And there I spied a pretty fair

miss, And all a-lone she_ cried.

1 As I were walking one fair May morning,
   All down by the greenwood side,
   And there I spied a pretty fair miss,
   And all alone she cried.

2 "You're welcome home, my pretty fair miss,
   You're welcome home with me,
   And you may have my oldest son,
   A husband for to be."

3 "Oh, I don't want your oldest son,
   For he's neither lord nor king,
   I never intend to be the bride of none,
   John over the Hazelgreen."

4 As I were riding an ink black road,
   The road run near to the town,
   All up stepped John my Hazelgreen,
   And helped his lady down.

5 His hair were long, his shoulder were broad,
   He was the flower of all his kin,
   His hair hang down like links of gold,
   John over the Hazelgreen.

6 'Tis forty times he kissed her cheeks,
   And forty times her chin,
   And forty times her red and rosy lips,
   And led his lady in.

7   "If ever I a vow break on you my love,
Oh, heaven will forsake on me,
And send me down to the torment place,
Where I never returntity."[1]

1. Mrs. Morris' last line is not entirely clear, but phonetically this seems to be what she said.   Perhaps she has confused two known readings: "Where I never return to thee" and "Throughout eternity."

46

TROOPER AND MAID
(CHILD, No. 299)

TBVa printed two good but slightly compressed texts of this ballad, with one tune. Added here is only a three-stanza text, without tune.

This is another of the five Child ballads excluded by Sargent and Kittredge from the one-volume abridged edition because of subject-matter. See also, in the present volume, the headnotes to "The Jolly Beggar" (Child, No. 279) and "The Gaberlunyie Man" (Child, No. 279, Appendix), pp. 328 and 333. Child tells the story thus: "A trooper comes to the house of his mistress in the evening and is kindly received. They pass the night together and are awakened by the trumpet. He must leave her; she follows him some way, he begging her to turn back. She asks him repeatedly when they are to meet again and marry. He answers, when cocker shells grow siller bells, when fishes fly and seas gang dry, etc. Similar question-and-answer endings occur in a number of ballads, among them "Edward" (Child, No. 13), "The Twa Brothers" (Child, No. 49), and "Lizie Wan" (Child, No. 51), in addition to "Trooper and Maid."

Child prints four texts and a one-stanza fragment, all from Scottish sources, and one tune from the Macmath manuscripts. His C text is also a fragment of three and a half stanzas. Child cites other ballads of a trooper and a maid named Peggy. Most of them are romanticized versions ending in marriage or the captain's death, as in "Pretty Peggy" or "Pretty Peggy O." See Sharp-Karpeles, II, 59-61; Belden, p. 169, and additional references there given.

There are no references to the song in Margaret Dean-Smith's index, and no version from English sources seems to have come to light since the date of her publication. The conclusion is that the ballad is extinct, or all but extinct, in contemporary English tradition. Greig-Keith (pp. 246-48, 278) report one thirteen-stanza version and a fragment collected in Aberdeenshire, and also print two tunes. As might be expected, the Scottish ballad still persists in Scotland, but is something of a rarity even there. Greig-

Keith describe it as "one of a number of amorous ballads on soldiers and maidens." The final fragment of their B text (p. 278) modifiies the casualness of the affair with a suggestion of the soldier's possible return:

> "An' gin ere I come this wye again,
> I will come in an' see ye."

Ord (p. 365) also reports a version from the North of Scotland in his *Bothy Songs and Ballads*. The single-stanza fragment in the Manx tongue published in *JFSS*, VII (1922-26), 216, may belong to this ballad or to "Geordie" (Child, No. 209). Manx, the language of the Isle of Man, is a subdialect of ancient Celtic, related to Irish and Scottish Gaelic. Translated, the stanza reads:

> There was a lady from the north
> When the moon shone bright and clearly
> A lady knew him by his horse
> Because she loved him dearly.

The American record is somewhat fuller but still sparse. First a correction: the Coffin reference (p. 161) to *The Sewanee Review*, XIX (July, 1911), 326, and the *TBVa* reference (p. 544) to the Shearin and Combs *Syllabus*, p. 9, do not concern this ballad but the related song of "Pretty Peggy, O," as Barry pointed out in *BFSSNE*, No. 7, p. 12. The first American texts to be announced were therefore the Virginia texts and tune listed in the *Bulletin of the Virginia Folklore Society*, Nos. 4, 7, and 8, and subsequently published in *TBVa*, pp. 544-46 and 606. They were compressed but good versions, of seven and six stanzas, respectively, of the Child story, not very close to any one of the Child texts but perhaps closest to Child B.

Campbell and Sharp (pp. 149-50) printed two texts, of four stanzas each, and two tunes, collected in North Carolina and Tennessee, respectively, during the summer of 1916. Both are reprinted, with an additional six-stanza text and tune from North Carolina, in Sharp-Karpeles, I, 305-7. Except for ... these texts are very close to those of *TBVa*, also from the Southern Appalachian region.

Barry, pp. 371-73, gives the first record from the North, a four-stanza text and a bagpipe tune from New Brunswick. He finds it closer to the Greig-Keith text than to any of Child's texts. "The melody," he says, "is of a strikingly archaic, not to say primitive, character, and is evidently a bagpipe air. It is distantly related to

the air printed in two variants by Greig . . . , but is more characteristically Scottish in that it has kept the upward skip of the octave in
the first phrase." Its language is broad Scottish. It ends with a
vague suggestion of the soldier's return, but with no mention of
marriage. Coffin makes it his Story Type B. In *BFSSNE*, No. 7
(1934), pp. 11-12, Barry adds a tune and a single stanza with a
nonsense refrain from Maine, the first and only trace of the ballad
from the Northeast section of the United States. The tune he
identifies as the usual American air to "Gypsy Davy" or "The
Gypsy Laddie" (Child, No. 200).

Brewster, pp. 166-69, gives a combination eight-stanza text and
tune from Indiana; half the stanzas (1, 4, 5, and 6) belong to
"Trooper and Maid," half (2, 3, 7, and 8) to "Young Hunting"
(Child, No. 68). In this corrupted text, after the trooper has told
the girl that he does not intend to wed her but does intend to see
his true love, the girl stabs him as he stoops to kiss her hand. This
is Coffin's Story Type D.

Coffin's Story Type C is supplied by the five-stanza text and
tune of Randolph, I, 213-14, in which the soldier replies affirmatively
to the girl's inquiry about marriage:

> "When peace is made an' the soldiers are at home,
>   Then it's oh my dear, we'll marry."

This is the only American text that is reminiscent of the one stanza
of Child, V, 307, "remembered by Miss Agnes Macmath, January
2, 1896, from the singing of her mother":

> "When will we twa meet again?
>   When will we meet and marry?"
> "When peace and truth come to this land,
>   Nae langer, love, we'll tarry."

We assume that the soldier is not a cynic about the coming of peace
    ⸱⸱th to the land!
            ⸱⸱ Carolina, the Brown Collection, II, 198-99, and
        ⸱ s two texts and two tunes, one text printed only
in part, the other a six-and-a-half-stanza text put together from
two sources—and, to be frank, not fitting together at all well. Indeed, the tune which is given for the last six lines only will not go
and was never intended to go to the first five stanzas at all. The
editor of the text, Professor Belden, comments in a footnote (II,
199): "It should be observed that the last six lines are metrically

of a different pattern from the preceding stanzas. They fit the situation well enough, but belong really to a different song." The musical editor, Professor Schinhan, adds his comment to the notation two volumes later (IV, 125): "This 'different song' we have here." Yes, and sung by two different people: Mrs. Polly Rayfield, and (later) Mrs. Peggy Perry. The text begins normally, but its ending is unreliable since it is introduced from another song. There is no need to classify it. It is a contaminated text, like Brewster's, but the contamination comes not from an old ballad but from a more recent and jauntier song.

The present Virginia text, also known as "The Bugle Boy," comes from the same Smith family which collected the North Carolina text described above. Its three stanzas correspond very closely, except for minor verbal changes especially in the third stanza, to the first three of the five stanzas collected from Mrs. Polly Rayfield. For this reason, there has been some hesitation about printing them. But since they represent a genuine additional trace of the ballad long resident in Virginia; since the variant was independently contributed to the Virginia collection by the Smiths; since there are variations, if only minor ones; since the text, so far as it goes, speaks well for the dependability of R. E. Lee Smith as a transcriber; and since there is no question of any contamination from any other song or from any other singer, it has seemed best to present the fragment here.

The fragment tells only of the coming of the soldier, his hospitable reception by the girl, and her high feeding of his horse and himself; there is no seduction, or riding away, or conversation about marriage. Perhaps the fourth and fifth stanzas of the North Carolina text should follow, telling of their going to bed together and their morning awaking to the soldier's departure and the girl's realization of her ruin. The rest of the North Carolina text would be an intrusion, as would its tune, in the ballad. Why R. E. Lee Smith did not send stanzas 4 and 5, one can only guess. It is possible that the first three stanzas represent the Southern fragmentation, Polly Rayfield and that the rest of the song belongs to Mrs. Peggy Perry? If so, we have an additional reason for printing the three stanzas here. But in the circumstances no such elaborate justification seems really necessary.

It should perhaps be said that, though R. E. Lee Smith usually indicates on his manuscript the source of the song, there is no notation to indicate that this song came from Zionville, N. C. Because of the similarity of the three stanzas with the Mrs. Rayfield text collected by his brother and because so many of the Smith family's songs originated in that vicinity, it is assumed that they may be the same song from the same source. It seems a reasonable assumption.

From the nature of its subject matter, it is quite likely that this ballad is more widely known and sung than given to collectors.

AA

"The Bugle Boy." Contributed by R. E. Lee Smith, of Palmyra, Va. Sung by his brother, Thomas P. Smith, of Palmyra, Va., and himself. Fluvanna County. May 19, 1931. Thomas P. Smith seems to have contributed these same stanzas, plus additional ones, to the Brown Collection in 1915. See the general headnote, above. The ballad has been resident in Virginia for many years.

1 She look-ed east and look-ed west,
     She saw the soldier a comin',
   She knew by the horse he rode
     Because she dearly loved him.

2 She took the horse by the rein,
     And led him to the stable,
   Saying, "Here's oats and corn for the soldier's horse,
     Feed high, for we are able."

3 She took him by the hand
     And led him to the table,
   "Here's cakes and wine,
     Eat and drink, we are able."

BIBLIOGRAPHY
With Abbreviations Used in the Headnotes

(Titles for which adequate bibliographical data are given in the headnotes where they occur are not necessarily repeated here, nor has it been thought necessary to include here the familiar older British collections before Child.)

Adventure or Gordon	*Adventure* [magazine]. "Old Songs that Men Have Sung," a department conducted by Robert Winslow Gordon, July 10, 1923—Nov. 10, 1927.
Baring-Gould	Baring-Gould, Sabine. *Songs of the West.* Revised edition. London, 1905.
Barry	Barry, Phillips, Fanny H. Eckstrom, and Mary W. Smyth. *British Ballads from Maine.* New Haven, 1929.
Belden	Belden, Henry M. (ed.). *Ballads and Songs Collected by the Missouri Folk-Lore Society.* (University of Missouri Studies, Vol. XV.) Columbia, Mo., 1940.
	Blackwood's Magazine. Edinburgh, 1817-.
Botkin	Botkin, Benjamin A. *American Play Party Song.* Lincoln, Neb., 1937.
Brewster	Brewster, Paul G. *Ballads and Songs of Indiana.* Bloomington, Ind., 1940.
Brown	*The Frank C. Brown Collection of North Carolina Folklore.* Newman Ivey White, general editor. 7 vols. Durham, N. C., 1952-.
Bronson	Bronson, Bertrand Harris. *The Traditional Tunes of the Child Ballads, with their Texts, according to the Extant Records of Great Britain and America.* Volume I. Ballads 1-53. Princeton, N. J., 1959.
	Bruce, William C. *Life of John Randolph of Roanoke.* 2 vols. New York and London, 1922.
BFSSNE	*Bulletin of the Folk-Song Society of the Northeast.* Edited by Phillips Barry. Nos. 1-12. Cambridge, Mass., 1930-37.

Bulletin   *Bulletin of the Virginia Folklore Society.* Nos. 1-12.
                    Charlottesville, Va., 1913-24.

                    Campbell, John C. *The Southern Highlander and His
                    Home.* New York, 1921.

Campbell   Campbell, Olive D., and Cecil J. Sharp. *English Folk
and Sharp   Songs from the Southern Appalachians.* 122 songs
                    and ballads and 323 tunes. New York and London,
                    1917.

Chappell   Chappell, Louis W. *Folk-Songs of Roanoke and the
                    Albemarle.* Morgantown, W. Va., 1939.

Child   Child, Francis James. *The English and Scottish Pop-
                    ular Ballads.* 5 vols. Boston, 1882-98.

Coffin   Coffin, Tristram P. *The British Traditional Ballad
                    in North America.* Philadelphia, 1950.

Combs   Combs, Josiah H. *Folk-Songs du Midi des États-
                    Unis.* Paris, 1925.

Combs   Combs, Josiah H. *Folk-Songs from the Kentucky
                    Mountains.* New York, 1939.

                    Comparative Literature. Vols. 1-10. Eugene, Ore.,
                    1949-.

Cox (1)   Cox, John H. *Folk-Songs of the South.* Cambridge,
                    Mass., 1925.

Cox (2)   Cox, John H. *Folk-Songs Mainly from West Virginia.*
                    New York: National Service Bureau, 1939. (Mimeo-
                    graphed.)

Davis   See *TBVa, FSVa, MTBVa,* below.

Dean-Smith   Dean-Smith, Margaret. *A Guide to English Folk
                    Song Collections 1822-1952, with An Index to Their
                    Contents, Historical Annotations and an Introduction.*
                    Liverpool, 1954.

                    Doerflinger, William M. *Shantymen and Shantyboys.*
                    New York, 1951.

Eddy   Eddy, Mary O. *Ballads and Songs from Ohio.* New
                    York, 1939.

                    English Studies in Honor of James Southall Wilson.
                    (University of Virginia Studies, Volume IV.) Char-
                    lottesville, Va., 1951.

Flanders   Flanders, Helen H., and George Brown. *Vermont
                    Folk-Songs and Ballads.* Brattleboro, Vt., 1932.

Flanders   Flanders, Helen H. *Country Songs of Vermont.* New
                    York, 1937.

Flanders   Flanders, Helen H., Elizabeth F. Ballard, George Brown, and Phillips Barry. *The New Green Mountain Songster*. New Haven, 1939.

Flanders   Flanders, Helen H. *Ballads Migrant in New England*. New York, 1953.

The Folk-Lore Journal. London, 1883-90. Successor to *The Folk-Lore Record, 1878-82*.

The Forget-Me-Not Songster. Boston, New York, Philadelphia, [1842?].

Fowke, Edith F., and Richard Johnston. *Folk Songs of Canada*. Waterloo, Ontario, Canada, 1956.

Friedman   Friedman, Albert B. (ed.). *The Viking Book of Folk Ballads of the English-Speaking World*. New York, 1956.

FSVa   Davis, Arthur Kyle, Jr. *Folk-Songs of Virginia: A Descriptive Index and Classification*. Durham, N. C., 1949.

Fuson   Fuson, Harvey H. *Ballads of the Kentucky Highlands*. London, [1931].

Gardner-Chickering   Gardner, Emelyn E., and Geraldine J. Chickering. *Ballads and Songs of Southern Michigan*. Ann Arbor, Mich., 1939.

Gerould   Gerould, Gordon H. *The Ballad of Tradition*. Oxford, 1932.

Gibbon   Gibbon, John M. *Melody and the Lyric from Chaucer to the Cavaliers*. New York, 1930.

Gordon   Gordon, Robert Winslow. *Folk-Songs of America*. New York: National Service Bureau, 1938. (Mimeographed.) See also *Adventure*.

Gray   Gray, Roland P. *Songs and Ballads of the Maine Lumberjacks, with Other Songs from Maine*. Cambridge, Mass., 1925.

Greenleaf and Mansfield   Greenleaf, Elisabeth B., and Grace Y. Mansfield. *Ballads and Sea Songs of Newfoundland*. Cambridge, Mass., 1933.

Greig, Gavin. *Folk-Song of the North-East*. Peterhead, Scotland, 1914.

Greig or Greig-Keith   Greig, Gavin. *Last Leaves of Traditional Ballads and Ballad Airs*. Edited by Alexander Keith. Aberdeen, Scotland, 1925.

Heart Songs   *Heart Songs*. Boston, 1909.

Henry   Henry, Mellinger E. *Songs Sung in the Southern Appalachians.* London, 1934.

Henry   Henry, Mellinger E. *Folk-Songs from the Southern Highlands.* New York, 1938.

Hoosier Folklore Bulletin. Bloomington, Ind., 1942-.

Hudson   Hudson, Arthur Palmer. *Folk Songs of Mississippi and Their Background.* Chapel Hill, N. C., 1936.

Hudson   Hudson, Arthur Palmer, and George Herzog. *Folk Tunes from Mississippi.* New York: National Service Bureau, 1937. (Mimeographed.)

Jekyll, Walter (ed.). *Jamaican Song and Story.* London, 1907.

JAFL   *The Journal of American Folk-Lore.* Boston, Lancaster, Pa., and New York, 1887-.

JEFSS   *Journal of the [English] Folk Song Society.* 8 vols.
or *JFSS*   London, 1899-1931.

JEFDSS   *Journal of the English Folk Dance and Song Society.* 7 vols. London, 1932-. Continuation of *Journal of the Folk Song Society,* 1899-1931.

Karpeles   Karpeles, Maud. *Folk Songs from Newfoundland.* Oxford, 1934.

Kidson   Kidson, Frank. *Folk Songs from the North Countrie.* London, 1927.

Kidson, Frank. *Traditional Tunes.* Oxford, 1891.

Last Leaves   See Grieg or Grieg-Keith, above.

Leach   Leach, MacEdward. *The Ballad Book.* New York, 1955.

Linscott, Eloise H. *Folk Songs of Old New England.* New York, 1939.

McCaskey, J. P. *Franklin Square Song Collection.* New York, 1881.

McGill, Josephine. *Folk Songs of the Kentucky Mountains.* New York, 1917.

Mackenzie   Mackenzie, W. Roy. *Ballads and Sea-Songs from Nova Scotia.* Cambridge, Mass., 1928.

MAFLS   *Memoirs of the American Folklore Society.* New York, 1894-. Also *Bibliographical and Special Series.*

Miller, Branford P. "The American Ballad List— 1952," *SFQ* (June, 1953).

MLN   *Modern Language Notes.* 74 vols. Baltimore, 1886-.

Morris Morris, Alton C. *Folksongs of Florida.* Gainesville, Fla., 1950.

Motherwell, William. *Minstrelsy, Ancient and Modern.* Glasgow, 1827; Boston, 1846.

MTBVa Davis, Arthur Kyle, Jr. *More Traditional Ballads of* or Davis *Virginia.* Chapel Hill, N. C., 1960.

Musical Quarterly. New York, 1915-.

Niles Niles, John J. *Seven Kentucky Mountain Tunes.* New York, 1928.

Ord Ord, John. *Bothy Songs and Ballads of Aberdeen, Banff, and Moray, Angus and the Mearns.* Paisley, Scotland, 1930.

Parsons Parsons, Elsie C. *Folk Tales of Andros Island, Bahamas.* (Memoirs of the American Folklore Society, XIII [1918].)

Pepys *The Pepys Ballads.* Edited by H. E. Rollins. 8 vols. Cambridge, Mass., 1929-32.

Pettigrew, Helen. *University of West Virginia Studies,* III (Philological Papers II). Morgantown, W. Va.

PMLA *Publications of the Modern Language Association of America.* 1885-.

Randolph Randolph, Vance. *Ozark Folksongs.* 4 vols. Columbia, Mo., 1946-50.

Records of Federal Writers' Project. Lincoln, Neb., 1937.

Reeves, James. *The Idiom of the People.* New York, 1958.

Rimbault, E. F. *Musical Illustrations of Bishop Percy's Reliques.* London, 1850.

Sandburg Sandburg, Carl. *The American Songbag.* New York, 1927.

Sargent Sargent, Helen C., and G. L. Kittredge. *The English* and Kittredge *and Scottish Popular Ballads.* Boston, 1904. A one-volume abridgement of Child.

Saxton-Dreyer-Tallant. *Gumbo Ya-Ya.* Cambridge, Mass., 1945.

Scarborough, Dorothy. *A Song Catcher in the Southern Mountains.* New York, 1937.

Scarborough, Dorothy. *On the Trail of Negro Folk-Songs.* Cambridge, Mass., 1925.

SFQ or *SFLQ* *Southern Folklore Quarterly.* Gainesville, Fla., 1937-.

Sharp-Karpeles Sharp, Cecil. *English Folk Songs from the Southern Appalachians.* Edited by Maud Karpeles. 2 vols. London, 1932.

       Sharp, Cecil. *English Folk Song: Some Conclusions.* London, 1907.

       Sharp, Cecil J., and Charles L. Marson. *Folk Songs from Somerset.* (First Series.) London, 1915.

       Sharp, Cecil. *One Hundred English Folk Songs.* Boston, 1916.

       Shearin, Hubert G. *British Ballads in the Cumberland Mountains.* Sewanee, Tenn. Reprinted from the *Sewanee Review,* July, 1911.

       Shearin, Hubert, and Josiah H. Combs. *A Syllabus of Kentucky Folk Song.* Lexington, Ky., 1911.

       Smith, Reed. "A Glance at the Ballad and Folksong Field," *SFQ,* I (June, 1937).

       Smith, Reed. *South Carolina Ballads.* Cambridge, Mass., 1928.

       Smith, Reed, and Hilton Rufty. *An American Anthology of Old World Ballads.* New York, 1937.

       The Southern Warbler. Charleston, S. C., 1845.

Stokoe   Stokoe, John, and Samuel Reay. *Songs and Ballads of Northern England.* London, [1899].

       Taylor, Archer. *Edward and Sven i Rosengaard.* Chicago, 1931.

TBVa   Davis, Arthur Kyle. *Traditional Ballads of Virginia.*
or Davis   Cambridge, Mass., 1929.

TFSB   *Tennessee Folklore Society Bulletin.* 25 vols. Marysville, Tenn., 1935-59.

       Texas Folklore Society Bulletin. Austin, Tex., 1916-.

       Thompson, Stith. *Motif Index to Folklore.* 5 vols. Bloomington, Ind., 1932-35.

       Wells, Evelyn K. *The Ballad Tree, A Study of British and American Ballads.* New York, 1950.

       Western Folklore. 18 vols. Berkeley, Calif., 1942-.

       Whittaker, W. G. *North Countrie Ballads.* London, 1921.

       Williams, Alfred. *Folk Songs of the Upper Thames.* London, 1923.

Wimberly   Wimberly, Lowry C. *Folklore in the English and Scottish Popular Ballads.* Chicago, 1928.

INDEX OF TITLES AND FIRST LINES

Ballad titles are given in italics, first lines in quotation marks. Inclusive pagination is given for each Child title, first page only for the title or first line of a particular version or variant. When the title of a version or variant is the same as the Child title, only the inclusive pagination for the Child title is given.

"A beggar man com' o'er yon lea," 337

"A little boy threw his ball so high," 235

"All in the merry month of May," 186

"A neat young lady comes tripping downstairs," 261

"A rich man who lived in England," 108

"As I walked over London's bridge," 265

"As I were walking one fair May morning," 354

"As Lady Margaret she was going to bed," 117

As Two Little Schoolboys Were Going to School, 98

"A way down yonders in London town," 197

Babylon; or, The Bonnie Banks O Fordie, 68-71

Barbara Allen, 185, 187, 189, 198

Barbry Allen, 193, 195, 196

Barbry Ellen, 191

Battle of Chevy Chase, The, 242

Beaulampkins, 218

'Beaulampkins was as fine a mason," 218

Beggar Man, The, 337

Black Cat Davy, 258

"Black Cat Davy came a-riding through the woods," 258

Black Jack Davy, 256

"Black Jack Davy come riding through the woods," 256

Bonnie James Campbell, 267-69

Bonny Barbara Allan, 182-98

Bow Ye Down, 49

Boy and the Devil, The, 15

Broken-Hearted Lover, The, 159

Brown Girl, The, 131

Bugle Boy, The, 360

Cambric Shirt, The, 13

"Carry a lady a letter from me," 13

"Cheer up, cheer up, my pretty fair maid," 285

"Cheer up, cheer up, my pretty fair miss," 284

" 'Come in, come in, love Henry,' said she," 114

" 'Come in, come in, Loving Henry,' she said," 115, 121

"Come in, come in, my old true love," 289

"Come in, come in, my own true love," 286

Cruel Mother, The, 81-83

Dandoo, 309

Dan-you, 314

Devil and the Nine Questions, The, or *The Devil's Nine Questions,* 5, 7

"Devil: 'I wish you out in yonder sea,' " 15

"Don't you see that little turtle dove," 206

Doom Ship or *Mermaid,* 346

Earl Brand, 26-34

Edward, 61-67

Elfin Knight, The, 8-13

Fair Ellen, 133

Fair Margaret and Sweet William, 138-45

Fair Sisters, The, 37

Farmer's Curst Wife, The, 316-27

Farmer's Wife, The, 326, 327

Fause Knight Upon the Road, The, 14-15

"First came down was dressed in red,"
178
"First night when I came home as
drunk as I could be," 304
"For eight long years I have served
the great King Orpheo," 91
Four Maries, 252

Gaberlunyie-Man, The, 333-38
Gallant Ship, The, 347
Gallows Tree, The, 226
Geordie, 262-66
George Collins, 203, 204, 205
"George Collins rode home one cold
winter night," 203, 204, 205
"Get you up, get you up, you seventh
sleeper," 30
"Go bring me a portion of your father's
gold," 21
"Go buy to me an acre of land," 10
"God prosper long our noble king," 243
"Go saddle me up my milk-white horse,"
260
Gyps of Davy, The, 259
Gypsy Laddie, The, 253-61

Hangman, 224
"Hangman, hangman, slack your rope,"
224
"Hangsman, hangsman, hold your
rope," 227
"Hangsman, Hangsman, slacken your
rope," 226
Hangsman's Tree, 227
Harvey Walker, 260
"He come whistling from his plow," 313
"He followed me up and he followed
me down," 18
"He mounted his horse, he rode to fair
Ellen," 129
Henry Martyn, 290-99
"High up in the mountains," 268
Highway Man, 227
House Carpenter, The, 274, 276, 278,
281, 285, 289
"How come this blood on your shirt
sleeve," 64
Hunting of the Cheviot, The, 239-44

"I came in the first night as drunk as
I could be," 302
"In Scarlet town where I was born,"
198
"I sail-ed east and I sail-ed west," 107

"It rained all day and it rained all
night," 238
"It rained a mist, it rained a rain," 233
"It rained, it rained, it rained a mist,"
231
"It was all in the month of May," 195
"It was early in the month of May," 32
"I've just returned, my own true love,"
277
"I went down to the old depot," 227

James Harris (The Dæmon Lover),
270-89
Jeems Randal, 57
Jellon Grame, 207-13
"Jellon Grame was in the Greenwoods,"
211
Jessel Town, 95
Jewish Lady, The, 233
Jew's Daughter, The, 231
Jewses' Daughter, The, 236
Johnny Randal, 56
Johnny Randolph, My Son, 55
John of Hazelgreen, 350-55
John of the Hazelgreen, 353
John Willow, My Son, 59
Jolly Beggar, The, 328-32

King Orfeo, 79-80
King Orpheo, 90
Kitty Lorn, 313

Lady Alice, 199-206
Lady Isabel and the Elf-Knight, 16-25
Lady Margaret, 116, 142
"Lady Margret was settin' in her bow'r
window," 142
Lamkin, 214-20
"Last night there were four Maries,"
252
Little Boy and the Ball, 234
"Little footpage was standing by," 175
Little Massey Grove, 172
Little Musgrave and Lady Barnard,
170-81
London's Bridge, 264
Lord Barney, 175
Lord Bateman, 108
Lord Batesman, 104
Lord Daniel, 178
Lord Henry, 120
Lord Lovel, 146-51
"Lord Lovel he stood at his castle gate,"
147, 151

"Lord Lovel stood at his castle gate," 149, 151

Lord Randal, 51-60

Lord Randall, 52

Lord Thomas, 124, 127, 129, 135

Lord Thomas and Fair Annet, 123-37

"Lord Thomas, Lord Thomas, take my advice," 128

"Lord Thomas was a brave young man," 125

"Lord Thomas was a gay young man," 135

"Lord William he rose about four o'clock," 33

Love Henry, 113

Loving Henry, 115, 121

Maid Freed from the Gallows, The, 221-28

Man in the Land, A, or The Dapple Gray, 23

Mary Hamilton, 245-52

Mermaid, The, 344-49

Miss Mary's Parrot, 21

Neat Young Lady, A, 261

"Now high, now high, now high holiday," 173

"O brother, O brother, can you play ball," 96

"Oh, I could have married the king's daughter dear," 278

"Oh, little did my mother think," 252

"Oh met, oh met, my old true love," 280

"Oh mother, dear mother, come riddle to me," 133

"'Oh Mother, oh Mother, oh Mother,' said he," 131

"Oh, where have you been, John Willow, my son," 59

"Oh, where have you been, Lord Randall, my son," 52

Old Bangem, 73

"Old Bangem would a-hunting ride," 74

Old Man That Lived in the West, The, 310

Old Man That Went Out to Plow, The, 323

Old Woman by the Seashore, The, 42

"Once there was an old man that lived in the West," 312

"One day I was sitting in my father's hall," 83

"One early morn our ship sailed," 347

"One night, one night, 'twas a moonshiny night," 155

On the Banks of the Sweet Willie, 284

"O sister, O sister, give me your hand," 47

Our Goodman, 300-304

"Out spoke the captain of our gallant ship," 348

Percy, 62

Riddles Wisely Expounded, 3-7

Ronald Barton, 298

Salt Sea, The, 279

Salt Water Sea, 17, 287

Seven Brothers, The, or Lord William, 33

Seven Horsemen, 32

Seven Sleepers, The, 27

Seventh Brother, The, 29

"She look-ed east and look-ed west," 360

"She thought it was her brother," 121

Sir Henry, 118

Sir Hugh, or The Jew's Daughter, 229-38

Sir Lionel, 72-78

Sweet Trinity, The (The Golden Vanity), 339-43

Sweet Wildee, 283

Sweet William, 139, 143

"Sweet William arose one merry mornin'," 140

"Sweet William rose one morning in May," 143

Sweet William's Ghost, 152-56

"Sweet William went down to get him a wife," 308

Sweet Willie's Ghost, 155

"Tell her to sew it up with a white thorn," 11

"The Devil went a-courting and he did ride," 5

"The farmer was guiding his plow one day," 326

"The miller's daughter went out one day," 46

"There is a lady, lady gay," 163, 167

"There is a wild hog in the wood," 76
"There's a wild hog in these woods," 77
"There was a certain beggar," 331
"There was a king lived in the west," 37
"There was a knight came riding by," 7
"There was a lady, a lady gay," 164
"There was a lady and a lady gay," 166
"There was a lady of beauty bright," 168
"There was a little ship, and she sailed on the sea," 342
"There was a man lived in the West," 50
"There was a man out in the land," 24
"There was an old man at the foot of the hill," 322
"There was an old man hired a farm," 326
"There was an old man in our town," 41
"There was an old man lived under the hill," 324
"There was an old man that lived in the West," 314
"There was an old man who had an old steer," 327
"There was an old man who had a wife," 309
"There was an old man who learned how to plow," 323
"There was an old man who owned a large farm," 319
There Was an Old Woman, 44
"There was an old woman in the North Countree," 45
"There was an old woman lived on a seashore," 47
"There was an old woman lived on the seashore," 43
"There was an old woman lived over the sea," 12
"There was an old woman who lived on the sea," 44
"There was a rich man lived in England," 104
"There was a wed lady lived on the seashore," 48
"There was a wild hog in the woods," 75
"There was three brothers," 298
"There was three ladies that lived in a town," 70

"There were three crows sat on a tree," 86, 87
"There were two brothers in one school," 94
Three Babes or Wife of Usher's Well, 164
Three Crows, The, 86, 87, 88
"Three crows they sat upon a tree," 88
Three Little Babes, The, 162, 165, 167, 168
Three Nights' Experience, 303
Three Ravens, The, 84-88
Three Sisters, 69
Trooper and Maid, 356-60
Turkish Lady, The, 106
Turkish Revelee, The, 341
Twa Brothers, The, 92-101
"'Twas in the late season of the year," 189
"'Twas in the merry, merry month of May," 188
"'Twas in the merry month of May," 192
Twa Sisters, The, 35-50
"'Twas late in the night when the landlord came," 259
"'Twas late last Friday night," 119
Two Brothers, The, 93, 100
"Two brothers, dear brothers, walked out one day," 101
Two Little Brothers from School One Day, 97
Two Little Devils, 318
Two Sisters, The, 40

Unquiet Grave, The, 157-60
"Up came the devil to the farmer one day," 325
"Up stepped the captain of our gallant ship," 349

"Wake up, wake up, you seven sleepers," 28
"Was the fourteenth day," 193
Wed Lady, The, 48
"We have met, we have met, my own true love," 275
"Well met, well met, you old true love," 282
"We will meet, we will meet, my old true love," 287
"What blood is that on your coat lap," 62

"What did you have for your breakfast," 57

"What did you have for your supper," 56

"What is that on the end of your sword," 65

What's On Your Sword?, 65

Where Have You Been?, 53

"Where have you been to, my dear son?," 54

"Where was you last night [nighheight]," 56

Whummil Bore, The, 89-91

Wife of Usher's Well, The, 161-69

Wife Wrapt in Wether's Skin, The, 305-15

Wild Hog, 74-78

Willie Campbell, 268

"Wind cold today, my love," 160

"Word has come from the kitchen," 250

Young Beichan, 102-10

Young Hunting, 111-22